AF674553

DISCOVERING BANDA BAHADUR

Discovering Banda Bahadur

SURINDER SINGH

MANOHAR
2010

First published 2010

© Surinder Singh, 2010

All right reserved. No part of this publication may be reproduced or transmitted, in any form or by any means, without prior permission of the author and the publisher.

ISBN 978-81-7304-892-0

Published by
Ajay Kumar Jain *for*
Manohar Publishers & Distributors
4753/23 Ansari Road, Daryaganj
New Delhi 110 002

Typeset by
Ajay Arts
New Delhi-110002

Printed by
Salasar Imaging Systems
Delhi 110035

Contents

Illustrations

Preface

After finishing my M.A. in History in 1952 from Panjab University and M.A. in Political Science from University of Delhi in 1954 I was engaged in research on Indian Constituent Assembly, when I was selected for the All India Allied Services in 1956. I thus drifted away from academic life to the mundane life of a government official. During a posting in Punjab in the late 1970s, I developed an interest in collecting old coins. When a few hundred coins had been collected, my instinct for research once again got awakened and I started planning to do research on some aspects of Indian coinage. The field of coinage being very vast and both the material in the shape of coins as well as documents being very scarce, I decided to conduct research only on Sikh coins, a subject which has remained unexplored by research scholars, especially the initial Sikh coinage issued by Banda Bahadur. I disposed off all other coins of the Mughal, Hindu and Indo-Greek periods and concentrated solely on collecting Sikh coins. During the course of my search for Sikh coins I got acquainted with Parkash Chand, a goldsmith of Guru Bazaar of Amritsar, dealing with antique jewellery, old coins, etc. Parkash Chand helped me in securing more than a thousand Sikh coins at a very reasonable price. I also started searching for books and documents on Sikh coinage, which were very scarce and I had to resort to collecting books on Sikh history and started gleaning what little numismatic information was contained therein.

The study of Sikh coinage encompassed three disciplines of social science—Numismatics, History and Political Science, besides a proficiency in Punjabi and Persian languages. I wished to pursue a doctoral degree in the above subject but was unable to secure admission to a nearby university primarily due to my failure to locate a university teacher conversant with my subject and willing to be my guide. But, I was not prepared to abandon the subject of Sikh coinage for which I had developed sufficient fascination and interest.

With the commencement of my study of Sikh coinage, I discovered that what little fragmented work was there, it was in the field of cataloguing only and not in the field of analytical study. It was only in the later half of the twentieth century that some numismatic work was actually carried out by a few scholars. Historians have been making fanciful remarks regarding Sikh coins based on very meagre evidence and at times with non-existent evidence in support of their contentions. Most of the writers who have commented on the Sikh coins while writing Sikh history have done so without any actual examination of those coins, which were even otherwise readily available.

The negligence on the part of historians at times resulted in baffling situations. Whereas the accounts in the books gave out a particular story about certain coins, the imprints of the legends and other inscriptions revealed a different story. Hence to arrive at the correct assessment about these coins became very difficult and time consuming. A novel method of dovetailing the historical data with numismatic investigation was adopted and where both sides lead to a common conclusion, the doubts stood clarified. Where the two sides did not match with each other, the situation came to be some form of historical disinformation and was to be further researched.

I started submitting research papers on issues in which all doubts stood clarified and presented my findings at conferences, seminars and other places wherever I could manage to squeeze in. In a decade, I was able to have to my credit over 25 research papers covering important aspects of Sikh coinage. My work was being appreciated by research scholars and especially Professor Himadri Bannerjee, who had been showing interest in my work by correspondence/discussions at conferences, etc. He guided me to go in for PhD in 'Sikh Coinage', and thanks to his encouragement received a PhD from Rabindra Bharati University, Calcutta in 2001 on my dissertation 'Studies in Sikh Coinage'. My book *Sikh Coinage: Symbol of Sikh Sovereignty* is based on my doctoral thesis and was published in 2004 by Manohar Publishers. The book has been very well received and is being used as a reference book by scholars and coin collectors.

During my study of Sikh coinage, the most difficult and time consuming aspect was the coinage issued by Banda Bahadur. Numismatists collecting and cataloguing Sikh coins generally commence their study with the Sikh coin issued in 1765 on the occupation of the capital city of Lahore by the Sikhs. Since there has been mention in historical records, about the coins issued by Banda Bahadur, I had to go through all available records on Banda Bahadur to locate the mention of his coins but more difficult was to locate the coins. While going through the work and time of Banda Bahadur, every aspect of his work as a commander of Sikh forces has been so remarkable in self-sacrifice and devotion to a cause that it has been a soul-stirring experience for me.

I began working on my next project, a comprehensive work on Banda Bahadur. Having done my earlier work on Sikh coins all by myself, I desired to join some nearby university for my research on Banda Bahadur. I made out a detailed draft of my research project and biodata and approached the Vice-Chancellor of Punjabi University, Patiala to consider me for some research fellowship/fixed grant so that I have the benefit of consultation with the professors and research scholars and the use of its libraries for my work. After waiting for the decision on my application for a few months, I moved another application to the Vice-Chancellor, Guru Nanak Dev University, Amritsar where also I had the same experience of no reply whatsoever. I made a last attempt, by submitting my project report to the Vice-Chancellor, Panjab University, Chandigarh. My application for the research was approved by the Department of History and the Dean of University Education but it remained unapproved at Vice-Chancellor's level and has by now been consigned to the waste-paper basket.

At my age and experience as a senior officer of Government of India, I can well understand that either the subject of my research or my ability to carry out the same has not been appreciated at their end. But a common courtesy of giving just a one line reply to cut short my endless waiting would not have been difficult for them to issue. The high priests of our temples of learning of our ancient civilization, seem to have lost their sheen and human courtesy. The above treatment has hurt me, but at the same time like the proverbial rise of the Phoenix, it has egged me on to greater affort to carry out and complete my work on Banda Bahadur. I am reminded of a couplet of Iqbal which aptly describe the above situation:

Sach keh doon eh brahaman, gar tu bura na manie
Tere sanam kadon kae butt ho gai puranae.

Tang aa kae main ne akhir dero heram ko chhora
Wahiz ka whaz chhora, chore tere fasanae.

MOHAMMAD IQBAL

During these five years, while I carried out my work, my family, my wife and my son have all along been a source of great assistance and encouragement to me. I have sought guidance and assistance during this period from a wide range of teachers, scholars of History and Political Science, religious men, numismatists, linguists and many others, some of whom went out of their way to help and encourage me. I visited various battle sites and spoke to the village elders. I felt myself like a bird, collecting straws of knowledge from all around to build a nest of wisdom to accomplish my work. I express my deep gratitude to all those persons from whom I was able to secure bits of knowledge.

2010 SURINDER SINGH

Introduction

> There was no such thing as a historian before the eighteenth century.
>
> R.G. Collingwood

In ancient times, history was more of fables and fiction than a realistic historical account. The Greeks brought to history a point of view about the world which we might call 'realism', a critical distinction from myths and fables that enabled them to discriminate between historical accounts and fiction-ridden stories. Methods of research were systematically explored; new techniques of reading documents were introduced.[1] In the seventeenth century, European historians would collect documents, make rational order of the chaos in which they were found and a reliable scientific criteria of discriminating among documents and other historical facts started emerging. Leopold Von Ranke was the first historian who turned history into a profession. More and more universities in Europe established chairs of history and historical associations sprang up everywhere on the continent, and with them the mark of the organized profession.[2]

In the ancient period of Indian history, there was no sense of history as such. Modern researchers have, however, tried to prove that this sense was not totally absent. But the fact remains that with the exception of Kalhana's *Rajatarangini* and *Mahavamsa* of Ceylon there is hardly any writing of a truly historical nature that has come from the ancient period.[3] The Puranas do contain historical elements but these too are submerged in a sea of myths, legends and supernatural sin. The dominant philosophy of life at that time was based on the orthodox Brahmanical view that the world was immensely old and on the decline, that things were impermanent and superhuman forces influenced the shaping of man's destiny.[4]

The Turks, Pathans and later the Mughals, who ruled for nearly seven centuries, had a sense of history. Muslim historians of the Sultanate period of India wrote with the conviction that true religion is to be found in the authoritative guidance of the divinely revealed Quran. They believed that the ideal history of Muslims was an act of heaven and their primary task was to illustrate this history, treating their source material as authorities to be cited rather than these being questioned. The Mughals who destroyed the Sultanate to establish their own empire in 1526 followed the same line as their predecessors. There was, however, a gradual drift towards writing biographical works during the Mughal period. The Mughal news writers and historians, by and large being employees of the ruling classes, wrote in their praise. They were greatly biased against the Sikhs, and would generally refer to call them as 'infidels', 'rebels', or 'curs'. Sikhs, in their own way, eulogized the actions of their own heroes and pulled down those who did not belong to their tribe. The eighteenth-century Muslims gradually made way for the British in this regard.

The British historians had a positive bias towards their own aggrandizements and an equally strong prejudice against the Sikhs of whose might they were greatly apprehensive. J.D. Cunningham, was an unbiased historian, whose frankness and authenticity of facts attracted condemnation from the British government, and he was sacked from his job for the same.[5] Many Europeans came forth to write about India and produced a large amount of historical literature. Most of the other writers were administrators who were chiefly motivated by the desire to write about their administration and local traditions. Historiography was making great advances in Europe but in India the colonial writers were not falling fully in line with the European scholars.[6] The British writers were biased and politically motivated, although the elements of analysis, discussion and interpretation were used in their writing. The same, however, was conspicuous by its absence in the writings of Indian scholars.

Historical scholarship in our country and elsewhere has taken long strides. New tools of research have been evolved and new points of view adopted. As in other areas of historical research, research in the field of Sikh history too has made reasonable advances. Emphasis is fast shifting from the old narrative and descriptive type of historical writing to critical and interpretative exposition of historical phenomena.[7] The pruning of Islamic and British bias from the recorded history as well as bringing the eulogizing of their heroes by Sikh writers to an authentic level is still a primary requirement for a genuine history of the Sikhs.

Guru Nanak (April 1469 to September 1539) the first Sikh Guru, who laid the foundation of the Sikh religion and the Sikh social order, which had a very smooth and steady development, especially during the half-century rule of Akbar, the Mughal emperor. The foundation of a Sikh centre at Amritsar was laid by Guru Ram Das and developed by Guru Arjan Dev. Sikh worship consisted of singing of the hymns composed by their Gurus. The dissident groups started making their own selections and distortions in the hymns of the Gurus. Guru Arjan Dev, therefore, felt the necessity of laying down the hymns of the Gurus in a single volume, so that distortions thereafter could not be inserted therein. The great task of compiling the hymns of Gurus, from Guru Nanak to Guru Arjan, was completed in August 1604 and the sacred volume was installed in the Harimandir in Amritsar the same year.[8] The most notable achievement of Guru Arjan was the compilation of the Sikh holy book known as the *Adi Granth* in Gurmukhi script designed by Guru Angad for the understanding of the common Sikh society. After the death of Akbar, Jahangir became the next Mughal emperor in October 1605. He was already biased against the Sikh Gurus and angered by the cordial treatment accorded by Guru Arjan Dev to the rebel prince Khusrau. He was also under the influence of the orthodox Naqshbandi Sayyads of Sirhind, who were against the rise of Sikh religious order in their area. In his autobiography, Jahangir writes:

> In Goindwal . . . , there was a Hindu named Arjan, in the garment of sainthood and sanctity, so much so that he had captured many of the simple-hearted Hindus, and even (some) of the ignorant and foolish followers of Islam, by his ways and manners, and they had loudly sounded the drum of his holiness. They called him Guru, and from all sides stupid people crowded to worship and manifest complete faith in him. For three or four generations they had kept this shop warm.

Many times it occurred to me to put a stop to this vain affair or to bring him into the assembly of Islam.[9]

Guru Arjan Dev was arrested and taken to Lahore in mid-1606. He was tied to a post in the open, exposed to the hot summer sun, burning sand and hot water was thrown on his naked body for five days continuously, next he was to be sewn in a raw hide. Just before that Guru Arjan sought permission to bathe in the nearby river Ravi. He plunged into the river Ravi and was lost therein for ever.[10]

Guru Arjan Dev had visualized the difficult times for the Sikhs in the near future and had started building a body of armed retainers. He had instructed Bhai Buddha to train his son in all the arts of war besides the study of literature and the sciences. The martyrdom of Guru Arjan Dev brought about a transformation in the Sikhs from a non-violent religious community to a military organization. Guru Hargobind successfully fought six battles with local Muslim commanders, but realizing that he was not in a position to fight with an imperial army, he moved his headquarters to Kiratpur, in the relative security of the Shivalik hills.[11] Guru Hargobind gave to the Sikhs a new confidence and organizational solidarity and demonstrated the possibility of Sikhs openly assuming an attitude of defiance against the Mughal government. Guru Hagobind expired in 1644.

Guru Tegh Bahadur, the ninth Sikh Guru (1664-75), after his stay in Bihar and Assam, finally settled down in Makhowal, adjoining the present site of Anandpur. Guru Tegh Bahadur tried to help the needy farmers of the Malwa region by helping them with provision of agricultural land, wells, animals and other farm implements to carry on their livelihood. These activities were, however, not liked by the Muslim landed nobility and zamindars. They sent distorted, biased and exaggerated reports of the activities of the Guru to the Mughal court. The Guru was summoned and on his way to Delhi, he was arrested and taken in an iron cage to Delhi.[12] Against all persuasion, Guru Tegh Bahadur refused to embrace Islam. His five companions were tortured to death in his presence to pressurize him into accepting Islam, but with no success. He was finally executed outside the Kotwali in Chandni Chowk on 11 November 1675.

Guru Gobind Singh took up the mantle of Guruship at the tender age of nine. In his period of about 33 years of Guruship from 1675 to 1708, he had to live a life of endless turmoil. He fought more then 21 defensive battles with the hill rajas and Mughal commanders. He created the Khalsas, the saint soldiers, on the Baisakhi day of 1699.[13] The five volunteers who were prepared to lay down their lives for him, were given *pahul*, i.e sugared water stirred with a *khanda*, to the accompaniment of *Gurbani* recitation. After they had all sipped the *pahul*, he took the *pahul* himself and thus merged his person in the Khalsa. During the last battle of Anandpur in 1704, he had to vacate the fort with the assurance of a safe passage by the Mughal emperor and the hill rajas. He, however, did not trust them, but after eight months of siege he had to vacate and was pursued by the Mughal forces during which time his family got dispersed.[14] He reached Damdama Sahib in Malwa from where he issued his letter *zafarnama* to Aurangzeb and was invited by the emperor for negotiation. While on the way, he got news of the death of Aurangzeb and planned to return to Anandpur.

However, on the recommendations of Bhai Nand Lal, Guru Gobind Singh helped Bahadur Shah in his battle against his younger brother Azim Shah at Jaiju for the imperial throne. Guru Gobind Singh sent his 400 *sawars* to help him. Bahadur Shah won the battle and invited Guruji at his court in Agra where costly gifts were exchanged.[15] The Guru, assuming that Bahadur Shah was having a helpful attitude, pleaded for the punishment to Wazir Khan, the *fauzdar* of Sirhind and some of his officials responsible for the atrocities committed on the Sikhs and the execution of Guru's two younger sons. In the meantime, Bahadur Shah's younger brother Kam Baksh had raised a standard of rebellion in the south and he asked the Guru to accompany him. At Nanded, the Guru realized that Bahadur Shah was not sincere in his assurance and was not likely to take any action against Wazir Khan and his officers.[16] This was a stage where all the efforts of the Guru in creating a Sikh religious-cum-martial order stood disturbed and their abode Anandpur Sahib and the surrounding areas were lost to them.

During Aurangzeb's reign, the frontiers of the Mughal Empire had expanded with the inclusion of Golconda and Bijapur kingdoms. The imperial rule was now over the entire subcontinent, but the authority of the central administration had become somewhat weak during this period. In the Mathura-Agra region, the Jat, *zamindars* and peasants repeatedly challenged the Mughal authority. In the Punjab, the Sikh movement was taking the shape of a significant force. The Rajput chiefs who had made contribution for the consolidation of the Mughal Empire were becoming lukewarm to the imperial cause.[17] The cracks and fissures in the Mughal system developed into breaches and chasms and the imperial edifice collapsed within forty years after the death of Aurangzeb.[18]

Aurangzeb (1659-1707) in his about half a century of rule, besides annexing the remaining southern territories to his kingdom, was a major factor in the decline and dissolution of the Mughal Empire. Aurangzeb's stay for a quarter century in the south made the general administration of the country weak. The enormous losses sustained by Aurangzeb in the Deccan wars have been described by Jadu Nath Sarkar thus: 'The wastage of the Deccan wars which raged intensely for nearly 20 years, was 100,000 soldiers and followers and three times that number of horses, elephants, camels and oxen on [the] Mughal side every year.'[19] Aurangzeb's Islamic bigotry and attempt to convert the Hindu populace to Islam by force was another great folly. The half-century work of Akbar in bringing about peace and harmony between the foreign Islamic rulers and the local Hindu population, was undone by Aurangzeb in his half-century rule of bigotry and fanatic orthodoxy. Muhammad Saqi Mustaid Khan in his *Masir-e-Alamgiri* (p. 81) writes, that in April 1669, 'Director of the Faith issued orders to all the governors of provinces to destroy with a willing hand the schools and temples of the infidels, and they were strictly enjoined to put an entire stop to the teaching and practicing of idolatrous forms of worship.'[20]

An account of the life of Banda Bahadur from his childhood up to his meeting Guru Gobind Singh, a period of 38 years does not seem to have been attempted by any contemporary or near contemporary historian. He hailed from an ordinary family in Techhal Nagar near Rajouri in the backward part of the Jammu region and his account of life spent there could not attract attention of any person in preserving it for posterity. A small accident, the killing of a doe, changed his very life. While cleaning the animal, two sibling offspring fell out and died within a few minutes. It touched the inner chords of his heart so much that he gave up hunting and started living the life of an ascetic, spending his time with *sadhus* and *bairagis* who passed through his village on their way to other religious places. He came under the influence of Janaki Prasad for a while.[21] While visiting the Baisakhi fair at the shrine of Baba Ranthaman near Kasur, Banda Bahadur detached himself from Janaki Prasad and joined another *bairagi* named Ram Das. Thereafter, there is no historical information available about the movements of Banda Bahadur till he set up his regular abode at Nanded.

Madho Das (soon to be known as Banda Bahadur) entered the unknown world of *sadhus* and ascetic warriors spread all over India, a world with which he had no acquaintance, a world which had greatly degenerated from an idealistic and ascetic way of life to a worldly way of life with all its failings and follies. His journey from the north to the south covered the most important formative and constructive period of his life (about 20 years) which is a dark period of his life, totally unknown to historians.

Two persons had come to Nanded almost at the same time, frustrated because of their ambitions having remained somewhat unfulfilled. One was Guru Gobind Singh, who had come to Nanded with Bahadur Shah, to seek justice against the excesses of Wazir Khan, the *faujdar* of Sirhind, and some of his officers, but he was disappointed with the attitude of Bahadur Shah and did not further accompany him down to Hyderabad. The other person was Banda Bahadur, who had also not been able to accomplish whatever he had desired to achieve.

Guru Gobind Singh initiated a meeting with Banda Bahadur in which he was able to convince him to leave the life of a *bairagi* and become a *karamyogi* under his guidance. Banda Bahadur became an ardent disciple of Guru Gobind Singh thereafter. After a short stay with the Guru, Banda Bahadur was sent to the Punjab with five advisers and a small detachment of soldiers to win back their lost territories and punish the guilty men of Sirhind.[22] A large number of historians have written about the encounter between Guru Gobind Singh and Banda Bahadur giving their own version of the conversation between the two. There is no authentic historical evidence available about what transpired between the Guru and Banda Bahadur, except the fact of the conversion of Banda Bahadur to Sikhism. At the risk of being accused of padding this book, a summarized assessment of the various accounts given by a large number of writers is placed in the text for the information and appreciation of the readers. It is considered a futile exercise on the part of historians to construct a dialogue between the Guru and Banda Bahadur for which there is no authentic historical record available. These dialogues based on various historians' imagination create unnecessary and avoidable distortions.

All that can be researched thereon is the final outcome of the meeting of the Guru with Banda Bahadur or the work and conduct of Banda Bahadur in bringing out a dormant Sikh power to a stage where it could challenge the might of the Mughal Empire. At this juncture, the Guru took another decision before his demise—to abolish the institution of personal Guruship and raised the level of the holy Granth to that of a living Guru called *Guru Granth Sahib.*[23] These two decisions of Guru Gobind Singh have been of tremendous value to the Sikh community in its advancement towards achieving of political sovereignty over the land of Punjab and the consolidation of Guruship in the holy book which otherwise may have led to an innumerable number of Gurus along with their *pothis* like the hundreds of religious Sikh *babas* who have come into existence so far. The succeeding chapters of this book will enable the readers to make their own assessment regarding these two momentous decisions taken by Guru Gobind Singh at the time of his demise and their contribution to the social and political advancement of the Sikh nation.

The chapter on 'The Concept of Sikh Sovereignty' may appear somewhat non-essential to the readers expecting only an account of the life and times of Banda Bahadur. But, it is the core of Sikh religion, political thought and backbone of the Sikh struggle. In fact, Guru Nanak laid down the concept of Sikh sovereignty. He laid down the conduct for the ruler and the ruled. He brought absolute democracy in his paying attention to the lowest amongst the lowly and bringing them at par with the highest among the high while seeking benediction for all alike from God Almighty.

His successors carried out the traditions set by him, thus consolidating the concept of human equality with the establishment of *langar* or partaking of same food sitting in a line (*pangat*). Guru Arjan, through his sacrifice and Guru Hargobind through his defensive warfare solidified the concept of human rights. Guru Tegh Bahadur espoused the principle of religious freedom with his martyrdom. The tenth Guru, Gobind Singh carried out the further implementation of these principles by creating the Khalsa to protect the faith as well as themselves from the atrocities of the Mughals. The concept of Sikh sovereignty had brought about absolute democracy which had not till then been fully adopted by the Western world. During the battles, the role of Bhai Kanhaiya to help the wounded friends and foes alike was a forerunner of the Florence Nightingale and the Red Cross.[24] Guru Gobind Singh in his famous letter *Zafarnama* to Aurangzeb—

چوں کار از ہمہ حیلتے در گذشت
حلال است بُردن بہ شمشیر دست

Choon kar az hama healtay dar guzasht
Halal ast burdan ba shamshir dast

When all efforts fail to dissuade an intolerant ruler, it is the right of the people to take up the sword to remove him.

had justified the right of the people to remove an unjust and intolerant ruler much before the Western world had embraced democratic practices and peoples' right to rebel against autocratic rulers. The idea of writing a chapter on this subject is to assess as to what extent Banda Bahadur and his *sardars* followed the principles laid down by the Sikh Gurus in the concept of Sikh sovereignty as some historians have cast aspersions on him in their accounts. In a widespread feudal system both with the Mughal government as well as the Hindu kingdoms bound down in a totally caste society; a fully democratic polity outside the caste system was propounded and established by the latter Gurus and early Sikh leaders. In this regard Banda Bahadur, in his short spell, that too amidst continuous conflict, had performed extraordinary achievements. It will also be a standard to measure the achievements of Sikh warriors like Kapur Singh, Jassa Singh Ahluwalia, Hari

Singh Nalwa and Maharaja Ranjit Singh, whose application and practice of the concept of Sikh sovereignty was on a dwindling scale than that of Banda Bahadur.

After the demise of Akbar, his successors Jahangir and others thereafter were not liberal minded and were bigoted and steeped in orthodoxy. Guru Arjan had visualized the coming difficult days and desired his son to be given all sorts of military training to defend himself and their faith. Jahangir had a bias against Guru Arjan and shortly after his accession to the imperial throne he got Guru Arjan arrested. He asked the Guru to join the Islamic faith which the Guru refused and consequently he was tortured to death. Guru Hargobind was initially jailed in Gwalior, but he managed to come out and even befriend Jahangir. Guru Hargobind fought six defensive battles, but realizing that he could not withstand the imperial forces, he shifted his headquarters to the relative security of the Shivalik hills. A similar situation arose after the execution of Guru Tegh Bahadur and Guru Gobind Singh who at the tender age of 9 had to face 21 defensive battles forced on him by the jealous hill rajas and Muslim state commanders. He had to leave Anandpur Sahib ultimately. In the battles fought both by Guru Hargobind and Guru Gobind Singh they have followed certain principles on humanitarian grounds totally divergent from the brutalities inflicted by the Mughal forces even on innocent civilians.

Banda Bahadur fought over twenty battles with Mughal forces under Mughal commanders and some even under the direct command of the Mughal emperors. In all these battles, the Mughal forces were far more superior as far as number of men, artillery, arms, ammunition, food stocks and replacement of men and materials were concerned. In comparison the Sikh forces were deficient in manpower, training, equipment and volunteers as were mostly running short of ammunition and food stocks. In spite of it they were able to win many battles and hold their own against the mighty Mughal forces. This was largely owing to the death-defying bravery of their men and the superior battle tactics adopted by their commander Banda Bahadur.

The tactics used by Banda Bahadur to change the fortunes of various battles in which the Sikhs were likely to lose was greatly similar to the tactics advocated in the books on 'art of war' and battle strategy written by Chinese authors. Sun Tzu's classic books *The Art of War* and *The Art of Strategy* were discovered in 1772 by a French Jesuit P. Amiot who translated them into French and presented them to Napoleon Bonaparte. These books were later translated by N. Conard into Russian and Captain E.F. Calthrop into English. The subject matter of these books has been read and practised by the commanders in European wars. In Central China there were about 50 countries who were perpetually at war with each other during 300 BC to AD 300. This constant fighting led to the coming into existence of Chinese experts on war helping various rulers in their wars and battle strategies. Sun Tzu was the first to put it down in writing in a book form called *Thirteen Chapters of Sun Tzu*.

Mahabharata, the epic war of India, and to a certain extent Kautilya's *Arthashastra* also throw light on the art of warfare and battle strategies. Since these are mixed with fables and fiction, the same have not been viewed as guiding principles. Banda Bahadur's application of strategy in wars fought hardly 300 years back with all the actual details of those battles being available, came out to be more useful than the Sun Tzu's classics which are very much wanting in details. The details of the battles fought by Banda Bahadur and the exposition of the battle strategies are given in a continuous form for the better appreciation of the situation and the strategy. This aspect appears to be dealt for the first time and needs more research thereon.

As soon as Banda Bahadur started occupying Mughal territories, his plan for a Sikh state commenced alongside. Banda Bahadur received information that an armed Mughal escort force was carrying treasure of revenue collections from a number of districts and was halting at the village of Bhuna on its way to Delhi. Banda Bahadur attacked the Mughal force accompanying the treasure, defeated them and took possession of the treasures. The matter was reported to the *amil* of Kaithal, a Hindu commander, who rushed with his troops to get back the treasure. Banda Bahadur and his men had hid themselves behind old walls, trees, etc. When they found that the *amil* and his troops had arrived, the Sikhs made a surprise attack and defeated them. They also took away all the horses and weapons from them. The *amil* was allowed to retain his office on behalf of the Khalsa, on payment of a requisite tribute and a detachment of Sikh soldiers was detailed with him for collection of revenue. The appointment of the *amil* of Kaithal as the revenue officer of the Khalsa was the first step taken by Banda Bahadur towards the establishment of a Sikh state.

Banda Bahadur after every occupation of large villages, towns, etc., appointed his own officials to administer the occupied territory. When Sirhind, the largest area in Punjab, was occupied, he appointed Baj Singh as the governor of Sirhind and Ali Singh was appointed his *naib* (assistant). Fateh Singh was appointed as the *faujdar* of Samana. Binod Singh and Ram Singh were jointly appointed governors of Thanesar. Hindu officials were appointed in all the subordinate posts in the place of Muslim officials. The Khalsa flag was hoisted on the fort of Sirhind. The battle of Sirhind is considered as the first major battle fought and won by the Sikhs against the Mughal forces.

Banda Bahadur seized all the landed estates and *zamindaris* and distributed them among the tillers and peasants cultivating these lands and declared them owners of those lands. He made the revenue system. Very simple revenue was collected twice a year at the site. The produce was divided into three parts. One part was taken by the Khalsa and rest of the two parts was given to the farmer. If the Khalsa needed the crop for their own consumption, they took the same as it is; otherwise the village *baniya* took the crop and gave its value to the Khalsa. This system was a great relief to the farmers as compared with the Mughal system in which 50 per cent of the crop value was taken as revenue by them, and from the other half as much as could be scrounged by the *zamindars*, and the farmers were left with very little. Banda's name struck terror in the hearts of lawless people, and thefts and dacoities became a thing of past. In all the parganas occupied by the Sikhs, writes Irvine,

> A low scavenger or leather dresser, the lowest of the low in Indian estimation, had only to leave home and join the Guru, when in a short time he would return to his birthplace as its ruler with his order of appointment in his hand. As soon as he set foot within the boundaries, the well born and wealthy went out to greet him and escort him home.

Arrived there, they stood before him with joined palms awaiting his orders. . . . Not a soul dared to disobey an order, and men who had often risked themselves in battlefield, became so cowed down that they were afraid even to remonstrate. Hindu who had not joined the sect were not exempt from these.[25]

Banda Bahadur made a Khalsa seal for the Sikh state, the legend on which was as under:

Degh, Tegh, Fateh o nusrat bedrang
Yaft uz Nanak Guru Gobind Singh.

Degh the economic power, Tegh the sword arm and Fateh the resultant victory, have been received from Guru Nanak to Guru Gobind Singh.

The imprint of this seal is available on the *Hukamnamas* issued by Banda Bahadur. It is a great irony that in the few battle-ridden years of his rule, he established the Khalsa state seal, whereas in the Misil period and the long reign of Ranjit Singh no state seal was ever made and used in the Khalsa rule. Banda Bahadur also issued a state coin in the name of the Sikh Gurus with the following legend:

Obverse:
Sikkah zad bar har do alam tegh-i-Nank wahib ast,
Fateh Gobind Singh Shah-i-Shahan Fazal Sacha Sahib ast.

A coin has been struck in both the worlds, herein and hereafter guaranteed under Guru Nanak's double-edged sword, the victories of Guru Gobind Singh has been with the grace of Lord all mighty.

Reverse:
Zarb ba aman-al-dahar musawarat
Shahar Zinat-al-takht Khalsa mubarik bakht.

Coin at the place of perfect peace, picture of a beautiful city, where the fortunate throne of the Khalsa is to locate.

These coins were issued for three years from 1710-12.

Banda Bahadur had converted a large number of Hindus and Muslim to Sikhism but he does not seem to have used any force to propagate his religion. Throughout the history of Sikhs it has been a glowing feature of the polity of various rulers to adopt a non-communal and tolerant policy towards those who agreed to be their subjects. When Banda Bahadur reached Kalanaur from Bahrampur, the Muslims of Kalanaur paid allegiance to him and joined his forces. Amin-ud-Daulah has stated that the authority of that deluded sect (of the Sikhs) had reached such extremes that many Hindus and Mohammedans adopted their faith and their rituals. Their chief, Banda Bahadur, captivated the hearts of all and whether a Hindu or a Mohammedan whosoever came into contact with him was addressed as a Singh. Accordingly, Dindar Khan, a powerful ruler of his neighbourhood, was named Dindar Singh and Mir Nasir-ud-Din, the official reporter of Sirhind, became Mir Nasir Singh. In much the same way, a large number of Mohammedans abandoned Islam and followed the misguided path (of Sikhism) and took solemn oaths and firm pledges to stand by Banda Bahadur.[26] This had been the result of religious tolerance shown to Muslim population of those places.

The character and development of the Sikh movement reveals that it had three main goals: (1) to build an egalitarian society, (2) to use the new society as a base to wage an armed struggle against the religious and political oppression, and (3) to capture political power.[27] The caste system among the Hindus was the greatest obstacle in the development of an egalitarian society. The Sikh Gurus concentrated on the elimination of the caste system in the development of an egalitarian society. Guru Nanak in his social order of the Sikhs brought the institutions of the *sangat*, *pangat* and *langar* in the service of common kitchen where everybody among the *sangat* has to sit in a *pangat* (line) and take the food prepared by the Sikhs in the *langar*. The third Guru, Guru Amar Das had made it obligatory for all the visitors to first take food in the *langar* and then meet the Guru. Sikh historical records show that Emperor Akbar took the food from the *langar* like everybody and thereafter met the Guru. Sikh Gurus considered that religion does not consist of mere words; he, who looks upon all men as equal, is religious. Radical *bhaktas* also subscribe to the theory of egalitarianism but they did not implement it in the manner the Sikhs carried out the same. Guru Nanak attacked the caste ideology and considered it perverse. He aligned himself with the lowliest of the low castes. 'There are lower castes among the low caste and some absolutely low. Nanak seeks their company. What hath he has to do with the high ones? For, where the lowly are cared for there is thine (God's) Benediction and Grace.'[28] Bhai Gurdas writes that Guru Nanak 'made the Dharma perfect by blending the four castes into one. To treat the king and the pauper on equal footing, and while greeting to touch the feet of other was made the rule of the conduct as a measure of humility.'[29]

Guru Gobind Singh chose five of beloved ones (*panj piaras*) as the leaders of the Khalsa community. One of them was a Khatri, one a Jat, one a barber, one a calico printer and one a water carrier. Guru stated that all embrace one creed and obliterate differences of religion. Let the four Hindu castes who have different rules for their guidance abandon them all, adopt one form of adoration and become brothers. Let no one deem himself superior to the others.

According to *Gurbilas Padshahi* 6, Guru Hargobind is said to have stated

> I will not give the hawk to them;
> I will get the crown and hawk from them.
> I will wrest from them the sovereignty of the country;
> I will bestow this all on the poor and the helpless.[30]

Guru Gobind Singh is said to have addressed Bhai Nand Lal as under:

> Listen, Nand Lal, to this plan:
> It will bring into being our Raj.
> I shall weld four castes into one;
> I shall make people remember God.
> The Khalsa under this plan, will ride horses and support hawks;
> The Turks will run away on seeing them.
> It will make one man fight a lakh and a quarter;
> He who dies (fighting) will be liberated . . .
> The drum will beat at every doorstep . . .
> The Khalsa will be victorious from one end to the other.
> The Khalsa will rule; no one will remain unsubdued.
> Everyone will join the Khalsa. For, they alone would be saved, who submit to the Khalsa.[31]

Rattan Singh Bhangoo in his *Sri Gur Panth Parkash* has brought out the saga of the Sikh struggle against the Mughal and Afghan rulers during the eighteenth century. Bhangoo has mastery over the language and poetic exposition.

Bhangoo has devoted about 50 episodes to Banda Bahadur out of a total of 189 episodes of the book, which took him over 30 years to complete. The portion pertaining to Banda Bahadur brings out the Mujhail bias against him in such abundance that it leaves a very bad taste with the reader.

Bhangoo was related to two major Mujhail families who made a great contribution in the fight against the Mughal forces. He states that he is writing (the account of the Sikhs) as narrated by his ancestors and forefather to him, and other elders, who had heard it from their elders. In these 50 odd episodes every conceivable effort had been made to belittle and ridicule Banda Bahadur wherever any opportunity occurred. False and baseless stories have been concocted almost in every episode. The extent to which this tirade has been carried out takes away the merit of the saga of sacrifices by the Sikhs when the tallest Sikh commander is being ridiculed and belittled much after his death by the thankless Mujhail soldiers who fought under his banner but never raised their bias against him during his lifetime.

Banda Bahadur has received praise for his valour and his character from numerous writers who have written detailed account of his getting initiated into Sikhism by Guru Gobind Singh and his role in leading the Sikh volunteers in the establishment of the initial Sikh state. He laid down the principle of land revenue to the maximum benefit to the peasants and farmers. In fact, he stands in the frontline of warriors of the world over.

Bhangoo's ancestors fought against the Mughals during the misil period and are remembered for their bravery and devotion. So for as the poetry and the general account of the battles is laudable, but his account of Banda Bahadur is full of fables and fictions laced with a high degree of Mujhail bias against him. Almost all his episodes on Banda Bahadur are full of unfounded allegations and records of events so much so that his work stands tainted far worse than the biased record of Islamic writers. In the chapter 'A Critique on Rattan Singh Bhangoo's *Sri Gur Panth Parkash*' gives in fair detail the false allegations and character assasination of Banda Bahadur carried out by Bhangoo.

ACKOWLEDGEMENT

At the time of my writing this book a very well written English translation of *Panth Parkash* by Prof. Kulwant Singh came out and has been very useful in my attempt to undo the damage done by Bhangoo to the reputation of Banda Bahadur. I am very obliged to Prof. Kulwant Singh for the use of his translation and a number of discussions on the subject with me.

NOTES

1. *Historians and Historiography of the Sikhs*, ed. Fauja Singh, New Delhi: Oriental Publishers and Distributors, 1978, Introduction, p. ii.
2. Ibid., p. iv.
3. Ibid., p. vi.
4. Ibid.
5. Ibid., S.S. Bal's account of J.D. Cunningham, pp. 129-33. Relevant excerpts are as under:
   'Lord Hardinge got Cunningham dismissed from Political Service that the latter had served with such great distinction for more than seventeen years.' It was a political decision and not on merit.
   Cunningham's assessment that the first Anglo-Sikh war began with the provocation given by the British agent on the frontier and won in collaboration with the leadership of the Sikh commanders. Cunningham's account came to be associated with the viewpoint that it did no credit to the British name and was put on *index expurgatrious*. For long time the book was looked upon as the outpourings of 'the apologist of the Khalsa' in which the author 'had done the English less than justice. . . .' While succouring his enemies, he was believed to have despitefully entreated his friends. It was almost taken for granted that the author had been clearly led astray by overweaning anxiety to do justice to our enemies. At places he had fallen short of truth, and at others drawn hasty conclusions from insufficient premises.
6. Ibid., pp. 7-8.
7. Ibid., p. 9.
8. H.R. Gupta, *History of Sikh Gurus*, New Delhi: U.C. Kapur & Sons, 1973, p. 97.
9. *Tuzuk-e-Jahangiri*, p. 35.
10. Gupta, *History of Sikh Gurus*.

11. Ibid., p. 121.
12. Ibid., p. 141.
13. Ibid., pp. 183-5.
14. Ibid., pp. 206-9.
15. Ibid., pp. 227-8.
16. Ibid., pp. 239-40.
17. Muzzaffar Alam, *The Crisis of the Empire in Mughal North India*, New Delhi: Oxford University Press, 1997, p. 1.
18. Ibid.
19. Elliot & Dowson, vol. VII, p. 183.
20. G.S. Deol, *Banda Bahadur*, Jullundur: New Academic Co., 1972, p. 16.
21. H.R. Gupta, *History of the Sikhs*, New Delhi: Munshiram Manoharlal, 1994, vol. I, p. 323.
22. Ibid., p. 326.
23. Harbans Singh, *Heritage of the Sikhs*, New Delhi: Manohar, 1994, p. 89.
24. M.A. Macauliffe, *The Sikh Religion*, New Delhi: S.Chand & Co., 1985, pp. 173-4.
25. Irvine William, *Later Mughals*, New Delhi: Taj Publications, 1989, pp. 98-9.
26. Teja Singh and Ganda Singh, *A Short History of the Sikhs*, Patiala: Punjab University, 1989, p. 86.
27. Jagjit Singh, *The Sikh Revolution*, Chandigarh: Bahri Publications, 1981, p. 115.
28. *Sri Guru Granth*, p. 15.
29. Bhai Gurdas, *Var I*, *Pouris* 23, 25.
30. *Gurbilas Chevin Patshahi*, p. 293.
31. *Rehatname*, ed. Piara Singh Padam, p. 47.

CHAPTER 1

The Early Life of Banda Bahadur (1670-1708)

Journey in Quest of Eternal Bliss

An account of the life of Banda Bahadur from his childhood up to his meeting with Guru Gobind Singh, from 1670 to 1708—a period of 38 years—does not seem to have been written about neither by any contemporary nor by any later writer. Maybe his being a person from an ordinary family did not attract any one to write about his antecedents and activities to be preserved for posterity. From childhood till adulthood, he lived an ordinary life in a remote village in Jammu close to Rajouri (Poonch area). With the commencement of his life of renunciation (*bairag*) some time from 1688 till 1708, he was lost in the wilderness of life in the company of *sadhus* and ascetic warriors. It was only when Guru Gobind Singh met Banda Bahadur and sent him to the Punjab that some contemporary accounts about him appeared, primarily through the accounts of suppression of the Sikh uprising under Banda Bahadur by the Mughal authorities.

Banda Bahadur spent some time between 1713 and 1715 at a very quiet place on the banks of river Chenab (now called Riasi). At this place his successors have set-up a small *dera* in his memory.

After Banda Bahadur's execution at Delhi in 1716, the Sikhs passed through a very difficult phase when the Mughal authorities would hunt them down everywhere and kill them mercilessly. With the coming of Misls and the deterioration in the Mughal administration due to inherent decay, Afghan attacks, as well as the Sikh resurgence, that the Sikhs were able to hold their own against the Mughal authorities. The successors of Banda Bahadur lived a quiet life in Riasi, till the rise of Sikhs and the downfall of

Plate 1: Banda Bahadur at the Dera at Riasi.

the Mughal administration perhaps to avoid detection by the Mughal authorities. Therefore, even in the period immediately after Banda Bahadur's execution, the times were very hard and nobody seemed to have time to record any account of Banda Bahadur's life.

The works of Rattan Singh Bhangoo, Santokh Singh, Bhai Gian Singh, Daulat Rai, Sohan Singh, etc., belong to a much later period, close to eighteenth and early nineteenth century. The accounts of Persian historians, namely, Khafi Khan, Ghulam Husain Khan and others are influenced by the pro-Islamic prejudices for their rulers and Islamic bias against the large-scale non-Muslim population. They have accepted false and flimsy rumours as historical truth and charged Banda Bahadur with cruelty and barbarity whereas the atrocities and barbarities of the Islamic rulers on the local population were far more severe and extensive.

Some bare facts of Banda Bahadur's life, collected and recorded, as available with us, are as under:

In the house of Ramdev, an ordinary ploughman and a Rajput of the Bhardwaj clan, a male child was born on 27 October 1670 at Rajouri in Poonch district of Jammu.[1] The child was named Lachhman Das. The period 1670-80 is generally taken as his childhood, 1681-8 as his adolescence and from 1688 to 1708 as his period of renunciation (*bairag*).

Ganda Singh states that the area to which Lachhman Das belonged was a very backward area and education was by and large restricted to the Brahmin community. Therefore, Lachhman Das had no regular schooling in the early years of his life.[2] In his adolescent age, he spent most of his time working in the fields like other boys and as he grew up he took to hunting and riding. He seems to have picked up quite a proficiency in the use of bow and arrow.[3] In their modest life, the special entertainment that a hillman could offer to a guest was a piece of 'shikar', for which these people were considered very hospitable.

There are a couple of theories about the original home of Banda Bahadur. Most historians hold that his birthplace was at Rajouri in Poonch district of Jammu. Over half a century after Banda's time, James Browne wrote that he was born at a village Pandori in the Jullundur Doab.[4] J.D. Cunningham wrote that he was a native of south India.[5] Hari Ram Gupta is of the view that Banda belonged to Sirmour, now in the district of Nahan (Himachal Pradesh).[6] He bases his conclusion on the ground that Guru Gobind Singh's field of activity has been the region lying between rivers Sutlej and Jamuna. He stayed at Paonta in Nahan district from 1685 to 1688. The Guru frequently went on hunting expeditions around Paonta as well as in the hilly areas south of Paonta and Nahan. This area was a famous hunting ground for wild animals. Banda was also a great hunter and during his hunting expeditions, Guru Gobind Singh seems to have met Lachhman Das (Banda) many a time.[7] Without any previous acquaintance, the Guru would not have undertaken a long journey of nearly 2000 km and selected Banda as his deputy at Nanded to guide the destiny of his beloved Khalsa.[8] The journey of 2000 km to the south taken by the Guru was *prima facie* on account of his meeting Aurangzeb and later on joining his successor Bahadur Shah at Nanded. This account is based on sufficient historical evidence. Hari Ram Gupta's account seems to be a piece of imaginative fiction and especially when he has not given any evidence in support of his contention.

Giani Bhajan Singh states that Ramdev was in-charge of a small fortress at Tachhal Nagar, 50 km from Rajouri.[9] As Lachhman Das grew up, his father arranged his education in elementary study of languages, arithmetic and use of weapons of warfare. He seems to have acquired some reasonable knowledge of Sanskrit, etc., during his childhood and during his period of *bairag*. The somewhat affluent status of the family of Ramdev, cannot be relied upon, it being the work of a devotee of Banda Bahadur and in the absence of any reliable evidence in support thereof.

Whereas historians have universally called Lachhman Das as unlettered and uneducated, he does seem to have had some education. While at Nanded he possessed a book of Tantrik powers given to him by Aughr Nath at Panchvati, from which he cultivated occult powers.

In one of his hunting expedition, it is said, Lachhman Das shot a doe and as he approached the injured animal, the pitiable looks of the dying animal struck a tender chord in his heart. When he opened its stomach to clean the animal, he saw two still-born offspring drop out of its womb and die before his eyes. This scene greatly disturbed his mental state and an urge arose in him from within eschewing hunting as a sport.[10] This was also the beginning of his turning away from other mundane things of daily life. Lachhman Das was now no longer a Rajput, but an ascetic in the making. Rajouri town was on the way to the shrines in the Kashmir valley and very often *sadhus* and ascetics would come to Rajouri, stay for a while and move on to the shrines of their pilgrimage. Lachhman Das started spending time with these *sadhus* and ascetics to understand their way of life and the rituals and austerities performed by them.[11]

Some time later Lachhman Das came under the influence of a *bairagi* Janaki Prasad, who greatly influenced the disturbed mind of the young lad. Abandoning his family and house Lachhman Das joined Janaki Prasad on his pilgrimage. A new name Madho Das was given to him to make a complete break with his past as has been the practice in all ascetic orders. For some time his first halt was at Sadhaura.[12]

Sadhaura is said to be a corrupted form of Sadhuwara, the place of *sadhus*. It is close to the Hindu pilgrimage centre called Kapalmochan, a few kilometres away on the bank of the then Saraswati River, which has since gone underground. Sadhaura was an important Buddhist centre but with the coming of Shankaracharya to the north, this place was taken over by ascetics and *sadhus* of Hindu religion. Lands around Sadhaura in the Jamuna basin being very fertile, were occupied by the Muslim zamindars with the advent of Islam in north-western India. In the early eighteenth century, Sadhaura was occupied by many sufi saints and one order amongst them was that of Pir Buddhan Shah, popularly called Pir Buddhu Shah, who became very friendly with Guru Gobind Singh. Hindu hill rajas, under the leadership of the raja of Garhwal, attacked Guru Gobind Singh, but the hill rajas were defeated at Bhangani in 1688. In this war, Pir Buddhu Shah sent his four sons and seven hundred of his disciples to the Guru's help.[13] Immediately after the Bhangani war, Guru Gobind Singh decided to leave Paonta, visited Pir Buddhu Shah at Sadhaura and then spent a few months in Kapalmochan and its surrounding areas before going back to Anandpur Sahib. Giani Bhajan Singh has ventured to state that although there is no evidence of Madho Das having met Guru Gobind Singh here, it is quite likely that he would have known about Guru Gobind Singh as they were living in close proximity for a few months.[14]

Although Madho Das had accompanied Janaki Prasad, somehow he was not getting the requisite guidance for his mental peace and solace and was still in a disturbed state of mind. In 1687-8, he accompanied Janaki Prasad to attend the Baisakhi fair at the shrine of Baba Ranthaman in the neighbourhood of Kasur (Pb.). Here he entered into the discipleship of another *bairagi* named Ram Das, but the real peace of mind was still as elusive from him as ever.[15] Madho Das entered the unknown world of *sadhus* and ascetic warriors spread all over India, a world with which he had no acquaintance, a world which had greatly degenerated from an idealistic and ascetic way of life to a worldly way of life with all its failings and follies. His journey from the north to the south covered the most important formative and constructive period of his life (about 20 years), i.e. from 1688 to 1708. Banda Bahadur's activities and associations with other groups of *bairagis*/ascetic warriors are totally uneventful as far as any happenings with Banda Bahadur or even any other historical events of this period.

A summarized account of rise and fall of the organization of ascetic warriors which seems to have existed in ancient times till the early eighteenth century is given in order to appreciate the situation in which Banda Bahadur had spent about 20 years of his life (1688-1708) and yet came out virtually unscathed from the viles and vices of ascetic warriors.

The people in ancient India understood the use of fire, made pottery, cultivated food grains and domesticated animals. The potter's wheel and the art of spinning and weaving are traced to the Neolithic period.[16] It is commonly believed that the present-day *adivasis* are descendants of them. The creation of Scheduled Caste is a post-Buddhist phenomenon. The present-day *adivasis* are descendants of the people who were called the Nagas and were Buddhist by faith. After the fall of Buddhism they were downgraded by the ruling priestly class because the Nagas had enmity with the Aryans and did not worship Aryan gods. The mention of Nagas in *Rigveda* shows that the Nagas were very ancient people. They were in no way aboriginals or uncivilized people. History shows a close association of inter marriages between Naga people with the ruling Hindu families of India. The Naga people occupied a high cultural level and were ruling a good part of India.[17] The present Andhra Pradesh and its neighbourhood were under the Nagas during the early centuries of Christian era. The term 'Dravidians' and 'Nagas' are merely two different names for the same people. The word 'Dravidia' is a Sanskritized form of the word 'Tamil' and was the name of the language of the people and does not denote the race of the people.[18] Before the seventh century BC, i.e. before the rise of Buddhism, all the kshatriya dynasties of Mahabharata times had been ruined, shattered and destroyed.[19] They were replaced by 'Dravidians'/'Nagas'. That 'Nagas' were sympathizers and followers of Buddha is well known.[20] Dr. Ambedkar had remarked that his selection of Nagpur was due to the historical association of the area with the Nagas who were friendly towards Buddhism. The devotion of the Nagas towards Buddhism is seen from the fact that they were among those who formed a body of guards protecting the Bodhisattva and his mother. At the Bodhisattva's birth, some Nagas came to bathe him, a scene that had long been a favourite theme among sculptors.

The non-Aryan Naga people were believers in the Buddhistic social culture. During their rule, they were a society based on social equality, because their cultural values were influenced by the Buddhist traditions. This social system of Nagas is noteworthy in contrast to the Brahmanical social system of inequality. All the members in the Naga society were treated with equal status and a casteless social order was the main basis of the social system of the Nagas. Naga culture played a great role in the process of establishing a casteless, egalitarian and integrated society in Indian cultural life.[21] With the advent of Aryans in India, the Nagas became a subject population under Aryan rulers. The introduction of caste system has been an Aryan institution which penetrated in the then casteless social order in India. Nagas had a public-oriented social system and unlike the Brahmanical system, their political system was also designed to give social justice to all the people.

During the pre-Gupta era, i.e. from the first to the fourth century AD, the countries in central India comprised strong republics of Nagas. Most of these were destroyed by Samudragupta.[22] K.P. Jaiswal has also stated that the administrative system of Nagas as well as their social system was based on the principle of equality. There was nothing like a caste system for them and all belonged to one and the same caste. There were also independent Naga kingdoms in the south.

Kashmir has always been considered as one of the principal centres of Naga worship in India. The Naga and Buddhist influence persisted till Mughal times as Abul Fazl tells in *Ain-i-Akbari* that during the reign of Akbar there were temples in Kashmir, 45 of Shiva, 65 of Vishnu, 3 of Brahma, 22 of Durga, but 700 of Nagas in active worship, all this has been gleaned from the architecture of the valley.[23]

Snake worship was an old and prevalent form of original faith all over India before the Aryans arrived and Aryans adopted it gradually as they inter-married with indigenous Naga people. Naga worship could have become the dominant faith in India, had it not been elbowed out from its place by Vaishnavism and Shaivism, as has been the case with Buddhism in India.[24]

Before the rise of the Guptas, important ruling dynasties were of the Nagas and also many republics. They were scattered all over India. In the Puranas, nine Nagas have been mentioned by name. Powerful king Virsen of Mathura was a Naga. The Allahabad pillar inscription mentions the marriage of Chandragupta II with a Naga princess Kuveranaga. Although the Guptas rose to power with the help of the Nagas, they demolished the Naga kingdoms and most of the Naga republics. Large-scale destruction of Naga republics was carried out by Samudragupta. The disappearance of Naga republics around AD 400 was due to the rise of Gupta imperialism. According to Jaiswal, Samudragupta, like Alexander, killed the free spirit of the country and all these independent kingdoms and republics came under the suzerainty of the Guptas.[25]

Where the Naga republics were subdued and merged with the Aryan kingdoms, the Nagas (ascetic warriors) continued to exist in batches and groups maintaining their existing way of life. These warriors were called Nagas, because they went around naked or with only a strip of cloth bound around their loin. They kept their beard parted in the middle and brushed over the cheeks to add to the fierceness of the appearance.[26] This type of depiction of the beard has been fairly common among the Rajputs of the later period. Their bodies were smeared with ash and their forehead painted with their sect marks. At times their bodies were smeared with oil so that they could slip away if their opponent tried to catch them. Their weapons were primarily bows and arrows (later replaced by the match-locks), shields, spears, and the murderous *chakras* worn one above the other around the neck. The other weapons used by them were a short sword or dagger: the 'rocket', a kind of glorified jumping cracker composed of a strong metal cylinder to which knives were attached; and the 'umbrella' consisting of a circle of iron balls suspended from a central rod, like a maypole, which when skilfully handled was said to be as impenetrable as a coat of mail, in addition to being a deadly weapon of offence.[27]

An important austerity practised by Naga *sadhus* was celibacy. According to Yoga-metaphysics, sexual energy, the fire passion, is the main potential source of spiritual energy. But as an aid to mental control of sexuality, physical restraint must be employed and one method was the continuous wearing of chastity belts. Upon joining, an apprentice-*sadhu* undergoes an initiation rite, which is regarded as a symbolic death—and a rebirth. He dies from his former, earthly life and is reborn into the divine life. The visible symbol of this rebirth is the shaven head of the novice. The guru is the father, mother and teacher—and the disciple worships his guru as God incarnate. In their nakedness, they do not emanate sexuality. On the contrary they control and inhibit the sexual vibrations, retaining its energy so that it can be mystically transformed into psychic and spiritual power. The wearing of chastity belts or tying some heavy objects to their penis or tying it around the body is done until the power of muscles and nerves is completely destroyed.

The Nagas made free use of *bhang*, opium and intoxicating liquors. When going into action their progress was less of a march than a kind of whirling dance, during which they became worked up to a pitch of uncontrollable excitement. Then, with ear-piercing yells, they rushed upon the enemy. Their frightful appearance, and the superstitious terror with which they were regarded contributed to the success of their army. In addition to being excellent swordsmen, Nagas were also skilled wrestlers, always eager to get hand to hand grips with their opponents. Their bodies were kept hard by severe physical exercises.[28]

Besides Nagas, other Aryan groups of ascetic warriors had also come into existence and they used to visit Kumbh Melas and also protect the properties of the *maths* and the temples. Occasionally they would impose levies on the pilgrims when they ran short of funds, but by and large they lived in a world of their own.

The successive tides of Mohammedan invasions from the twelfth century onwards had brought into India swarms of reckless adventurers of every description in the train of conquering armies. Among these were a large number of Muslim *faqirs* or *derveshes* whom the religious wars of the time had made familiar with the use of arms. Equipped with a spear and a battle-axe they roamed at large throughout the subdued territories, murdering and pillaging at will.[29] The Hindu ascetic orders were amongst the worst sufferers at their hands. Places of religious pilgrimage with steady flow of pious offerings were a favourite hunting ground for the fanatical *faqirs*. Murderous assaults were made on parties of defenceless pilgrims bathing at the sacred spots. The sympathies of the Muslim authorities were for the most part on the side of the aggressors.[30]

In the absence of any administrative action by the rulers to redress the grievances of the public against these foreign free-booters, this wanton violence greatly disturbed the large peace-loving Hindu population and especially the ascetic warriors who stood in defence of the pilgrims. They had to suffer greatly at the hands of these fanatic marauders. The ascetic warrior groups also carried out large-scale recruitments in which a number of rules and regulations were given a go-by in order to collect a large number of able-bodied volunteers to fight against these fanatics. Some of the important *deras*/organized orders are given in the following paras.

Yogis were one of the well-known Hindu ascetic orders of the disciples of Gorakhanath, popularly known as *kanphata* (split-eared) on account of the heavy pendants worn in their ears. Both in theory and in practice, these *yogis* did not follow the Hindu doctrine of *ahimsa* (harmlessness) as compared to other religious orders. This cult was associated with dark and fearsome rites in which the sacrificial sword played an important part, and human sacrifice was quite common.[31] The *yogis* were also great practitioners of magic and were widely credited with possession of occult powers, a reputation which enabled them to influence those people who aspired for temporal powers. These *yogis* with tantrik powers became the trusted advisors of kings and nobles, and often acted as secret agents in the advancement of their designs. They had been attached since early times with the courts of several Rajput princes, such as Bappa Rawal of Mewar (Udaipur) and Rao Jodha of Marwar (Jodhpur).[32]

The famous order of *yogis* was the first to offer armed resistance to the Muslim oppression. Besides fighting against the Muslim aggression, these *yogis* being attached to various Hindu rulers fought on behalf of those rulers against Hindu co-religionists as well. Professor J.N. Farquhar states that in the case of a *yogi* king who had his lands in western India around AD 1500, he kept a considerable body of *yogis*. Once in three or four years, some 3,000 of these warriors would go on pilgrimage and lay the whole country under contribution.[33] Kabir has given a description of these ascetic warriors in his *Kabir-Bijaka*

Never have I seen such *yogis*, Brother.
They wander mindless and negligent
Proclaiming the way of Mahadeva.
For this they are called great *mahants*.
To markets and bazaars they bring their meditation,
False *siddhas*, lovers of *maya*.
    When did Dattatreya attack a fort?
    When did Sukadeva join with gunners?
    When did Narada fire a musket?
    When did Vyasadeva sound a battle cry?
These make war, slow-witted.
Are they ascetics or archers?
Become unattached, greed is their mind's resolve.

Wearing gold they shame their profession,
Collecting stallions and mares and
Acquiring villages they go about as tax collectors.[34]

Another important group was the *sannyasis*. The *sannyasis* as reorganized by Sankaracharya in the ninth century, were divided into ten sections each with its own special designation. Monasteries of all the ten sub-orders are still found in the south, their *sannyasis* were all brahmins; but in the north only few monasteries were of brahmins only and others were a mix of brahmins and non-brahmin warriors.[35]

The armed *sannyasis* were generally known as Gosain (Goswami), lord of the cattle and also as Dasnamis, members of the order of ten names. In violation of the rules of their order, they accepted money and also like the *yogis* indulged freely in the use of flesh and intoxicating liquor. Unlike the *sannyasis* proper, they were keen disciples of the God Shiva and sworn enemies of the worshippers of Vishnu.[36] It is said that two notorious Gosain leaders who had taken a vow to slay two *bairagis* (Vaishnava ascetics) daily before tasting food. When unable to achieve their purpose, their custom was to make clay models of their foes, affix the appropriate sect-mark, and destroy them in effigy. This was believed to result in the death of the victim.[37]

Another major group of Hindu devotees, the Vishnu worshipping sect, whose members were called *bairagis* (one who had subdued his passions) resorted to the arming of their members and became the third main group of Hindu ascetic warriors.[38]

The *sannyasis* were by far the most numerous as well as the most aggressive. Not only the twice-born, but braves of all ranks and classes, seem to have flocked to their standards. There were continual armed clashes between the *sannyasis* and the *bairagis*, generally over the policing of the religious fairs, and the collection of pilgrim dues.[39]

The *bairagis* were divided irrespective of the sect into seven sections, each attached to a separate *akhara*, its military headquarter, presided over by a *mahant*, who was recognized as its military leader. The member of each sect continued to use their own sect-mark, worshipped their own special deities and retained their connection with their own temple, but for defensive purposes, they belonged to their respective *akharas*. The seven *akharas* later rose to sixteen.[40] Among the fighting *bairagis*, the caste distinctions were put aside and members of the various groups shared a common kitchen. This relaxation of caste rule extended to only the actual combatants. *Bairagis* were nominally vegetarian, but this rule was fairly disregarded. Free use of opium, hemp, and other narcotics was very common.[41]

Early in the reign of Sawai Jai Singh, the founder of Jaipur city, a strong body of armed Ramanandis were permanently established in a small fort, which is still known as the temple of Balanand at the base of Nahargarh. *Sannyasis* were to be found in great number in Bundelkhand and other adjoining districts of the Mughal Empire.[42]

By the eighteenth century, the monastic movement which began as a measure of self-protection entered its last phase, that of professional military service. The Rajput kingdoms torn by internal dissension and bled white by endless Mughal exactions, stood in constant need of military reinforcement in their desperate struggle. The armed ascetics clung obstinately to their own methods of warfare, and to the last refuse to join the regular armies. Many were only too ready to exchange the precarious life of a freebooter for steady employment with some ruling prince, or military adventurer. The usual pay of such mercenaries at that time was only half an *anna* a day, but it was the smallest part of their earnings.[43]

With the passage of time an increasing number of religious places like temples, *maths*, *deras*, etc., had come into existence and they had amassed large and valuable assets. They became an easy prey for robbers and other such elements. So ascetic warriors were engaged by these religious places to protect themselves. As a natural growth of the country, a number of new groups of ascetic warriors also came into existence.

To overcome the continual damage done by these lawless fanatics which had come with the Mohammedan armies, the existing ascetic orders were made to rise to the occasion. Fresh recruitments were made in which the requirements of caste, training, etc., were relaxed and virtually a number of armies consisting of armed ascetics and others came into existence to protect the religious places and the defenceless pilgrims bathing at these sacred spots. As already stated, the Hindu ascetic orders of Nagas, *yogis*, *sannyasis*, *bairagis*, etc., made a major contribution by increasing their strength and converting them into large-scale armies fully armed to fight the marauding menace of Islamic fanatics. This situation brought a major change in the ascetic orders and in place of following of ascetic taboos and directions, the habits of normal armies fighting such battles came into existence. The use of opium and other drugs, consumption of meat, collection of money and all other worldly vices became part and parcel of the ascetic world with a virtual good-bye to the rigorous and religious asceticism.

The term *gosain* derived from *goswamin* meant the one who had mastered his passions and was originally conceived of as a person who was to honour God and for the benefit of his own soul had completely mastered his passions and could devote his whole life to devotion and austerity. The *gosains* had derived their spiritual descent from the religious leader Shankaracharya.[44]

In a due space of time, the armies of *gosains* set aside the following of religious asceticism and took to worldly life in full measure. Some of these devotees who settled down in Bengal were engaged in moneylending and trade. In north India they took to the activities as tax farmers, moneylenders and traders.

The French traveller Tavernier makes reference to these doughty warriors, but little attempt is made to establish their identity. The standard books on Indian history are almost silent on this subject. In the troubled years that witnessed the decline and downfall of Mughal power in India, a large part of north India was overrun by marauding bands of armed religious ascetics, who usually travelled in large companies of horse and foot taking a heavy toll in the name of alms from the habitations through which they passed. They were ready to give battle to anyone who opposed their progress. In the ranks of warrior ascetics were to be found representatives of all the chief religious orders then established in north India.[45] In times of imminent danger, rival sects, forgetful of their differences, turned to the military leader who, in the role of *mahant* presided over the *akhara* or monastic settlement, and was best able to afford effective protection. Nevertheless the opening of the doors of the religious order to this undisciplined rebel of nominal devotees could not but have a profound influence on their later history.[46]

In the reign of Emperor Akbar (1556-1605), a famous *sannyasi* scholar of Benares approached the emperor with a request that his order be permitted to take suitable measures for its own defence. It was proposed that 'twice-born non-brahmins (that is, men of the warrior and mercantile castes) should now be enrolled as fighting *sannyasis*'. The emperor is said to have given his consent. Of these ten *sannyasis* orders only three and half are pure, that is, consisting entirely of brahmins. Hardly had the *sannyasis* got permission to bear arms than dissensions broke out amongst them. History relates that in a camp at Thaneswar in 1567 Akbar witnessed with keen enjoyment an armed encounter between the members of the 'giri' and 'puri' sub-orders and even sent some of his own men to aid the weaker side.[47] In the times of Akbar, the Mughal army had two battalions of Naga warriors who were paid double the salary as compared with normal wages in the Mughal army. During the 35th year of Aurangzeb's reign, i.e. 1692-3 an imperial decree was issued authorizing five Ramanandi commanders to move freely about the whole empire with standards and kettledrums, at the head of companies both of horse and foot' and instructing *subedars* and zamindars 'that no obstacle or hindrance be put in their way so that they may travel without molestation from one province to another'.[48] The success of Saiva ascetic (*gosains*) arms depended on the effectiveness as mercenaries—Naga *sadhus* and the *gosains* that led them in the eighteenth century had to be willing to serve with one another regardless of caste and status, and to serve states regardless of the religious foibles of the monarch and his allies. The most obvious reflection of this is the fact that the *gosains* were allied with the major powers of north India, including the Mughal emperor, the Nawabs of Awadh, and the British, and turned their backs on the one military force, the Marathas. While in the service of the Nawabs of Awadh alongside the Mughals and Durrani Afghans in the battle of Panipat of 1761, Maratha fortunes in northern India were dealt a heavy blow. The *gosain* ascetics did not take any offence when

Ahmad Shah Durrani complained to Shuja-ud-Daula, just before the battle of Panipat in 1761, that he could not stand the presence in his camp of naked infidels, parading around with their genitalia in full view for all to see. Significantly, the *gosains* respected the religious sensibilities of the Afghan, removed their battalions to a respectable distance, and then proceeded to contribute in a major way to the slaughter of the Marathas.[49]

With the death of Aurangzeb in 1707 organized persecution came to an end, but this change brought no corresponding reduction in the war-like activities of the Hindu ascetic orders. By this time, the militant movement had begun to lose even the semblance of a religious war. The existence of such a mighty host of professional warriors, called into being for a special purpose and required to maintain itself by means of forced levy on the local inhabitants inevitably led to violence and pillage on an extensive scale. The prevailing disorder was highly favourable to the designs of the monastic militants. Strong bands of naked warriors ravaged the country, striking terror in the hearts of the inhabitants. They were no longer united against a common cause and their arms were now turned against one another.[50]

The famous *gosain* leader, Himmat Bahadur, with a large body of fighting ascetics, joined the service of Mahadaji Sindhia and at a later date aided the British in the conquest of Bundelkhand. Himmat Bahadur had his headquarters at Jhansi. A disciple of Himmat Bahadur by name Kampta Giri with a strength of 1,500 horsemen joined the camp of Daulat Rao Sindhia in Rajputana in 1809. After his breach with Himmat Bahadur, many of the *gosain* fighters remained with Kampta Giri. Mahadaji Sindhia was the first Maratha leader who employed *sannyasis* in large numbers. A strong force of *gosains* joined the services of Shuja-ud-Daula, the *nawab wazir* of Oudh. This gave a sort of identity to the 5,000 fanatics, all perfectly naked, covered with paint and ashes in the attack on British lines in 1764. In the battle of Patan in 1790, the forces of Jodhpur and Jaipur allies had 5,000 *faqirs*, called Brakys and Attyles, which shows that a mixture of Muslim fanatics and Hindu fanatics were fighting in a team against the enemies. We find the *sannyasis* and *bairagis*, once sworn enemies, fighting cheerfully side by side, and often winning high distinctions in the armies of Bijay Singh and his successors.[51]

As regards *yogis*, they seldom chose to serve as professional soldiers, not from lack of courage, but through fear of injury to their *mudras* or earrings, the loss of which was looked upon as an irreparable disaster. They preferred diplomacy and intrigue to open warfare. Some distinguished themselves as leaders of considerable bodies of armed men, both hired mercenaries or ascetic warriors of their own or other's persuasions. The spiritual head of Mahamandir, the famous Nath fortress on the outskirts of Jodhpur, used to have a larger cavalcade than that of any feudal lord of Marwar.[52] Some 7,000 *Dadupanthis* were kept employed by Maharaja Partap Singh of Jaipur for suppressing revolts and collecting revenues.

Of the fighting orders, the *sannyasis* were by far the most numerous, as well as the most aggressive. Not only the 'twice born', but bravos of all ranks and classes, seem to have flocked to their standard. There were continual armed clashes between the *sannyasis* and the *bairagis*, over the policing of the great religious fairs and the collection of pilgrim dues. It is said that while a company of *bairagis* were performing their ablutions in the Shipra River at Ujjain, they were suddenly overwhelmed by a deadly rain of arrows from the *gosain* fort popularly called 'monastery of Bhairongarh' overlooking the river. It is said that the brutal murder of a trusted Ramanandi leader while on a peaceful journey led to the final mustering of the *bairagi* forces at the Galta. Under the able leadership of Balanand, a Rajput from Delhi, the four *sampradayas*—the Ramanandis, the Madhvas, the Vishnuswamis, and the Nimbarkas—were welded into a strong confederacy which was able to meet the Dasnamis on equal terms.[53]

At Kotah, in an encampment of several hundred *gosains*, in commodious modern tents, well provided with horses, camels and other means of transport, at intervals they marched out in procession, headed by their naked and ash-smeared leader mounted on an elephant, in a manner strongly reminiscent of the old fighting days as described by various writers. Several months of each year were thus spent in pilgrimage to Hardwar, Benares, and other holy places, the expenses of the journey being defrayed by the offerings of pious votaries. These prosperous 'pilgrims' were generally attached to one of the larger Naga monasteries scattered over central and north-western India.[54]

The deterioration in the conduct of the ascetic *sadhus* had happened to such a vile extent, in spite of their suppression by the British, that they remained unrepentant as can be observed from their conduct on the *maha-kumbh mela* of 1954. Early on the morning of 3 February 1954, the *Prayag maha-kumbh mela*, India's premier festival, descended into utter chaos. At the centre of the commotion were armed Naga *sadhus*, who tore indiscriminately into the throng of jostling, hapless pilgrims, over a frivolous right as to who was to bathe first. A stampede ensued with great losses of life, as the pressure forced the people to tread over the bodies of the injured and the dead.[55] The Naga ascetics had by then degenerated to become the scum of the once laudable ascetic warriors.

Banda Bahadur passed through the world of ascetic-hood and spending a period of about 20 years moving from the north to the south and ultimately settling down at Nanded. About this period of Banda Bahadur's life we have no available account as to how he spent these years and to which group he was aligned and in which battles he had participated except the little account of the last few years of his stay at Nanded. Banda Bahadur with his ideals of embracing *bairag* at an adolescent age was based on certain established principles of asceticism, must have found himself a total misfit in the armies of ascetic warriors in the most depraved and degenerated conditions of asceticism. Otherwise had he joined these ascetic warriors, he would have certainly risen to be the leader of one of these groups and would have left a definite mark on his role in the history of ascetic warriors. It appears to be a circumstantial assessment that he was a disappointed man who had set-up his *dera* at Nanded to bless people with 'Dudh-put'.

NOTES

1. Ganda Singh, *Life of Banda Singh Bahadur*, Amritsar: Khalsa College, 1935, p. 1.

2. Ibid., p. 2.
3. Ibid.
4. James Browne, *Indian Studies Past & Present*, vol. II, no. 4, Calcutta, 1961, p. 568.
5. J.D. Cunningham, *History of Sikhs*, Delhi: S. Chand & Co., 1972, p. 77.
6. Hari Ram Gupta, *History of Sikhs*, New Delhi: Munshiram Manoharlal, 1978, vol. II, p. 2.
7. Ibid., p. 3.
8. Ibid.
9. Bhajan Singh Giani, Smarika Golden Jubilee, Rohtak, n.d., n.p.
10. Ganda Singh, op. cit., p. 3.
11. Ibid., pp. 3-4.
12. Ibid., p. 4.
13. Hari Ram Gupta, *History of Sikh Gurus*, New Delhi: Kapur & Sons, 1973, p. 153.
14. Bhajan Singh Giani, op. cit.
15. Ganda Singh, op. cit., p. 4.
16. V.D. Mahajan, *Ancient India*, Delhi: S. Chand & Co., rpt., 1972, p. 28.
17. K. Jamanadas, *Adivasis Were Buddhist Naagas*, p. 3.
18. Ibid.
19. Ibid.
20. Ibid.
21. H.L. Kosare, *Prachin Bharat Naag*, Nagpur: Pradip Prakashan, 1989, p. 251
22. Jamanadas, op. cit., p. 6.
23. James Fergusson, *Tree and Serpent Worship*, London: India Museum, 1868, p. 47.
24. Ibid., p. 114.
25. V.D. Mahajan, op. cit., p. 201.
26. W.G. Orr, 'Armed Religious Ascetics in Northern India', *Bulletin of the John Rylands Library*, p. 94.
27. Ibid.
28. Ibid., pp. 94-5.
29. Ibid., p. 83.
30. Ibid.
31. Ibid.
32. Ibid., p. 84.
33. Ibid.
34. D.N. Lorenzen, 'Warrior Ascetics in Indian History', *Journal of the American Oriental Society*, 1978, p. 61.

35. Orr, op. cit., p. 84.
36. Ibid., p. 86.
37. Ibid.
38. Ibid.
39. Ibid., p. 88.
40. Ibid., p. 89.
41. Ibid.
42. Ibid., p. 90.
43. Ibid.
44. B.S. Cohn, 'Role of Gosains in the Economy of the 18th & 19th Century Upper India', *IESHR*, p. 175.
45. Tavernier (a French Traveller), *Travels in India*, 1989 edition in an encounter with powerful armed faqirs, p. 10.
46. Orr, op. cit., p. 85.
47. Ibid.
48. This *farman* issued by Aurangzeb is in the possession of the Balanand Math and Mandir in Jaipur, W.G. Orr has quoted this in his article 'Armed Religious Ascetics in Northern India', *Bulletin of the John Rylands Library*, p. 25.
49. Ghulam Ali Khan Naqwi, *Imad-us-Sa'adat—Aid to Bliss*, Lucknow: Newal Kishore, 1864, p. 84 translated in *A History of the Dasnami Naga Sannyasis*, p. 158 'How could the kafirs have so much liberty as to walk with their things and buttocks exposed before the Moslems. In any case, the gosains did in fact comply with Abdali's request, moved their tent to a polite distance, and notwithstanding the Durrani affront, acquitted themselves on the battlefield with large scale massacre of the Marathas.'
50. Ibid., p. 88.
51. Ibid., p. 91.
52. Ibid., p. 93.
53. Ibid., pp. 88-9.
54. Ibid., p. 99.
55. William R. Pinch, *Political Ascetics in Indian Myth, Memory and History*, Wesleyan University, 'Peasants Symposium', Hauserfestschrift, p. 1.

CHAPTER 2

The Die is Cast

Banda Bahadur's Encounter with Guru Gobind Singh

Guru Gobind Singh evacuated Anandpur Sahib in December 1704 in an unequal fight with the Mughal forces assisted by the Hindu hill rajas. The safe passage offered to him was a deception. The Guru and his followers were pursued by the Mughal troops,[1] the moment they came out of Anandpur Sahib. In this battle, he lost all his four sons, his mother and a large number of his followers, besides most of the literature which he had compiled.[2] Somehow the Guru reached Talwandi Sabo (near Bhatinda) in early 1705.

During his stay of about a year and a half at Damdama Sahib, he got a copy of the *Guru Granth* made. Copies of his works with his disciples were also collected and compiled into a single volume called the *Dasam Granth*, by Bhai Mani Singh.[3] At this stage, the principal aim of Guru was to get Wazir Khan punished for his treachery and cruelty. After the Guru had written the famous letter 'Zafarnama' to Aurangzeb, he was invited by the emperor to meet him. He started for the south in October 1706.[4] But while still in Rajasthan, he got the news of Aurangzeb's death at Ahmadnagar on 20 February 1707,[5] and decided to return back.

Soon he moved to Delhi to be with his wives and stayed in the Moti Bagh area. Prince Mauzzam who had come from Kabul to stake his claim for emperorship to the Mughal throne sought his help. Consequently, a few hundred Sikh cavalrymen joined the Prince in the battle of Jajau in June 1707.[6] Prince Mauzzam won the battle and became the Mughal emperor and assumed the title Bahadur Shah. He invited the Guru to Agra and received him warmly.[7] He also gave him some costly presents. The Guru again

Plate 2: Banda Bahadur submitting to Guru Gobind Singh.

raised the issue of punishment to Wazir Khan and some of his associates with the emperor. He wrote to the *sangat* at Dhaul that negotiations with the emperor are on and he shall soon be returning to Punjab.[8] Meanwhile Kam Bakhsh, the younger brother of Bahadur Shah, rose in rebellion at Hyderabad against him, hence Bahadur Shah moved to the south taking the Guru along with him.[9]

The Guru remained in and around the Mughal camp almost for a year, but no definite decision was forthcoming from the emperor against Wazir Khan. The Guru now became convinced that the emperor was using delaying tactics and no just decision was likely to be taken by the emperor, more so, when the entire Mughal court was hostile towards the Guru.[10]

When Bahadur Shah moved to Hyderabad in the Deccan to chastise his rebellious brother Kam Baksh, the Guru decided to stay at Nanded and set-up his camp on the bank of the Godavari.[11] Nanded is an old habitation initially called Nau Nand Dera, the place where nine *rishis* had lived in earlier times. During his journey, the Guru was informed by Jait Ram, the Mahant of Dadudwara (Jaipur state) about *bairagi* Madho Das of Nanded and some of his pranks.[12]

On 3 September 1708, the Guru called at the *bairagi's dera* situated on top of a small hillock on the bank of river Godavari.[13] The meeting between the Guru and the *bairagi* after which the *bairagi* became a disciple of the Guru has been variously recorded by almost all historians while writing about Banda Bahadur. There are, however, serious differences of opinion in these accounts. A large number of such accounts have been studied and relevant portions have been recorded in a summarized form. A further summing up at the end of each account has been given in italic print. A total of 57 accounts have been scrutinized. Some of these are short while some give more details. Some are historical novels/ long poems and some appear to be virtual copies of others. The crucial meeting between the Guru and Banda Bahadur is said to have taken place in the later part of 1708 and the first account thereof appeared in the *History of the Origin and Progress of the Sikhs* by James Browne in 1783, seventy-five years after the above-said crucial meeting. The meeting appears to have taken place between two responsible individuals both being quite competent to take the decision on their own without any consultation with anybody else. Moreover, these decisions were not state matters where record had to be maintained or sanction of any higher authority like the emperor, etc., had to be obtained or any court historian had to enter the same in government records. The poet Sainapet who was in the Guru's camp during this period and has accounted for various activities of Guru Gobind Singh has made no mention of Banda Bahadur in his writings.[14]

Since all accounts have some fable/fictional aspects as well as, these are wanting in historical evidence, and none of these can be taken as a true account in accordance with the modern standards of historiography. The study of history requires evidence in support of every statement made about the past and the application of relevant methods in the assessment of evidence. Nothing is accepted on faith.

Since no such account can be taken as an authentic evidence, all these accounts have been placed in a year-wise format in a summarized form for the reader to make his/her own assessment about their relevance and authenticity.

VARIOUS ACCOUNTS OF THE GURU'S MEETING WITH BANDA BAHADUR

Guru Gobind Singh meets Banda Bahadur

List of Historical Accounts under reference:

1. Major James Browne
2. William Murray
3. W.L. M'Gregor
4. Kanhiya Lal
5. Gian Singh Giani
6. Karam Singh Historian
7. Khazan Singh
8. Rattan Singh Bhangoo
9. Sohan Singh
10. C.H. Payne
11. H.H. Rose
12. Ganda Singh
13. Gokul Chand Narang
14. John Clark Archer
15. Indubhushan Banerjee
16. G.S. Chhabra
17. Ranbir Singh
18. Gobind Singh Mansukhani
19. Narain Singh
20. J.S. Grewal and S.S. Bal
21. Bhagat Lakshman Singh
22. J.D. Cunningham
23. Bakhshish Singh Nijjar
24. G.S. Deol

25. Hari Ram Gupta
26. W. Owen Cole and Piara Singh Sambhi
27. Pritam Singh Gill
28. Bhagat Singh
29. Gopal Singh
30. Bhai Kahn Singh
31. Sohan Singh Seetal
32. Pritam Singh Safeer
33. Bhai Parmanand
34. Max Arthur Macauliffe
35. P.K. Nijhawan
36. Anil Chander Banerjee
37. Khushwant Singh
38. Gurbaksh Singh
39. Dalbir Singh Dhillon
40. Muhammad Latif
41. William Irvine
42. Khafi Khan
43. Sunita Puri
44. Harbans Singh
45. The Encyclopaedia of Sikhism
46. Kaisar Singh Chhibar
47. Patwant Singh
48. M.L. Ahluwalia
49. Surjit Singh Gandhi
50. Harbans Kaur Sagoo
51. Dalip Singh
52. Kuldeep Bhatnagar
53. Sukhdial Singh
54. Harish Dhillon
55. M.S. Chandla
56. Harinder Singh Dilgir
57. M.S. Ahluwalia

MAJOR JAMES BROWNE

History of the Origin and Progress of the Sikhs, London: East India Company, Logographic Press, 1783.

Major James Browne was for some time the English Minister at the Court of Emperor Shah Alam. He was there for a short time before he was removed by the Governor-General of East India Company. During his period of stay at Delhi and Agra, he tried to collect information about the sect of the Sikhs. He came in contact with Budh Singh Arora of Lahore, the author of *Risala-i-Nanak Shah*, and Lala Ajaib Singh of Maler (Kotla) who was a collaborator of Budh Singh in this work. According to the colophon of this treatise, it was written at the instance of Major James Browne in 1197 A.H. (AD 1783). [British Museum, London, Pers. Ms. Add. 26273]. Major Browne has stated that he had added information which he had collected from other channels regarding the Sikhs and accompanied the whole with a map, specifying the extent of their territories, etc.

One Bundah, a Biragee Fakeer, and the native of a village Pundory, in the Doab of Beit Jalinder, had been for many years the intimate friend of Gooroo Gobind;* and hearing of the destruction of his defenceless family, it gave way to the deepest impressions of grief and resentment, which at length settled into a fixed determination to seek revenge; for this purpose. He went to all the most powerful and zealous of the Sicks, who had been the followers of Gooroo Gobind, and having excited in them the same spirit with which he himself was actuated, and enrolled himself in the fraternity of the Sicks, he, with surprising diligence and activity, and aided by uncommon abilities, collected the sect together in arms from all quarters, and inspired them with the most ardent spirit of revenge.

Fortunately for the execution of Bundah's design, about this time, Aurungzeb died in Deckan, and the succession to the throne being disputed between his sons (as it is well known to those who are conversant in the history of Hindostan,) great confusion arose in all parts of the empire. Bundah taking advantage of this opportunity, and having collected together a large, though irregular army of Sicks, marched to attack Navab Vizier Khan, who was then at Sirhind, the seat of his government. Vizier Khan came out to give them battle with all the troops he had, and the armies coming to action near Alwan Siray, the Sicks, inspired by enthusiasm and revenge, gave the Mussulmans a total defeat: Vizier Khan was killed upon the spot, and the greater part of his army was cut in pieces.

Sum-up: *During September/October 1708 Guru Gobind Singh met Madho Das, converted him to Sikh faith, gave him the name Banda Bahadur and sent him to Punjab to fight against the atrocities of the Mughal forces. He is also said to have been an intimate friend of the Guru for many years.*

* Guru Gobind Singh stayed at Nanded, where Banda Singh (then known as Madho Das) had his monastery, for not more than a fortnight, from the last week of September to 6 October 1708. It was during this period that he converted Madho Das into Banda Singh and despatched him to the Punjab.

William Murray

History of the Punjab: The Sikhs, London: H. Allen & Co., 1846

The confusion which took place in the Indian provinces on the death of Aurungzeb, in 1707, was favourable to the designs of Banda, whose grief at the fate of Guru Govind is said by Sikh authors to have settled into a gloomy and desperate resolution to avenge his wrongs. The severities which had been inflicted upon the Sikhs, instead of crushing them, exalted their fanaticism, whilst they extinguished the humane and merciful feelings which Nanuk had laboured to instil. After plundering the country, and defeating most of the petty Mahomedan chiefs that were opposed to him in the Punjab, Banda though himself sufficiently strong to contend in a pitched battle with Foujdar Wazir Khan, the governor of the province of Sirhind, a man abhorred by the Sikhs, as the murderer of the infant children of Guru Govind Singh. The Mahomedans fought with valour, the Sikhs with all the desperation which the most savage spirit of revenge could inspire; and this, aided by the courage and conduct of their leader, gave them the victory, after a severe contest. Foujdar Wazir Khan fell, with most of his army; the enraged Sikhs gave no quarter, nor was their thirst for vengeance satiated by the destruction of the Mahomedan soldiers; they put to death the wife and children of Wazir Khan (who was concerned in the murder of Govind's family), and almost all the inhabitants of Sirhind.

Sum-up: *Guru Gobind Singh selected Banda Bahadur and sent him to Punjab to fight against the Mughal forces. There is some account of his battles but there is no account of the Guru's meeting and selecting Banda as commander of the Sikh forces.*

W.L. M'Gregor

The History of the Sikhs, New Delhi: Rupa & Co., 2007 (1st published in 1846)

Before the death of Govind, it is related that some of his followers told him one day, that there was a fukeer, of the Byragee caste, who was not only a great warrior, but likewise a magician. They added, 'whoever attempts to sit in his presence without his permission, he makes him fall down from the couch.' The curiosity of Guru Govind Singh was raised at hearing this account of the Byragee, and he determined on paying him a visit, and conversing with him.

Next day he proceeded with a number of Sikhs to Bunda's hut, and entering it, seated himself without asking the *Bairagi's* leave. Bunda observed this unwarrantable freedom, and was very angry. He began to use his art in the hope of unseating Guru Govind Singh. He in vain read munter after munter; the Gooroo ji kept his seat firmly. When Bunda observed this, he rose and prostrated himself before Guru Govind Singh, entreating that the latter would explain to him the cause of his honoring his poor abode with a visit, asking at the same time his name. Guru Govind Singh replied, 'You know who I am'. The *Bairagi* rejoined, 'How should I know?' Govind merely added, 'Think over this matter.' Then Bunda enquired if he were Gooroo Govind Singh. The latter responded, 'Yes'. Bunda again asked the purport of his visit; and Govind Singh answered 'To make you a convert'. Bunda immediately consented, received the Pahooldee (*pahul*), and became a Sikh. Govind Singh then took Bunda along with him. Some days after this occurrence, Govind sent for Bunda, and having seated him, delivered to him his dying words (*wusseequt*), 'You are appointed my successor', exclaimed the Gooroo: 'You must be a warrior, and avenge the blood of my father and grandfather, as well as that of my sons. Do not fear death'. Govind then took five arrows from his quiver, and delivering them to Bunda, added, 'Do not approach a woman, and keep these five arrows: so long as you obey this order, no misfortune will happen to you; if you forget my orders, or disobey them, then you shall die.' Bunda received the arrows, and promised to obey faithfully the injunctions of the Gooroo.

Sum-up: *The Guru came to know about a* bairagi faqir *living nearby at Nanded. He went to Banda's hut and seated himself on his couch. Banda's attempt to unseat the Guru failed and he sought pardon from the Guru. He readily consented to become a disciple of the Guru for which he received* pahul *and the Guru gave certain instructions to*

Banda Bahadur and sent him to Punjab to fight against Mughal atrocities.

KANHIYA LAL

Tarikh-i-Panjab (History of Panjab), Patiala: Punjabi University, 1987 [1st published Lahore: Victoria Press, 1881]

During tour of Deccan, Guru Gobind Singh ji while having a walk on the bank of Godawari river, entered a beautiful garden. This was the dera of Madho Das Bairagi. The Guru sat down on the couch of Madho Das. The disciples of the Guru, who had been accompanying him, slaughtered a goat belonging to the *Bairagi's* dera for their meal.

Bairagi had some captive spirits in his control, with whose help he intended to topple the couch on which the Guru was sitting but he could not succeed in his attempt. When he came close to the Guru, his entire power was drained and he remained standing in front of the Guru totally awe stricken. He fell down at the feet of the Guru and stated that he is his Banda (slave).

The Guru told him that in case he is Guru's Banda then he should work accordingly. Banda requested that he be so ordered. The Guru took five gold-tipped arrows from his quiver and also five senior Sikhs as an advisory council, told him to go to Panjab and all those who killed the Guru's friend Budhu Shah faqir, should be punished and their habitations destroyed. Thereafter, destroy the Samana and Kunjpur. The Guru also asked Banda to punish Wazir Khan, *faujdar* of Sirhind along with his officers who were responsible for the execution of his young sons and his followers. Their part of the city should also be destroyed. The Guru also gave some further instructions to Banda Bahadur and sent him to Panjab.

Sum-up: ***The Guru went to the*** dera ***of Madho Das Bairagi and sat on his couch; his followers killed some goats for their meal. When Madho Das could not dislodge the Guru from his cot he became his disciple. The Guru gave him some instructions and sent him to Punjab to avenge the atrocities committed on Sikhs.***

Gian Singh Giani

Shamshir Khalsa Wa Twarikh Guru Khalsa, part II, Sialkot, 1892

Banda Bahadur was born in October 1670 in the house of Ramdev Rajput in Rajouri (Poonch). His name was Laxman Dev. In young age he was very fast and had an athletic body. He was very much interested in learning the art of warfare. He was also very keen on hunting animals. His life took a turn when he saw the young ones of a doe hunted by him dying in his presence.

He took a revulsion to hunting etc. and became an ascetic. After some time he got persuaded by Janki Prasad Bairagi and joined his group. Later on, he went to the *dera* of Baba Ram Thaman in Kasur and met his grandson Haridas. He was greatly influenced by Haridas and he became his disciple and went to the South with him. He spent a few years in Panchvati and became disciple of Auger Nath, an occult yogi.

After the death of Auger Nath, he set up his own *dera* on the bank of river Godavari. Since then many people in the area used to come to him with their problems, and he used to satisfy them with his occult powers. He had set up a nice house and a big garden and was living a very luxurious life. When Guru Gobind Singh reached Nanded, he disengaged himself from Emperor Bahadur Shah who was going to Hyderabad (Deccan) in pursuit of his younger brother Kam Baksh. The Guru stayed back and set up his *dera* on the bank of river Godavari. Guru Gobind Singh went to see the Bairagi where in a short time Bairagi realized that under Guru Gobind Singh's patronage he could do something worthwhile and thus became his disciple. The Guru gave him five arrows from his own quiver and sent five senior Sikhs as advisors with him and a small contingent of about 20 soldiers along with few *hukamnamas* issued to the *sangats* in Punjab.

Sum-up: *Guru Gobind Singh went to meet the* bairagi *and in a short time converted him as his disciple. The Guru gave him five arrows from his own quiver and sent five senior Sikhs as advisors and a small contingent of about 20 soldiers to proceed to Punjab.*

KARAM SINGH HISTORIAN

Biography of Banda Bahadur, Amritsar: Jaidev Singh, 1907

On reaching Nanded the Guru set up a separate camp near the Godavari River. The Guru was attacked by a Muslim from Sirhind while he was resting. The assailant and his companion were caught and killed, but the Guru was badly wounded. His wound was stitched by the royal surgeons. Karam Singh states that doctors suggested rest to the Guru and, therefore, he was advised to stay back at Nanded for some time.

During this period, people used to visit the Guru and he was apprised of the activities of the Bairagi Madho Das, who had set up his *dera* at the bank of river Godavari. The Guru went to the Bairagi's *dera* along with some of his Sikhs. Madho Das was not in the *dera*. The Guru knew fully well that Madho Das was a strict vegetarian, yet he ordered his Singhs to slaughter some of the goats to cook meat for their refreshment. This news reached Madho Das and he was greatly disturbed.

On coming to the *dera*, he saw meat being cooked and the Guru was sitting on his bed. He tried his best with his tantrik powers to overturn the bed or the cooking pot, but he failed in his efforts. A realization came on him that he was faced with a person of very great powers and he was going to be his master and he himself his Banda. He fell at the Guru's feet and said that I am your Banda. He entreated the Guru to take him under his patronage. The Guru accepted him as his Banda and his name became 'Banda Singh'.

After few days the Guru tried to pull a bow string and his wound got opened which was not possible for anybody to stitch. The Guru expired on 18 October 1708. A very important fact emerges in this regard that Banda was not given *pahul* by the Guru and yet Sikhs had a lot of respect for him. After the funeral ceremonies, Banda moved towards Panjab.

Sum-up: *The Guru went to Madho Das Bairagi's* dera *at the bank of the river Godavari. He sat on his couch and ordered his men to kill some goats and cook them for their refreshment. Madho Das on arrival was greatly disturbed but he could not overturn the couch on which the*

Guru was sitting. Madho Das submitted to the Guru and became his disciple. The Guru was grievously injured by some Pathans and he expired on 18 October 1708. After the performance of the last rites, Banda Bahadur left for Punjab. He was not given pahul *by the Guru.*

KHAZAN SINGH

History of the Sikh Religion, Patiala: Language Department, 1st published in 1914

After the death of yogi Agar Nath, Narain Das travelled southwards and put up at Nanded on the bank of river Godavari and constructed a beautiful little hut in a garden. He changed his name from Narain Das to Madho Das and became known and greatly respected in that neighbourhood. Guru Gobind Singh had heard about the *bairagi* during his travel from north to the south. The Guru one day went to *bairagi's* place and sat on the magical couch. He ordered the Singhs to slaughter a couple of goats and cook the same. Madho Das was informed by his disciples and he came greatly inflamed and tried his magical powers to upset the couch, but all his powers failed to affect the Guru. He came in and stood before the Guru with folded hands.

Guru	: 'Who are you?'
Madho Das	: 'I am your humble servant (Banda)'.
Guru	: 'Are you a true banda, or banda merely by the empty words of the mouth?'
Madho Das	: 'Truly in body, as well as in mind'.
Guru	: 'A banda must serve his master.'
Madho Das	: 'I am quite prepared to serve you in any way'.

Thus Madho Das was thenceforward named Banda. The Guru found in him a very useful, competent and reliable person, and explained to him the various tricks, cheating and oppression committed by the hill rajas and the Imperial Muhammadan commanders. These details made a deep and indelible impression on Banda's mind and Banda was soon after that deputed to bring all the oppressors to book. He was given all the necessary instructions and a plan for his operations in the Panjab.

The Guru gave Banda five arrows and various other weapons to wear, and at the same time conferred upon him the title of 'Banda Bahadur'. The Guru did not consider it necessary to give him the *pahul*, but he was asked to strictly follow the under-mentioned instructions:

1. He should not marry, nor indulge in sexual intercourse.
2. He should ever be truthful, never resorting to falsehood.
3. He should not start a new religion of his own.
4. He should never use a cushion in a Sikh Temple.
5. He should not allow himself to be called Guru.
6. He should always live in brotherly love and peace with the Singhs, never arrogating his might in their presence.

Twenty-five Singhs were told to accompany him, and he directed his course towards the Panjab. At the same time the Guru issued edicts to the Singhs in the Panjab, to join him for the prosecution of the grand undertaking with which he was entrusted. He came to the Panjab in rapid marches and, as soon as his arrival was known, thousands began to gather round his banner in small detachments.

Sum-up: *The Guru went to* bairagi's *place, sat on his couch, ordered some goats to be slaughtered for refreshment. Banda came greatly annoyed, tried but could not overturn the couch. Banda submitted to the Guru, became his disciple and after suitable instructions he was sent to Punjab by the Guru. He was instructed to observe celibacy. He should not start a religion of his own.*

RATTAN SINGH BHANGOO

Prachin Panth Prakash, completed 1808-41, 1st published by Bhai Vir Singh in 1914 (tr. in English by Professor Kulwant Singh)

Rattan Singh Bhangoo, in his book *Sri Gur Panth Prakash*, has devoted four episodes covering 15 pages over Guru Gobind Singh's meeting with Banda Bahadur. A brief summary thereof is given as under:

Guru Gobind Singh and his men were given a reception by Mahant Jait Ram of Dadu Duar (Narayana, Jaipur). During discussion, Jait Ram mentioned about Narain Das, a *bairagi*, who makes visiting saints sit on a splendid bed and then upturns the bed on the visitors, feeling delighted over the discomfort to the visitors. Jait Ram advised Guru Gobind Singh to avoid meeting him, to which Guru replied that how he could avoid meeting with him when it was ordained by God.

> 'Since Narain Dass Bairagi used to be a pauper in his early life,
> He had joined a troupe of homeless wandering saints,
> While moving along for a long time with these mendicants,
> He came across a saint possessing powers of necromancy.'
>
> 'Mahant Jait Ram narrated a new incident during this discussion,
> About a place which he had visited some time back.
> A person named Narain Dass was the occupant of that place,
> Who belonged to the sect of Bairagi saints of that place.'
>
> 'After making saint Jait Ram sit on this splendid bed,
> He toppled the bed upside down on the noble saint.
> After playing this very obnoxious mischief on his guest,
> He felt extremely delighted and broke into guffaws of laughter.'
>
> 'Saint Jait Ram advised the Guru to avoid a visit to his place,
> And follow another route during his journey to the South.
> The Guru remarked that everything happened according to God's Will,
> How could the Guru avoid whatever is ordained by God?'

R.S. Bhangoo devotes a great deal of space on the book of necromancy written by Ilumia Sidh, which Narain Dass obtained at the time of the death of his master Necromancer. He explains the powers of how to capivate women, convert base metals into gold, walk in the air and on water, break siege of fortified forts, change human sex, and so on. Bhangoo's account appears like a fairytale told by a wandering *sadhu* to the village children.

After a short stay at Nanded, Guru Gobind Singh went to the *dera* of Bairagi Narain Dass, who was not present there. The Guru occupied the controversial bed and pressed its four bedposts down with his four arrows. The accompanying Singhs cut some goats and started cooking meat for their meal. When Banda Bahadur came back, and saw this, he was greatly enraged and used all his powers to topple the bed on which the Guru was sitting and also topple the meat that was being cooked. His attendant/captive spirit told him of their helplessness against the Guru. Banda Bahadur finally accepted the greatness of the Guru, and went with all humility and bowed before him. Narain Dass declared himself as a humble servant of the Guru and beseeched him to be taken in his fold as a humble disciple (*banda*). The Guru told him the strict rules of the Khalsa to be followed by him. Narain Dass accepted all the stipulations. The Guru then accepted him as a disciple and named him Banda Singh Bahadur.

'Feeling outraged at the sight of the Guru sitting on his bed,
The Banda ordered his captive spirits (Birs) to dislodge the intruder.
But as these captive spirits tried to lift up the bedstead,
The Guru pressed its four bedposts down with his four arrows.'

'Although the attendant spirits tried their best to lift the bedstead,
They failed to lift the bed even by one inch from the ground.'

'Feeling extremely incensed and outraged at the immobility of the bed,
The Banda burst out in anger at his captive attendant spirits:
They must dispatch that intruding occupant to his death,
Without wasting any more time in disobeying out his orders.'

'When Banda's spirits returned without harming the Guru's Singhs as well,
Then alone the Banda was convinced of Guru's Divine powers.
He declared the Guru to be a perfect Divine Satguru,
And accepted his own inferior status to the Guru's Singhs.'

'Thereafter, the Banda bent down on his knees before the Guru,
Which made the Guru to address him in these words:
What was his saintly Order and who his spiritual guide?
Why did he play nasty tricks on the saints?'

'Then Banda declared himself to be the humble servant of the Guru,
And declared the Guru to be his spiritual guide and master.
He begged forgiveness of the Guru for his past misdeeds,
And promised never to indulge in any of his past activities.'

'He proclaimed himself to be the humble servant of the Guru,
And promised to carry out any command of the Guru.
He beseeched the Guru to take him into his fold,

And consider him as the most intimate disciple of the Guru.'

'Whatever conditions the Guru laid down before the supplicating Banda,
The Banda accepted all those stipulations in complete humility.
The Guru, then, named him as Banda Singh from his earlier name,
Which the Guru's new disciple accepted in all humility and reverence.'

'Satguru remarked that if Banda Singh was really worthy of a great task,
He must set out and destroy the murderers of Guru's Sahibzadas.
The Guru directed him to destroy the Hill principalities after destroying Sirhind,
As that was the task assigned by the Guru to him.'

'Thereafter, the Guru blessed Banda Singh with five of his arrows,
Remarking that these five arrows were invested with miraculous powers.
Whenever he felt it extremely necessary to shoot these arrows,
He should shoot only one of these arrows in extreme situations.'

Sum-up: *The Guru went to the* dera *of Bairagi Narain Das, occupied his bed and fixed it with four arrows. The Singhs then slaughtered some goats for their refreshment. When Banda came back and saw all this he tried to topple the couch but failed. He realized the situation and became a humble disciple of the Guru. Banda agreed to follow all the conditions laid down by the Guru. The Guru then sent him to Punjab.*

SOHAN SINGH

Life and Exploits of Banda Singh Bahadur, 1st published from Muzang Lahore in 1915, Patiala: Publication Bureau, Punjabi University, 2000

The struggle of the Sikh Gurus with tyrant Mughal rulers was a movement which neither the execution of the Gurus and their many descendants and Sikhs could suppress, nor any other means on earth could put an end to. These persecutions and murders rather fanned the fire of opposition into higher flames. Thus the martyrdom of Ajit Singh and Jujhar Singh and murders of Zorawar Singh and Fateh Singh simply added to the courage of the over-courageous Guru who hit upon many other means to crush the cruel. But now finding the land of the five rivers unable to afford him a safe refuge and relief even after so many severe skirmishes and battles, he found his way towards the South, where he hoped to secure a good field for his future operations against the oppressor (a rather incorrect amusement).

After Aurangzeb's death in 1707, Prince Mauzzam was given some help by Guru Gobind Singh at the battle of Jaijou in the war of succession. They were on good terms. The Guru had raised the issue of punishment to Wazir Khan of Sirhind for his atrocities on the Sikhs and his children. Bahadur Shah asked the Guru to accompany him to the south. The Guru went up to Nanded with the emperor. But when it was realized that emperor was using delaying tactics and was not interested in any kind of settlement; the Guru stayed back at Nanded and set up his own *dera* on the bank of river Godavari. Madho Das a *bairagi* from Rajauri had also established a *dera* on the bank of river Godavari. He used to crack coarse jokes on *sadhus* visiting to his *dera*, when they were made to sit on a particular couch, Madho Das would overturn the same with his occult powers and enjoyed the discomfiture of the visitors.

The Guru had heard about the *bairagi's* activities and decided to meet him. So he went to the *bairagi's dera* and seated himself on the very same magic couch. He also told his accompanying Sikhs to slaughter a couple of goats of the *dera* and prepare refreshment. Madho Das who was out nearby heard the news and became greatly disturbed. He came to his *dera* and tried all his occult powers to overturn the couch, but could not accomplish the same. Thus baffled, the poor and helpless Madho Das felt convinced of the superiorty of his visitors. Hence, finding no alternative, he fell at the Guru's feet and sincerely apologized for the mischief he had done. Thereafter he promised that henceforth he would serve the Guru as his slave (*banda*). It is since then that Madho Das has been named Banda Singh. The Guru finding him suitable for his purpose and seeing in him just the person he was in search of, granted him pardon and admitted him into his fold.

'Do make any command and I shall obey. I am thy slave'. The Guru took Madho Das to his *dera* and explained to him the situation in Panjab and ways and means to handle the same. The Guru gave him five trusted followers and also letters to all his Sikh *sangats* of the land of five waters, immediately to assemble under his flag with a laudable object of punishing the murderers of the Sikhs. The Guru gave him five arrows from his quiver and 25 soldiers. The Guru gave him the following instructions:

1. Not to take rest until the Muslim anarchy had entirely stopped;
2. To do everything in consultation with five Sikhs, and to begin every action with an *ardas*, the prayer to God;
3. Never to disregard the position of the community, and never to style himself as Guru;
4. Never to start a separate sect;
5. To remain celibate and avoid women.

Thus Banda Bahadur moved from Nanded to Panjab to face the new life.

Sum-up: *The Guru went to Bairagi's* dera *and seated himself on the magic couch. The Guru told some of his Singhs to slaughter couple of goats and prepare refreshment. Madho Das came back, tried to overturn the couch but failed. He fell at the Guru's feet and became his humble disciple. The Guru gave him five advisors and about 20 soldiers to go to Punjab and avenge the atrocities of the Mughals. Banda was told not to style himself as a Guru and remain celibate.*

C.H. Payne

A Short History of the Sikhs, Delhi: S. Chand & Co., 1960 [1st published London: Nelson & Sons, 1919]

All we know is that Guru Gobind Singh went as far south as the Godavery, and that he made Nanded, on the banks of that river, his headquarters. Here he spent much of his time in the company of a Bairagi hermit afterwards known as Banda the 'slave', whom he converted to his own faith and baptized, and to whom he became so much attached that he nominated him his successor, not as guru, but as commander of the forces of the Khalsa.

Govind Singh was not destined to return to his native country. One day, after preaching his doctrines at Nanded, he was stabbed by a Pathan assassin; and though the physicians of Bahadur Shah were sent to attend him, they were unable to save his life. He died at the age of forty-eight, in the year 1708, having reigned as guru for nearly thirty-three years.

On the death of the last of the gurus, Banda assumed the arms of his master, and the leadership of the Sikh community. Acting in accordance with the instructions he had received from Govind Singh, he at once set out for the north; and at Buria, to the east of Ambala, he was joined by the main body of the Sikh army. The soldiers promised allegiance to their new commander on condition that they should receive the arrears of pay due to them. To satisfy this demand, Banda took the only course open to him, that of plundering the surrounding villages, a course which his troops appreciated more than the villagers, who dispatched an urgent appeal for protection to the Governor of Mustafabad. The latter immediately set out to their assistance with two thousand imperial troops; but his march had scarcely commenced when it was intercepted by Banda and his army. The governor's force was dispersed with great slaughter, and his capital was entered and sacked by the victorious Sikhs. Banda next laid siege to and captured Samana in the Patiala district, and then proceeded to Sirhind.

Sum-up: *While at Nanded the Guru met a Bairagi hermit who was afterwards known as Banda Bahadur. He was converted to Sikh faith and baptized and nominated him his successor, not as Guru, but as the commander of the Khalsa forces. Immediately after the demise of the Guru Banda moved to Punjab.*

H.H. Rose

A Glossary of the Castes and Tribes of the Punjab and the North Western Province of India, Lahore: Punjab Government Printing, 1919

This man (bairagi) had a curious history. By birth a Rajput of Rajouri in Kashmir, he changed his name of Lachhman Bal to

Naraindas at the shrine of Baba Ram Thamman (a cousin of Guru Nanak near Kasur, District Lahore) and became a *bairagi* in 1686 AD. But in 1691 AD he became a jogi and adept in occult sciences with the new name of Madhodas. Meeting the Guru probably at Nanded, he was given the title of Bahadur with that of Banda which he had already earned by submission to the Guru, together with five arrows and other weapons.

Rose has given another account of Banda Bahadur stating Banda was a Panjabi khatri of Sialkot district, perhaps of the Kapoor section. The verses quoted (Hakim Rai's Aywal Lachhman Dass urf Banda Sahib Chela and Guru Singh) also makes him a khatri of the Sodhi clan. He was married in a Marwaha or Mehra family.

Sum-up: *Madho Das Bairagi met the Guru at Nanded and was given the name Banda Bahadur after submission to the Guru and was sent to Punjab.*

GANDA SINGH

Life of Banda Bahadur, Amritsar: Khalsa College, 1935

During his journey to the South, while at Dadudwara (Jaipur State), Guru Gobind Singh had heard from Mahant Jait Ram of a peculiar occultist Bairagi Madho Das of Nanded who delighted in practicing unpleasant tricks on *sadhu* visitors to his *dera* to their great annoyance. Jait Ram had himself been ridiculed by Madho Das. Guru Gobind Singh had kept this in his mind and shortly on reaching Nanded he went to the *bairagi's dera* along with few of his men. The *bairagi* was not present. The Guru occupied the only cot available which Madho Das used to overturn with his tantrik powers and enjoyed the discomfiture of the visitors. The Guru ordered his men to slaughter some goats of the *dera* and prepare meat for their refreshment. This news reached *bairagi* and he came to his *dera* very angry over what had happened. He tried to use his tantrik powers but failed to achieve any result against the Guru. This happening softened the *bairagi* who then approached the Guru.

Madho Das	:	Who are you?
Guru Gobind Singh	:	He whom you know.

Madho Das	:	What do I know?
Guru Gobind Singh	:	Think it over in your mind.
Madho Das (after a pause)	:	So you are Guru Gobind Singh!?
Guru Gobind Singh	:	Yes!
Madho Das	:	What have you come here for?
Guru Gobind Singh	:	I have come so that I may convert you into a disciple of mine.
Madho Das	:	I submit, my Lord. I am a *banda* (a slave) of yours.

(The above dialogue is recorded in the *Zikr-i-Guruan wa Ibtida-i-Singhan-wa Mazhab-i-Eshan* by Ahmad Shah of Batalvi).

The erstwhile proud and invincible Bairagi Madho Das submissively fell down at the feet of Guru Gobind Singh and accepted to be his disciple without any argument. Guru Gobind Singh clearly perceived what was yet vital in the youthful ascetic. He availed himself of this psychological moment, dressed him like a Sikh, and administered to him the *Amrita* of the Khalsa Church, and baptized him with the *Pahul* ceremony.

Sum-up: *While at Nanded, the Guru went to Bairagi's* dera. *The Guru sat on the Bairagi's couch and ordered his men to slaughter some goats and prepare refreshments. The Bairagi tried to topple the cot but could not. Ganda Singh has quoted a dialogue between the Banda and the Guru recorded by Ahmad Shah Batalvi. Bairagi submitted to the Guru, became his disciple. The Guru administered* pahul *to the Bairagi and sent him to Punjab.*

Gokul Chand Narang

Transformation of Sikhism, Lahore: New Book Society, 1945

'Banda Bahadur had ceased his wanderings and settled down in a quiet village of Nanded situated on the bank of river Godavari. It was here [that] the meeting between him and Guru Gobind Singh took place in September/October 1708 AD. The Guru, while traveling in the Deccan, happened to halt at Nanded, and hearing [a] great deal about the ascetic went to see him. He at once found out what stuff the Bairagi was made of, and the Guru fixed upon him as the future leader of the Khalsa who would carry out his great designs. An intimate friendship soon grew up between them, and the persuasive eloquence and religious zeal of the Guru made such a deep impression on the mind of Madho Das that he became a disciple and called himself his *banda* or slave, and threw himself entirely at his service. The Guru was exceedingly pleased at this triumph and at once accepted the offer of Madho Das's services. The Guru had told him all about his aims and ambitions, his sufferings and disasters. He now instructed his new disciple to take up his work, avenge the blood of his father and his innocent children, and strike a blow at the Moghul despotism and emancipate his race from the yoke of thralldom.'

The Guru gave him a sword and five arrows from his own quiver and enjoined upon him the following five commandments:

1. Do not approach a woman, but lead a life of chastity and celibacy.
2. Always think the truth, speak the truth and act the truth.
3. Regard yourself as a servant of the Khalsa and always act in accordance with its wishes.
4. Do not try to found any sect of your own.
5. Do not let victories elate you or kingly pride turn your head.

The Guru gave him letters addressed to the Sikhs in Punjab to accept Banda as their leader and fight under his flag. He also gave him a drum and a banner and twenty five chosen followers to go with him to Punjab.

Sum-up: *At Nanded the Guru went to the Bairagi's* dera. *Bairagi submitted to the Guru and became his disciple. The Guru gave him some of his weapons, five advisors and twenty soldiers to accompany him to Punjab. The Guru also instructed him to lead a life of chastity and celibacy. He was instructed not to form a sect of his own but should serve the Khalsa.*

John Clark Archer

The Sikhs, Wisconsin: Princeton University Press, 1946

Banda was born of Khatri stock in Kashmir, where learning was, in those days, 'the exclusive monopoly of brahmans'. He became disciple of a *bairagi*, or adherent of the Hindu Ramanujist fraternity, acquired a new name (he had been known as Lachhman Dev and Madho Das) and journeyed to Bengal. There he attached himself for a while to a yogi skilled in Tantric science, until he had himself gained some mastery of Tantric yoga, a form of Shakti exercise in the name of the goddess Durga. Thereupon he settled in Nanded in a math, or 'monastery', of his own, maintaining the Tantric yoga discipline and gathering about him chelas (pupils) to share the training. It was in Nanded that he met Guru Gobind Singh who had drawn aside from the campaign in Hydarabad, and where he soon declared himself the Guru's 'slave' or *banda* – his designation ever afterward, it becoming a title equivalent among Sikhs to the Moslem *abd* or to the Hindu *das*, although Sikhs did not resort to any wide use of, e.g. Gurbanda, the 'slave of the Guru'. In becoming 'Banda', says Ganda Singh, 'the dross of the Bairagi was at once transformed into the gold' of the Sikh order. Gobind himself initiated him by pahul and a draught of amrit into the Khalsa, making him 'a full-fledged Singh'.

Upon the death of Guru Gobind Singh, Banda Singh returned to the Panjab, bearing all the essential tokens of Sikh leadership, including the five arrows from Guru's own quiver, a flag (nishan), a drum (nagara), five duly appointed aides (pyaras – who constituted a panchayat?) and a guard of twenty other Singhs. He had also, as tradition holds, *hukmnamahs*, 'warrants', from the Guru, bidding all Sikhs to support him.

Sum-up: *At Nanded, the Guru met the Bairagi who became his disciple. He was given* pahul *and made a full-fledged Singh with the name Banda Singh Bahadur. After the death of the Guru Banda came to Punjab with five advisors and twenty soldiers.*

INDUBHUSHAN BANERJEE

Evolution of the Khalsa, vol. II, Calcutta: A. Mukherjee & Co., 4th edn. 1980.

The Guru reached Nanded in the last week of September 1708. Sainapat gives us a fair idea as to how about three weeks' time in Nanded was passed by the Guru. It appears very significant that

Sainapat does not say anything about Banda or his conversion to Sikhism.

According to Sikh tradition, the Guru reclaimed Banda and brought him within the fold of the Khalsa on the very first day of his arrival at Nanded and this was virtually the only important act that he did there. It seems curious that Sainapat should be totally silent about this vital matter.

Irrespective of the fact that Sainapat had ommitted the Guru's meeting with Banda Bahadur, the historical factual position stands that Banda did convert from Bairagi ascetic to a Sikh and came to Panjab and was the leader of the Sikh struggle against the Mughal rulers from 1709 to 1716.

Sum-up: *The Guru met Banda and brought him within the fold of Khalsa and he came to Punjab as leader of the Sikh struggle against the Mughals.*

G.S. Chhabra

Advanced History of the Panjab, vol. I, Jullundur City: New Academic Publishing Co., 1968

Many writers of Indian History deal with the subject. But the accounts of almost all such writers seem to be based on Elphinstone's *History of India*.

Banda, who became a *bairagi* at a fairly young age, roamed from place to place meeting saints and yogis and came to Nasik where he came in contact with Yogi Augher Nath from whom he learnt occultism. After the death of Yogi Augher Nath, Banda moved along the Godavari River and settled down on the bank of river Godavari at Nanded. It is here that Banda came in contact with Guru Gobind Singh. It is said that Banda used to take delight in practicing tricks on the visitors with the help of his occult powers. When Guru Gobind Singh visited his monastery, he tried to play the same trick on him but the same would not work on the Guru. When his occult powers failed he fell at the Guru's feet and begged for his pardon. The Guru asked him who he was, and in utter humility Madho Das replied that he was the Guru's *banda* or his slave. Pleased with his humility, the Guru patted him and giving him the title of *Banda*, and commissioned him to go to Panjab.

At the time Banda was commissioned, the Guru gave him five arrows out of his quiver, and handed over to him his drum and banner as emblems of his authority. The Guru instructed Banda to remain pure of heart and honest. He was not to touch another man's wife, was to look upon himself as a servant of the *Khalsa* who would be his true Guru. He was to undertake no important task without an *ardasa*, or a prayer to the Almighty. Whatever he did, he was to take the advice of the 'Five Sikhs'. Among the 'Five Sikhs' who were asked by the Guru to accompany Banda, were Baj Singh, Binod Singh and Kahan Singh. Banda was not to found any sect, nor call himself a *Guru*. He was not to permit his victories to elate him, nor his defeats should depress him. These were in brief the instructions which the Guru gave to Banda.

Sum-up: *With the failure of his occult powers against the Guru, Banda begged pardon and became a disciple of the Guru. The Guru gave him some of his weapons, five advisors and some soldiers to accompany him to Punjab.*

RANBIR SINGH

Glimpses of the Divine Masters, New Delhi: International Traders Corpn., 1964

A secluded hut stood in a beautiful spot on the bank of the river Godavari. Guru Gobind Singh had journeyed a long way to Deccan perhaps to retrieve the soul of this ascetic and convert him to his faith, so that he might continue to fight the Mughal oppressors and thus deliver the country from their cruel hands.

When the Guru came to the hut, *bairagi* was not there. He occupied the *bairagi*'s couch. The *bairagi*'s men hastened to inform him about the strange visitor, his followers had also killed two wild goats and were cooking them in the forbidden square of the *bairagi*. Madho Das, an orthodox vegetarian was mad with anger and rushed back to his hut. But facing the Guru his fury wilted. He asked his visitor as who he was and what was the purpose of his visit. The visitor answered that he was Gobind Singh and he had come to take him out of the evil deeds and to convert him and retrieve his soul. The divine light from the Guru's eyes dispelled the flickering darkness from the mind of the *bairagi*, who immediately knelt before the Master and surrendered himself heart and soul stating that he was his *banda*, the slave. The Master instructed him in the tenets of Sikh religion and administered *amrit* to him and thus initiating him into the fold of the faith and named him Banda Singh. The Guru some time before his demise granted Banda Bahadur wish to go to Panjab and take revenge from Wazir Khan and his friends. The Guru equipped him with his own bow and arrows, a flag of saffron colour, a battle drum, he deputed five of the Khalsa to accompany him and help with their counsel and advice. Banda Singh was to be the secular leader of the Sikhs. Banda Singh bowed to the Master and left for Panjab with his party.

Sum-up: *The Guru went to Bairagi's* dera, *sat on his couch, got his goats slaughtered for refreshment. Bairagi came in anger but on seeing the Guru his fury got wilted and he became a disciple of the Guru. He was sent to Punjab to take revenge on Wazir Khan.*

GOBIND SINGH MANSUKHANI

The Quintessence of Sikhism, Amritsar: SGPC, 1965

Banda Singh whose original name was Lachman Bairagi was born in 1670 in a small village in Poonch (Kashmir). At an early date, he renounced the world and became a *sadhu*. He settled at Nanded in the Hyderabad State. Guru Gobind Singh met him in 1708 and enlisted him in the Khalsa Panth. The Guru gave him a new name, Banda Singh Bahadur. He gave him a sword and five arrows and asked him to respect the following five commandments:

1. Lead a life of *Brahmcharya*. Do not touch a woman.
2. Speak the Truth.
3. Serve and obey the Khalsa Panth.
4. Do not establish a new sect.
5. Be humble. Let not victory make you haughty and vain.

Having taken the Guru's blessings, Banda, with a band of Sikhs, proceeded to the Panjab, dreaming of revenge against the Nawabs and rulers and who had done wrongs to the Guru and his family. He first attacked Sarhind where the Nawab had ordered the live-burial of the two young sons of Guru Gobind Singh. Many villages were razed to the ground. The Muslim rulers caught fright and united together to ward off Banda Singh's attacks. Wazir Khan, Governor of Sarhind, assisted by Khawaja Ali of Malerkotla, fought a decisive battle with Banda Singh's forces in May 1710. The Muslims were defeated; Wazir Khan was killed in battle. The Sikhs plundered Sarhind. Banda Singh appointed Baj Singh as Governor of Sarhind.

Sum-up: *The Guru met Laxman Bairagi at his* dera *in Nanded and enlisted him in the Khalsa Panth and gave him the name Banda Singh Bahadur. He was given commandments to remain a* brahmacharya, *not to establish a new sect, be humble and obey the Khalsa Panth. With five advisors and a few soldiers he was sent to the Punjab.*

NARAIN SINGH

Guru Gobind Singh Re-told, Amritsar: Narain Singh, n.d.

At Nanded, the Guru went to see a *bairagi* named Lachhman Dass. The *bairagi* was the son of a Rajput, Ram Dev, of Bhardwaj clan. At his young age, he was fond of hunting but he was very tender hearted too. Once, he killed a doe and when he cut its body open he found within it two cubs alive that died soon after. He was so deeply touched that he renounced the world and became a *bairagi*, renamed as Madho Dass. He learnt occultism from a Yogi, Aughar Nath, but later he set up his own monastery in Nanded. People had come to believe that, through the practice of austerities, he had achieved occult and miraculous powers. If, for instance, an intruder ever made the mistake of lying on his couch, it was regarded as an act of sacrilege and the *bairagi* would punish the intruder by overthrowing him from the couch. His magic skill seemed to work on people through the power of the mind, practically in the same manner as the hypnosis of the modern age works.

When the Guru was in the hut of the *bairagi*, the *bairagi* was away. As the Guru was very much fatigued, he rested his limbs on the couch, which, for the *bairagi*, was the throne that represented the spiritual authority of his Guru from whom he had acquired the so-called powers. The *sadhus* in the ashram were requested to provide food to the Guru and to his companions. But they refused to do so before the *bairagi* had been served first. One of the goats in the *dera* was slaughtered, cooked and served to the party. This was another act of sacrilege. When the *bairagi* heard the story, he was in rage. He tried his so-called occult powers and his magic on the intruder but it did not work in casting any spell on his powerful mind that remained wholly unmoved. When the *bairagi* looked at the intruder's face, the same reflected peace, light and calm. The eyes were shining brightly, casting a sweet and radiant look that seemed to snap the peculiar cast of the *bairagi*'s heart. He saw clearly that behind the lustre and radiance of the face there rested the peace and glory of the great soul that had already started to affect his own heart. He was overpowered, fell on the Guru's feet and called himself his *banda* (slave). In Nanded, the Guru found himself in the lap of nature and felt happy and at home. The exquisite beauty of the place and its secluded location had drawn him, because it could make his communion with the Creator easy. So he decided to make it his headquarters.

Nanded had really become a place of pilgrimage. Saiyyad Khan, now a devotee, came all the way from the Panjab for the Guru's darshan. Soon after, a message was brought from Nasiran to say that her husband Budhu Shah was declared a rebel and the whole town of Sadhaura was ransacked and that she was also preparing that very day to die fighting as a true soldier of the Guru. In this atmosphere, the *bairagi* too was a changed man. He was baptised and renamed as Gurbux Singh. He had realised by that time that the life of austerities was of no real value because it did not stir up man for action in the service of the afflicted humanity.

Banda heard the atrocious tales of cruelty carried out in Panjab. He was deeply affected about the cruel killings of the Guru's sons and his Sikhs. The dormant Rajput spirit grew up within him and it wanted an outlet. He realised that he had wasted his life and had now found the way. The Guru also felt that he had, after all, found a man who could be entrusted to carry on the work he had left unfinished in the Panjab.

Sum-up: *The Guru came to Bairagi's* dera, *sat on his couch, one goat was cooked for refreshment to the accompanying Sikhs. Bairagi when heard the story was enraged. His occult powers failed to topple the couch. He fell on the feet of the Guru and became his disciple. He was baptized and renamed as Gurbaksh Singh and sent to Punjab to carry out the work which the Guru had left unfinished.*

J.S. Grewal and S.S. Bal

Guru Gobind Singh, Chandigarh: Panjab University, 1967

Towards the end of September 1708, imperial army halted near Nanded, a place of pilgrimage on the river Godavari and about a hundred fifty miles to the north of Hyderabad. Guru Gobind Singh selected for his residence a congenial spot overlooking the river; and started addressing congregation, besides offering the usual daily prayer.

Guru Gobind Singh's missionary activity among the inhabitants of Nanded led to an armed fight between the Khalsa and the followers of a *bairagi*, later to be known as Banda.* The followers of Banda were worsted in the encounter, and his own encounter with Guru Gobind Singh resulted in Banda's conversion to Sikhism. He accepted the *pahul* and the *rehat* of the Khalsa.

Sum-up: *Guru Gobind Singh's missionary activities in Nanded led to an armed fight between the Khalsa and the followers of Bairagi. Bairagis were worsted in the encounter and the Bairagi became a disciple of Guru Gobind Singh. He accepted the* pahul *and* rehat *of the Khalsa.*

* J.S. Grewal and S.S. Bal, *Guru Gobind Singh (A Biographical Study)*, Chandigarh: Panjab University, 1967, p. 154. Banda's meeting with Guru Gobind Singh is a highly controversial point. It cannot be discussed here, but we are aware of the conflicting views expressed by several writers. Our statement on Banda's meeting with Guru Gobind Singh is based primarily on evidence presented by an anonymous Persian ballad called *Amarnama* which has been published by Gurdit Singh from Patiala.

BHAGAT LAKSHMAN SINGH

Guru Gobind Singh, Patiala: Language Department, 1970

There was a thinking going along that Guru Gobind Singh was soliciting help from Marathas and Rajputs to start agitation against the Mughal rulers which he would also reciprocate by starting the same in Punjab. This assumption does not seem to be correct. There is no historical evidence for the same. However, the conversion of a *bairagi* subsequently in history as Banda Bahadur more than outweighed the advantages of a possible alliance with the Rajputs or the Marathas.

Banda was a great genius of his age. In learning and worldly wisdom, in military valour and religious fervour, few surpassed him. Hearing of the Guru's arrival at Nanded he went to see him and was so deeply impressed with his divine grace that he immediately became his disciple and remained, till death, his very ardent admirer and devoted follower.

Commissioned by the Guru to carry on the work of freeing Panjab from the tyrannous yoke of the Muslims and of the arrogant ruling castes and priestly classes he immediately left for that country (Panjab).

Sum-up: *Hearing of the Guru's arrival at Nanded, the Bairagi went to see him and was deeply impressed with his divine grace that he immediately became his disciple. He was sent by the Guru to Punjab to lead the Sikh struggle.*

J.D. CUNNINGHAM

History of the Sikhs, Delhi: S. Chand & Co., 1972.

Banda, the chosen disciple of Gobind, was a native of the south of India, and an ascetic of the Bairagi order; and the extent of the deceased Guru's preparations and means will be best understood from the narrative of the career of his followers, when his own commanding spirit was no more. The Sikhs gathered in numbers round Banda when he reached the north-west, bearing with him the arrows of the Guru as the pledge of victory. Banda put to flight the Mughal authorities in the neighbourhood of Sirhind, and then attacked, defeated, and slew the governor of the province. Sirhind was plundered.

Sum-up: *Banda, a native of south India, became a disciple of Guru Gobind Singh and was sent to the Punjab to lead the Sikhs in their struggle against the Mughals.*

BAKHSHISH SINGH NIJJAR

Panjab Under the Later Mughals, Jullundur: New Academic Publishing Co., 1972.

Banda Bahadur known as Lachhman Dass in his childhood was born in October 16, 1670 at Rajouri in the Poonch district of Jammu & Kashmir. His father Ramdev was an ordinary ploughman Rajput of Bhardwaj class. Lachhman Dass developed into a youth of very active habits, full of energy and fond of shooting and hunting. At the age of 16 years Lachhman Dass took sudden abhorrence to the hunt of animals and his normal daily life. He became the disciple of a *bairagi*, Janaki Prasad, who was touring in J&K. After some time he lost his interest and went to Kasur and became the disciple of Ram Thamman. His wanderings took him to Deccan and ultimately he set up his *dera* at Nanded on the bank of river Godavari. After some time Guru Gobind Singh also went to the south with Bahadur Shah, but having lost interest in the emperor for his not agreeing to punish Wazir Khan, Guru Gobind Singh settled down at Nanded and did not go further with the emperor into Deccan. At Nanded Guru Gobind Singh formed first acquaintance with Madho Das and soon they became intimate friends. The persuasive eloquence and religious zeal of the Guru made such a deep impression on the mind of Banda that he was initiated into the '*pahul*' and became a disciple of the Guru. Banda by his devotion inspired the Guru with confidence and became his most staunch disciple. Although he was not acknowledged as Guru's successor in apostleship, yet the Guru declared that after him the Sikhs would look upon him as their leader and protector.

The Guru's injunctions to Banda Bahadur were that he should remain a warrior and avenge the blood of innocents. He must not fear death, he was given five arrows by the Guru as emblems of victory. The Guru further told him that he should not approach women. So long as you follow my instructions no misfortune will happen to you; if you forget them or disregard them you shall answer for non-performance with your life. Banda solemnly promised to obey the commands of the dying Guru. Acting in accordance with the instructions received from the Guru he at once set out for Panjab.

Sum-up: *At Nanded the Guru met Madho Das and became friends. Banda became a disciple of the Guru and was given* pahul. *He was given certain instructions by the Guru and sent to the Punjab to lead the Sikhs in their struggle.*

G.S. DEOL

Banda Bahadur, Jullundur: New Academic Publishing Co., 1972

Guru Gobind Singh accompanied by some of his Sikhs went to the *dera* of Bairagi Madho Das. *Bairagi* was not there. The Guru sat on the resplendent bed of Madho Das. He instructed his Singhs to slaughter some goats and cook meat for their meal. It is said by some of the historians that the Guru deliberately asked for the slaughter of some goats to ascertain as to what extent Madho Das gets excited over the same. Some disciples of *bairagi* went to him and told him of the situation. Madho Das ordered his '*birs*' to go and overturn the bed and the cooking pot, but these powers could not succeed in either of them. Madho Das is said to have attempted his own power, but with no result. Madho Das seem to have realized that his guest is some great personality and himself approached the Guru.

Madho Das	:	Who are you?
Guru Gobind Singh	:	He whom you know.
Madho Das	:	What do I know?
Guru Gobind Singh	:	Think it over in your mind.
Madho Das (after a pause)	:	So you are Guru Gobind Singh!?
Guru Gobind Singh	:	Yes!
Madho Das	:	What have you come here for?

Guru Gobind Singh	:	I have come so that I may convert you into a disciple of mine.
Madho Das	:	I submit, my Lord. I am a *banda* (a slave) of yours.

(The above dialogue is recorded in *Zikr-i-Guruan wa Ibtida-i-Singhan-wa Mazhab-i-Eshan.*)

After the above conversation, Madho Das came to be known as Banda, and became a disciple of the Guru. He became a Sikh after having been baptized, whereafter he was named Banda Singh Bahadur. Banda Bahadur was taken by the Guru to his camp. For some days, Banda and the Guru had lot to discuss over the situation in Panjab and how the same was required to be handled. The Guru conferred the title of 'Bahadur' on Banda whereby he came to be known as Banda Singh Bahadur or Banda Bahadur. The Guru gave him five of his arrows and some other weapons. The five commandments given by the Guru to Banda Bahadur are as under:

- Not to approach a women but to lead a life of chastity and celibacy.
- Not to resort to falsehood but to think, speak and act the truth always.
- Not to start a new religion or a sect.
- Not to use a cushion in a gurdwara and allow himself to be called a guru.
- To regard himself as a servant of the Khalsa and always to act in accordance with its wishes and live in peace with the Singhs.

He was also given him a drum (nagara) and a banner. Five senior Singhs, representing the *Panj Piaras*, were sent with him as advisors. Twenty Sikh soldiers were also sent with him. The Guru's last advice was 'If you don't obey the Khalsa, you will fail. If you keep the Khalsa happy, you will always be happy. If you trouble the Sikhs, you will also be in trouble.'

Sum-up: *The conversation between the Guru and Madho Das as given by Ahmad Shah Batalvi is reproduced in Deol's account also. Madho Das became disciple of the Guru and after baptism was named Banda*

Singh Bahadur. Banda stayed for a short time with the Guru, received instructions and then was sent to Punjab to lead the Sikhs. In various instructions, he was asked to lead a life of chastity and celibacy.

According to Guru Nanak, leading the life of a householder was an essential characteristic of a Sikh, the enforcement of chastity on Banda Bahadur, a baptized Sikh sounds a discordant note.

HARI RAM GUPTA

History of the Sikhs, vol. II, New Delhi: Munshiram Manoharlal, 1978

The Guru expressed his disappointment at emperor's attitude of not deciding the issue of Wazir Khan and unnecessary prolonging it. The Guru set up his own independent *dera* about a kilometre outside the city in a colony known as Afzalnagar by purchasing a plot of land from Sayyid Sabir Shah Faqir. The place was named Abchalnagar. This took place some time in August 1708.

On September 3, 1708, the Guru called at *bairagi's* cottage situated on the top of a hillock on the bank of river Godavari. The *bairagi* not being there, the Guru sat on his couch. When *bairagi* came back he was overawed by the presence of the Guru whom he could recognize. The Guru asked him 'Who are you?' 'Your Banda (slave)' was the reply. The Guru observed: One is not virtuous, who while possessing strength, retires from the world like you have. The honour, life and property of your countrymen are unsafe. Innocent people are being slaughtered, unwilling persons are forcibly converted to Islam. Women are forcibly being seized and violated. Children are mercilessly killed. There is no freedom of thought, expression and conscience. My own father was executed, my children and my mother and thousands of my Sikhs have been killed.

My dear, brave Rajput! Throw away these hermit's clothes. Put on Rajput's uniform. Wear your arms in place of ashes which you rub on your body. You have a lot of strength and magnetic power in you, that is why, thousands of people are devoted to you. In the new life, you will be served by tens of thousands. My Khalsa is awake. It is waiting for a man like you. You have the ability of a hero and the capacity of a giant. Our motherland lies bound in fetters. Smash them to pieces and liberate the mother who has nursed you. In this lies your good and that of the nation. Banda quietly submitted. Daily Banda went to the Guru and carefully studied the workings of his mind. He tried to absorb the Guru's national spirit and prepared himself to take charge of his unfinished work in Punjab. Meanwhile, the Guru was badly wounded by a Pathan from Sirhind. Banda felt enraged at the treachery and infidelity. He expressed his eagerness to leave for Panjab at the earliest. Banda became a disciple of the Guru. The Guru did not baptize him according to his new ceremony of administering *pahul*.

The Guru held a *darbar*. It was attended by all the Sikhs and the leading men of the place. The Guru declared that he was investing Banda with authority to complete his work of national struggle in Panjab. He conferred the title of 'Bahadur' on him. He was given an advisory council of five devoted Sikhs, Baj Singh, Binod Singh, Ram Singh, Vijay Singh and Kahan Singh. Twenty-five other Sikh soldiers were chosen to accompany him. He was supplied with a standard and drum as a symbol of temporal authority. A *hukmnama* or a letter of authority from the Guru was given instructing the Sikhs to join Banda Bahadur in his national war against religious and political tyranny. The Guru gave Banda his own sword, green bows and five arrows from his quiver. Three hundred Sikh cavaliers in battle array accompanied Banda's party to a distance of 8 kms to give him a final send off.*

Hari Ram Gupta in an another book of his states, 'Banda seems to have travelled in disguise and by circuitous routes to avoid detection by the widely prevalent Mughal spy system. Had he followed the normal route between Nanded and Hissar, about 1,600 kms long, at the rate of 16 kms or 10 miles a day on an average, he should have taken not more than three months. But Banda and his party took a year to reach Punjab. It means that he might have been frequently changing his course and hiding in places to avoid detection by the Mughal authorities.' This account when read with that the grand darbar held at his farewell, some

* In case a *darbar* as stated above, was held on Banda Bahadur's departure, it would certainly have come to the notice of the Mughal authorities and every effort would have been made to stop the same.

part of it seems apparently incorrect and contradictory to the earlier statement of a grand farewell *darbar*.

Sum-up: *The Guru called on Banda's cottage on 3 September 1708. The Guru sat on his couch. Banda could recognize the Guru and submitted to him and became his disciple. Banda would daily go to the Guru to apprise the situation and the role being assigned to him. The Guru did not baptize him by administering* pahul. *The Guru held a* darbar *and entrusted him with the work of national struggle. He was given the title of Banda Bahadur, some personal weapons of the Guru, five advisors and twenty-five soldiers. After the* darbar, *Banda and his party were escorted by the Sikh soldiers and public up to 8 km.*

In his another book, History of Sikhs, *vol. II, 1978, Hari Ram Gupta stated that Banda travelled in disguise and circuitous routes to avoid detection by the Mughal spy system, where he could have conveniently reached Hissar in three months' time, it took him almost a year to cover 1,600 km. His above-quoted second version seems to be more mature and correct.*

W. Owen Cole and Piara Singh Sambhi

The Sikhs: Their Religious Beliefs and Practices, Delhi: Vikas Publishing House, 1978

At what point, militant Sikhism came to have the aim of winning independence from the Mughals, it is difficult to say. It first expressed itself in Banda Singh's war cry of 1710, '*Raj Karega Khalsa*', the Khalsa will rule!

From the Sikh point of view, their history during the 18th century was a painful but eventually successful attempt to implement the slogan, '*Raj Karega Khalsa*', the Khalsa will rule. These words are associated with Banda Singh's capture of Sirhind, a town in Panjab in 1710. The city's governor was killed in the battle outside the town and until Banda Singh was captured and executed in 1716, Panjab was intermittently under Sikh control. Banda Singh had been one of the Guru Gobind Singh's companions at Nanded. When the Guru expired Banda Bahadur moved to Panjab and organized his successful revolt.

Sum-up: *Banda Singh had been one of the companions of Guru Gobind Singh at Nanded. When the Guru expired, he moved to the Punjab and organized his successful revolt.*

PRITAM SINGH GILL

History of the Sikh Nation, Jullundur: New Academic Publishing Co., 1978.

The child was born in 1660 in the house of Ram Dev, a farmer and was named Lachhman Dev. Lachhman Dev was fond of *shikar* and was a very good marksman in the use of bow and arrow. One day, he killed a pregnant doe and when her stomach was cut, two live young ones fell out and died in a short time. This had a great effect on the young mind of Lachhman Dev. He took such a revulsion to hunt that he became a vegetarian detached from all manly activities he was indulging in, became a *bairagi* and moved out of his home and Rajouri with a group of *sadhus*. His mind was not yet reconciled to his new master that he changed to another group of ascetics. In these wanderings he reached Nasik and came in contact with a yogi Aughar Nath who dealt in occult practices. His devotion was very much liked by the yogi and at the time of his death, the yogi gave him his books and also left his establishment under the charge of Madho Das. Madho Das soon became very famous all around for showering his blessings on those who came to his dera with their problems both spiritual and mundane.

Guru Gobind Singh who had recently come to Nanded heard of the *bairagi* and his occult practices and therefore decided to meet him. One day the Guru went to his dera, sat on his famous couch, instructed his Sikhs to slaughter couple of goats and cook meat. Disciples of Madho Das reported the matter to him and the *bairagi* tried to play those very tricks on the Guru which he used to play on other visitors by upturning the couch. Here all his occult practices failed to have any effect on the Guru. The *bairagi* finding that the visitor has far superior powers as compared to his, he went before the Guru and fell on his feet and called himself his Banda, the slave of the Guru.

Thus, Madho Das, *bairagi* became a disciple of Guru Gobind Singh. He was baptized and made familiar with the tenets of Sikhism. Thereafter Madho Das was called Banda Bahadur or Banda Singh Bahadur. For some days the Guru explained to him the situation in Panjab and how that the same was to be tackled and how he should deal with the Sikh volunteers. The Guru, thereafter, ordained Banda to proceed to Panjab. The Guru gave him his own bow and arrows and a flag and a battle drum, five senior Sikhs as advisors and a small contingent of twenty soldiers. The Guru also gave him *hukamnamas* for the Sikh *sangats* in Panjab to join under Banda's banner to deal with the Mughal forces. The Guru also gave few more injunctions to Banda Singh before his departure.

1. Do not approach a woman.
2. Do not resort to falsehood. Think, speak and, act truth.
3. Do not start a new religion or a sect.
4. Do not use a cushion in the gurdwara; do not call yourself as Guru.
5. Regard yourself as a servant of the *Khalsa* and act in accordance with their wishes and live in peace with the Sikhs.

Sum-up: *The Guru went to Bairagi's* dera, *sat on his couch and asked his followers to slaughter a couple of goats and prepare refreshments. Bairagi's occult powers could not dislodge the Guru from the couch and he submitted and became his disciple. He was baptized and made aware of the tenets of Sikhism. After some more instructions he was sent to Punjab with some of the Guru's arms and an advisory of council of some senior Sikhs and about 25 soldiers. He was also told to maintain chastity, not to create his own sect and to serve the Khalsa.*

BHAGAT SINGH

Sikh Polity, New Delhi: Oriental Publishers and Distributors, 1978

After the death of Guru Gobind Singh, the Sikhs soon developed into a political power under the leadership of Banda Singh who came to Panjab, not as Guru but as commander of the forces of the *Khalsa*. Before Banda Singh's departure from the Deccan the

Guru bestowed upon him a battle drum and a flag as emblems of temporal authority and five arrows from his quiver. He was blessed with victory provided he considered himself to be a comrade, a servant, of the *Khalsa* with whom would rest in future the supreme authority of the community. Persons like Binod Singh, who were to assist him in his activities and future programme, accompanied him to the Punjab.

Arriving in northern India Banda Singh despatched the *Hukamnamas* of Guru Gobind Singh to prominent Sikhs in the Punjab. His main target, to begin with, was Wazir Khan, the *faujdar* of Sirhind, the killer of Guru Gobind Singh's young sons. The cold-blooded murder of the innocent children of the Guru had given the Sikhs a shock and they were burning with rage against him. The leading Sikhs of the Punjab, Bhai Fateh Singh, Karam Singh, Dharam Singh, Nagahia Singh, Aali Singh and Mali Singh, flocked round him along with their followers. According to Khafi Khan, in two or three months' time, four or five thousand horsemen and seven or eight thousand foot soldiers joined him, and their number gradually rose to 40,000.

Sum-up: *The Guru made Banda commander of the Sikh forces, and not his successor or a Guru. He was given some personal weapons, five advisors and sent to the Punjab to lead the Sikh struggle. In a couple of months, four to five thousand horsemen and seven to eight thousand foot-soldiers joined under his banner.*

Gopal Singh

History of the Sikh People, New Delhi: World Sikh University Press, 1979

Guru Gobind Singh travelled with Bahadur Shah hoping that Bahadur Shah will take a proper decision for the punishment of Wazir Khan. Since the Guru lost hope of Bahadur Shah honouring his commitment regarding Wazir Khan, he did not accompany Bahadur Shah any further and settled down in Nanded on the bank of river Godavari. The Guru went to the house of the *bairagi* Madho Das, about whom he had heard while in Rajasthan. The Guru entered into his hut and lay on his couch in his absence.

Madho Das was told about the visitor and the slaughter and cooking of a goat by his followers. *Bairagi* wanted an explanation from the visitor for violating norms of the *dera*. The Guru replied that he was too tired and having come to the house of one who is known for his hospitality he reclined on the couch. The Guru also told him that he had come to reclaim him from the life of a recluse. Madho Das looked into the Guru's eyes and asked him who he was, to which the Guru said he was Guru Gobind Singh in person. At this, Banda Bahadur fell at the feet of the Guru and declared himself as his slave (*banda*). You have honoured me by your visit. I pray give me the command of yours that I can carry out. You are saviour of our race.

After listening to the Banda's story of his childhood and the period of *bairag* the Guru baptized him and named him Banda Singh Bahadur. The Guru gave him detailed instructions and a advisory council of five elder Sikhs and twenty soldiers along with some of his own weapons and *hukamnamas* for the people of Panjab and directed him to go to Panjab and punish Wazir Khan and his officers responsible for the persecution of the Sikhs.

Sum-up: *At Nanded, the Guru went to the* dera *of Bairagi Madho Das. He sat on his couch and asked his followers to slaughter a goat and prepare some refreshment. When Banda came he was greatly agitated, but his agitation cooled down when the Guru told him that he was too tired and was taking some rest in his place. Banda felt sorry and became his disciple. The Guru gave him detailed instructions, an advisory council of five elder Sikhs and twenty soldiers along with* hukmnamas *for the people of Punjab. Thus equipped, he was sent to the Punjab.*

BHAI KAHAN SINGH

Maha Kosh, Patiala: Language Department, 1981

Born in Rajouri (Poonch) in October 1670 in the house of a Rajput farmer Ram Dev: he was named Laxman Dev and from childhood he was very fond of use of weapons and going on hunts. One day over the death of the young ones of a hunted doe, Laxman Dev developed an abhorrence to killing of animals and he became an ascetic at a young age of about 15 years. He left his interests and hunts and became the disciple of Janki Prasad and moved with his group thereby leaving his home and people for good.

Moving from place to place he reached Deccan, he set up his own *dera* at the bank of river Godavari. Guru Gobind Singh reached Nanded in 1708 and Madho Das came in contact with the Guru. He was so much impressed by his meeting with the Guru that he became his *banda* (disciple). Banda became a Sikh and the Guru gave him *pahul* and named him Gurbaksh Singh, but his name remained Banda Bahadur in popular use. To punish the perpetrators of the heinous crime against Sikhs, the Guru sent Banda Bahadur to Panjab with five senior Sikh advisors and a small contingent of 25 men and *hukamnamas* in the name of Sikh *sangats* all over Panjab to join Banda Bahadur in his crusade against the Mughals. The Guru also gave him the following instructions:

1. To observe chastity.
2. To abide by the desires of the Khalsa.
3. Never call himself a Guru.
4. Eat only after others have been fed.
5. Help the despondents.

Sum-up: *At Nanded, Bairagi came in contact with the Guru and soon became his disciple. Banda was baptized, given* pahul *and named Gurbaksh Singh, but his name remained Banda Bahadur in popular use. He was sent to the Punjab with an advisory council and some soldiers. He was also instructed to observe chastity and not to call himself Guru.*

SOHAN SINGH SEETAL

Rise of the Sikh Power in the Punjab, Ludhiana: Lyall Book Depot, 1982

Sohan Singh has also given a somewhat detailed account of the meeting between Guru Gobind Singh and the Bairagi. The Guru reached in his absence, sat on his bed, got a goat slaughtered for the refreshment for his men, which greatly disturbed the Bairagi.

When the Bairagi came face to face with the Guru, his anger dissipated and he stood spell-bound and addressed the Guru 'Your Holiness, I have lost all my merit and rectitude at the hands of such a high saint as yourself'.

The Guru :	What do you mean?
Madho Das :	Your honour, I am a confirmed vegetarian saint. You have killed lives and shed blood in my own house and you have desecrated my seat on which I sit, while worshipping my gods.
The Guru :	Does the shedding of blood profane your seat?
Madho Das :	That is the principle of my *Vaishnav* creed.
The Guru :	Is that so in spite of the fact that the blood has flowed in one corner of your large compound while your couch stands in a distant corner? How did that make your seat unhaloed?
Madho Das :	Your lordship, when blood has been shed in the hermitage, no seat in any corner of it can escape the curse of impurity.
The Guru :	Then tell me one thing: When in India rivers of blood of its guiltless inhabitants happen to flow over every inch of its soil, how was it that your hermitage in this locality could remain unprofaned so far in spite of it all?

These words went home and shook him out of complacency. His very soul was shaken out of its deep slumber and all his powers were up in revolt against his past. Thus staggered altogether, he exclaimed: 'Well?'

The Guru replied in a firm tone: That is that.

A new and bright light had dawned in the inner soul of the *bairagi* now. He bowed and fell at the feet of the Guru and spoke with tears welling in his eyes: Pardon me, my Lord, I am your humble votary (*banda*).

The Guru: And I am raising my *banda* (servant) to the status of Banda Singh Bahadur.

Madho Das: At your service and at your sacred feet, your Holiness.

The Guru administered holy, Sikh baptism to Madho Das with his hands. Madho Das was now no longer a Bairagi. He had now become a full-fledged Sikh – a disciple of Guru Gobind Singh – a member of the Khalsa brotherhood.

Sum-up: *The Guru went to the Bairagi's* dera, *sat on his couch and got a goat killed for refreshment. Bairagi was greatly disturbed, but when he came face to face with the Guru and after a short discussion he became his disciple. The Guru administered him holy baptism and sent him to Punjab to lead the Sikh struggle.*

PRITAM SINGH SAFEER

The Tenth Master, New Delhi: Guru Nanak Foundation, 1983

Two armies—one functioning under Bahadur Shah and the other under the tenth Guru—continuing their march reached Nanded in September 1708. The Sikhs set up their camp at some distance from the Mughals. Accompanied by his devotees the Guru decided to make Nanded the place of his permanent residence. A spot, exceptionally beautiful on the banks of river Godavari attracted him. Sanctified by his presence, the new *dera* began to attract flocks of worshippers from far and near.

At a short distance Madho Das Bairagi was living with his followers. It was believed that he possessed super-natural powers. The tenth Master went to his place. A decorated bed was prominently spread-out there. Madho Das was away. When the Guru sat on the decorated bed, Madho Das who became aware of it, exerted his supernatural power. He firstly raised the bed on one side and then he succeeded in raising the three corners thereof. The tenth Master took out one of his gold-tipped arrows and pressed the bed down with its tip. As soon as the bed became stationary the *bairagi* rushed to the place. It is stated that the Guru's followers had slaughtered a goat and were in the process of cooking non-vegetarian food. The disciples of Madho Das were in a state of frenzy.

Historians record a strange coincidence. As soon as Guru Gobind Singh looked into the eyes of the *bairagi*, he asked him as to who he was. Madho Das instantly fell at the feet of the Master and said that he was his 'banda' i.e. captive at his feet. The tenth Master observed:

'Very well, if you are my 'banda', then you will have to accept baptism at my hands.'

The *bairagi* joyfully agreed. He was baptised and given the name of Banda Singh. In course of time, he came to be known as Banda Singh Bahadur.

Guru Gobind Singh imparted exceptional knowledge to Banda Singh, who received a touch of divinity not transmitted to anyone else. He was told that he was to go along with a chosen contingent to the Panjab. He was made aware that Sikh warriors in large numbers were to join him there. The Master gave him his own sword and five gold-tipped arrows from his quiver. Every Sikh who was to see the arrows was expected to extend his support to the personage possessing them.

The tenth Master told Banda Singh that no harm will come to him if, he will remain absolutely chaste and will not marry. He was not to start any sect. He was not to have any territorial kingdom. He was to remain devoted to his cause. All the Sikhs were to be taken as his own brothers. He was never to allow anyone to worship him. Before undertaking any important task, he was to say his prayers before God Almighty.

The tenth Master gave a *hukamnama* addressed to the Khalsa enjoining upon all the Sikhs to unite under the command of Banda Singh. It is stated that amongst those who accompanied Banda Singh were the trusted devotees of the great Guru named Baj Singh, Binod Singh, and Karam Singh. Banda Singh carried in himself the unique spirit ignited in him to achieve victories all the way.

Sum-up: *The Guru went to the Bairagi's* dera, *sat on his couch and his Sikhs slaughtered a goat for refreshment. The Bairagi could not dislodge the Guru from his couch and ultimately became his disciple. The Guru gave him some of his own weapons, instructed him to observe chastity and not to conduct as a Guru. He was sent to Punjab along with five senior Sikhs to lead the Sikh struggle.*

Bhai Parmanand

Veer Vairagi, New Delhi: Rajpal & Sons, 1984

Banda had set up his *dera* at the bank of river Godavari and was having quite a prosperous life with a large following seeking his blessings. Guru Gobind Singh also came up to Nanded along with Bahadur Shah. Since the negotiations with Bahadur Shah had virtually broken down, the Guru decided to stay back at Nanded and set up a *dera* of his own. Guru Gobind Singh, while passing through Rajasthan, met a saint of Daduduara who told him about the character and acts of a *bairagi* settled at Nanded. The account given by Narain Das left an impression on the mind of the Guru that this person seems to be having some exceptional qualities.

The Guru on reaching Nanded went to the *dera* of the *bairagi* who had become very famous in that area. In the very first meeting they seem to have liked each other to an extent that *bairagi* became a disciple of the Guru and the Guru in his own mind decided to send him to Panjab to lead the Sikhs in their struggle against Mughal authorities. The Guru gave him five arrows from his own quiver and five Sikh advisors and a small contingent of soldiers to go to Panjab. He was also given some *hukamnamas* of the Guru to the Sikh *sangats* in Panjab to join under the banner of Banda Bahadur.

Sum-up: *The Guru went to Bairagi's* dera *and in the very first meeting they seem to have liked one another and the Bairagi became the Guru's disciple. He was sent to Punjab along with five senior Sikhs as advisors and a small contingent to lead the Sikh struggle against the Mughal authorities.*

Max Arthur Macauliffe

The Sikh Religion, New Delhi: S. Chand, 1985

Guru Gobind Singh arrived at Nanded in July-August 1707 with some infantry and two or three hundred cavalry. He went to the hut of Madho Das, a *bairagi* hermit. Finding the *bairagi* absent he sat on his couch. The accompanying Khalsa slaughtered the goats kept at the *dera* and cooked the same for their meal. A disciple went to inform the *bairagi* of the Guru's proceedings. It was a sacrilege to kill an animal at *bairagi's* seat and another sacrilege to take possession of his couch. *Bairagi* came to demand an explanation of the intruder's strange conduct. The Guru replied that he had arrived fatigued in Nanded and having heard of *bairagi's* hospitality and philanthropy took the liberty of testing the favourable accounts he had received. The *bairagi* accepted the Guru's explanation, recognized from his words and manners that he was a great man and called himself his *banda* (slave), the name by which he was subsequently known.

The Guru instructed Banda in the tenets of Sikh religion, and in due time baptized him according to the new rites. On that occasion, Banda received the name Gurbakhsh Singh, but continued to be known as Banda. Banda developed great attachment with the Guru and one day asked him if there was any service he could perform for him. The Guru after reflection found that he had an account to settle with the Mohammedans of the Panjab, and replied, 'I have come into the world to consolidate the faith and destroy oppressors. Are you prepared to assist me?' Banda promised to undertake any enterprise suggested by the Guru. Upon this he was enjoined to proceed to the Panjab and wreak vengeance on the enemies of the Khalsa. Saying this the Guru presented him five arrows and thus addressed him, 'As long as thou remainest continent, thy glory shall increase. He who is continent, turneth not away from the combat, and his opponents cannot withstand him. The continent man succeedeth in everything'.

Sum-up: *The Guru went to the bairagi's* dera *with his men, sat on his couch, asked his men to kill some goats to make refreshments. When the bairagi saw what was happening he was greatly agitated, tried to topple the bed, but could not accomplish it. He was soothed by the Guru's words and soon became his disciple. The Guru instructed him in Sikh tenets and baptized him in due course. He gave the name Gurbaksh Singh, to him, though his name remained Banda Bahadur in popular use. The Guru advised him to remain continent and sent him to the Punjab to lead the Sikh struggle.*

P. K. NIJHAWAN

Sri Guru Gobind Geeta, New Delhi: Army Educational Stores, 1985

Banda Bahadur was born in 1670 in the house of Ram Dev and he was named Lachhman Dev. Not much is known of education of Lachhman but we understand that he showed an instinct for skills and craft of warfare. He was particularly good in archery and enjoyed hunting games. As story goes, he shot a pregnant doe and when he ripped open its belly, two unborn calves emerged out and died after a little while. The gory episode filled him with futility of violence and he instantly turned Goutama. He thereafter left his home and set out on his spiritual wanderings which took him from place to place in search of real peace. He was just about 16 when in 1686 he met a *sadhu* named Janaki Prasad, but his inquistive mind was not satiated and he left his Guru and came to Kasur where a *sadhu* of great reputation named Ram Thamman lived. Here Lachhman Dev renounced the world and assumed the name of Madho Das, the name he held until his encounter with Guru Gobind Singh in 1708. Madho Das wandered his way to Nanded on the bank of Godavari. Here he met Aughar Nath, a *bairagi* known for his yogic *siddhis* and occult powers. Madho Das became his disciple and on the death of Aughar Nath, he became the head of the hermitage. As his fame spread, people in spiritual and mundane distress started coming to him and had their wishes granted on his blessings. What happened between Guru Gobind Singh and the *bairagi* is a long poem covering 111 pages of the book. Guru Gobind Singh in his meeting with the *bairagi* was able to convince him about his requirement for the Sikh *panth* which was fighting a long war with the oppressive Mughal Government. Madho Das submitted before the Guru as his *banda* and prepared to carry out all his commands.

The message of the Guru aimed at bringing back to life of action and commitment those who were already confirmed in asceticism, having covered good many stages on the path. The idea perhaps was that the men who were spiritually evolved were inevitably the men born to lead the rest of the mankind. Rather, they should be made to participate in life, thus restoring mankind to the path of *dharma*. Never before that were the ascetics reclaimed in this manner. In fact, one having eschewed the world of affairs was never again to participate in it. But in Sikhism, Guru Nanak had initiated the process. He went to the siddhas in their abode in Himalayas and debated with them as to which path was more correct – his or theirs. It is just befitting that the last Guru succeeded in bringing back a very venerable ascetic, a *bairagi* to where the conflict between *dharma* and *adharma* was at its fiercest. The salvation was to be won for all the forces of *dharma*, *bairagi* not only took up the leadership of the relentless struggle against tyranny that Sikhism was waging, but also became a house holder by marrying and begetting children. To a votary of the old Indian tradition, it would mean a fall from a high pedestal. But to the Guru *panth* it was a matter of real glory. This subtle but obvious distinction between the old brand of Hinduism and Sikhism is seldom so well appreciated either by the Hindus or by the Sikhs. The last few cantos of the poem are given as under:

Banda: But before I begin my mission, O Guru!
Baptise me into your Panth
As you did thousands of your sons,
The Khalsa
So that I be one of your very own,
One of the Khalsa only,
So that I do not waver
Or err, or falter,
In carrying out your exalted mission.

Guru: You are my very special man, O Banda!
Talked we have
So much between us.
You alone have been given
Explanations by me
For each act of mine.
You alone know
Why I did what.
I have convinced you so long and hard
That baptized you already are
In spirit!
Yet, a formal baptismal is necessary
And I administer you one

With full ceremony
Because when in power
You act as the Khalsa would want you.
The Khalsa should be able to judge you
On your acts
And not as my viceroy among them,

Not answerable to anyone but me.

(The Guru then duly administers *Amrit* to Banda).

Now, the final act:
Let me do you the greatest honour,
The honour you so richly deserve.
Let me confer upon you
The order of the Khalsa,
Which means Fearless as the Lion!
And bequeath to you
My own arrows
As a token of that.
So henceforth, O Banda!
People shall forget you as a Bairagi.
Hereafter, they will remember you
As Banda Bahadur,
Or Banda Singh Bahadur,
Or Banda, the Lion,
Or Banda, the Fearless.

Banda: O Sodhi Sultan!
O the best of the great race of Raghus!
From today onwards
You are my father,
Not as you are
To your countless sons, the Khalsa
But my own father,
My real father,
Whose name and lineage
My own sons shall carry in the world.
Today I disown my own proud lineage of
The great *Agnikula* Rajputs.
Today I become a Sodhi and a Raghu
Born of you from the seed of your mind,
The nectar of immortality that I've sipped
From your sacred hands

Has made me to be reborn
In you and to you.
Guru: Blessed are you, O my son!
Not you,
I too am fulfilled.
But no more talking,
No more display of emotions,
No more wasting of time.
I, therefore, order you
To go and prepare yourself
For your journey tomorrow –
The journey of destiny!
You shall report to me in the morning
When my *firmans* and my men,
Your companions,
And the *Panj Piaras*
Will all be ready
To join you.
May you be victorious!
May the Khalsa be victorious!
Ever, ever victorious!!

– SAT SRI AKAL –

Sum-up: *It is a long poem, very well composed with poetic imagination and at the same time remaining in tune with the prevalent account. Some important cantos of the poem have been given.*

ANIL CHANDER BANERJEE

Khalsa Raj, New Delhi: Abhinav Publications, 1985

Lachhman Das, son of a Rajput farmer was born in 1670 at Rajouri (Poonch). In his youth, he became a *bairagi* and took the name of Madho Das and wandering from place to place he came to Nasik on the bank of Godavari. He became the disciple of a yogi Aughar Nath and took lessons in occultism. After the Guru's death Madho Das moved to Nanded and set up his own *dera* and practiced magical tricks on visitors to his *dera*. Guru Gobind Singh while at Nanded came to his *dera*, but Madho Das's tricks failed to have any effect on the Guru. He submitted to the Guru and became his disciple and vowed to continue the struggle against the Mughal Government.

The Guru gave him a battle drum and a banner as emblem of temporal authority and also gave him five arrows from his quiver as a pledge of victory. On parting he enjoined on him to remain pure in conduct, to be true in word and in deed, to look upon himself as a servant of the Khalsa, who would be the Guru in future, and to act always upon the advice of the five Sikhs sent along with him. Sainapat, who gives us a fair idea as to how the Guru passed his days at Nanded, does not say anything about Banda or his conversion to Sikhism.

A.C. Banerjee is unable to understand as to why Guru's choice fell upon a new convert who had no previous experience in the use of arms. He states that what Banda achieved in the reign of Bahadur Shah could certainly have been achieved by the Guru, but he chose to compromise instead of confrontation. These fanciful remarks of A.C. Banerjee are not based on any historic understanding and are in a way uncalled for regarding spiritual sagacity and the ability of Guru Gobind Singh to face any adversity.

Sum-up: *The Guru went to Bairagi's* dera *and sat on his couch. Madho Das's tricks could not dislodge the Guru. He submitted to the Guru and became his disciple. The Guru gave him some of his personal weapons, five advisors and sent him to the Punjab with a small contingent.*

KHUSHWANT SINGH

A History of the Sikhs, vol. I, Delhi: Oxford University Press, 1987

Guru Gobind Singh tried for many months to persuade Bahadur Shah to take action against Wazir Khan before he arrived at the conclusion that he would not obtain any justice from the Mughals. He continued to negotiate with the emperor, but decided to send one of his commanders back to Panjab to rouse the peasantry in the event the negotiations failed.

Although there were many old and trusted disciples, the Guru's choice fell on a comparative stranger whom the Guru had known for only a few weeks. He was an ascetic named Laxman Das who had spent the last 15 years in a hermitage on the banks of Godavari.

The Guru caught the fanatic gleam in the hermit's eyes and felt that in the spare frame of the ascetic smouldered the Promethean fire which could be fanned into a flame. He summoned Laxman Das and charged him with the duty of punishing the men who had persecuted the Sikhs and murdered his sons. He gave Laxman Das a new name which the latter had himself chosen, that is, Banda or the slave.

Guru Gobind Singh armed Banda with five arrows from his quiver and gave him his own standard and battle drum. He also issued orders (*hukamnamas*) for the Sikh *sangats* urging them to join service under Banda Bahadur.

Sum-up: *The Guru selected a comparative stranger, a bairagi, ignoring many an old and trusted disciples. The Guru saw a fanatic gleam in the hermit's eyes and felt that in the spare frame of the ascetic smouldered the Promethean fire which could be fanned into a flame. He summoned Laxman Das and charged him with the duty of punishing the men who had persecuted the Sikhs and murdered his sons. He was given some personal weapons by the Guru along with* hukamnamas *for Sikh* sangats *to join Banda Bahadur.*

GURBAKSH SINGH

Tarik-i-Punjab, Patiala: Punjabi University, 1988

Guru Gobind Singh while at Nanded decided to set up his dera on the bank of Godavari and named it Abchalnagar. He did not accompany Bahadur Shah any further into Deccan as the negotiations between them had virtually broken down. The Guru had heard of the *bairagi* also having a *dera* on the bank of Godavari who had a couch on which when people would sit, he would topple them with his occult powers and enjoyed their discomfiture.

The Guru decided to meet this *bairagi* and with a small number of Sikhs he went to the *bairagi's dera* and occupied the particular couch. *Bairagi* when saw the Guru accompanied by some Sikh soldiers occupying his couch; his blood boiled and he tried all his occult powers to topple the couch but he failed. At this moment, it dawned on *bairagi* that the person sitting on the couch was some great personality and could be he is Guru Gobind Singh. When the Guru confirmed the same he fell at his feet and he declared himself his 'banda' (the slave). The Guru seemed to have made up his mind to convert him to Sikhism to which he readily agreed.

The Guru brought Banda to his *dera* and gave him the *pahul* and made him a Khalsa. The Guru placed all the Sikhs under his command to stop the tyranny of the Mughal rulers.

The Guru expired within few days and Sikhs started dispersing. Banda Bahadur collected as many Sikhs as he could and moved towards Punjab with five Sikh advisors and small contingent of soldiers and *hukamnamas* of the Guru to the Sikh *sangats* in Punjab.

Sum-up: *The Guru went to the bairagi's* dera *and occupied his couch. Banda failed to topple the couch and wisdom dawned on him regarding his guest and he submitted to the Guru and became his disciple. The Guru brought him to his camp, gave him* pahul, *and made him a Khalsa. The Guru expired in a few days and Banda moved to the Punjab with five elder Sikh advisors and a small contingent.*

DALBIR SINGH DHILLON

Sikhism: Origin and Development, New Delhi: Atlantic Publishers and Distributors, 1988

According to the Sikh chroniclers, at Nanded, Guru met an ascetic named Lachhman Das, who had spent about fifteen years of his life in a hermitage on the banks of the river Godavari. The ascetic was impressed and attracted to see and hear the religious discourses of the Guru. He became a devotee of the Guru to the extent that he called himself the *banda* or the slave of the Guru.

One day the Guru summoned him and entrusted him with the duty of punishing the men who had persecuted the Sikhs and murdered his sons. It is said that 'Guru Gobind Singh armed Banda with five arrows from his quiver and gave him his own standard and a battle drum. He also issued orders (*hukamnamas*) to the Sikhs, urging them to volunteer for service'. This added a new era in the history of the Sikhs, in which now the Sikhs fought not only for protection but also for the sovereignty. It took place in the early years of the 18th century after the demise of Guru Gobind Singh.

Sum-up: *The Guru met Bairagi at Nanded who became his disciple. The Guru entrusted him with the duty to punish the persecutors of the Sikhs and the murderers of his sons. He gave him some of his weapons and* hukamnamas *for Sikh* sangats *to join him. A new era was thus added to Sikh history to fight for Sikh sovereignty.*

MUHAMMAD LATIF

History of Punjab, Ludhiana: Kalyani Press, 1989

Guru Gobind Singh during his stay at Nanded (Deccan) formed his acquaintance with Banda, an ascetic of the *Bairagi* order. *Bairagi* had hundreds of followers and lived in a princely fashion. The Guru and Banda soon after initial meeting became intimate friends. The Guru by his persuasive power and religious zeal, made such a deep impression on mind of the Banda that he was initiated into the *pahul* and became a disciple of the Guru. Banda by his devotion soon inspired the Guru and became his most staunch disciple. Though he was not acknowledged as a Guru's successor in the apostleship, yet the Guru declared that after him the Sikhs would look upon Banda as their leader and protector. His dying injunction to him was that he should remain a warrior and avenge the blood of his father, as well as of his innocent sons.

He told him that he must not fear death, and taking five arrows from his quiver delivered them to Banda as emblem of victory. He further instructed Banda: Don't approach a woman if you are Guru's true disciple, and keep these five arrows with you. So long as he follows Guru's instructions, no misfortune should happen to him; if he forgets them or disregards them, he would answer for the non-performance with his life. Banda received the arrows with profound reverence and solemnly promised to obey the commands of the dying Guru.

Banda, having yet to carry out the dying wishes of the Guru, determined to redeem to the very letter the promise given by him to avenge the wrongs of his late leader. He now in order to accomplish his design issued orders to the Sikhs (in the name of Guru Gobind Singh) to prepare for hostilities and assemble at a place appointed by him, for the purpose of overthrowing the Mohammedan rule. The Sikhs broke from their retreats and flocked in numbers round the banner of Banda who assumed the title of Guru.

Sum-up: *The Guru, while at Nanded, met the Bairagi Madho Das, who became his disciple. The Guru sent him to the Punjab to punish the persecutors of the Sikhs. He converted the Bairagi to a Sikh and instructed him to refrain from women. Sikhs came out from their retreats and joined Banda in large numbers who now assumed the title of Guru.*

WILLIAM IRVINE

Later Mughals, Delhi: Taj Publication, 1989

William Irvine is the author of a monumental work *Later Mughals*, which is widely read and appreciated as a fairly authentic book on Mughal history. In this book, William Irvine has given a very short account of Banda Bahadur as under:

On the death of Govind, his family and followers brought forward a man, who exactly resembled the deceased. It is not very clear who this man was; he is generally spoken of either as *banda* (the slave) or as the False Guru. Two contemporaries call him Fath Shah, and if this be correct, it points perhaps to his passing as Fath Singh, the son of Govind. Some say he was a *bairagi* faqir, a native of village, Pandor, in the Baith Jalandhar Duaba, who for many years had been the intimate friend of Guru Gobind. A more recent account called him Madhu Das, alias Narayan Das, and tells us he was born in October 1670 being the son of Ram Deo, Rajput of Rajouri Garh in Poonch. The name given to him at birth was Laxman Deo.

He formed a friendship with Janki Prasad Bairagi with whom

he went to the monastery of Baba Ram Thamman. This math is in a place not far from Qasur, which is itself a little way south of Lahore. Authority was at that time exercised there by Baba's grandson, of whom Laxman Deo became a *chela*, or disciple receiving the name of Laxman Bala alias Narayan Das. In the end he found his way as a pilgrim to the Deccan and there met Guru Govind Singh and became his *chela*.

This man was now sent off secretly from the Dakhin to Hindustan. At the same time letters were written to the Panjab, informing the disciples that the Guru had been slain in the Emperor's camp by the dagger of an Afghan. But just before his death, their leader had announced that in a short time, through the power of transmigration, he would appear again clothed with sovereignty, and whenever he should raise the standard of independence, sikhs would be joining him to secure prosperity in this world and salvation in the next. Immediate collections of cash and goods must be made. Expectation was thus aroused, and the new manifestation awaited.

Suddenly there appeared in the town of Kharkhoda, thirty-five miles west of Delhi, a man who gave himself out to be Guru Govind Singh. According to some accounts, he asserted that others believed that he had been restored to life by God's power.

[This account has been given verbatim to show as to what extent leading scholars of Mughal history, were totally deficient of Sikh history and of its heroes.]

Sum-up: *On the death of Guru Gobind Singh, his family brought a man who resembled the Guru. He was generally called Banda or false Guru. Some say that he belonged to Rajouri (Jammu) and reached Nanded (Deccan) where he met the Guru and became his disciple. He was secretly sent to Punjab, soon thereafter the Guru expired from the wounds inflicted on him by an Afghan. Just before his death, the Guru had announced that he shall rise again clothed with sovereignty. Suddenly in Kharkhoda came a man calling himself as Guru Gobind Singh making people to believe that he has been restored to life by God.*

Khafi Khan

Muntakhabu-Lubab, History of India by its own historians, Elliot & Dowson, vol. VII, Delhi: Low Price Publication, 1990

At the time Bahadur Shah marched towards Hyderabad, Guru Govind Singh, the chief Guru of the sect came to join him with two or three hundred horsemen bearing spears and some footmen. After two or three months he died from the wounds of a dagger and his murderer was not discovered. When the news of his death reached Panjab where the bulk of the Sikhs were living, an obscure member of the sect called Banda to whom there are various statements, gave out that in the course of transmigration, in which the Sikhs believe in and call Avatar, he had taken the place of the murdered Guru Gobind Singh, who had come to life again as a bearded man in his body, for the purpose of taking revenge. This worthless dog having published this statement stirred up disaffection in the sect and raised the standard of rebellion. By jugglery, charms, and sorcery he pretended to perform miracles before credulous people and gave himself the name of *Sacha Padshah*, true king. He began to plunder in the Punjab and the country about Sirhind, and in the course of three to four months, he gathered around him four or five thousand pony riders and seven to eight thousand footmen. His numbers daily increased and much plunder fell into his hands until he had eighteen or nineteen thousand men under arms, and carried on a predatory and cruel warfare. He fought with two or three *faujdars* who went out to punish him, defeated them and killed them.

Khafi Khan's account is very widely referred to in Sikh history. The above account of Banda Bahadur, as for as the quality of its historical authenticity is the poorest in all the fable/fiction ridden accounts mentioned in this chapter.

Sum-up: *When Bahadur Shah marched towards the Deccan, Guru Gobind Singh joined him with two or three hundred horsemen. After two to three months he died of a stab wound. When news of his death reached Panjab, an obscure man named Banda took place of Guru*

Gobind Singh. He raised a rebellion and gave his name as Sacha Padshah. He started plundering Punjab and even fought and defeated a few faujdars.

SUNITA PURI

Advent of Sikh Religion, New Delhi: Munshiram Manoharlal Publishers, 1993.

Lord Krishna, the exponent of the Bhakti and Sankhya Yoga (Knowledge) in the *Bhagavadgita*, also advocated a life of action (Karmayoga) and urged Arjuna to take up arms for the protection of his right and to fight against injustice.

In this context, it is significant to note that Guru Gobind Singh himself while wanting Banda Bairagi (Madho Das Bairagi) to give up his life as a hermit and instead take up the 'battle of Dharma', which was then being fought in the Punjab, invoked the memories of the days when, in this very land, Lord Krishna had taught man 'the primacy of action'. Guru Gobind Singh, in the same context, reminded Banda Bairagi of the task that had beset Guru Nanak viz., 'to restore to man the greatness that is man's. To make man protest against tyranny and injustice'. The Guru also revealed to the *bairagi* his reasons for adopting the 'cult of the sword' 'when tyranny reigns supreme, it is no use slipping rosary beads through your fingers and meditating over issues of soul and Brahma in remote forest groves.' He added that is the time when 'every saint must wield the sword'.

Guru Gobind Singh's aim was to serve the cause of righteousness and, more specifically, to protect the Dharma enunciated by Guru Nanak. In his compositions one finds the same insistence on the worship of the one True Lord, the same delineation of devotion and surrender and the same glorification of Name as found in Guru Nanak's hymns. 'The core of Sikhism remained unaffected by the political turmoil through which its votaries passed under his leadership during seventeenth century.'

Sum-up: *Guru Gobind Singh advised Banda (Madho Das Bairagi) to give up the life of a hermit and instead take up the battle of dharma, to protest agains tyranny and injustice. The Guru revealed that when tyranny reigns supreme, it is no use slipping rosary beads and meditating in remote forest groves. It is the time when every saint must wield the sword.*

HARBANS SINGH

The Heritage of the Sikhs, New Delhi: Manohar, 1994

On reaching Nanded Guru Gobind Singh came to the hermitage of a *bairagi sadhu*, Madho Das, who was believed to possess magical powers. Finding him absent from his hut, the Guru sat down on his couch to wait for him, while his Sikhs slaughtered a goat to cook meat for the evening meal. Madho Das was furious at this profanation of his monastery and burned with the desire to chastise the strange visitor for his temerity. But no sooner did he set his eyes on the Guru than all his anger was gone: so was his sorcerous will of which he was greatly proud. He fell at the Guru's feet and called himself his *banda*, or slave. The brief conversation which took place is set down by Ahmad Shah Batalia in his *Zikr-i-Guruan wa Ibtida-i-Singhan wa Mazhab-i-Eshan*, based on contemporary records of his ancestors:

Madho Das	: Who are you?
Guru Gobind Singh	: He whom you know.
Madho Das	: What do I know?
Guru Gobind Singh	: Think it over in your mind.
Madho Das (after a pause)	: So you are Guru Gobind Singh.
Guru Gobind Singh	: Yes
Madho Das	: What have you come here for?
Guru Gobind Singh	: I have come so that I may convert you into a disciple of mine.
Madho Das	: I submit, my Lord, I am a *banda* (slave) of yours.

Madho Das was baptized on 3 September 1708, with the rites and vows of the Khalsa and given the name of Banda Singh. The Guru gave him five arrows from his own quiver and an escort, including five of his chosen Sikhs and directed him to go to the Punjab to carry on the campaign against the provincial overlords.

Sum-up: *While at Nanded, Guru Gobind Singh went to the hermitage of the Bairagi Madho Das, and his Singhs slaughtered a goat for their evening meal. Bairagi was greatly enraged but when he set his eyes on the Guru his anger was gone and he submitted to the Guru in extreme humility. Madho Das was converted to Sikhism and baptized on 3 September 1708 and named Banda Singh Bahadur. The Guru gave him some of his weapons, five elder Sikhs as his advisors, along with a small detachment and sent them to the Punjab.*

THE ENCYCLOPAEDIA OF SIKHISM

Harbans Singh, Editor-in-chief, Punjabi University, 1995

Banda Bahadur after roaming around the country for many years settled down at Nasik where he learnt the occult art from Yogi Aughar Nath. After the death of Yogi Aughar Nath, Banda moved to Nanded and set up his own *dera* on the bank of river Godavari. Here he had an encounter with Guru Gobind Singh who happened to visit his hermitage on 3 September 1708, at the end of which he, as the chronicler records, fell at his feet, pronouncing himself to be his *banda* or slave.

Guru Gobind Singh escorted him to his own camp, administered to him the vows of Khalsa and gave him the name of Banda Singh, from the word *banda* he had used for himself when proclaiming his allegiance to the Guru. Guru Gobind Singh gave him a battle drum, a banner and five arrows as emblem of authority and accompanied by five senior Sikhs he set out towards the north determined to chastise the tyrannical Mughal faujdar of Sirhind. As he reached Panjab, Sikhs began to rally round his standard. The ancestors of Phulkian rulers provided him some material help.

Sum-up: *The Guru went to the* dera *of Bairagi who got so impressed that he became his disciple. The Guru escorted him to his camp and administered him the oaths of Khalsa and gave him the name Banda Singh. The Guru gave him some war material, five elder Sikhs as advisors and a small contingent and sent him to Punjab. As soon as he reached Punjab, Sikhs began to rally around his standard.*

KAISAR SINGH CHHIBAR
Bansawalinama, Amritsar: Singh Brothers, 1997

Lachhman Das Bairagi was called Banda. He had come from Peroja Nagar in eastern India. Banda had remained there for 80 years as *sanyasi*. Thereafter he came to the south and stayed at Haripur for 60 years. From there he came to Majha, the land of the Jats with the name Lachhman Das. People were calling him '*Wali*'. But Guru Gobind Singh (Sahib Puran) had recognised him.

The Guru asked him to join his Sikhs and go to Panjab. Banda was initially not willing, but the Guru convinced him that he should serve the country against the tyranny of the Mughals.

On the way the Banda and his group was questioned by the Mughal authorities, but he was able to dodge them with the story of his being a Lubana trader. In this way he was able to dodge Mughal authorities at other places with different stories. Banda and his party had a safe journey due to the *bakhshish* of the Guru and they reached near Delhi.

Lachhman Das was a *bairagi*, but he became a Sikh of Guru Gobind Singh.

Sum-up: *It is a short story full of fable/fiction and with hardly any historical evidence. The only fact that comes out is that Banda was sent by the Guru to the Punjab and he reached there dodging the Mughal authorities.*

PATWANT SINGH
The Sikhs, New Delhi: Harper Collins Publishers India, 1999

By the time the Mughal and the Sikh contingents reached the southern town of Nanded in September 1708, it was obvious that the emperor was avoiding issues that most concerned the Sikhs. Seeing the futility of any further discussion with the emperor, Guru parted company with Bahadur Shah at Nanded and set up his *dera* at a vantage point on the bank of river Godavari.

One of those converted by the Guru in Nanded, was a man then named Madho Das Bairagi, a *sadhu* of some standing with a following of his own. *Bairagi's* men had clashed with some of the Khalsa in which Madho Das's followers had been defeated. His conversion was a momentous event for Sikhism. Banda Singh served the faith with exemplary dedication and valour, and in the process shook the Mughal empire to its very foundations.

Sum-up: *The Guru parted company with Bahadur Shah and set up his camp on the bank of river Godavari. A bairagi named Madho Das had his own* dera *nearby. Bairagi's men had clashed with the Khalsa but were defeated. The bairagi was converted to Sikhism and he served the faith with exemplary dedication and valour and in the process shook the Mughal empire to its foundations.*

M.L. AHLUWALIA

Landmarks in Sikh History, New Delhi: A I Publishers, 1999

Lachman Das alias Madho Das whom the Guru Sahib energised to involve himself in the practical *tapasaya* of leading the struggle in the north against the fundamentalist Mughal regime had pledged to do that as the 'servant to order' or the *banda* of the Guru. The Guru also did not insist on Banda taking the *Khande da pahul*. In spite of the Sikh tradition to the contrary, there is no mention of that fact in the *Akhbarat-e Durbar-e Mualla*. That goes to prove that the Guru–Madho Das meeting was held in secrecy and the only thing to be decided in such a secret meeting was how Madho Das should have to operate for the success of a very difficult programme he had undertaken. The factors which favoured his choice were, that besides being a Rajput, he belonged to the north in Jammu. Another weighty consideration must have been that as a *bairagi sadhu* he would have no difficulty in getting around him most of the *bairagis*, who held extensive jagirs in north India from Banaras to Jammu. In their religious beliefs the *bairagis* were not much different from the Nanak Panthi *sadhus*.

That Banda had not become an *amritdhari* Sikh is also fully proved by the news reports in the later day *akhabarat* according to which during his military campaigns Banda's personal flag had Goddess Durga and Hanuman painted on it on a green cloth having *Gota-kinari* embedded on the corners. Moreover his becoming an *amritdhari* or not was not of any material consequence even other wise. What mattered was how and under what circumstances he was to collect a large volunteer force which swelled to four to five thousand horsemen and seven or eight thousand foot soldiers within only three or four months of his coming on the scene. All of them certainly were not *amritdhari*. In the estimate given by Khafi Khan Banda's force is described between seventy thousand to one lakh though it was very much on the higher side.

Sum-up: *The Guru did not insist on administering 'Bairagi Khande Ki Pahul' and there is no mention of the same in 'Akhbarat-i-darbar-i-Mualla'. This is further established by the fact that Banda's personal flag had goddess Durga and Hanuman painted on a green cloth. In three to four months he collected four to five thousand horsemen and seven to eight thousand foot-soldiers.*

SURJIT SINGH GANDHI

Sikhs in the Eighteenth Century, Amritsar: Singh Brothers, 1999

Banda was born on October 27, 1670 at Rajouri in the Poonch district of western Kashmir. While a child, he was called Lachhman Dev. His father, Ram Dev, being a Rajput ploughman, the boy had to do various odd jobs connected with farming which a peasant boy often does in a village. During his early years, it appears that he had attained high degree of efficiency in archery, swordsmanship and horse-riding. He also developed taste for hunting. At the age of fifteen, an incident is said to have occurred which changed the whole course of his life. In one of his hunting excursions, he killed a female deer on the bank of the Tavi River. When its stomach was opened, the two young ones which she was carrying fell from her womb and writhed in pain and died.

The scene was too pathetic to bear and Banda resolved, thenceforward, to lead an ascetic's life. He became disciple of Janki Prashad, *bairagi* ascetic who resided at Rajouri.

In accordance with the custom of the *bairagis* he changed his name to Madho Das. Like the *sadhus* of this order, he wandered from place to place until he came to Nasik on the bank of Godavari, where he entered the hermitage of an old yogi, Aughar Nath, and learnt occultism from him. Aughar Nath was much impressed by the service of Madho Das and as a token thereof he presented to him a rare yogic book, *Sidd Anunia*, compiled by a disciple of Guru Gorakhnath. After his preceptor's demise, he moved to Nanded (Maharashtra) and established a monastery of his own where he worked for fifteen years. It is here that Banda came in contact with Guru Gobind Singh who paid a visit to Nanded, one of the religious centres of the central India, possibly to acquaint the religious leaders with his mission. From the chronology of the Guru's travels, it appears that he did not live more than one month in Nanded. During this short sojourn, according to Muhammad Latif, 'Govind and Banda soon became intimate friends, and the former, by his persuasive eloquence and religious zeal, made such a deep impression on the mind of Banda that he was initiated into the *pahul* and became a disciple of the Guru'. Soon, Banda won the Guru's confidence and became his most staunch adherent. The Guru found in him the fire for the Sikh cause, sincerity for upholding it and the capability to spearhead the Sikh Movement. After baptism, the Guru gave him a new name Banda Singh which the latter had himself chosen to consecrate his relationship with the Guru.

Then the Guru commissioned him to go to the Punjab to lead the Sikhs. He armed Banda with five arrows from his quiver and gave him his own standard and battle drum as emblem of victory. He also issued orders (*hukamnamas*) to the Sikhs urging them to volunteer for service. Five Sikhs—Binod Singh, Kahan Singh, Daya Singh, Ram Singh and Baj Singh—representing 'Five Piaras' were sent with Banda for help and to act as his counsel. Twenty more Singhs were also sent with him to render him assistance. Then the Guru advised Banda, 'As long as thou remaineth continent, thy glory shall increase. He who is continent, turneth not away from the combat, and his opponents cannot withstand him. The continent man succeedeth in everything.'

Sum-up: *During the short stay of Guru Gobind Singh at Nanded he and Bairagi Madho Das became friends. After his baptism, the Guru named him Banda Singh Bahadur. The Guru gave him some of his personal weapons, five elder Sikhs as advisors and a small contingent. He also gave him* hukamnamas *for Punjab* sangats *to join him in his fight against the Mughal forces in the Punjab.*

HARBANS KAUR SAGOO

Banda Singh Bahadur and Sikh Sovereignty, New Delhi: Deep & Deep Publications, 2001

In 1708 AD Guru Gobind Singh while accompanying Mughal Emperor stopped at Nanded. One day he went to the monastery of Bairagi Madho Das about whom he had heard a fairly detailed account from Jait Ram of Dadu Duara. Madho Das being not present, the Guru sat down on *bairagi's* couch and ordered some of his Sikhs to cook a few goats for their refreshment. When the matter was reported to the *bairagi*, he felt greatly offended over the conduct of the Sikhs and immediately came back to his *dera*. *Bairagi* used all his tricks to topple the couch on which the Guru sat, but in spite of his best efforts he could not succeed. He came to the Guru, saw him and the presence of Guru greatly fascinated him. His anger seemed to have melted away and he had become an admirer of the Guru. The conversation between Madho Das and the Guru as recorded by Sagoo appears in certain earlier accounts.

Guru administered holy, Sikh baptism to Madho Dass and after taking the *amrit* from the Guru, he was named Banda Singh Bahadur. He had now become a full-fledged Sikh and a disciple of Guru Gobind Singh and member of the Khalsa brotherhood. The Guru gave him five arrows from his quiver with five senior Sikhs as advisors and about 20 soldiers Banda Bahadur moved towards Panjab to take up his task as assigned by Guru Gobind Singh.

Sum-up: *Banda could not topple the couch and became the Guru's disciple. He was administered holy baptism and sent to the Punjab.*

DALIP SINGH

Life of Sri Guru Gobind Singh Ji, Amritsar: B. Chattar Singh Jiwan Singh, 2002

As we shall note from the accounts of events given in *Amarnamah*, that the Guru met with Banda at Nanded on the solar eclipse day, which was observed on 3 September 1708 (The Guru had been dealing with Banda, more than one month, since his arrival at Nanded). Near to the Guru's place, there used to live a mendicant (*bairagi*), who was ill tempered. This *bairagi* had attained magical powers through the practice of yogic techniques, and like all other yogis used to dominate the simple minded people of the jungle nearby, by threats of curses and show of his magical powers. The *bairagi* had established his domain which rivalled the domain of kings. Obviously, the people were greatly fear stricken from his so called tyrannical rule.

At Nanded Guru Gobind Singh witnessed the same situation of domination of the *bairagi* over the people, who were living in awe of him. Nathmal further states that the *bairagi* possessed wooden sandals and a vessel of milk, believed to be endowed with miraculous powers. He was full of vanity and devoid of love altogether. He hated those who loved God and were Truthful Persons. He was jealous of the Guru's nearness to the emperor. This *bairagi* was later named Banda.

The Guru's popularity amongst the tribal people created extreme jealousies in the mind of Banda, as he saw his following dwindling. One day Banda had gone to the other side of Godavari River, and in his absence no one was occupying his seat at his place. The Guru asked the Sikhs accompanying him to slaughter all the goats, which they did. The people in the nearby jungle saw this, rushed to the Banda's place to get the goats' meat, which they very much relished. . . . The Guru had caused slaughter of the goats to provide meat to these poor people.

On his return, Banda saw all his goats had been slaughtered, sent five of his fighting men to kill the Guru. As the Guru had

God's protection, they could not harm him, but were themselves over-powered by the Sikhs. They were bleeding profusely due to the wounds received in fighting with the Guru, reported back to Banda their helplessness. They stated, 'countless other warriors were prepared to sacrifice their lives for the Guru, and even the unseen horsemen were supporting him.' They further stated that they had become helpless and submitted themselves to the Guru and offered to join his Panth.

Banda then rushed to nearby Nanded town, collected a large number of Hindus to support him against the Guru. He told them that the Guru had killed his goats at the auspicious time of the Solar Eclipse. The Hindus got infuriated and approached Emperor Bahadur Shah, who was also at that time at Nanded, and lodged a complaint on behalf of Banda. Hindus pleaded that they had been ruined by the Guru's act and requested for justice. Since they passionately and most resentfully placed their grief to the emperor, it made him seriously consider their case. Nand Lal, an advisor to the emperor, suggested to him to discuss the matter with the Guru personally. This Nand Lal was different person, and not Bhai Nand Lal, who was one of the poets in the Guru's Court.

The emperor and all the Hindus in their anxiety came to see the Guru on the banks of Godavari River. The Guru at that time was in deep meditation. The emperor made an offering of a couple of diamonds and a costly pearl. The Guru, however, threw the pearl into the river and told the emperor that the river had sought the offering of the pearl from him. The emperor on hearing this folded his hands in courtesy. The Guru then offered him a seat besides himself.

The emperor then stated about the complaint of Hindus lodged with him. The Guru then explained the reality, and said that he had only got the goats killed as he wanted to give to the needy people the food they relished most. The Hindus thereupon asserted that at that the solar eclipse was caused as the demons engulfed the Sun. There is mythical Puranic story describing conflict between Sun and demons, the latter devouring the former, as it had some debt to clear. The Guru, however, explained that Sun Eclipse was a natural phenomenon, when Moon comes in between

Sun and Earth, and till such time Moon does not move away from the said position, till that time that portion of the Sun, which we cannot see, appears to us eclipsed.

Banda then submitted to the Guru and begged for mercy and grace. 'The Guru deputed five independent minded Singhs to accompany him, and commanded him to proceed to the Punjab.' This all took place on 3 September 1708.

The Guru elsewhere in Amarnamah stated, 'Sikhs have been granted Sovereignty of both the worlds, and must retain high spirits under all circumstances.'

Sum-up: *The fictional aspects of this long story takes away from it whatever material facts are related therein. The sum total is that bairagi was administered* pahul *and sent to Punjab.*

KULDEEP BHATNAGAR

Banda Singh Bahadur, Chandigarh: Lokgeet Parkashan, 2002

Guru Gobind Singh went to the *dera* of the *bairagi* on the bank of Godavari. *Bairagi* was not there. The Guru sat on his couch and told Binod Singh to make provision for the refreshment for the Sikhs, if necessary by slaughtering a few goats of the *dera*. The sevaks of the *dera* got greatly frightened and went to locate the *bairagi* and informing of the visitors. Madho Das came back to his *dera* and entered his cottage to see a person of grand personality was resting on his couch.

Madho Das spoke in a irritated voice: Who are you?

The Guru in a very sedate voice said: I am the same person whose arrival you have been awaiting.

Madho Das again asked: Whom am I awaiting?

The Guru said: Think carefully.

At this, Madho Das realized and said: Are you Guru Gobind Singh, to which the Guru replied, Yes, he is Guru Gobind Singh.

The knowledge about the Guru came welling up in his mind. Madho Das very politely said: What is the purpose of your coming here?

The Guru said: I have come here to avail of your services, to which Madho Das with folded hands pleaded that I am your Banda (Das) and you can order me for my services.

The Guru and Madho Das spent a lot of time in the *kutiya* alone getting conversant with the problems faced by the community. When he came to know about the execution of younger sons of the Guru he virtually broke down and resolved that he will take revenge on the people who carried out such heinous crime. On the suggestion of the Guru Madho Das resolved to go to Panjab at the earliest and take vengeance on those who committed the crime against Sikhs. The Guru smilingly asked Madho Das: What will happen to your *dera*?, to which Madho Das said: I am leaving it with you, you know, what will happen to it.

After about two weeks a sevadar came running and told Madho Das that the Guru has been attacked by two Pathans sent from Sirhind by Wazir Khan. So Banda rushed to the Guru's *dera* where the wound had been stitched and bandaged by that time. The Guru asked for a *darbar* the next day where the Guru declared Madho Das as the leader of the Sikhs. He was given the title of Bahadur. He was also given five senior Sikhs as advisors and twenty-five soldiers to accompany him. The Guru also gave him his own sword, the green bow with five arrows, and a *hukamnama* to the people of Panjab to join Banda Bahadur in his struggle for the freedom from Mughal atrocities.

Sum-up: *Kuldeep Bhatnagar's account is in the form of a historical novel woven around the subject of Banda being converted from a bairagi to a Sikh and sent to the Punjab.*

SUKHDIAL SINGH

Banda Singh Bahadur (Punjabi), Patiala: Punjabi University, 2003

Guru Gobind Singh reached Nanded in September 1708. Sukhdial Singh contends that all the earlier accounts of Guru Gobind Singh meeting Banda Bahadur are unbelievable. He has come with a fresh account. He states that Prince Mauzzam had a section of Sikh soldiers in his army, which was increased to about few thousand during his passage through Panjab while moving from Kabul to Delhi after the death of Aurangzeb.

Since it was a large contingent it had its commander who was named Banda. While at Nanded this Sikh section of the Bahadur Shah's army went to Guru Gobind Singh's camp when he was seriously injured by some Pathan sent for the purpose by Wazir Khan of Sirhind. When Bahadur Shah moved to Deccan along with his army, the Sikh contingent stayed back in Guru's camp.

It was in Nanded Banda Bahadur came in contact with Guru Gobind Singh and was selected to lead the Sikh forces in Panjab. Banda left for Panjab shortly after the demise of Guru Gobind Singh. It is not understandable that a few thousand strong Sikh contingent under the pay of the Mughal emperor, of their free will, stay back at Nanded without there being any reaction in the Mughal camp.

Sum-up: *There is no other account showing a Sikh force of a sizeable strength (stated to be in thousands) with Prince Mauzzam who became the Mughal emperor after the death of Aurangzeb. That Sikh contingent could leave the Mughal camp with impunity and would not join the Mughal imperial forces in their march towards Deccan seems very strange and that the Mughal commanders had no control over this force, selected and in the payroll of the Mughal authorities is unbelievable. Further it is surprising that its commander just leaves for Punjab to fight against the Mughal forces without any reaction from the Mughal authorities.*

HARISH DHILLON

The Legend of Banda Bahadur, New Delhi: UBS Publishers Distributors Pvt. Ltd., 2004

The Guru on reaching Nanded heard about the Bairagi Madho Das, and went to meet him in his *dera* on the bank of river Godavari. When the Guru went to his *dera*, he sat on that magical couch and asked his Singhs to slaughter couple of goats and prepare it for their meal. The disciple of Madho Das who saw all this happening went to Madho Das and informed him thereof. Madho Das was greatly disturbed at cutting of the goats in a vaishnavite hermitage. From the details of the Guru said by his followers gave him an impression that it could be Guru Gobind Singh. When he did come into the Guru's presence he was struck by the Guru's radiance and he greeted the Guru by touching his feet.

The Guru and Madho Das discussed over the happening in Panjab where thousands and thousands people have been killed by the Mughal intolerant rulers. The Guru pointed out that two goats killed in a corner of your Ashram can be washed with the Ganga water, what waters you will sprinkle to wash away the blood that stains the vast land of ours. Gradually the inner peace the Madho Das had found on that first day strengthened itself and replaced completely the earlier restlessness. He knew that the Guru had given him a purpose in life and would now show him the path that he must take to achieve this purpose.

Over the following days Madho Das sought every opportunity to be with the Guru. He listened closely every word that the Guru spoke in his discourses and in private meetings. The Guru emphasized that the overthrow of the tyrannical rulers would only be the beginning. Once the same is achieved they must destroy the zamindari system which squeezes the poor farmers.

Before his departure the Guru said that considering the role that Madho Das would now be called upon to play in Panjab, it was good that he had been bound by the vows of chastity. The Guru advised him not to break these vows. For a soldier, a rebel, a wife and children would be hostages to fortune, forcing him to make compromises that he would not otherwise have made. *Hukamnamas* had been sent to all the Sikh leaders of Panjab – they were to marshal as strong a force as each of them could muster and wait for the Guru's return to join him in his war against the Mughals. Phulkian Sardars have promised large contingents. The baptism ceremony was a simple one. Sugar crystals were added to water in an iron cauldron and the water was stirred with a sword to the reciting of prayers till all the sugar had been dissolved. The Guru gave of this *amrit* to Madho Das to drink and also the name Gurbaksh Singh. Banda Bahadur was given a nigara and a flag by the Guru and five advisors and 20 soldiers. He was advised that he should proceed with caution, taking care to avoid any encounter or confrontation with the enemy or his representatives on the way, even if this means that you have to take a longer and more circuitous route to reach your destination.

Sum-up: *Harish Dhillon's account is a historical novel which is woven around the story of the Guru converting Madho Das from a bairagi to a soldier and sending him to Punjab to fight against the tyranny of the Mughal authorities.*

M.S. CHANDLA

Banda Bahadur, Chandigarh: Aurva Publications, 2006

M.S. Chandla contends that Guru Gobind Singh had got made a complete dossier on Madho Das Bairagi. Certain emissaries had done some field work between the Guru and the *bairagi*, but that had failed. However, this did not dishearten the Guru. Accordingly, the Guru accompanied by some of his followers went to Madho Das's *dera*. M.S. Chandla mentions the most popular conversation between Madho Das and Guru Gobind Singh given by Ahmad Shah Batalvi as under:

Madho Das	:	Who are you?
Guru Gobind Singh	:	He whom you know.
Madho Das	:	What do I know?
Guru Gobind Singh	:	Think it over.
Madho Das	:	(After some pause) so you are Guru Gobind Singh
Guru Gobind Singh	:	Yes, you are right.
Madho Das	:	What have you come here for?
Guru Gobind Singh	:	I have come to make you a Sikh.
Madho Das	:	I submit. I am your 'Banda'.

Chandla adds that Bandai Sikhs believe that Madho Das used this word 'Banda' in a very different context and he meant that he was totally devoted to God and as such was God's Banda.

Chandla further says that both these accounts are purely imaginary. The warrior saint Guru Gobind Singh reclaimed the misdirected energies of the ascetic and made them flow in the channels of Khalsa brotherhood, strenuously working for the emancipation of humanity suffering under the oppressions of the age.

Sum-up: *M.S. Chandla gave an account of the conversation between Madho Das and the Guru as given by Ahmad Shah Batalvi, and Banda Bahadur's selection also by the Guru. After giving these accounts he calls them purely imaginary.*

HARINDER SINGH DILGIR

Mahan Sikh General Banda Singh Bahadur (Punjabi), Amritsar: Singh Brothers, 2007

Guru Gobind Singh was on a dharma parchar mission in Doon valley in 1695 when Laxman Dass (Banda) had a short meeting with him. In this meeting, the Guru advised him to leave yog and take to the life of karma. It being a very short meeting the issue did not progress any further.

In mid July the Guru understood the duplicity of Bahadur Shah in not settling the issue against Wazir Khan and using delaying tactics. The Guru dropped any further negotiations, and when Bahadur Shah moved towards Deccan, the Guru decided to settle down at Nanded.

The Guru came to know about Laxman Dass staying nearby where he had set up a *dera* of his own on the bank of Godavari River. The Guru went to the *dera* and convinced him for the need to serve the country facing Mughal atrocities. Banda was duly convinced and immediately became the Guru's disciple. Banda Singh took *khanda pahul* on 4 September 1708. The Guru gave him the dress of the Khalsa and converted him from a *bairagi* to a Khalsa Singh.

Sum-up: *While at Nanded the Guru went to the* dera *of Bairagi Laxman Das and convinced about the need to serve the country facing Mughal atrocities. The Guru administered him* khanda pahul *on*

4 September 1708, and gave him the uniform of the Khalsa and converted him from a bairagi to a Khalsa Singh.

M.S. Ahluwalia

History and Religion of the Sikh People, vol. II, SGPC, 2009

Guru Gobind Singh had helped Mauzzam in the battle of Jaijou against his brother. The Guru had asked him, in return, to punish Wazir Khan for crimes against the Sikhs and his children. But Bahadur Shah asked him to accompany him to Deccan to finalize the same. By the time they had reached Nanded the Guru was convinced that Bahadur Shah was not sincere to the settlement and he dropped at Nanded while the emperor moved to Deccan.

The Guru set up his dera on the banks of river Godavari. It was in Nanded that the Guru heard of Madho Das and decided to meet him. Madho Das had a big monastery and a magic couch on which he used to seat his *sadhu* visitors and then topple the couch by his occult powers and enjoy the discomfiture of his guests. Madho Das tried to play his trick on the Guru but all his power failed to have any effect. Madho Das realizing his encounter with a great personality submitted to the Guru and sought acceptance as a disciple. The erstwhile proud *bairagi* was baptized as a Sikh and given the new name Banda Singh.

Banda was sent to Panjab as the commander of the Sikh forces. Five senior Sikhs were sent with him as an advisory council along with a small contingent of 20 Sikhs. The Guru gave him some of his weapons and *hukamnamas* to the Sikh sangat in Panjab to join Banda Bahadur in his campaign against the Mughal rulers.

He was also asked to maintain personal purity and chastity.

Sum-up: *The Guru went to the* dera *of Madho Das and sat on his couch. Madho Das attempted to topple the couch but his occult powers failed to dislodge the Guru. The proud bairagi submitted to the Guru and was baptized as a Sikh and given the name Banda Singh. Banda was sent to Punjab as commander of the Sikh forces. Five veteran Sikhs were sent with him as advisory council along with a small contingent. The Guru gave him some of his personal weapons and* hukamnamas *to the Sikh* sangat *in Punjab. He was asked to maintain personal purity and chastity.*

The dearth of historical literature in ancient period of Indian history has led to the common belief that there was no sense of history among the Indians in that age. The fact remains that there is hardly any writing of a truly historical character coming from the ancient period. The historical element that existed to some extent was submerged in the sea of myths and legends.[15] There is only one exception of *Rajatarangini* by Kalhana. Its author reveals that in composing his work he studied eleven existing historical books on Kashmir. He also corrected errors in them by going through the ordinances of former kings and laudatory inscriptions and written records. Further Kalhana held the view that a true historian should recount the events of the past after having discarding personal bias as well as prejudice.[16]

With the advent of Islam (Sultanate period), their historians had a some sense of history. But most of them being connected with various kings and courts, they indulged in panegyrics in praise of their Patrons. Their blind faith in the superiority of Islam led to rhetoric and exaggerations. Hence, accounts of these historians cannot be accepted at their face value.[17] The Mughals who destroyed the Sultanate to establish their own empire in 1526, broadly followed the line of their predecessors, though among the Mughal historians a gradual drift towards a growing interest in biographical works is discernible.[18]

In the eighteenth century, Muslims gradually gave way to the British who consolidated their power in the nineteenth century. The British historians also had a positive bias towards their actions and a prejudice against the Sikhs and other similarly placed Indian people.

J.D. Cunningham was an unbiased historian, but his forthright approach and authenticity of facts was condemned by the British government and he was sacked from his job for the same.[19]

After Independence, historical scholarship in our country and elsewhere has taken long strides. New tools of research have been evolved and new viewpoints adopted. As in other areas of historical research, research in the field of Sikh history too has made advances. Emphasis is fast shifting from the old narrative and descriptive type of historical writings to critical and interpretative expositions of historical phenomena. Similarly, social and economic aspects of history are now receiving more and more attention. All this has been possible because in recent years the problems of the Punjab, particularly of Sikh history, have attracted the notice of a large number of scholars, both Indian and foreign. All this has made notable contributions to the field of historiography.[20] It is the considered opinion of the author that all these stories with varied facts about a single event are not relevent, they being not based on authentic historical facts. Banda Bahadur's period is a very crucial part of Sikh history and all the fables, fiction, exaggerated accounts are required to be gleaned away to arrive at a correct historical account.

J.S. Grewal, an eminent Sikh historian, has laid down a standard for the collection of evidence and its interpretation:

> The modern student of history aims at interpreting the past modes of life and processes of change in rational and human terms. . . . He demands evidence in support of every statement made about the past and insists on the application of valid techniques and methods in interpreting evidence. He accepts nothing on faith.[21]

However, Grewal, has given himself the concession of implementation of the above directions when he writes 'Banda accepted the *pahul* and the *rehat* of the Khalsa without any authentic evidence in support thereof'. There is obviously no contemporary historical evidence about Banda Bahadur being administered the *pahul* by Guru Gobind Singh.[22] In fact, some of the historians have stated that he was not baptized by Guru Gobind Singh; they furnish a reason that his not being given the *pahul* was to avoid his becoming a successor Guru.[23] Sukhdial Singh, Punjabi University, Patiala states that all accounts of the Guru's meeting Banda at Nanded are unbelievable. Further, the statement that Banda Bahadur was earlier a *bairagi* is equally unbelievable.[24] Using the modern techniques of interpreting evidence, all these accounts fall in the category of fable and fiction and cannot be taken as authentic.

The unassailable situation that emerges from these accounts and historical facts has been: the Guru had gone to Nanded in late 1708 and had set up his *dera* on the bank of river Godavari. This fact stands established from the historical gurdwara set-up by him in Nanded and his demise at Nanded. Banda Bahadur's (Bairagi's) stay in a *dera* of his own on the bank of river Godavari, in those times stands established from historical accounts and ground realities. The Guru's meeting the *bairagi*, converting him to Sikh faith, and sending him to Punjab is also an unassailable fact of history and cannot be denied by any standards of historical interpretation.

The problem that stands before our historians is: What transpired between the two—How was the situation handled; whether the *bairagi* was baptized by Guru Gobind Singh or he was not baptized to prevent him from becoming a successor Guru to Guru Gobind Singh; whether he belonged to north India or south India; and various other somewhat similar questions have been raised by our historians. Guru Gobind Singh took three very momentious decisions in his lifetime. These decisions complement each other in the development of the Sikh community and its long drawn fight with the mighty Mughal Empire. These decisions have made a great contribution to the formation of the independent Sikh state and towards the downfall of the Mughal Empire in India. The first momentous decision has been the creation of the Khalsa in 1699. The Guru created a very well-knit army of saint soldiers with a distinctive bearing which played a major role in all the battles in the Khalsa state. (A detailed account is given in Chapter 4 on the concept of sikh sovereignty.)

The meeting between the Guru and *bairagi* was a very crucial factor in the future development of Sikh identity and Sikh faith at that stage of time. Sikhs had received a serious blow after the battle of Anandpur of 1704. The Guru was in a situation that his going back to Punjab would not have been appreciated by the Mughal government and in all probability he would not have been allowed to return to Punjab. Even if his move to Punjab was not interrupted, he would not have been allowed to raise an armed force large enough to create any serious problem for the Mughal administration.

The second crucial decision of the Guru, in his wisdom was the selection of Banda Bairagi, over the rights and claims of many of his old followers. In the absence of historical evidence for various reasons which led to such an unexpected choice, it is not possible to reconstruct the same to a logical conclusion. Further, there is no conclusive evidence of assertion of a claim to this position by any of the associates of the Guru during the lifetime of Banda Bahadur. The selection of outsiders on merit had been in existence during the Guru's period.

Khushwant Singh, in his account, has stated that 'the Guru caught the fanatic gleam in the hermit's eyes and felt that in the spare frame of the ascetic smouldered the Promethean fire which could be fanned into a flame'. This assessment seems to be somewhat close to the thinking of the great saint soldier. But then it is only a conjecture and not a historical fact. There have been instances where *karamyogis* took to *bairag*, generally in the later part of their lives, but it is a very rare phenomenon where a *bairagi* of long standing is persuaded to become a *karamyogi* and makes a laudable contribution to the struggle of the Sikh community against the Mughal tyranny and barbarianism in a very short period. The use of battle strategies almost in every battle by Banda Bahadur was a rare gift not possessed by any of the other Sikh warriors of distinction. The death defying courage of the Khalsa combined with the battle strategies of Banda Bahadur led to the victories of the Khalsa against the Mughal forces and the creation of the initial Sikh state to a great extent. Although Banda Bahadur failed in the battle of Gurdas Nangal but he was able to arouse in the Sikhs the desire to rule their own country and the ability to make every sacrifice for its achievement. As a result, the Sikhs who were in a state of depression rose to such heights of courage and valour that the great Mughal and Afghan armies had ultimately to succumb to their indomitable courage and determination.

The third vital decision taken by Guru Gobind Singh shortly after the despatch of Banda Bahadur to Punjab was to abolish personal Guruship. The period between the two was very short as Guru Gobind Singh was attacked by some hired Mughal assassins, and was badly injured. The wound did not heal and after some days, the Guru announced that his end was near.[25]

The Sikhs accepted *Guru Granth Sahib* as the Guru incarnate immediately after the passing of the tenth Guru. *Guru Granth* was considered the repository of *Shabad*, the source of enlightenment and guide in spiritual pursuit. Sikhs, from the moment of their great grief on losing the tenth Guru, held strongly to the belief that the *Guru Granth* was henceforth their living Guru and seem to have rejected any claim by any individual who even remotely tried to claim the spiritual mantle. This acceptance of the decision of the tenth Guru to accept the *Guru Granth Sahib* as their living Guru is supported by earlier developments in Sikh religious tradition. Guru Arjan Dev who compiled the Holy Granth, then called the *Pothi*, had brought it to Harimandir Sahib and it was placed on a higher pedestal than the seat on which the Guru himself sat, listened to the Bani being recited and sung by the *sangat* and explicated it in their discourses. The Sikhs therefore, had accepted the Granth over a long period as encapsulating the Guru's thought and thus acting as a bridge between them and God and to guide them in their spiritual quest. The Granth was opened at random and the verse revealed through such a random opening of the book was taken as divine response or advice by the Guru in person. This practice is continuing as an important tradition among the Sikhs till date. The house of the *Guru Granth* was treated as a place to congregate, be a part of the *sangat* and *pangat*, listen to the *kirtan* and explication of the Guru's thoughts, perform *seva*, bring their *daswandh* for the projects undertaken by the Guru and learning what the term *Guru Maanyo Granth* really means to a Sikh.

These three decisions of Guru Gobind Singh were the cardinal pillars of strength to the fledgling Sikh community for a great source of inspiration to take them forward to their goal of a Sikh state of their own. The Guru collected his Sikhs around him and gave them his parting instructions. He opened the Granth, placed a five *paisa* coin and a coconut, bowed before it, and declared that henceforth the holy book would be the Guru for all times to come and thereby he abolished the institution of personal guruship. He is also said to have composed the following verse:

> *Agya bhai Akal ki tabhi chalayo Panth,*
> *Sab Sikhan ko hukm hai Guru Manio Granth.*
> *Guru Granth je manyo pargat Guru ke deh.*
> *Jo Prabho to milbo chahe khoj shabad me le.*

> The Panth was founded under the order of the Immortal God. All Sikhs are enjoined to accept the Granth as their Guru, consider the Granth as representing the Guru's body. Those who desire to contact God can find Him in its hymns.[26]

Guru Gobind Singh had earlier said in the *Bichhittar Natak*.

> Installed on Nanak's throne as Guru tenth,
> When assumed the scripture of my sovereignty
> I promoted religion to the best of my power.

Guru Gobind Singh states that when he assumed the spiritual sovereignty of Guru Nanak, he served the *piri* aspect, the *dharma*, with all his devotion.[27] He also states in Bhai Nand Lal's rendering of the Guru's remarks:[28]

> The Granth is my second self.
> And it should be taken as me.
> A Sikh who wants to see me
> Should have a look at the Granth.
> One who wants to talk to me,
> Should read the Granth and think over it.

Guru Gobind Singh had, in his vision of the coming times, anticipated the mushroom growth of false gurus and this foresight of his would have also contributed to the abolition of the personal guruship.[29]

Guru Gobind Singh placed the temporal aspect of his sovereignty in the hands of the Khalsa. This goal had already been partially achieved with the creation of the Khalsa and when he selected the 'five beloved ones' and gave them the *khandah-ki-pahul*. Thereafter he personally sought the *khandah pahul* from the five chosen ones, thus merging his person with the Khalsa whereby the Guru and the Khalsa became one and the same. He states, 'Where there are five Khalsas to take a decision I am present in spirit with them'. He had submitted to the will of the Khalsa against his own personal opinion to give sanctity to the decisions of the Khalsa. When he was asked to leave Chamkaur, he left in submission to the will of the Khalsa against his own desire to lay down his life along with his Khalsa. Now when he was leaving his mortal frame, he placed his temporal sovereignty in the collective wisdom of the Khalsa, knowing fully well that as the need arose it would throw up its own leaders. That the Guru's hopes were not belied is shown by the part that even such obscure men like Kapur Singh and Jassa Singh Ahluwalia fought in the Sikh war of independence.[30]

These three decisions of Guru Gobind Singh in difficult circumstances were so momentous that they lifted the Sikh community from its depression to the ambition to rise and rule.

Guru Gobind Singh defines his temporal sovereignty in the *Krishan Avtar*:

> Great death be thou my protector;
> All steel I am thy slave.
> Deeming me thy own, preserve me.
> Single out and destroy my enemies.
> Let both my free kitchen and my sword.
> Prevail in the world.
> Preserve me and let none trample me.
> Be thou my cherisher.[31]

When Guru Gobind Singh gave his temporal sovereignty to his Khalsas, he issued a stern warning to them to preserve the Sikh identity in its uniqueness, as stated in the *Sarbloh Granth:*

> *Jab Lag Khalsa rahie niara, Tab lag jas dion men sara.*
> *Jab aye gai bipran ke reet, Man na karun in ke partit.*[32]

> The Khalsa shall continue to be blessed with all my power, so long as it preserves its identity and uniqueness. But when the Khalsa strays from the path of righteousness, the Guru will not stand by them.

Nihar Ranjan Ray rightly states that the integration of the temporal and the spiritual has been the most significant contribution of Guru Gobind Singh to the way of life which he laid down for his Sikhs.[33] Guru Hargobind and the Sikh community felt that for the development of the Sikh faith they would have to vindicate Nanak's message of resisting the evil of tyranny. Bhai Gurdas refers to the martial response of Guru Hargobind to the martyrdom of Guru Arjan as hedging the orchard of the Sikh faith with hardy and thorny *kikar* trees.[34] The two sovereignties of the Godhead—the spiritual and temporal—remained centred in the Guru's person up to the time of Guru Gobind Singh who, on the eve of his death, bestowed the temporal sovereignty on the Panth and the spiritual sovereignty on the Granth. The Panth became the Guru Panth and the Granth became the *Guru Granth*. The revealed word as such was formally installed as the eternal Guru, leaving no room for any physical/corporeal Guru in Sikh society.[35] The concept of the sovereignty of the Khalsa provides the motivating spirit for the relentless struggle against the state. It also gives the principle of unity, cohesion, and organization to the Sikh people in the form of voluntary submission to the supreme collective authority of the Guru Panth.

All that can be examined at this stage is the end result, i.e. the success in various aspects of social and political life of the Sikh society brought about by Banda Bahadur in a few years. For such like assessment, all historical facts of sufficient authenticity are available and an examination thereof gives abundant credit to Banda Bahadur *vis-à-vis* similarly placed situations of great heroes and commanders worldwide. The credit for the achievement of the Sikhs during 1709 to 1716, in spite of the final defeat, goes to Banda Bahadur. The choice of Banda Bahadur by Guru Gobind Singh in that precarious and difficult situation was a mature act, right and proper in all aspects, most probably with the divine blessings.

The Guru's selection of Banda Bahadur gave the Sikhs a taste of self-rule where absolute equality prevailed at all levels of Sikh society. Banda Bahadur in a short spell of five years took the Sikh struggle to such heights, that in spite of his failure at Gurdas Nangal the Sikh spirit generated by Banda Bahadur could not be suppressed by the mighty Mughal empire and has been a major contribution in the downfall of Mughal rule in Punjab and the establishment of independent Sikh state.

NOTES

1. Hari Ram Gupta, *History of Sikh Gurus*, New Delhi: Munshiram Manoharlal, 1984, p. 291.
2. Ibid., p. 293.
3. Ibid., p. 311.
4. Ibid., p. 312.
5. Ibid.
6. Ibid., p. 314.
7. Ibid., p. 315.
8. Ibid., p. 316.
9. Ibid.
10. Ibid., p. 317.
11. Ibid., p. 319.
12. Ibid., p. 312.
13. Ibid., p. 320.
14. A.C. Banerjee, *Khalsa Raj*, New Delhi: Abhinav Publishers, 1985., p. 31.
15. Fauja Singh, *Historians and Historiography of the Sikhs*, New Delhi: Oriental Publishers and Distributors, 1978, p. vi.
16. R.K. Majumdar and A.N. Srivastava, *Historiograph*, Delhi: SBD Enterprises, 1988, p. 294.
17. Ibid., p. 306.
18. Fauja Singh, *Historians and Historiography of the Sikhs*, p. vii.
19. Majumdar and Srivastava, op. cit., p. 354.
20. Fauja Singh, *Historians and Historiography of the Sikhs*, p. ix.
21. J.S. Grewal, *From Guru Nanak to Ranjit Singh*, Amritsar: Guru Nanak Dev University, 1982, p. 82.
22. J.S. Grewal and S.S. Bal, *Guru Gobind Singh*, Chandigarh: Panjab University, 1967, p. 154.
23. Banerjee, *Khalsa Raj*, p. 31.
24. Sukhdial Singh, *Banda Singh Bahadur*, Patiala: Punjabi University, 2003, p. 17.
25. Macauliffe, *The Sikh Religion*, New Delhi: S.Chand & Co., vol. V, p. 245.
26. Hari Ram Gupta, *History of Sikh Gurus*, p. 237.
27. Macauliffe, *The Sikh Religion*, vol. V, p. 303.
28. Hari Ram Gupta, *History of Sikh Gurus*, p. 237.
29. Louis E. Fenech, *The Darbar of the Sikh Gurus*, New Delhi: Oxford University Press, 2008, p. 202. Conversation between Guru Gobind Singh and Bhai Nand Lal.

'O Bhai Nand Lal ji, the standard of conduct which [is generally observed] during the Kaliyug cannot be explained completely I will [therefore] offer a summary. This [summary] will be dictated as follows: In this period fathers and sons and sons and fathers together will oppose each other. So too will wives and husbands and husbands and wives, and brother and brother. All of these relatives will plot against one another. Their desires will be profoundly chaned to greed for money. And for the sake of [fulfilling such] desires people will regularly perform sinful acts [in the Kaliyug]. And other sins too such as (*dimbhu*) will know no limits. Such pride will regularly culminate in people who will call themselves gurus. They will tell many falsehoods and so too engage in pointless discussions [which distract and lead one astray].

30. Indu Bhushan Banerjee, *The Evolution of Khalsa*, 1980, vol. II, p. 154.
31. Dharam Pal Ashta, 'Poetry of Guru Granth', Ph.D. thesis, Panjab University, Chandigarh, p. 26.
32. J.S. Ahluwalia, *The Sovereignty of the Sikh Doctrine*, p. 48.
33. Nihar Ranjan Ray, *Sikh Gurus and Sikh Society*, p. 59.
34. Sunita Puri, *Advent of Sikh Religion*, Munshiram Manoharlal, 1993, p. 219.
35. J.S. Ahluwalia, *The Sovereignty of the Sikh Doctrine*, p. 181.

CHAPTER 3

The Concept of Sikh Sovereignty

The Core of the Sikh Struggle

This inclusion of an elaborate chapter on the concept of Sikh sovereignty in the book on Banda Bahadur might appear to some readers as an unnecessary addition. But, the Mughal administration covering a large part of India as well as the administration in the non-Muslim kingdoms were based on feudal and *zamindari* system in which the peasants and tenants were literally squeezed of their earnings from the land and were treated almost like slaves. In the midst of this long established feudal system, the Sikh Gurus propounded a democratic polity and set-up an administrative system of government with an egalitarian social set-up and upliftment of the plebeian social society. The rulers were made responsible for the good of the general public, and the people's right to remove an autocratic ruler was upheld.

Banda Bahadur came on the scene when Guru Gobind Singh and his Sikhs were displaced from their principality at Anandpur by the Mughal authorities in 1705. He was sent to the Punjab by Guru Gobind Singh to reclaim the lost territories and also punish Wazir Khan, *faujdar* of Sirhind for his atrocities on the Sikhs and the Guru's minor sons. He was instructed to follow the rules and regulations laid down by the Gurus for social and political conduct. The inclusion and study of the Sikh sovereignty in the book on Banda Bahadur, becomes necessary as after the Gurus, he was the first Sikh commander to set-up the initial Sikh state and administer it in accordance with the concept of Sikh sovereignty in the few years of his rule, in which most of his time was spent in battles with the powerful Mughal armies.

Sikh Gurus were primarily religious preachers, yet they have made a great contribution in the field of social and political

Plate 3: Guru Gobind Singh with poets.

thought and in setting up a democratic egalitarian state in a world of feudal system. Banda Bahadur's contribution was great in the battlefield but in the social and political field it was greatest amongst the various commanders who have contributed in the establishment of an independent Sikh state in the north-western territories of the Mughal Empire. It has therefore been considered necessary to include a chapter on Sikh sovereignty so as to assess the contribution of Banda Bahadur in its implementation.

The study of Banda Bahadur's activities give definite indication that he was very conscientiously following the concept of Sikh sovereignty almost in all aspects of his government. Therefore for a proper appreciation of the theory and its practical application, the inclusion of a chapter on Sikh sovereignty has been considered very necessary.

The court (*darbar*) of the Sikh Gurus though structurally raised on the model of the Mughal court, was very different in principle. Whereas in the Mughal government, the emperor was supreme and his orders were the law, in the *darbar* of the Sikh Gurus, God Almighty was the supreme authority. It was run on the principles laid down by Guru Nanak and his successors and put into practice by the later Gurus. The nature of the Sikh state, the conduct of its rulers and the duties of its citizens were guided by the principles of the concept of Sikh sovereignty, and not by the absolute authority exercised by the ruler, as in the case of Mughal government. It has been termed as *Halemy* raj by the Gurus.

A recent writer Louis E. Fenech in his book *The Darbar of the Sikh Gurus* has given it a second title *The Court of God in the World of Men*. In the *darbar* of the Sikh Gurus decisions were taken not on the authority of the Guru alone, but in accordance with the concepts laid down by the Sikh Gurus for the conduct of the individual Sikhs. The principle of egalitarian character and the democratic spirit was incorporated in the Sikh society, though it was surrounded all around by absolute feudalism both in the Islamic as well as Hindu states all over the Indian subcontinent. The democracy established by the Sikh Gurus was at a time when even the European nations had not taken seriously to democratic traditions. In the *Nasihatnama* by Nand Lal, the Tenth Master begins, 'Listen Nand Lal and hear this; I shall establish my [i.e.

the Khalsa's] rule in which all human beings will be treated equally (the four varnas will become one).'[1]

The Sikh Gurus, as the head of the Sikh *darbar*, were dealing with the spiritual aspect of the Sikh social order by expounding the *bani* written in the *Guru Granth Sahib*; the temporal aspect was dealt with separately in accordance with the principles of equality and dignity of man in a world of feudalistic social order everywhere.

Shortly before his demise, Guru Gobind Singh converted a *bairagi* to Sikhism and sent him to the Punjab to reclaim the lost territories for which he seems to have been given some elementary instructions during the very short period of a few days only that he was with the Guru. The personal Guruship was also abolished and the holy book was given the status of *Guru Granth Sahib* for the spiritual guidance of the Sikhs. Banda Bahadur, in a short time, conquered sizeable territories and set-up the initial Sikh state, fixed a state seal and issued coins and maintained an egalitarian structure of the Sikh society. Certain historians have stated in their accounts that Banda Bahadur maintained a regal style and lived in palaces. It therefore becomes very important to assess as to what extent Banda Bahadur followed the principles of the concept of Sikh sovereignty in laying down the structure of the initial Sikh state in contrast to the existing feudalistic system of the authority vested in the ruler and the *zamindari* system in which the cultivators and the peasants were treated like slaves.

GURU NANAK (APRIL 1469–SEPTEMBER 1539)

The time when Guru Nanak lived has been considered as the 'dark period' of Indian history. The social, religious and economic conditions of the people had deteriorated beyond recognition. The emperors at Delhi and other political authorities far from doing anything for peoples' welfare indulged in political lawlessness and sought to prosper at the expense of their subjects. Guru Nanak in one of his bitter moments has given vent to his feelings in the following words:

> In this age of darkness,
> Men have become dogs;

They eat the ill-gotten gains,
And bark at their lies;
Giving no thought to righteousness,
They have no honour in life,
And leave a evil name after death.

As the word of the Lord descendeth upon me,
So I make it known friend Lallo;
With evil as his best man,
Bringing a crowd of sins as his bridal procession,
Like a bridegroom Babar hath hastened from Kabul,
To seize by force as his bride, O Lallo,
The wealth of Hindustan.
Modesty and righteousness have both vanished away,
Falsehood leading the van, holds the field, O Lallo;
Both the Qazi and the Brahmin are out of work,
The devil reads the marriage services.
Muslim women who read the Koran
In their agony will cry on God, O Lallo;
Hindu women of high caste or low caste.
Will meet with the same dire fate.
Men will sing hymns in praise of murder, O Nanak;
And instead of saffron smear themselves with blood.[2]

Guru Nanak had witnessed with his own eyes the atrocities committed by the Mohammedan rulers on the innocent people and he questioned God as to why he allowed such a state of affairs to prevail.

This age is a knife, kings are butchers,
Justice has taken wings and fled,
In this completely dark night of falsehood,
the moon of truth is never seen to rise.
I have become perplexed in my search;
In the darkness I find no way.
Devoted to pride, I weep in sorrow;
How shall deliverance be obtained.[3]

Guru Nanak was primarily a religious and a social thinker and hence adequate attention has not been paid to the study of his life and teachings with a view to understanding his ideas about politics and political institutions. But while he did not systematically deal with the affairs of the state, out of the volume of his personal experiences and reactions to the organized political authority which he came across throughout his travels in various parts of India and in foreign lands, we are in a position to assess the political conditions of those times and form a picture, even if somewhat hazy, of things political he advocated.[4]

The degeneration which had taken place in the whole body politic, had brought about a revulsion in him not only against the ruling authorities but even against the servility of the people. The Hindus had become prey to atrocities and developed a pessimistic resigned attitude. Some of them gave ungrudging obedience to their rulers, the others accepted their living condition as a divine dispensation. They were, therefore, quite readily exploited by the unscrupulous rulers and selfish priests. The same was also true of the Muslim society. It was Guru Nanak who attempted to awaken the individual from this lethargy, to help him in understanding his own moral strength, to rekindle in him the failing religious and divine fire and to guide him to lead a useful life for the realization of his personality and enjoyment of the divine bliss.[5]

The sultanate of Delhi had declined and broken up; provincial kingdoms had emerged and the *amirs* and *maliks* of the larger provinces became independent rulers.[6] These rulers had little interest in public welfare, they were careless in financial and administrative matters, and were addicted to the pleasures of the flesh and tried to govern mainly by force.[7] The government fell into anarchy, and civil war raged. The internal political instability quite naturally invited foreign invaders.[8] An assignee did not have to apply to a governor or other official to coerce his recalcitrant debtors, but coerced them himself with forces raised at his own cost. The most effective method was to kill the debtors and reduce their families to slavery—a most cruel system of local tyranny.[9] Guru Nanak describes the deep suffering of the common people in four of his verses called the *Babur Vani*:

> Compassion is not exercised by merely beholding a suitor.
> There is no one receiveth or giveth not bribes.
> The king dispenseth justice when his palm is greased.
> He does not move in the name of God.[10]

Greed and sin are ruler and village accountant.
Falsehood is master of the mint.
Lust his minister summoneth and examineth men.
And siteth in the judgement on them.
The subjects are blind and without divine knowledge
And satisfy the judges' greed with bribes.[11]

Guru Nanak's emphasis on the divine position of the individual was a revolutionary idea. It helped the people to view things in an altogether different light. It encouraged them not only to compose themselves but to get inspiration from the idea that all are equal before God and hence are entitled to participate on the basis of equality in the affairs of the community. The Guru had said:

We are all children of the self-same father. . . .
Allah created light first. All creatures are from him. From one light springs the whole universe, who is good and who is bad.[12]

'Great jealousy and hatred existed in those times between the Hindus and the Mohammedans, and the whole of the non-Muslim population was subjected to persecution by the Mohammedan rulers.'[13] Guru Nanak had also advocated that the status of woman should be raised and she should be given equal rights.

Of a woman we are conceived,
Of a woman we are born,
To a woman we are betrothed and married,
It is a woman who is friend and partner of life,
It is a woman who keeps the race going,
Another companion is sought when the life-partner dies,
Through woman are established social ties.
Why should we consider woman cursed and condemned
When from woman are born leaders and rulers.
From woman alone is born a woman,
Without woman there can be no human birth.
Without woman, O Nanak, only the True One exists.
Be it men or be it women,
Only those who sing His glory
Are blessed and radiant with His Beauty,
In His Presence and with His grace
They appear with a radiant face.[14]

Guru Nanak witnessed Babur's attack on Sayyadpur and the atrocities committed by his soldiers greatly distressed him. He states in his *Vani*:

> The kings are like whores, the courtiers like dogs,
> For they awaken those asleep in God's peace.
> The king's servants tear (the docile subjects) with their nails.
> And like curs lick all the blood they spill.[15]

Hindu society suffered from depression and stagnation as a result of rigid casteism and the ritualistic tyranny of the brahmins. The springs of true religion had been choked by the weeds of meaningless rites, rituals, and superstitions, the selfishness of the priests, and the indifference of the people. The true spiritual nature of Hinduism lay buried under ostentation and sectarianism.[16] Guru Nanak was greatly troubled by the barbaric social and political tyranny of the Islamic rulers and invaders, on the one hand, and the ritualistic dominance of the brahmins, on the other. Guru Nanak taught that the one who inflicts torture and the one who submits to tyranny are both equally guilty in the eyes of God, and he preached the vision of a self-reliant society devoid of fear whose members worship one God with absolute devotion. After centuries of subjugation, Nanak was the first amongst the Hindus to raise his voice against tyranny and oppression.[17]

The emphasis on the worth of the individual brought about an awareness of the potentialities of human personality and gave an impetus to the downtrodden and the afflicted to assert themselves. It also tore to shreds the distinction between the Hindus and the Muslims which had been exploited by the Mohammedan rulers for their personal advantage. Similarly, it also undermined the position of the brahmins who by preaching caste had saddled themselves on the Hindu masses and had exploited them for their personal ends. The Guru did not believe in distinctions of caste or creed:

> Caste and birth will not be of avail,
> Go and ask those who know the truth.
> That is the caste and that descent,
> Which is defined by deeds.
> What can the caste do? Ascertain truth

Plate 4: Guru Nanak with disciples.

> Value the light within, ask not of caste,
> For caste there is none hereafter.[18]

The doctrine of equality and brotherhood brought home to the people an awareness of their true position in society and thus released them from the shackles of centuries old taboos, customs and superstitions. It also paved the way for rational and concerted action against organized authority which came in due course of time. By imbibing the virtues of justice, purity and good action, it laid the foundations of a society of people who would not like to be cowed down by the tyrannical action of any organized authority.[19]

The seventy years of Guru Nanak's life may be divided into three well-defined periods:

Period of Inward Struggle and Enlightenment on the Banks of the Kali Bain in 1469

After gaining enlightenment on the banks of the Kali Bain, Guru Nanak resigned his assignment under Daulat Khan and proceeded on his travels saying, 'There is no Hindu and no Musalman', meaning that both Hindus and Musalmans had strayed away from true religion. When some *qazis* posed questions to him, Guru Nanak advised them:

> Make kindness thy mosque,
> sincerity thy prayer carpet,
> what is just and lawful thy Quran.
> modesty thy circumcision, civility thy fasting
> so that thou be a Musalman.[20]

Period of Travel, Propagation of Faith, and the Establishment of *Dharamsalas* at Numerous Places from 1496 to 1521

1. To south-west Punjab for one year, 1496-7
2. To the Gangetic plains up to Dacca, 1497-1510
3. South India, including Sri Lanka, from 1510-15
4. To the Himalayas, 1515-17
5. To West Asia, including Baghdad, 1517-21

Guru Nanak's extensive travels included visits to the holy places of the Hindus, Buddhists, Muslims, Sufis, and Sidhs, where he held discourses on his gospel of one God and won over many disciples. *Dharamshalas* were opened at the places he visited where the *sangat* sang hymns in praise of one God. Bhai Gurdas states that a *dharamshala* was opened in every house and *kirtan* was held as if it was an unending Baisakhi festival.[21] Some Western historians believe that Guru Nanak undertook these extensive travels to attain wisdom by practising penitent meditation, through study, and through an enlarged social intercourse with humankind.[22] This assumption has been refuted by later historians who argue that the journeys were not in search of truth, but rather were meant to propagate the truth he already knew. In his talks with brahmins, *jogis*, *pirs*, Jain *munis*, and other holy men, Guru Nanak was never a student; he was always the teacher who points out falsehood and indicates the path of truth.[23]

Settled Life in Kartarpur from 1521 to 1539

After his long tours of India and beyond, Guru Nanak settled down in Kartarpur in AD 1521. He lived the life of a householder, joined by his wife and two sons, and soon his disciples joined him. In this period he gave practical expression to his ideals, combining the life of disciplined devotion with normal daily activities.[24] Guru Nanak followed the same rules which he had laid down for his disciples, which encouraged equality and democracy amongst them. In the *dharamshala* hymns were sung both in the mornings and evenings. The disciples, who came from far and near, were called the *sangat*. The congregation sat in *pangat* and partook in the food from the free kitchen called the *langar*. These institutions broke down the barriers of caste and class and all individuals stood before the Guru in perfect equality. Guru Nanak said:

> Castes are folly, names are folly.
> All creatures have one shelter, that of God.
> Man, no matter what his caste or social position may be,
> is exalted by devotion.[25]

The lowest of the low castes,
The lowliest of the lowly,
I seek their kinship
Why emulate the so-called higher ones?
Thy elevating grace is where
the downtrodden are looked after.[26]

Guru Nanak denounced the practices of asceticism and renunciation. A Sikh must work and earn his living and share his savings with others. Exploitation of the labour of others is like eating the forbidden.

Oh Nanak, he alone realizes the way
Who eats the fruits of toil,
Sharing with others.[27]

To exploit the rightful due of others
Is like eating the forbidden.
Cow for one (Hindu) and swine for the other (Muslim).[28]

Guru Nanak placed great emphasis on the unquestioning obedience and absolute surrender of the disciple to the Guru. He taught this lesson through the nomination of Lehna who unquestioningly obeyed the orders of the Guru.[29] Guru Nanak said:

If thou desire to play the game of love with me,
Come my way with thy head on the palm of thy hand.
Put thy feet on this road.
Give thy head and regard not human opinion.[30]

Guru Amar Das has said: 'Entrust thy body, soul, and wealth to the Guru, and obey his orders, so shall you succeed'.

This idea, with the passage of time, became a living force in the Sikh community and was beautifully illustrated when the five beloved Sikhs (the *panj piaras*) came forward at the call of Guru Gobind Singh at Keshgarh, with their heads virtually in the palms of their hands.[31]

The last important aspect of Guru Nanak's work was the nomination of a successor. It has aptly been called the key event in the history of Sikhism.[32] Guru Nanak considered Lehna, one of his most devoted disciples, for this onerous responsibility. Lehna became Angad, literally a part of Guru Nanak's body and metaphorically an extension of his mission. It was the establishment of an effective line of succession of the Gurus which, above all other factors, ensured the transmission of the first Guru's leadership and the cohesion of the newly established religious community. The nomination and formal installation of Guru Angad was the first step in the process which resulted in the founding of the Khalsa and ultimately in the emergence of a Sikh nation.[33]

The uniqueness ascribed to Guru Nanak's position lies in the continuity of his work through his successors. The immediate successor of Guru Nanak was also called Nanak and so were all the other successors. The mingling of 'the light' of Guru Nanak with 'the light' of Guru Angad is in accordance with God's *raza*.[34] Guru Gobind Singh is quite emphatic about this unity; in his presentation, Guru Nanak becomes Guru Angad and Guru Angad becomes Guru Amardas and Guru Amardas becomes Guru Ramdas. Indeed, only 'the foolish failed to understand that the Gurus were all manifestations of one form and were not distinct from one another'.[35] G.C. Narang writes 'the sword that carved the Khalsa's way to glory was undoubtedly forged by Gobind, but the steel had been provided by Nanak'.[36] J.D. Cunningham notes that 'it was reserved for Nanak to perceive the true principles of reform, and to lay those broad foundations which enabled his successor Gobind to fire the minds of his countrymen with a new nationality and to give practical effect to the doctrine that the lowest is equal with the highest, in race as in creed, in political rights as in religious hopes'.[37] Ernest Trump argues that the disciples of Guru Nanak would no doubt have soon dispersed and gradually disappeared, as well as the disciples of many other Gurus, after Nanak, if he had not taken care to appoint a successor before his death.[38]

Bhai Gurdas conceives of the position of the Guru in terms of sovereignty. The true Guru is the true king. The Guru Panth is his coin.[39] Bhai Gurdas compares the Panth to an eight-metal coin.[40] The Guru as the true sovereign commands exclusive allegiance; those who do not submit to the Guru are rebels.[41] Bhai Gurdas does not make any distinction between Guru Nanak and his successors for they too are the Padshah of both *din* and *dunia*.[42]

A.C. Banerjee writes that Guru Nanak created a higher moral force which brought about all the virtues of the Sikh community and enabled it not only to survive but also to create a state in a period of ruthless strife.[43] J.C. Archer argues that there was something positive and realistic in the reforms of Guru Nanak, something that made a religion and a state.[44] Kapur Singh notes that the order of the Khalsa, far from being a contingent phenomenon dictated by the exigencies of the moment, appears to be the logical development and antelechy of the teachings of Guru Nanak.[45] Sher Singh writes 'who knows that given the means which Guru Gobind Singh had at his disposal, with the work of ten generations which had prepared the ground for him, Nanak would have met the situation in the same way in which the former did in his own time afterwards'.[46] Nihar Ranjan Ray observes that 'to achieve the integration of temporal and spiritual seems to me to have been the most significant contribution of Guru Nanak to the totality of the Indian way of life in medieval India'.[47]

POLITICAL AUTHORITY

On quite a few occasions Guru Nanak had given answer to the question as to where the political authority comes from. He argued that authority in every sphere flows from God:

> I am gifted by one God
> Whose gifts every one enjoyeth.
> Whoso looketh up to human support,
> Loseth both matter and his soul.
> There is but one Giver, all others beg.
> Those who forget Him and look to others, lose all honour.
> Kings and Sultans are all made by Him;
> Hear O Babar Mir, What Nanak saith:
> Foolish is the Faqir who begs of thee.[48]

On another occasion he had said:

> Though this is a city of corpses, Nanak exalteth the Lord in it, and uttereth this true saying:
>
> The Lord who made men, gave them their different stations
> He sitteth aloof from their doings and watcheth them all.

Just and true is the Lord; just and true is His judgement.
Just and true is the Judgement He meteth out
As a warning to us all.[49]

This does not mean, however, that God may act arbitrarily in bestowing such positions. In reply to the question of Mardana as to who created this man (Sheikh Wajid) who rideth in a sedan of ease while the bearers have no shoes to their feet, he said:

They who perform austerities in their former lives, are now kings and receive tribute on earth. They who were then wearied, are now shampooed by others. O Mardana, whoever is born hath come naked from his mother's womb, and joy or misery is the result of actions in previous states of existence.[50]

This political authority, however, can be maintained only if the king performs his functions justly and for the good of the people. If he indulges in worldly pleasures, he forfeits his claims to be the ruler. The Guru had blessed Babur and his descendants with the power to rule the country 'as long as they governed with justice' adding that 'when they departed from justice they shall lose the Empire'.[51] If the political authority digresses from its true functions, God, in his wrath, may even send an outside authority to deprive the ruler of his office.[52] In reply to Lalo who had complained of the oppression of the Pathans, the Guru had mentioned that Babur was on his way to India to teach the Pathans a lesson and to remove them from power.[53] In other words, resistance to an oppressive regime may even be considered as a religious duty.[54]

Guru Nanak believed that every aspect of one's life must be governed by divine wisdom. This is equally applicable to those who deal with the affairs of the state. The kings or men in authority must imbibe the divine and moral virtues and by putting them into practice they must contribute their share in the spiritual and material uplift of the community. Like Plato's philosopher kings, Guru Nanak wanted the rulers to be above the temptations of this world:

Men set in authority,
Let devotion to God be thy service,
Let thy toil be faith in the Name.
Check thy mind from wandering after temptation,

Stand alert on guard against all evil.
So from all men thou shall earn the praise.
And the Lord, the Kind, will delight in thee
With a fourfold increase of this Love.[55]

Only if a ruler is guided by the divine light, can he be of real service to the people. Such an authority should not be swayed by material pleasures but should create conditions in which love for God and spiritual values may flourish. He should also apply the laws impartially and selflessly. An ideal ruler must have the betterment of his subjects at heart. On his trip to the south, Guru Nanak commended the queen of Sri Lanka for her love of her subjects. In reply to her query, he said: 'You gather your revenue and return it for the benefit of your subjects. The Chief who does not appropriate everything to himself but gives to others in the name of God, is blessed.' [56] Similarly, he criticized those who indulged in corruption. The king should honour his office and do his duty conscientiously. Referring to the Pathan administration, he had said: 'The king ministers justice if his palm is greased', meaning thereby that the whole paraphernalia of government was corrupt and people at every rung of the governmental machinery indulged in such acts.[57]

An ideal king must, therefore, be an embodiment of virtue and above the temptations of this world. Only then he can perform his duties properly. The same is true of the soldiers who in order to protect their motherland must also morally equip themselves and play their due role towards that end. To Nanak, a true kshatriya is one whose valour shows itself in every detail of his being:

A true soldier protects his motherland to deserve a well earned salary;
He works for God and gets the real good;
He frees his mind of selfishness, greed and all other evils of material possession,
He lives in the divine fort and is never defeated.He is the servant of God only and faces all troubles bravely;
Verily a soldier who loses his salary never mounts the throne of *atma*.[58]

Guru Nanak laid a good deal of emphasis on honest living, for, in his view, a society cannot be stable and prosperous unless the people engage their energies in constructive pursuits and in right channels. That is why he ridiculed the brahmins who earned their livelihood by preaching all sorts of falsehood and who exploited the people for their personal gains. Such persons, he thought, were hypocrites and enemies of the society:

> A true Brahmin is one who grasps Brahm.
> Meditation on God and self-control are his daily routine
> His religious observances are right conduct
> And an unfretting heart.
> He removes the sensual chains that bind the soul.
> Such a Brahmin deserves all praise and honour.[59]

A truly religious man was he who acted on the religious plane in everyday life. To Gorakhnath, the Guru said:

> Religion consisteth not in patched coat, or in a Jogi's staff, or in ashes smeared over the body;
> Religion consisteth not in earrings worn, or a shaven head, or in the blowing of horns;
> Abide pure amid the impurities of the world; thus shalt thou find the way of religion.
> Religion consisteth not in mere words;
> He who looketh on all men as equals is religious.
> Religion consisteth not in wandering to tombs or places of cremation, or sitting in attitudes of contemplation;
> Religion consisteth not in wandering in foreign countries, or in bathing at places of pilgrimage;
> Abide pure amid the impurities of the world; thus shalt thou find the way of religion.[60]

It is clear that for Guru Nanak religious and ethical purity are complementary to each other and must be practised in the day-to-day affairs.[61]

In a similar vein, he criticized those who exploited other people's labour in order to make gains for themselves. A typical example of the same is furnished by his personal experience in refusing to dine at Malik Bhago's and instead, enjoying Lalo's ordinary and coarse bread, thus bringing home to the people that Lalo's bread had been earned by honest means and was pure while that of Malik Bhago's had been obtained by bribery and oppression and was therefore impure.[62] Honest productive work and sharing of the fruits of the same with others is an essential attribute of a religious person and is a sure passport for the realization of truth. This is implicit in the Guru's saying:

> The oxen are disciples, the ploughman is their Sheikh;
> The earth is a book, the furrow the writing.
> The sweat of the ploughman's brow falleth to his heels,
> And every one eateth of his earnings.
> They who eat the fruit of their earning and bestow a little from it,
> O Nanak, recognize the true way.[63]

In conformity with his ideas on productive labour, the Guru established at Kartarpur a model farm where he used to spend a considerable time in manual labour. The idea is symbolic in the sense that one must devote his time to honest living because it is through honest conduct that one can realize God and fulfil his personality.

Guru Nanak believed that the ultimate goal of human personality was to enjoy divine beatitude. But unlike many of his contemporaries who had advocated renunciation for the achievement of this goal, he stressed the need for the reconstruction and improvement of the worldly order. An individual should not be encumbered by ignorance, superstition and other vices. Rather he should imbibe divine and moral virtues and should put these into practice in everyday affairs. Only in a society of fellow human beings can one fulfil his personality. The unique position in which the Guru held the conduct of an individual is clear from his statement which says: 'Truth is higher than everything but higher still is the true living'.[64]

GURU ANGAD (1539-1552)

A short while before his demise in 1539, Guru Nanak nominated his most devoted and sincere disciple, Bhai Lehna as his successor.[65] To him Guru Nanak said, that between him and Nanak there was no difference. None of his Sikhs have such faith and confidence in him, as he and therefore he loved him most of all. 'You are verily *angad*, a part of my body. I congratulate you.' The appointment of Angad was a step of far-reaching significance. Nanak had rejected the claim of his eldest son Srichand because he could not match

Lehna in his devotion to the Guru. The younger son Lakshmidas was not interested in spiritual matters.

Guru Nanak held a large congregation on 2 September 1539, twenty-days before his demise. He praised Lehna for his single-minded devotion and service. He called Lehna to come near him, placed five *paise* and a coconut before him, put his head at Lehna's feet and appointed him his successor and declared that the new Guru shared his spirit and soul as well.[66]

Guru Angad born in March 1504 and served as Guru from 1539 to 1552. He shifted from Kartarpur to Khadur in Amritsar district situated 5 km away from the Beas River in order to avoid the impending conflict with Guru Nanak's sons. During the first six months, he remained virtually hidden in the house of a devotee near Khadur. Then at the persuasion of Bhai Buddha he assumed the responsibilities of the Guru's office.[67]

First of all he gave his attention to the collection of Guru Nanak's hymns which were either written in Lande Mahajani or committed to memory by some of Nanak's disciples, particularly the Guru's old companion Bala Sandhu as well as some devotional composition of his own.[68] Lande Mahajani is rather rough and crude and cannot be easily and properly deciphered as vowel sounds are omitted in it.

Guru Angad beautified the Lande alphabet by giving them better shape, like the alphabet of Devanagari script used for Sanskrit. He also modified the order of the Lande alphabet. The new script came to be called Gurmukhi (coming from the mouth of the Guru). It was in this script that Guru Angad wrote the hymns of Guru Nanak. He personally gave lessons to the village children in Gurmukhi. He penned down his own compositions in Gurmukhi.

Following the example of Guru Nanak the *langar* was continued. It was looked after by his wife Mata Khivi and its expenses were met out of the offerings of the Sikhs. Guru Angad earned his living by twisting course grass (*munj*) into strings used for netting cots.[69]

Guru Nanak's son Srichand had renounced the world, and he and his disciples practised celibacy and asceticism. He professed to belong to Sikhism but Guru Angad emphatically declared that there was no place for passive recluses in Guru Nanak's teachings. In this manner he tried to preserve the purity and originality of the Sikh religion.

The Sikh tradition says that while fleeing to Iran, Humayun waited upon Guru Angad at Khadur seeking his blessings for his sovereignty. As the Guru was immersed in deep thought, Humayun who was standing drew out his sword, to which Guru Angad remarked that his sword should have been better used against his rival Sher Shah Suri rather than against the men of God who could not be forced to grant a boon.[70] It was a period of uncertainty and restlessness leaving ugly scars on people's life, as is explained in the following well-known verse:

> Every beggar today would be a king.
> Every blockhead sets up as a pundit.
> The blind man would be a connoisseur of gems,
> That is the modern way of talking of things
> The really bad men set up as spiritual leaders
> The liar is judged the perfect type of man
> So it is in this iron age.[71]

GURU AMAR DAS (1552-1574)

Shortly before his demise, Guru Angad nominated his 73 year old devout disciple, Amar Das, born on 5 May 1479, as his successor, who held this office from 1552 to 1574. Guru Amar Das moved to Goindwal situated not far away from Khadur. He did so to avoid the impending conflict with Guru Angad's sons who had not approved of their father's decision. Even there, he was harassed by one of the sons named Datu who went to Goindwal and said: 'Only yesterday thou wert a water-carrier in our house, and today thou sittest as a Guru'. Saying this he kicked the Guru off his seat. The Guru humbly said, 'Oh Great King, pardon me, thou must have hurt thy foot'. The Guru retired from Goindwal and stayed in a house at Basarka, his home village. Datu set himself up as the Guru. Guru Amar Das was persuaded by Bhai Buddha to return, and Datu, finding no following, went back to Khadur.[72]

Where Guru Nanak laid the elementary basis of the Sikh society, Guru Amar Das carried out a number of institutional developments to make Sikh society more self-reliant and to engender greater cohesion amongst its rapidly growing membership. His major contributions were:

The *langar* was made more elaborate and all Sikhs and non-Sikhs were fed. In fact, it was made obligatory for all those desirous of meeting the Guru to partake of *langar* food before they could meet him. According to Sikh tradition, even Emperor Akbar had to partake of the food of the *langar* before meeting the Guru.[73] When Akbar offered some rent-free lands for the maintenance of the *langar*, the Guru politely declined, stating that he received sufficient resources from his creator.[74] Contributions to the Guru's *langar* could only be made by the Guru's disciples. The compulsory partaking of food at the *langar* was also a great social leveller, since it encouraged the abolition of the class/caste system amongst the Hindus, and the slogan often used was *pehle pangat pichhe sangat*.

Guru Amar Das laid great emphasis on the physical fitness of his disciples. He declared that human beings were created in the image of God. The human body was the temple of God. It was the duty of his Sikhs to keep the body fit uptil the last. It was a valuable gift of God, and must not be spoilt by bad habits. He sanctified human life by condemning torturing of the body.[75]

The Guru abolished the prevailing practice of *sati* (widow burning on the funeral pyre of her dead husband) amongst his disciples.[76] He also persuaded the womenfolk not to use *purdah* to cover their faces. The Guru composed the 'Anand', a song of joy to be recited at the time of weddings and other occasions of happiness.[77] Guru Amar Das collected the hymns of Guru Nanak, Guru Angad, and his own songs and left this collection in the custody of his son Mohan.

The Sikhs were rapidly increasing in number and were spread all over the Punjab and the surrounding areas. Guru Amar Das established separate centres of *sangats* called *manjis* and selected his representatives to address these gatherings. They also collected offerings for the Guru and conveyed these twice a year on Baisakhi and Diwali at his headquarters.[78] According to Sikh tradition, 22 *manjis* were on the model of 22 provinces of the Mughal state. The institution of the *manji* was later developed into the institution of the *masand* by Guru Arjan Dev and remained in operation till the end of the seventeenth century, when it was abolished by Guru Gobind Singh as having become redundant and riddled with corruption.

Guru Amar Das, eager to meet his Sikh disciples, invited them with their families and friends twice a year on Baisakhi day during March-April and again during Diwali during October-November. He constructed a large *baoli* at Goindwal where the disciples could recite the *Japji* at each of the eighty-four steps leading to the water's edge.[79] This institution became so well entrenched with the passage of time that the largest congregations at Amritsar now assemble on these two festivals. He also debarred the Sikhs from performing the usual Hindu ceremonies at cremations, which created much resentment amongst the brahmins who relied on their ritualistic roles at these rites to earn their livelihood.[80]

The Udasis were eager to join Sikhism. They were ascetics and non-householders. The Guru emphatically declared that there was no room for the Udasis in the Sikh religion.[81]

The abolition of useless and meaningless Hindu customs and ceremonies related to weddings and cremations led to the severance of links with the general body of the Hindus. This gave the Sikhs a distinct identity and marked their separate corporate character; as Cunningham writes, 'they were preserved . . . from disappearing as one of the many sects of Hinduism'.

The Guru's growing influence and his rejection of wasteful Brahminical customs and traditions annoyed the brahmins and the Khatris who complained to Emperor Akbar against the Guru, giving out distorted information. Akbar invited the Guru for a discussion but the Guru refused to go personally to the emperor for this purpose. He, however, sent Bhai Jetha, his son-in-law and the future Guru, who explained to the emperor that the Sikhs had no hostility against the Hindus. The emperor was convinced and rejected the plea of the Hindus. The regulations made by Guru Amar Das during his long tenure accentuated the differences between the Hindus and the Sikhs which became more pronounced, and the Sikhs began to gradually drift away from the orthodox Hindu society and formed a new brotherhood of their own.[82]

Guru Amar Das states:

Even in a gale and torrential rain,
I would go to meet my Guru.
Even if an ocean separates them,
A Sikh would go to meet his Guru.
As a man dies of thirst without water,
A Sikh would die without his Guru.
As parched earth exults after a shower,
A Sikh rejoices on meeting his Guru.[83]

These words of the third master emphasize the great influence of the Sikh Gurus among their followers and underline their strong inner urge to be in constant communion with the founders of their faith.

According to the Sikh traditions, Emperor Akbar visited Guru Amar Das at Goindwal. In accordance with the practice recently established the emperor was requested to dine in *Guru ka langar* in *pangat* before meeting the Guru. The emperor willingly agreed and ate food prepared in the *langar*. The Sikhs, both men and women, working in the community mess so deeply impressed Akbar with their humility, spirit of service, feelings of reverence for the Guru as well as for the emperor, and devotion to God that he offered a few villages revenue-free for the support of the *langar*. The Guru did not accept it. It is said, writes Cunningham, 'that he found an attentive listener in the tolerant Akbar'.[84]

Guru Amar Das being highly pleased with the single-minded devotion of his daughter Bibi Bhani and son-in-law Bhai Ram Das, shortly before his demise conferred the Guruship on Bhai Ram Das. The claims of his own sons were turned down. Guru Amar Das died on 1 September 1574 at the ripe old age of 95.

GURU RAM DAS (1574-1581)

Guru Ram Das was born in Lahore on 24 September 1534. In order to avoid family feud on account of Guru Amar Das's sons,

Guru Ram Das did not stay at Goindwal. Following the practice of his predecessor, he decided to select a new place for his headquarters. According to the gazetteer of Amritsar district in 1577, he obtained a grant of the site together with 500 bighas of land from Emperor Akbar on the payment of Rs. 700 Akbari to the zamindar of *tung* who owned the land.[85] Akbar granted the Jhabal area, 15 km south-west of Amritsar to Bibi Bhani.

There Guru Ram Das dug a pool to which he gave the name of Amritsar, the pool of nectar. This was constructed under the supervision of Bhai Buddha. A number of habitations grew around the tank. The whole place was popularly called Guru ka Chak or Chak Ram Das or Ramdaspura. Some petty traders and shopkeepers settled near the tank. The commercial place came to be known as Guru ka Bazar.[86]

During his short tenure, Srichand, Guru Nanak's eldest son, visited him. Guru Ram Das received him with great regard. Guru Ram Das, however, did not allow the Udasis to join the Sikhs or the Sikhs to join the Udasis. The Udasis, however, consider themselves to be part of the Sikh community. Shortly before his demise in 1581, Guru Ram Das selected his youngest son Arjan as his successor, i.e. as the fifth Nanak. The principle of hereditary succession was taking root, yet the selection was on the old principle of devotion and service to the faith.

GURU ARJAN (1581-1606)

During the quarter century of his Gurudom, Guru Arjan carried out the consolidation of the fledgling Sikh *panth* which was now rapidly coming of age. In this task, Guru Arjan faced many difficulties, including the lifelong hostility of his disinherited and embittered elder brother Prithia. Prithia tried to administer poison to the infant Hargobind, founded his own sect called the Minas, started writing his own scripture, aided and abetted Sulahi Khan against the Guru, joined hands with Chandu Shah, the *diwan*, against the Guru, and indulged in similar intrigues and conspiracies against his younger brother. The Sikh community was thus faced with profound sectarianism and deep divisions within the family of the Guru himself. The other threats to the Sikh community were posed by the growing hostility of the orthodox Hindus and the fanatic Naqshbandi Sufi, Shaikh Sayyed Ahmad Sirhindi. Despite these internal schisms and external threats to the survival of the Sikh community, the extraordinary genius of Guru Arjan was able to consolidate the Sikh Panth to a considerable extent.

Guru Nanak's novel method of selection of his successor, in his lifetime and himself becoming a disciple of the newly annointed Guru did help in the smooth continuity of the guruship. But as human nature is, the rejected children of the Gurus created problems, even to the extent of manhandling the newly established Gurus. In the ruling Mughal dynasty, every new emperor had been eliminating every likely rival to ensure his emperorship. Faced with similar situation, no action was taken up against the dissenting claimants of the guruship. This shows the scale of tolerance observed by the Sikh Gurus against their rivals over the issue of succession as compared with the Mughal emperors.

Guru Arjan's first task was the completion of the city of Ramdaspur, the tank of nectar (Amritsar), and the Harimandir located in the centre of the tank. According to tradition, the foundation stone of the holy temple was laid by the Qadiri sufi saint Mian Mir of Lahore, but there is no contemporary record to support this claim.[87] Guru Arjan also built his quarters in the precincts of the temple. The tank, the temple, and the Guru fostered psychological integration amongst the Sikhs as a continuous process.[88]

According to Dabistan, 'before the fifth period no tribute was exacted from Sikhs, but presents were given by them according to their own discretion to their Guru'. The voluntary contributions from the Sikhs proved to be insufficient for the various construction works then in progress and the running of the *langar*. Guru Arjan named his agents *masands*, presumably a corruption of the word *mansad-i-ali*, and these *masands* were sent to each town to collect tribute. Each Sikh was asked to donate one-tenth of his income (*daswandh*) to the Guru every year and the *masands* were called upon to bring this tribute to the Guru in the month of Baisakh.[89] Although the *masands* were initially supposed to collect funds, they also became missionaries and guides on religious matters. Thus developed a system of tax collection which in later times resembled a system of parallel government. The Guru came to be looked upon by his Sikhs as exercising temporal authority in addition to providing spiritual guidance.[90] Guru Arjan also commenced the construction of a large tank at Tarn Taran and a temple by its side.

The most notable achievement of Guru Arjan was the compilation of the holy book known as the *Adi Granth*. Sikh worship consisted of the singing of hymns composed by their Gurus. The dissident groups made their own selections and also distorted the hymns of the Gurus to suit their ill intentions. Guru Arjan now felt the necessity of laying down rules of conduct for the guidance for his followers in the performance of their daily religious duties and expiatory rites.[91] This would bring about consistency in the practice of the Sikh religion and restrict the entry of divergent beliefs and rituals. Prithia's distortion of Guru Nanak's hymns was causing anxiety. Guru Amar Das had ordained that only the real hymns of the Guru should be repeated and revered by the Sikhs, and he made the collection of hymns from the time of Nanak to his own time, which he then left with his son Mohan. Guru Arjan's action was the final step in this direction of consolidation and authentication of proper Sikh religious practices. Guru Arjan needed the earlier collection from Mohan who was reluctant to part with it to his envoys Bhai Gurdas and Bhai Buddha. Guru Arjan thereafter personally went to Mohan and sat singing the hymns outside his house. The Guru's melodious voice softened the heart of Mohan and he gave the *pothis* to him.[92] When the collection of hymns was completed, Guru Arjan dictated them to Bhai Gurdas in a tent set-up on a selected spot near Amritsar. The great task was finished in August 1604 and the sacred volume was installed in the Harimandir in Amritsar.[93] The *lokbhasha* (language of the people) thus permanently replaced the *devabhasha* (the language of God's) and religion was brought to the heart of the masses. There was no need at all for a priest to guide or misguide and exploit the illiterate or ill-educated people. Religion ceased to be a mystery hiding behind a linguistic curtain, and now became a matter of daily experience by the individual worshipper.[94]

Guru Arjan began living in a grand style for the inspiration of his disciples. He considered the spiritual life and worldly living as two aspects of a single reality. He erected lofty buildings in Amritsar, wore rich clothes, kept fine horses and elephants, and had retainers in attendance. His personal life was otherwise very simple. The Sikhs venerated their Guru and called him *Sacha Padshah*.[95] Guru Arjan encouraged his disciples to take to trade and commerce and with the settling of traders, Amritsar soon grew into a prosperous city. The number of Sikhs also greatly increased, and according to Mohsin Fani, in almost all towns in the country a few Sikhs were found.[96]

Abul Fazl writes in the *Akbarnama* that the emperor crossed over the Beas at Goindwal and called on Guru Arjan on 24 November 1598. Sujan Rai Bhandari states that the emperor was highly pleased to meet the Guru who greeted him with the recitation of hymns composed by Baba Nanak in praise of God. Guru Arjan told Akbar that during the stay of his troops the price of grain had gone up and now that the troops were leaving, the peasants would not be in a position to pay the enhanced revenue. The emperor ordered that the land revenue be reduced by one-sixth.[97] Indu Bhushan Banerjee states that the exemption of land revenue was one-twelfth, and G.C. Narang states that the remission was for the whole year's revenue.

With the installation of the *Granth Sahib* in 1604, the enemies of the Sikhs complained to the emperor that it contained some passages offensive to Islam. The emperor called for the *Granth* and the holy book was carried to him by Bhai Gurdas and Baba Buddha. Akbar got the alleged offensive passages read out and found nothing objectionable, and instead he appreciated the hymns in praise of God.[98] But with the death of Akbar in 1605, the half century of peaceful co-existence of the Sikhs with the Mughal government came to an end.

During the reign of Akbar, the Sikh Gurus Amar Das, Ram Das, and Arjan had very cordial relations with the emperor who was greatly appreciative of their activities. The important measures of the Gurus were the consolidation of the community; complete separation of the Sikhs from the Udasis and the orthodox Hindu community; the development of Amritsar into a sacred place and the centre of the Panth's authority; the large-scale expansion of the Sikh community; and the compilation of the *Granth*. During this period, voluntary contributions from the disciples were made compulsory at the amount of one-tenth of their income (*daswandh*) and the collections were made through authorized agents called *masands*. This was more or less a revolutionary arrangement with far-reaching consequences.[99] The Guru could now arrange the budget with much more certainty as the dues of the Guru were paid more readily and unfailingly than even the collection of Mughal revenues. The large *sangat*, increased resources, palatial buildings, tents, horses, and the splendour and magnificence of the *darbar* all gave it the appearance of a princely court.[100] A state, peaceful and unobtrusive, had been slowly evolved, and the Guru as its head was called the *Sacha Padshah* of the Panth. The Sikhs had already become accustomed to a form of self-government within the empire.[101]

Jahangir, who became emperor in October 1605, was already biased against the Sikh Gurus due to his orthodox Islamic leanings. In his autobiography, Jahangir writes:

> In Goindwal . . . , there was a Hindu named Arjan, in the garment of sainthood and sanctity, so much so that he had captured many of the simple-hearted Hindus, and even of the ignorant and foolish followers of Islam, by his ways and manners, and they had loudly sounded the drum of his holiness. They called him Guru, and from all sides stupid people crowded to worship and manifest complete faith in him. For three or four generations they had kept this shop warm. Many times it occurred to me to put a stop to this vain affair or to bring him into the assembly of Islam.[102]

Jahangir was also alleged to have been angered by the cordial treatment accorded to the rebel prince Khusrau by Guru Arjan. He, therefore, ordered him to be produced and his property and family handed over to Murtaza Khan and the Guru be put to death.[103] The Guru's enemies, Prithia, Chandu Das, and Naqshbandi Sayyad of Sirhind also became active and the fanatic and orthodox Farid Bukhari was made governor of the Punjab.

The Guru was arrested and taken to Lahore. He was also fined Rs. 2 lakh and ordered to remove those hymns in the *Granth* which opposed Hinduism and Islam. Father D. Jarric states that some Sikhs intended to intercede on his behalf but the Guru declined and prevented his disciples from raising the required amount for the fine. Fines, he said, were for thieves, adulterers, and slanderers, the men devoted to religion never paid fines.[104] Guru Arjan was imprisoned in the Lahore Fort. He was tied to a post in the open, exposed to the hot sun of June, burning sand and hot water were thrown on his naked body for five days, and he was next to be sewn up in raw hide. Guru Arjan sought permission to bathe in the nearby river Ravi. He plunged into the Ravi and never appeared again.[105]

The second part of Jahangir's order concerning Guru Arjan's properties and family was not implemented, presumably on the intervention of Mian Mir, a Muslim saint of Lahore. Jadunath Sarkar in his short account of Sikhs has made some very uncharitable and incorrect remarks. His comments on Guru Arjan —that he was a common revenue defaulter and this collision of the Sikhs with the Mughals in Jahangir's time was entirely due to secular causes—have been debated threadbare by later historians and rejected. Indu Bhushan Banerjee has reacted very strongly to Sarkar's claim that there was nothing exceptional in the punishment meted out to the Guru as it was the usual punishment accorded to revenue defaulters in those days. Banerjee argues that to call Guru Arjan a revenue defaulter because of his incapability or refusal to pay fine and then to justify the tortures inflicted on him on the ground of current usage, ignoring all other circumstances connected with his death, show a perversity of judgement which can hardly be excused in a historian of Sarkar's eminence.[106]

GURU HARGOBIND (1606-1644)

Guru Hargobind became the sixth Nanak, as decided by Guru Arjan, at the age of 11 years. Some historians argue that Guru Hargobind brought about the transformation of the Sikh community from a non-violent religious organization to a military organization.[107] This is not correct, as it was Guru Arjan who had quite clearly foreseen the difficult times ahead. During the half-century-long reign of Akbar the orthodox Islamic fanatics had been kept under control, but their re-emergence after the death of Akbar and under the rule of the orthodox Jahangir was foreseen by Guru Arjan. He changed the style of his *darbar* from a princely court to a more modest one. He arranged for horses and armed retainers.[108] He instructed Baba Buddha to train his young son Hargobind in the use of all defensive and offensive weapons, riding as well as languages, arts, and sciences.[109] Shortly before his death, he sent word through his Sikhs that his son Hargobind should sit fully armed on his throne and maintain an army to the best of his ability.[110] What Guru Hargobind carried out was what had already been started by Guru Arjan and what he did was in accordance with the instructions of his teacher Bhai Buddha as directed by Guru Arjan. Hence the work of Guru Hargobind was merely the continuation of the work of Guru Arjan. Guru Arjan introduced and imparted military training not only to his son Hargobind and other boys of his age, but he also employed skilled and accomplished warriors to build the nucleus of Guru Hargobind's army. According to Bhai Mani Singh, the concept of *miri* and *piri* was also introduced by Guru Arjan.

Guru Arjan had conceived of Sikhism essentially as a state—*Halemi Raj*—(egalitarian dispensation) right from the very beginning, the most significant aspect of Sikh sovereignty, founded by Guru Nanak. The new socio-political order described by Guru Arjan as *Halemi Raj* places great value on equality amongst human beings, liberty to all and ready justice without any discrimination on the grounds of caste, creed, race, sex and social position.[111] Bhagat Ravi Dass has stated his concept of an ideal city in his verses included in *Guru Granth Sahib*.

> I have sought thine protection,
> O Lord, quickly meet thy servant and make no delay.
> Begampura is the name of the town.
> At that place there is no pain or worry
> There is no fear of tax on goods there
> Neither awe, nor error, nor dread, nor decline is there.
> I have now found an excellent abode

My brethren, there is everlasting safety there.
Firm, stable and for ever is the sovereignty of God.
There is no second or third, He alone is there.
Populated and ever famous is that city.
The wealthy and the content dwell there.
As they please so do they stroll about.
They are the knowers of the Master's Mansion,
So none does obstruct them.
Says Ravi Dass, the emancipated shoemaker,
he, who is my fellow citizen, is a friend of mine.[112]

Nihar Ranjan Ray has very correctly concluded that Guru Nanak laid the main foundations on which the edifice of Sikh society was to be built. The later Gurus walked on these foundations and a few of them—Guru Arjan, Guru Hargobind and Guru Gobind Singh—strengthened them by buttressing and expanding them.[113]

Guru Hargobind at his succession ceremony wore two swords on either side—one symbolizing *miri*, the temporal power, and the other *piri*, the spiritual power.[114] He stated that in the Guru's house, the spiritual power and the mundane power shall be combined and his rosary would be the sword belt and that on his turban he would wear the emblem of royalty.[115] He inherited 52 bodyguards, 700 horses, 300 horsemen, and 60 gunners.[116] In front of the Harimandir, he built a 12-feet-high platform in 1606 called the *Akal Takht*, God's throne, on which he sat in princely attire. The Harimandir was the seat of spiritual authority from where he provided spiritual solace to his disciples. The Akal Takht was the seat of temporal authority from where he administered justice like a king in court, accepted gifts, awarded honours, and meted out punishments. Court bards used to sing songs in praise of the great Indian heroes.[117] Thus the Sikhs came to occupy a kind of separate state within the Mughal state, the position of which was established by the independent fiscal policy of Guru Amar Das and Guru Arjan and his system of armed self-protection.[118] Sikh consciousness was based on an unprecedented quest for a sovereign Sikh identity which would establish and strengthen the uniqueness of Sikhism.[119]

The Guru created a government of his own like that of the

Mughals. All his disciples formed a separate and independent entity, and had nothing to do with the agencies of the government of the day. Thus the Sikhs came to occupy a kind of a separate state within the Mughal state, the position of which was securely established by the fiscal policy of Guru Amar Das and Guru Arjan and his own armed system.[120]

No clear account of Guru Hargobind's relations with Jahangir during his reign (1606-27) is available. It is historically true that Guru Hargobind was imprisoned by the Mughals in Gwalior Fort. The reasons for the arrest of the Guru are not clear, nor is the date of his arrest; the period varies in different accounts from 40 days to twelve and a half years.[121] The role of Mian Mir, a revered Muslim saint of Lahore is not clear, who was also a friend of the Guru's family, in bringing about a rapprochement between the two leaders. The most reasonable period of confinement seems to have been only a few years. Guru Hargobind is said to have gone to Kashmir with Jahangir. His visit to Kashmir and Baramula is historically true. For how long and what assignment did the Guru hold under Jahangir is once again not clear. He would not likely have taken a minor post as he was quite wealthy, with his own resources and it is likely that he merely accompanied Jahangir, as Guru Gobind Singh later had accompanied Bahadur Shah in his travels in 1707. The Guru had also visited Sikh places in what is present-day north-western Uttar Pradesh. Guru Hargobind's good relations with Jahangir are seen from his handing over Chandu Shah to the Guru for punishment and also the imprisonment of Shaikh Ahmad Sirhindi in 1619.[122] During this period the Guru was able to soften the Mughal emperor with diplomatic moves and friendly relations. However, the details of this relationship between the Guru and the emperor are not recorded.

Actual hostility between Mughal troops and the Guru broke out in the early years of Shah Jahan's reign, based on rather flimsy grounds. Guru Hargobind decided to defy the Mughal authorities and fought six engagements against the Mughal officials from 1633 to 1638. He kept on shifting his headquarter from Amritsar to Hargobindpur, then to Kartarpur, then to Phagwara, and finally to Kiratpur[123] in the relative safety of the Shivalik range in order to get away from the plains where a major attack by the Mughal forces was quite likely.[124]

The battles of Guru Hargobind have been as under.

Battle of Jallo 1633

Guru Hargobind and Shah Jahan were hunting in the same forest, when a quarrel occurred amongst their followers, in which Mughal followers were beaten back by the Sikhs.[125]

Battle of Sangrana 1633

A large force was sent against the Guru. A battle occurred in Sangrana in which the Mughal force was beaten back.[126]

Battle of Amritsar 1634

A much larger force was sent to chastise the Guru. After a sharp scuffle the Guru shifted to Jhabal, where he performed the nuptial ceremony of his daughter, rather in haste and waited for the Mughal army. The pursuing Mughal saw the enormous quantities of sweets and were feasting on the same when the Guru gave a surprise attack and defeated the Mughal army, killing many, including their commander. Macauliffe writes, 'In this battle seven hundred Sikhs defeated an army of seven thousand Mughal troops.'[127] Muhammad Latif writes: 'Mukhlis Khan marched from Lahore at the head of seven thousand troops, who were, however, signally defeated near Amritsar, their leader being killed in the engagement. The defeated army returned to Lahore after losing many killed and wounded. This was the first combat in the annals of Panjab which was fought between Mohammedans and the Sikhs.'[128] The Guru's fame spread far and wide. Jadunath Sarkar writes: 'Many men came to enlist under the Guru's banner. They said that no one else had power to contend with the Emperor.'[129]

Battle of Lahara 1637

A disciple of the Guru had gone to Kabul and Balkh to secure some fine horses for the Guru. He collected three fine Arab horses and on his return journey Mohsin Fani was also accompanying him. At Lahore two horses were seized by the governor Khalil Khan. Bidhi Chand, a decoit turned disciple of the Guru, was sent to secure back the horses and he manoeuvred to secure back those horses.[130] Khalil Khan sent a large force after the Guru who had moved to Lahara. The Mughal force was repulsed with losses. Mohsin Fani who witnessed all this has squarely blamed Khalil Khan.[131]

Battle of Gurusar 1637

Guru Hargobind was aware of the great power of the Mughal emperor and had temporarily moved into the Lakhi jungle. Kumar Beg and Lal Beg were sent with a large force. The Sikhs laid an ambush and made a sudden attack and defeated the Mughal force but at a heavy cost of 1,200 Sikh soldiers.[132] Kumar Beg and Lal Beg were sent from Lahore at the head of an army which crossed the Sutlej; but want of provisions and the difficulties of the march had a disastrous effect on the imperial troops. The scene of the battle is now called Gurusar situated at 5 km from the Rampura Phul railway station.[133]

Battle of Kartarpur 1638

A Mughal force was sent under the command of Mir Badehra and Paindah Khan against the Guru who had only 5000 men with him. A tough battle was fought in which both the enemy commanders were killed.[134] In this battle Guru's son Tyagmal showed exemplary courage and he was named Teg Bahadur.

Mohsin Fani says that by God's grace, the Guru had escaped unhurt, though whatever he had was lost fighting against the larger forces. It was impossible for the Guru with his slender resources to maintain a constant struggle against powerful Mughal government.[135] He, therefore, moved to the relative safety of the Shivalik hills and set-up an establishment named Kiratpur.

After these battles the Guru realized that his resources were not adequate for the open defiance of the Mughal forces and hence he decided to retreat into the relative security of the Shivalik hills at Kiratpur (an establishment set-up by Gurditta at the instance of the Muslim saint, Pir Buddhan Shah), and there were no further confrontations with the Mughals during the last decade of the Guru's life.[136] Guru Hargobind gave the Sikhs a new confidence in themselves and organizational solidarity. He demonstrated the possibility of the Sikhs openly assuming an attitude of defiance against the Mughal government, which did occur after a little over half a century when Guru Gobind Singh confronted the Mughals; this attitude ultimately led to the emergence of the Khalsa and the establishment of the Sikh sovereign state in the eighteenth century.[137] During the tenure of Guru Hargobind, Bhai Buddha expired in 1628 at the age of 120 years and Bhai Gurdas expired in 1637 at the age of 88 years. Guru Hargobind expired in 1644 after nominating Har Rai as the seventh Nanak. Mohsin Fani says: 'The Sikhs believe that all the disciples of the Guru go to the heaven.'[138]

GURU HAR RAI (1644–1661)

Guru Har Rai succeeded his grandfather at the age of 14 and in accordance with the advice of Guru Hargobind, he maintained a force of 2,000 armed Sikhs and his court had the pomp of a semi-independent chieftain. When Mughal forces invaded the territory of Raja Tarachand of Kahlur, the Guru moved further into the interior of the Shivalik hills and stayed for about twelve years in Nahan.[139] Guru Har Rai took a keen interest in organizational and missionary work. Since many *masands* had become corrupt and indifferent to their missionary work, he entrusted the task of preaching in the east to Bhagat Gir who is said to have established about 360 *gaddis*. Another disciple was sent to the central Punjab. Thus two *bakshishes* were established and many more were set-up during the tenures of the ninth and the tenth Gurus.[140] These agencies reduced the importance of the *masands* and paved the way for their eventual abolition by Guru Gobind Singh.

Aurangzeb summoned Guru Har Rai to his court, but instead the Guru sent his 14-year old son Ram Rai.[141] The Guru is reported to have stated, 'I am not a king who payeth thee tribute, nor do I desire to receive anything from thee, nor do we stand in relationship of priest and disciple to each other, so why has thou summoned me?' In explaining a hymn of Guru Nanak, Ram Rai deliberately misinterpreted a passage to avoid causing annoyance to the emperor. When this transgression of the Sikh religion came to the notice of the Guru, he disowned Ram Rai, considering his offence unpardonable. Guru Har Rai observed that the Guruship is like tiger's milk which can only be contained in a golden cup. Only he who is ready to devote his life thereto is worthy of it. 'Let Ram Rai not look at my face again.'[142] Har Rai passed away at Kiratpur in October 1661 at the young age of 32 years. He had nominated his younger son Harkrishan, a five-year-old boy, while suppressing the claim of Ram Rai to the *gaddi*.

GURU HARKRISHAN (1661-1664)

Guru Harkrishan, born in 1656, assumed the *gaddi* as the eighth Nanak and was called a 'child saint'. Since Ram Rai had appealed to the Mughal court against the suppression of his claim to the *gaddi*, Guru Harkrishan was summoned to the imperial court and Mirza Raja Jai Singh was sent to escort him. Guru Harkrishan refused to meet the emperor on the plea that his father and predecessor had forbidden him to meet Aurangzeb. However, within a short time Guru Harkrishan suffered from a severe attack of smallpox and expired on 30 March 1664. While in delirium, Harkrishan pointed to Baba Bakala as his successor.[143]

GURU TEGH BAHADUR (1664-1675)

Tegh Bahadur became Guru at the age of 43. He was bitterly opposed by dissidents. Dhir Mal attacked him and gunshots scraped his shoulder. He went to Amritsar with his few followers but the temple gates were closed on him by Harji, the grandson of Prithia.[144] He went to Kiratpur and his jealous relatives did not let him stay there. At Delhi Ram Rai got Guru Tegh Bahadur arrested on the charge of being a pretender to power and as a disturber of peace.[145] Mirza Raja Jai Singh of Jaipur, who cherished great reverence for the house of Gurus, sent his son Raja Ram Singh who pleaded for the Guru's innocence and thus the Guru was released.[146] The difficulties confronted by Guru Tegh Bahadur at the very beginning of his guruship indicate that the organizational cohesion based on the Guru's undisputed leadership which had been the glory of Sikhism was now in the decline and the movement was weakening.[147] Instead of settling down at one place, the Guru toured the Majha and Malwa areas for a year and then returned to Kiratpur. He laid the foundation of a new settlement which grew into the town of Anandpur.[148]

The Guru found that the Sodhi relations settled in Kiratpur would not leave him in peace and he moved towards the east via Prayag and Banaras and reached Patna where he decided to stay. It was at Patna that Mirza Raja Ram Singh met the Guru and persuaded him to accompany him to Assam.[149] On receiving the news of the birth of his son, the Guru returned to Patna. Guru Tegh Bahadur stayed for some time in Patna and on hearing of Aurangzeb's fanaticism towards Hindus and Sikhs he decided to return to the Punjab. He initially moved alone, not sure of the reception that awaited him at the hands of his enemies, but he soon called for his family and finally settled down in Makhowal.[150]

During Aurangzeb's rule, orders were passed to demolish all schools and temples of the infidels and to put down their religious practices and teachings; the magnificent temples of Somnath, Mathura, and Banaras were demolished and *jaziya* was re-imposed.[151] The Sikhs, who were also regarded as infidels, could not expect better treatment than the Hindus. Aurangzeb ordered the temples of the Sikhs to be demolished and the Guru's agents (*masands*) who collected the tithes and gifts from the faithful to be expelled from the cities.[152] Such was the situation when Guru Tegh Bahadur returned to Anandpur. Kashmiri Pandits who were being converted or being put to the sword by the specially appointed governor, Afghan Khan, approached Guru Tegh Bahadur who took up their cause. The Guru took to touring the Malwa area between the rivers Sutlej and Ghaggar. The simple but hardy farmers were cowed down by the Muslim officials during the emperor's stay in the Punjab. The Guru worked for the physical and spiritual needs of the people of Malwa. Where fields were barren and dry, he got wells dug. Where there was scarcity of milk, he procured cows and gave them free of cost to the people. For the landless peasants he procured some land and urged them to live courageously as free people. In barren areas he got trees planted.[153]

Distorted and exaggerated reports of the activities of the Guru were sent to the Mughal court and the Guru was summoned.[154] While the Guru was on his way to the Mughal court, he was arrested along with his five companions at Agra and was put in an iron cage on the way to Delhi. The governor and *qazi* tried to persuade the Guru to embrace Islam but he resolutely rejected their overtures. The companions of the Guru were tortured to death in his presence and the next day he was beheaded outside the *kotwali* in Chandni Chowk on 11 November 1675.[155] In the confusion, a low caste Sikh named Jaita carried away the Guru's head to Anandpur, 340 km away, and presented it to his son Gobind, a nine-year child, who bestowed all affection and love on this hero and remarked, *Rangrete Guru ke bete*, meaning that all the low caste Sikhs were Guru's own children. A Labana Sikh, Lakhi Shah, stole the decapitated body of the Guru in a cart laden with cotton/straw and carried it into his house in his village named Rakab Ganj (near the present Parliament House) and set fire to his house. The ashes of the body were collected and placed in a vessel and buried underground on that very spot.[156] Nearly a hundred years later, a Gurdwara was built at that place by Baghel Singh.

GURU GOBIND SINGH (1675-1708)

Gobind, born in Patna in 1666, remained in that city under the care of his mother and his uncle Kirpal in the absence of his father Guru Tegh Bahadur. He was brought to Makhowal, a settlement set-up by Guru Tegh Bahadur, and at the age of 9 years in 1675 he succeeded as the tenth Nanak after the execution of his father.[157] Shortly after the assumption of guruship by Gobind, the Sikhs were divided into two camps, i.e. Kirpal and the devotees of the Guru *versus* the powerful *masands* who were keen that the Guru should move out of Makhowal and go to Amritsar. The Guru, aided by Kirpal and others, resisted the move of the *masands* and decided to stay on in Makhowal. The next nine years were comparatively peaceful and this period of calm helped Gobind to tide over the initial shock of his father's cruel execution and he grew to manhood a determined person.[158] Kirpal methodically and tactfully went about his work to keep the *panth* intact. He prevailed upon the Sikhs and the Guru's family to accept the martyrdom of Guru Tegh Bahadur with philosophical resignation and to avoid giving any offence, at least for the time being, to the hill rajas or to the Mughal administration. At the same time, he encouraged more and more Sikhs to come to Makhowal and give their undivided devotion to the young Guru. Bulleh Shah, a celebrated Sufi Muslim saint of Punjab was a contemporary of Guru Gobind Singh. He has stated, 'I neither say of the past, nor do I speak of the future, but I talk of the time of Guru Gobind Singh and declare openly, that but for him all the Hindus would have been converted to a foreign culture and religion.'[159]

Kirpal arranged to carry out the wishes of Guru Tegh Bahadur regarding Gobind's marriage to Jito, daughter of a businessman of Lahore. The marriage was solemnized at a small settlement raised nearby which was named 'Guru ka Lahore' to avoid any confrontation with the Mughal rulers at Lahore or the powerful *masands* on the way.[160] A small army soon grew around the Guru and a more strategic place was selected in 1678 and the settlement established there was named Anandpur. This change was also reflected in the Guru's *darbar*. The Guru would meet his daily congregation in an expensive tent, with a trained elephant and horses as part of his retinue. Guru Gobind sat on a raised platform wearing princely attire and an aigrette on his turban. The Sikhs called him *Sacha Padshah* and princes from distant places visited him; the whole setting was that of a royal court.[161]

The life of Guru Gobind Singh is a story of unparalleled sacrifice, which began at the age of nine, and traversing a flaming course which involved the martyrdom of his father and all his four sons, ending at the age of 42. In a short but crowded span of life, he had changed the character and destiny of a whole people. The meek, lowly and cowardly serfs were transformed into invincible warriors and invested with dignity and dream. Assuredly, here the human form was only a corporeal proof of the divine spirit operating in the temporal world. Such indeed was the mark of Guru Gobind Singh addressed as *Mard-i-Kamal*, the perfect man by Bhai Nand Lal.[162] Guru Gobind Singh forcefully exhorted his followers to translate the cardinal principles of religion into their day-to-day lives. The Guru taught that religion was a way of life. It was neither a set of dogmas, beliefs or rituals, nor an academic probe or enquiry into the unknown. Religion according to him was the noble life lived amongst one's fellow beings. A life enlivened by religion, with purity, love, service and sacrifice as its goals, was real life; the rest was all unreal.[163] Guru Gobind Singh created such a religious revolution in the social set-up of those days that the dry bones of an oppressed peasantry were stirred into life. It gave his followers a distinct national character in opposition to the ways of other people. It aroused a new sense of purpose and gave a new direction to faith.[164]

Similarly, when he assumed charge of the spiritual leadership of the Sikhs at the age of nine, he pondered deep over the then existing situation. He came to the conclusion that the Hindu religion, as it then existed, could not meet the great challenge of the time. People were so much over-awed by the tyranny of the ruling class that they had lost faith in themselves. The priestly class and the religious guides to whom they could look up for help were completely demoralized. Guru Gobind Singh felt pained when he saw that even the high priests of religion were behaving timidly and spinelessly. Timidity and belief in God, he held, were irreconcilable, a negation of an alive religion. Guru Gobind Singh could not remain passive under the circumstances. He told his men that it was irreligious to submit to oppression and tyranny.

Cowardice and helplessness, according to him, were the worst types of sins, and ran counter to all religious beliefs. It has been emphasized in one of his favourite couplets:

> Sweep away the filth of timidity and
> Cowardice from the deep recesses of your
> Mind with the broom of Divine Wisdom.[165]

Long before him, other Sikh Gurus and men of God had told their devotees that they could attain the highest love provided they were prepared for the highest type of sacrifice. It was Guru Nanak who had said:

Plate 5: Guru Gobind Singh at the battlefield.

Desirest thou the game of love to play?
Put they head on thy palm,
With a heart resolute and calm,
Steadily follow me on this way.

If choosest thou this path to tread,
Be prepared, O dear,
Without wavering or fear,
In perfect joy to lay down thy head.[166]

A huge kettledrum called the *ranjit nagara* was installed at the gate of Guru Gobind's residence. It was beaten regularly every morning and evening as a symbol of Sikh sovereignty. Bhim Chand, the Raja of Bilaspur, objected to the use of the kettledrum, the same being the prerogative of the ruler only, but the Guru paid no heed to the raja's protests. Guru Gobind had made great strides in literary studies, excelled in the martial arts, and had grown to full maturity and responsibility. The *masands* had been isolated and made ineffective. An especially trained elephant was sent by the Raja of Assam and Sikhs from Kabul brought the Guru a costly tent for holding his *darbar*.[167]

A quarrel with Bhim Chand was inevitable. He was a year younger to the Guru but far less mature. Bhim Chand's pride was wounded and he could not tolerate a sovereign state coming up within his state.

In a span of 23 years (1682 to 1705), Guru Gobind Singh fought nine battles before the creation of the Khalsa in 1699 and 11 battles after the creation of the Khalsa. A short account thereof is as under.

First Battle of Anandpur 1682

Bhim Chand Raja of Kahlur was greatly unhappy with the large Sikh gatherings and war-like activities in the vicinity of his capital. Bhim Chand demanded the white elephant and the Persian tent given to the Guru by his devotees. Guru refused it doubting his intentions to return the same. Bhim Chand led an expedition against Anandpur, but was badly defeated with huge losses.[168]

Second Battle of Anandpur 1684

Bhim Chand formed alliance with the Raja of Kangra and of Guler. They attacked Anandpur in the beginning of the year but were again badly beaten.[169]

Cordial relations had existed with the Raja of Sirmaur since the time of Guru Har Rai. Raja Medni Parkash invited Guru Gobind Singh to come to his state. The Guru was not willing to leave Anandpur but under pressure from his mother and uncle Kirpal, he agreed and his camp consisting of 500 soldiers, and a large number of animals left Anandpur in April 1685 and settled down at Paonta, a place on the banks of the Yamuna about 50 km equidistant from Nahan and Dehra Dun. The Guru built a fort at Paonta. The Guru's literary and martial activities flourished during his stay of about three years at Paonta. Sikh disciples brought money, arms, and horses in plenty and war games and martial exercises were carried out. On the literary front the Guru had 52 poets in his *darbar* who sang their martial compositions.[170] The Guru composed *Var Sri Bhagwati*, *Chandi di Var*, *Krishan Avtar* and other hymns. He had employed Muslim mercenaries who deserted him in the battle of Bhangani, an experience similar to the one which his grandfather had had with Painda Khan.[171] During this period, his poets or disciples gave him a new title *Padshah Darwesh* (the saintly ruler) and this title is in use at several places.

Battle of Bhangani, October 1688

Bhim Chand's son was to get married with the daughter of Raja Fateh Shah of Garhwal. They along with Kirpal Chand of Kangra, Sidh Sain of Mandi and some more hill rajas planned to attack the Guru's camp.[172] Medni Parkash of Sirmaur was persuaded to remain neutral.[173] Firstly they seduced away all the 500 Pathans in the Guru's employment. The Guru sent word thereof to Pir Buddhu Shah who immediately sent seven hundred of his men under the command of his four sons to assist the Guru.[174]

The enemy force crossed Yamuna a few miles ahead of Paonta. As the Guru was aware of the entire area, he planned to meet the hill army in the valley of Bhangani and himself occupied a small hillock facing the field of battle which gave him a strategic advantage. Some of his army was kept behind the hillock to be brought into operation at an appropriate time.

At this juncture, the Guru's position became very weak. A large number of armed *masands* had deserted him before the battle. The Pathans, who were also familiar with the Guru's resources, changed sides and joined Fateh Shah.[175] Fateh Shah, aware of the Guru's position, expected only a nominal resistance. But this first major battle fought by Guru Gobind Singh was a marvel of war tactics and he gained success over the overwhelmingly larger enemy. The Guru chose to meet Fateh Shah on the banks of the rivulet Gir at Bhangani, about 10 miles north of Paonta. Having marked the correct position, he asked Medni Parkash and Buddhu Shah of Sadhaura to march to Bhangani and himself occupied a hillock to check the Garhwali army. The bulk of the Guru's troops were hidden behind the hillock, from where the battlefield manoeuvres could be manipulated.[176]

The Pathans who had deserted the Guru now joined the Garhwalis, and were placed in front. The Guru put a major part of his army in the attack against the Pathans, which they could not withstand; in their retreat they put the entire Garhwal army in disorder. By evening, the Guru himself plunged into the battle and killed Hari Chand, the best general of the enemy. Fateh Shah and his men fled and the Guru won the battle; Buddhu Shah and his men had joined him in the afternoon.[177] Medni Parkash and his troops never moved to the battlefield.[178] Although the victorious Sikhs wanted to pursue the Garhwalis, the Guru in his wisdom, took the victorious army to Sadhaura and from there sent the soldiers to Makhowal.

The Guru soon realized that there was a long-standing feud between Garhwal and Sirmaur for the previous few generations. Medni Parkash chose Paonta for the Guru's camp, which, in fact, was located midway on the route which lay conveniently between the two states. The Guru did not like his headquarters being sandwiched between two rival states.[179] Fateh Shah decided to occupy all territories which were disputed between Medni Parkash and himself, and to achieve this goal he had to dislodge the Guru from Paonta. He moved to Ramgarh and met the Rani of Raipur, through whose intervention he entered into an agreement with Bhim Chand and was back in Anandpur in 1688.[180]

The neutrality of Sirmaur was not liked by Guruji and he decided to leave Paonta and go back to Anandpur. He raised his camp in November 1688 and sent most of his army to Anandpur and with some troops moved leisurely stopping at Kapalmochan and Sadhaura where he expressed condolences to Pir Buddhu Shah's family. He also stayed at Naraingarh, Raipur Rani. He returned to Anandpur via Ropar and Kiratpur.[181]

The stay in Paonta gave Guru Gobind an insight into the psyché of the Hindu hill rajas whose mutual jealousies and rivalries dated back to many generations. They could not overcome their mutual animosity and make a joint front against the foreign rulers. They preferred to accept foreign suzerainty. The Guru also witnessed the duplicity and disloyalty of his armed *masands*. He came to the conclusion that he had no place to stay other than Anandpur and that all his energies should be devoted to bolstering his bastion to repulse a combined attack by the Hindu hill rajas and the Mughal forces. The Guru utilized the changed situation and sought the good offices of Bhim Chand to build-up his headquarters which he did with remarkable speed and boldness. He weeded out those who had been unfaithful and had not joined the Bhangani battle.[182] He renewed his contacts with his disciples in Malwa and Doaba. He reorganized his *darbar* and rapidly strengthened his army. He built a chain of forts around Anandpur and garrisoned them with trained musket men and mounted two guns, viz., *Bhangani* (Tigress) and *Vijay Ghosh* (an announcer of victory) on the fort walls.[183]

Battle of Nadaun, 1690

Kangra hills was under the charge of the Mughal governor at Jammu who sent Alif Khan with a force to subdue some recalcitrant hill rajas. Alif Khan set-up his camp at Nadaun on the banks of river Beas. A coalition of hill rajas was made to fight Alif Khan. The Guru's help was also solicited. Alif Khan was defeated by the hill rajas with the active support of the Guru's army.

Without consulting the Guru, Bhim Chand and Kirpal Singh of Kangra made peace with Alif Khan and agreed to pay tributes to the Mughals. This was not liked by the Guru.

Rustam Khan's Expedition against Anandpur, 1691

The governor of Lahore was apprised of the increasing strength of the Sikhs who sent a strong force under Rustam Khan to chastise the Guru. Rustam Khan planned a surprise attack on the Sikhs. He camped in the dry bed of a seasonal rivulet opposite Anandpur. Sikhs who used to have an early bath saw the Mughal troops. They immediately reported to the Guru and a Sikh force was hastily collected and made a forceful attack on the enemy. The Mughal force could not hold against the attack and ran away leaving behind their weapons, etc.[184]

The Husaini Battle of Guler, 1693

Dilawar Khan, governor of Jammu, sent another stronger expedition under Hussain Khan in early 1693. In internal expeditions, the general rule was that war must be made to pay with war. Hussain Khan subdued nearby all the hill rajas and charged levies from them to subdue the Sikhs. Hussain Khan was supported by Kirpal Katoch, Bhim Chand, Himmat Singh, Hari Singh and on the opposite side was Raja Gopal helped by the Guru and Raja Ram Singh. In the fight, Hussain Khan, Kirpal Katoch and Himmat Singh were killed. The Guru recalls the Husaini Battle in *Bachittar Natak* as 'victory was won and the battlefield was left deserted. Talking about the fighting, all went home. God Almighty saved us. He made the cloud of lethal blows burst upon the enemy' (*Bachittar Natak*, Section XI, Chaupais 1-69).[185]

Battles of Anandpur, 1694 and 1696

A newsletter stated: News from Sirhind. Gobind declared himself to be Guru Nanak. *Faujdars* were ordered to prevent him from assembling Sikhs at Anandpur. A special order was issued to the governor of Sirhind to admonish Gobind, son of Tegh Bahadur. Expeditions were planned in 1694 and 1696 but these failed to achieve any success. No definite details of these battles are available.

Jujhar Singh's Operation, 1697

Jujhar Singh, a Rajput prince was sent to chastise the Guru. He was assisted by Rustam Khan, a representative of the governor of Lahore. Gaj Singh of Jaswal was sent by Guruji with his men, who laid an ambush at Bhalan village and drove away the invading force with heavy casualties. The enemy failed to reach Anandpur.[186]

Guru Gobind Singh now asked his disciples not only to come in greater numbers to Anandpur, but also to make Anandpur their home. The Guru was engaged in giving the large influx of Sikhs suitable training and making them observe a proper code of conduct. The increased strength of the Sikh forces under the Guru, unnerved the Kangra *faujdar* as well as some rajas who now sought Aurangzeb's advice on how best to meet the rising Sikh power. In November 1693, Aurangzeb directed the *faujdar* to prevent the Guru from assembling his Sikhs.[187] A large expedition was sent under Hussain Khan. The Guru sent a well-armed contingent to the aid of the hill rajas and in the ensuing battle Hussain Khan and some hill rajas were killed. This encouraged the hill rajas not to pay the tribute. In 1694, 1696, and 1697 small forces were sent against the Guru, all of which failed in their objective. Aurangzeb was a very suspicious person, especially of his sons and other relatives who he considered were capable of raising a rebellion against him; he used to keep them at widely dispersed locations and away from the throne. Aurangzeb sent Prince Mauzzam to the north under some scheme of his and it was rumoured that he had been sent to subdue the hill rajas and the Guru. Actually Mauzzam reached Lahore in August 1696 on his way to Kabul and sent some forces to collect tributes from the hill rajas. The entire force of Mughal wrath fell on the rajas and the Guru's headquarters were left unharmed.[188] Mauzzam's arrival had been a cause of great anxiety to the Guru, and his departure now gave him much relief.

CREATION OF THE KHALSA, 1699

The Mughal forces had suppressed the Jats of Tilpat, the Satnamis of Narnaul, the Rajputs of Jodhpur and Udaipur, and the Marathas in the south. The loss in the Deccan wars which raged intensely for nearly 20 years, was 1,00,000 soldiers and followers and three times that number of horses, elephants, camels, or oxens on the Mughal side even year. Guru Gobind Singh after a most determined meditation on the sad state of affairs came to the conclusion that to tyrannise was bad, but to bear tyranny patiently was even worse. The country did not belong to the king. The king belonged to the country and the country belonged to the people. If the king was bad, the people must rise in revolt. Without political liberty, religious, intellectual, social and economic freedom could not be achieved. Political freedom could be won by armies. Armies of the suppressed people were non-existent. For these reasons all the rising against tyranny stated above was suppressed by the Mughal government. Guru Gobind Singh realized that he would have to depend entirely on his own resources. The hill Rajputs whom he wanted to use in the national cause had failed. With the above situation in mind Guru Gobind Singh created the Khalsa. He instituted *khanda pahul* in place of *charan pahul*. *Pahul* given by the Guru to the five Sikhs was reciprocated by the five Sikhs by giving the same *pahul* to the Guru. That is how, it is said: *Waha Guru Gobind Singh, aape Guru te aape chela*. Thus he brought perfect equality among the Sikhs. He totally abolished the out-dated caste system. The religious aspect was no less important than the martial aspect. The disciples of Guru Gobind Singh were therefore called saint soldiers. The creation of Khalsa was an epoch-making event in the religious and political history of the country. It marked the beginning of the rise of a new people destined to play the role of a hero against all oppression and tyranny. The severities of high caste people over their brethren, the shudras were set at naught. As soon as one joins the rank of the Khalsa all were equal and ready to render one another every help and useful service.

> No people can have self-rule as a gift from another.
> It is to be seized through their own strength.[189]
>
> GURU GOBIND SINGH

During the next two years 1697-9, hectic literary activity took place. Still the Guru struggled hard to come to some important decisions. During this outwardly peaceful interval, the Guru abolished the office of the *masand* and instituted the Khalsa on Baisakhi on 30 March 1699. As a true successor of Nanak, Guru Gobind believed himself to have been chosen by God to establish the *Panth* of Nanak.

> The Divine Guru sent me for religion's sake:
> On this account I have come into the world.
> Extend the faith everywhere;
> Seize and destroy the evil and the sinful;
> Understand this, holy men, in your souls.
> I assumed birth for the purpose
> Of spreading the faith, saving the saints,
> And extirpating all tyrants.[190]

For the fulfilment of his mission, Guru Gobind Singh first tried to set his own house in order. The *masands*, who at one time, were the representative agents of the Guru, were an important link between the Guru and a large number of his Sikhs. The organization of the Sikh *Panth* greatly depended on the performance of their duties by the *masands*, but these *masands* had lost the confidence of the Guru. Guru Gobind Singh had witnessed their insolent attitude at his assumption of Guruship, their refusal to join the Battle of Bhangani, their ill-treatment of the Sikhs, and their dishonesty and corruption, which have been directly portrayed by the Guru himself in the thirty-three *savvaiyas*.

> If any one serves the *masands*, they will say
> Fetch and give us all the offerings.
> 'Go at once and make a present to us of whatever property is in thy house.
> 'Think on us night and day, and mention not others even by mistake.'
> If they hear of any one giving, they run to him even at night, they are not at all pleased at not receiving.
> They put oil into their eyes to make
> people believe that they are shedding tears.
> If they see any of their own worshippers
> Wealthy, they serve up sacred food
> And feed him with it.
> If they see him without wealth, they

give him nothing though he begs for
It; they will not even show him
Their tears.
Those beasts plunder men, and
Never sing the praises of the Supreme Being.[191]

The intervening role of dishonest and corrupt *masands* between the Guru and his followers was most undesirable because of their influence among a large number of Sikhs. The Guru, therefore, decided to establish a direct connection with the Sikhs through freshly appointed agents and by removing all the *masands* whose integrity or loyalty was questionable.[192] In most of the *hukamnamas* issued by Guru Gobind Singh to the Sikh *sangats* after the Baisakhi of 1699, the Sikhs were asked to send their offerings directly to the Guru through authorized persons (not the *masands*) or to bring these personally to Anandpur.[193]

In the time of Guru Hargobind the Sikhs who were directly linked with the Guru's household and who remained his permanent companions were called his Khalsa. The *sangat* of the East was called the Khalsa of Guru Hargobind. Likewise, the *sangat* at Pattan was called the Khalsa of Guru Tegh Bahadur and the *sangat* of Machhiwara was called the Khalsa of Guru Gobind Singh even before the Baisakhi of 1699.[194] It is possible that the term 'Khalsa' for Sikhs in general was derived from its earlier usage. Guru Gobind Singh could not have chosen a more auspicious occasion than the Baisakhi of 1699 and the *sangats* were asked to come in large numbers. In a dramatic and soul-stirring speech, Guru Gobind Singh selected five Sikhs willing to lay down their lives for *dharma*. The first man was a Khatri from Lahore, the second was a Jat from Delhi, the third was a washerman from Dwarka, the fourth was a cook from Jagannath, and the fifth was a barber from Bidar. Each man represented five different regions of the country. The Guru dressed them in fine clothes and initiated them into Khalsa Panth by giving them *khandah-ki-pahul*, i.e. sugared water stirred with a double-edged *khanda*, and consecrated by recitation of the Gurbani, rather than and not by the earlier method of *charan pahul*, water with which the feet of the Guru had been washed. After administering the *khandah-ki-pahul* to his five Sikhs, thereafter called the five beloved ones (the *Panj Piaras*), Guru

Gobind Singh himself took *pahul* from each of them, thereby merging his person with the persons of his disciples.[195]

He created 'an Order of the Purified Ones (The Khalsa) of the wonderful Lord' who were to have faith in the Supreme Being and in none else. Guru Gobind Singh defines the type of faith that his Purified Ones, i.e. the Khalsa were to have:

> He who keeps alight the unquenchable torch
> of truth and never swerves from the thought
> of one God;
> He who has full love and confidence in God,
> and does not put his faith, even by mistake
> in fasting or in the graves of Muslim saints,
> Hindu crematoriums, or Yogic places of sepulchre;
> He who only recognizes the one God and no pilgrimages,
> non-destruction of life, penances or austerities;
> And in whose heart the light of the Perfect One
> Shines—he is to be recognized as a pure
> member of the Khalsa.[196]
>
> GURU GOBIND SINGH

Everyone who was to join this order had to undergo an initiation ceremony called the 'baptism of the sword' (*khand-ki pahul*). Baptism of the sword was proclaimed and effected not only to arm his men and instill in them 'esprit de corps', but also to completely transform their psychology, outlook on life and attitude towards their fellow beings. They were to be ever-prepared crusaders of the Lord, ready to dedicate their lives to the love and service of humanity, ready to fight tyranny whenever and wherever it became overt and intolerable. They were enjoined to preserve the corporate life of the community called the Panth. The highest ideal which the Guru placed before them was that they should merge themselves completely in the Guru, and in token thereof, they were to cut themselves off completely from the past. Accordingly, they were required to take four principal vows:

1. that they will have no pride of their occupation or position (called the *kritnash* vow);
2. that they will have no pride of high birth, etc. (called the *kulnash* vow);

3. that they will discard all superstitions and traditional beliefs in the false *dharma*, rituals, etc. (called the *dharmnash* vow);
4. that they will discard all old social customs and practices; and instead fashion their lives according to the injunctions of the Guru (called the *ritinash karmnash* vow).[197]

The method of initiation which had been hitherto current among the Hindus was the *charan pahul*, i.e. the feet or the toes of the Guru were washed with water and the disciples were to drink a portion of it. Guru Gobind Singh rejected such a system of initiation, as it ran counter to his fundamental ideology, i.e. nothing should be done in the name of religion wherein man may have to make a compromise with his self-respect. He, therefore, adopted an entirely new initiation ceremony. After he had baptized his chosen five, Guru Gobind Singh himself stood up and asked them (his five beloved ones) to initiate him in the same manner. Thus, the Guru was also administered *khande-ka-pahul* and just as he had merged the Khalsa in the Guru, he merged the Guru also in the Khalsa and he expressed the same in these words:

> The Khalsa is the Guru and the
> Guru is the Khalsa.

The oft-repeated phrase *apai Guru apai chela* beautifully depicts the communion between the Guru and his Khalsa. Like the Guru himself, his baptized Sikhs were to wear their *keshas* (uncut hair) as well as their arms. The wearing of uncut hair was the most important injunction of the Guru to his Khalsa. The Khalsa thus stood distinguished from the rest of the world. After the five beloved ones baptized the Guru, the principle that emerged was that any five baptized Sikhs could initiate novice Sikhs into the Khalsa. Thus the Khalsa became the Guru and the Guru became the Khalsa.[198] J.D. Cunningham writes, 'the last apostle of the Sikhs effectually roused the dormant energies of a vanquished people and filled them with a lofty though fitful longing for social freedom and national ascendancy, the proper adjuncts of that purity of worship which had been preached by Nanak.' Contemporary estimates indicate that about 80,000 people were baptized in a few days. Guru Gobind Singh describes his feelings about his Khalsa in one of the *Shabad Hazare*.

All the battles I have won against tyranny
I have fought with the devoted backing of these people;
Through them only have I been able to bestow gifts.
Through their help I have escaped from harm;
The love and generosity of these Sikhs
Have enriched my heart and home.
Through their grace I have attained all learning
Through their help in battle I have slain all my enemies.
I was born to serve them, through them I reached eminence.
What would I have been without their kind and ready help?
There are millions of insignificant people like me.
True service is the service of these people.
From top to toe, whatever I call my own,
All I possess and carry, I dedicate to these people.[199]

POST-KHALSA BATTLES

First Battle of Anandpur, 1699

The Viceroy of Delhi sent a force of 10,000 men under Paindah Khan, Din Beg, and some hill chiefs joined them at Ropar. Guru Gobind Singh met them near Anandpur. In the battle, Paindah Khan was killed and Din Begh and the hill rajas ran away.[200]

Second Battle of Anandpur, 1699

The hill rajas under Bhim Chand's leadership and without Mughal assistance sent a message to Guru to leave Anandpur and settle somewhere else. The Guru prepared his Sikhs to fight for their survival. The siege lasted about three months. The Raja Kaiser Chand and Ghamand Chand of Kangra lost their lives. The survivors fled.[201]

Battle of Nirmohi, 1700

A strong contingent of Mughal army joined by hill rajas advanced on Anandpur.[202] The Sikh forces intercepted them at Nirmohi, 5 miles short of Anandpur, and drove them away.

Battle of Bharsali, 1700

Wazir Khan of Sirhind personally assumed the command and attacked Anandpur. The Sikhs suffered defeat and retreated towards

Bharsali about 40 km from Anandpur. The invaders pursued the Sikhs and another engagement took place at Bharsali. After some time, the invading force left for Sirhind and the Sikhs again occupied Anandpur.[203]

Third Battle of Anandpur, 1702

The Mughal commander Sayyad Beg and Alif Khan were going back to Delhi. Bhim Chand persuaded them to help him expel the Sikhs from Anandpur on payment of Rs. 1,000 per day. After a couple of skirmishes differences arose in the invading parties and they left the area.[204]

Fourth Battle of Anandpur, 1703

Bhim Chand again made an alliance of few hill rajas and marched on Anandpur. The Sikhs met them outside the town and a tough battle ensued. The hill rajas fell back and dispersed.

Fifth Battle of Anandpur, 1703

Bhim Chand again sought the help of the Mughal Viceroy at Delhi. A strong force was dispatched and Guruji came to know of it when they had reached Thanesar. The defence of Anandpur was organized. Sayyad Beg and Maiman Khan stood with the Guru. The enemy forces were able to drive the Sikhs out of Anandpur and plundered the town. The Sikhs returned back when the heavily laden enemy troops were moving out. A fierce battle was fought and the Sikhs recovered back Anandpur.[205]

The institution of *masands* had got corrupted over the passage of time and was abolished by Guru Gobind Singh. The notorious *masands* were severely punished. Others had to pay fines.[206]

Sixth and Last Battle of Anandpur, 1704

Anandpur was closely besieged in September 1704 by the Mughal forces from Delhi, Sirhind, Lahore and Jammu and the Hindu hill rajas of Guler, Kangra and others. Wazir Khan, *faujdar* of Sirhind, assumed the command of the entire force.[207] The Sikhs had mounted two guns on the fort and they took a heavy toll of the enemy troops. Wazir Khan lost 900 men on the first day.[208]

All the routes of ingress and egress were cut-off. Besides acute shortage of food, supplies of war material were also getting exhausted. There occurred certain desertions also. Wazir Khan and the hill rajas gave promise of safe passage in case the Guru left Anandpur.[209]

Under pressure the Guru decided to leave Anandpur on 20-1 December 1704.[210] Wazir Khan attacked the Guru's camp. There were lots of casualties on the Guru's side both on account of the enemy attack and the swollen rivulet. Guru's party of 400 men was left with only 43 persons. The Guru's family was also separated. The Guru was in a very delicate position with the Mughal forces both in front and at the back and the hill rajas on the left pursuing them like wild dogs. Guru turned to the right, reached Chamkaur where he occupied a mud-built double-storeyed house with a large compound.[211] By next morning the house was besieged by 700 cavalry with artillery. An envoy was sent to the Guru asking him to surrender and negotiations for the same started. By evening only five Sikhs were left with the Guru. His two elder sons had also died fighting. The five Sikhs met in a conclave and took the decision that the Guru should escape. The five Sikhs thereafter announced the decision to the Guru and the Guru accepted the same with reluctance.[212]

GURU ESCAPES TOWARDS MALWA DESERT

By instituting the Khalsa, Guru Gobind Singh took the most vital decision of his life, thus reaffirming the faith promulgated by Nanak; he consolidated the Panth, and inspired the Sikhs to defend their faith and stand on their own feet. All these preparations were likely to invite the intervention of the Mughal government.[213] A newsletter from the imperial court to the *faujdar* of Sirhind admonished the Guru.[214] Since the Baisakhi gathering had passed off peacefully the Guru was not disturbed for a couple of years, during which period he continued to consolidate his position. The large congregations of armed Sikhs which assembled during Baisakhi, Holi, and Diwali were sources of great annoyance to the hill rajas. Bhim Chand, the most powerful hill raja, again asked for tribute from the Guru, which was refused, as had been the case on an earlier occasion. From 1699 to 1703, seven attacks were made on Anandpur by the combined forces of the hill rajas[215] and at times also supported by Mughal contingents, and even by Wazir Khan of Sirhind during the Battle of Bharsali. The Guru successfully faced all these combinations, defeated the hill rajas, and maintained his sway over Anandpur and the surrounding villages which came under the Guru's control due to the ever-increasing influx of Sikhs to Anandpur.[216] Ahmad Shah Batalvi states that Guru Gobind Singh was in occupation of the territory of about 100 sq miles around Anandpur and was determined to create a dominion for himself and his Sikhs.[217] The views of Ahmad Shah Batalvi are confirmed by a dialogue between Guru Gobind Singh and Bhai Nand Lal. After the establishment of the Khalsa, Guru Gobind Singh explained his aims to Bhai Nand Lal in the following manner:

> Listen, O Nand Lal, to this truth:
> Our own Raj I would manifest;
> The four castes I would make into one;
> God's Name would then on all lips be;
> And my men would be riding horses and flying hawks;
> A sight that would put the Turks to rout.[218]

The long-standing conflict between Bhim Chand and the resolute Guru came to a climax in late 1704. Bhim Chand is believed to have made a personal representation to the emperor giving his point of view and emphasizing the potential danger from the Khalsa. Aurangzeb ordered Wazir Khan, *faujdar* of Sirhind, and other Mughal forces from the nearby areas to extend full assistance to his rajas. Thus a formidable combination was formed against Guru Gobind Singh in this trial of strength between the Khalsa and the Mughal Empire.[219]

The allied forces failed to take Anandpur. The Sikhs emerged from the town and put up a stiff resistance and repulsed the attack. Anandpur was, therefore, placed under a long-drawn siege. The allies concentrated all their resources on imposing a complete blockade. After about eight months of the siege, food became very scarce and it became increasingly difficult and unrewarding to make nightly forays into the nearby villages. In the meantime Wazir Khan and the hill rajas started negotiations with offer of a safe passage and all sorts of assurances, even on behalf of the emperor.[220] The Guru also faced pressure from his own relatives and the Sikhs. Guru Gobind Singh left Anandpur during the night of 21 December 1704.[221] The hill rajas did not pursue him, but the Mughal forces under Wazir Khan soon caught up with the Guru and his forces in the rear while they were crossing the swollen Sirsa stream. The situation resulted in a disaster for the Guru. Along with his two older sons and some followers he was separated from Mata Gujari, his mother, and his two younger sons who fell into the hands of Wazir Khan. Mata Sundari, his wife, was, however, safely escorted to Delhi by Bhai Mani Singh. The Guru lost his two older sons in an unequal fight with the Mughal forces at Chamkaur, near Ropar. Guru Gobind Singh, under pressure from the few surviving Khalsa left with him, had no option but to escape.

In early 1705, the Guru wandered from place to place in the Malwa area either alone or with a few followers with the Sirhindi troops in active pursuit after him.[222] At Jatpura (in present-day Ludhiana district) he received the news of the execution of his two younger sons by Wazir Khan and the death of Mata Gujari having died of grief.[223] Even though he was passing through a hopeless period of destruction and defeat, the Guru responded in a remarkable manner. His immediate need was to establish contact with the Khalsa, which gradually started joining him and moved from place to place in search of a suitable location to establish a settlement. Wazir Khan, who was chasing the Guru, came to know the Guru's location and attacked the Khalsa at Khidrana. The Khalsa fought with such great determination and devotion that the larger force of Wazir Khan was severely defeated and Wazir Khan retreated without any further battle with the Guru.[224]

The Guru now settled down at Talwandi Sabo. Slowly his old disciples started coming to him and a small force was established. During about a year's stay at Talwandi Sabo, the Guru dictated a new recession of the Holy Granth. Here the Guru received Aurangzeb's messages in reply to the *Zafarnama* which the Guru had written to the emperor, who was now anxious to meet him in Deccan. The Guru, with a large number of his followers, moved towards the Deccan via Rajasthan. Near Baghaur, he heard of the death of Aurangzeb and planned to return to the Punjab. Prince Muazzam had also rushed from Peshawar to Delhi to stake his claim to the throne against his brothers. Guru Gobind Singh, who was heading towards Delhi, met Muazzam before or after the Battle of Jaju. Guru Gobind Singh was given an honourable reception by Bahadur Shah, the new emperor and he was allowed to go fully armed in the emperor's presence and was given lavish and expensive gifts.[225] Guru Gobind Singh informed his Khalsa that his other matters were being settled satisfactorily and that he intended to go to Kehlur and not the Punjab.[226] But it appears that no final decision was taken and Guru Gobind moved with the emperor to Nanded.

Nearly all wars, in history, have been fought for money, woman or territory. Guru Hargobind and Guru Gobind Singh fought many wars but they did not make any personal gain out of them. They fought against tyranny and to defend the rights of human beings. The following laws have been practised by the Sikh Gurus:

1. *Not to Attack the Unarmed or the Weak*

- When Guru Hargobind attacked Paindah Khan, the latter's horse was killed, in keeping with the ethics of the war the Guru also dismounted to fight at equal level.[227]
- When Guru Gobind Singh, came face to face with Harichand of Hindur, he gave him a fair chance to fight. Harichand's first arrow killed the Guru's horse. The second arrow grazed past the Guru's ear and the third penetrated the buckle of Guru's waistbelt and just pricked his body. Thereafter the Guru took aim at Harichand and struck him with an arrow. He died instantaneously and his soldiers ran away.[228]

2. *To Challenge before Attacking*

Enemy should not be taken unawares of and not to be attacked from the rear. Banda Bahadur also used to issue *parwanas* and send these through a messenger, and on refusal of the opposing party to submit, he would attack.[229]

3. *Not to Plunder Private Property of Peaceful Citizens*

Sikh Gurus all along enjoined on their soldiers not to plunder private property or property of private citizen.

4. *Women and Children are to be Accorded Proper Treatment*

At one stage the Sikh soldiers told the Guru that Muslim soldiers have raped Hindu women. Why not the Sikhs also take revenge. The Guru said that 'I have to take you much higher, I don't want you to go downwards, that is why I forbid you to commit sins'.[230]

5. *To Help the Opposing Party for the Cause of Righteousness*

This is a unique convention set by Guru Gobind Singh to help even the enemy for the cause of righteousness. Though Guru Gobind Singh fought the Battle of Bhangani led by Bhim Chand yet he had no hesitation in making a common cause with those very hill chiefs when the latter was attacked by the Mughal force. The joint army of the hill chiefs and the Guru repelled the attack in the Battle of Nadaun.[231]

6. *No Violation of Treaty or Agreement*

According to Sikh thought, once one has made some commitments, he should not back away from his words. This condition applied during wars as well. Aurangzeb promised Guru Gobind Singh that he would not attack the Guru if the latter vacacted the fort of Anandpur. The emperor went back from his promise and his forces attacked the Guru when he left Anandpur.[232]

7. *No General Massacre*

Indian history is replete with numerous examples, wherein Muslim invaders have killed the general public in mass massacres. In his *Zafarnama* Guru Gobind Singh asked Aurangzeb not to commit cruelties on the humble and the general public who had not committed any sin against the emperor.[233]

8. *Not to Damage the Places of Worship*

The history of Islamic rule in India is full of instances of demolition of Hindu temples and raising mosques in their place. This was because the Muslims took the Hindus as infidels and treated them as their slave.

> The temples are razed to the ground,
> And mosques are erected in their place
> The sin is prevailing
> The temple and the mosque are the same.
> The Hindu worship and the Muslim prayer are the same;
> All men are the same;
> It is through error they appear different.[234]

9. *Not to Harm Persons who have Surrendered*

The Sikh Gurus laid down the rule that whosoever surrenders must be protected and not harmed. Whosoever seeks Lord's refuse, He hugs to His bosom: This is the innate nature of the Lord.[235]

10. *Treatment of the Injured after the Battle*

Some of the disciples complained to the Guru that a Sikh called Kanahaiya had been giving water and aid not only to the wounded Sikhs but also to the wounded enemies. The Guru asked Kanahaiya if this was true. 'Yes, my Lord, it is true in a sense,' said Kanahaiya 'I have been giving water to everyone who needed it on the field of battle, but I saw no Mughal or Sikhs there. I saw only the Guru's face everywhere.' The Guru was pleased with his reply, blessed him and told his Sikhs that Kanahaiya had understood his teaching correctly. Thus, started the Red Cross of the Sikhs at the battle front.[236]

Guru Gobind Singh had become aware of the hostility of the court, especially over his dispute with Wazir Khan of Sirhind. At this juncture, the Guru met a *bairagi* who became his ardent disciple, and who was later named Banda Bahadur. The Guru chose him as the commander of the Sikh forces to chastize Wazir Khan and others.[237] How Banda came in contact with the Guru, how the Guru was able to ascertain his capabilities, whether they were known to each other are questions shrouded in mystery and no authentic account regarding their veracity is available. But what stands established as historical fact is that there could not have been a better choice for the purpose for which Banda Bahadur was sent. Shortly after Banda's departure for the Punjab, the Guru was attacked, apparently by some hired assassins, and was badly injured. The wound did not heal and after some days, the Guru announced that his end was near.[238]

The Guru collected his Sikhs around him and gave them his parting instructions. He opened the *Granth*, placed 5 *paisa* and a coconut, bowed before it, and declared that henceforth the holy book would be the Guru for all time to come and thus he abolished the institution of personal guruship. He also composed the following verse:

Agya bhai Akal ki tabhi chalayo Panth,
Sab Sikhan ko hukm hai Guru Manio Granth.
Guru Granth je manyo pargat Guru ke deh.
Jo Prabho to milbo chahe khoj shabad me le.

Under the order of the Immortal God, the Panth was founded.
All Sikhs are enjoined to accept the Granth as their Guru.
Consider the Granth as representing the Guru's body.
Those who desire to contact the Guru can find Him in its hymns.[239]

Guru Gobind Singh had earlier said in the *Bichhittar Natak*.

Installed on Nanak's throne as Guru tenth,
When assumed the scripture of my sovereignty
I promoted religion to the best of my power.

Guru Gobind Singh states that when he assumed the spiritual sovereignty of Guru Nanak, he served the *piri* aspect, the *dharma*, with all his devotion. He also states in Bhai Nand Lal's rendering of the Guru's remarks:[240]

The Granth is my second self.
And it should be taken as me.
A Sikh who wants to see me
Should have a look at the Granth.
One who wants to talk to me,
Should read the Granth and think over it.

Guru Gobind Singh defines his temporal sovereignty in the *Krishan Avtar*:

Great death be thou my protector;
All steel I am thy slave.
Deeming me thy own, preserve me.
Single out and destroy my enemies.
Let both my free kitchen and my sword.
Prevail in the world.
Preserve me and let none trample me.
Be thou my cherisher.[241]

When Guru Gobind Singh gave his temporal sovereignty to his Khalsa, he issued a stern warning to them to preserve Sikh identity in its uniqueness, as stated in the *Sarbloh Granth:*

Jab Lag Khalsa rahie niara, Tab lag jas dion men sara.
Jab aye gai bipran ke reet, Man na karun in ke partit.[242]

The Khalsa shall continue to be blessed with all my power, so long as it preserves its identity and uniqueness. But when the Khalsa strays from the path of righteousness, the Guru will not stand by them.

Guru Gobind Singh had made himself the master of the imagination of his followers. His death triggered such an enormous popular response that the first sovereign Sikh state came into existence within two years over the *subah* of Sirhind and the surrounding territories. The coins struck and the seal adopted by the Sikh state closely reflect the Sikh concept of sovereignty. As unique symbols of Sikh sovereignty these differed from contemporary coinages and remained unchanged during the entire period of the Sikh state till its annexation by the British in March 1849.[243]

Guru Gobind Singh lived a very active life. Ever since he was designated as the Guru at the tender age of 9 up to the time of his death at 41, he came into continuous conflict with the existing social and political order and had to wage a war against the Hindu as well as the Mughal rulers. In order to vindicate his views on many of these matters, he organized the Khalsa and attempted to put his ideals into practice. He was an extremely well-read man and many of his observations on the then existing political order provide us with a wealth of material.[244]

The views of Guru Gobind Singh on the main aspects of political ideas are elaborated in the next section.

THE RULER AND HIS DUTIES

In conformity with the teachings of Guru Nanak, the tenth Guru had argued that authority in every sphere ultimately derives its validity from God and not from any human source. In the *Zafarnama* which was addressed to Aurangzeb, the Guru had mentioned that God is the true emperor of the earth and heaven and that He is the master of both the worlds.[245] He has further stated in this regard:

> The successors of both Baba Nanak and Babur
> were created by God Himself.
> Recognize the former as a spiritual,
> And the latter as a temporal king.[246]

This idea is further elucidated as under:

> By his (God's) *hukum* are all things formed,
> Not one is blessed, save by his *hukum*, and
> by his *hukum* alone nature doth run her course,
> All serve beneath his *hukum*, and none may act
> without it.
> Under Thy *hukum*, O God, hath all been done,
> And naught is of itself alone.[247]

Guru Gobind Singh believed in the divine origin of authority. But he had made it clear that while the person in authority exercises this power as a mandate from God, so that he may continue to enjoy this boon, he must always act according to the dictates of God. If he does not abide by the God's mandate, if he annoys the weak, if he plunders the people, if he engages in activities prejudicial to the general welfare, if he puts the fulfilment of personal material pleasures as the prime motive of life and digresses from religious and moral teachings and from the principles of justice, he incurs the wrath of God, who may then deprive him of his position and bestow the sameon someone else.[248] The Guru had made it clear in unmistakable terms that a secular ruler must always be responsible to God for all his activities. Condemning the religious bigotry and political intolerance of Aurangzeb as inconsistent with divine mandate, he said:

> Smite not any one mercilessly with the sword, or a sword from the high shall smite thyself. O Man, be not reckless, fear God, he cannot be flattered or praised. The King of Kings is without fear. He is the true emperor of earth and heaven. God is the master of both worlds. He is the Protector of the miserable and Destroyer of the reckless.[249]

In the *Zafarnama*, the Guru said: 'God will grant thee the fruit of the evil deed thou designed—I do not deem thou knowest God, since thou hast done acts of oppression.'[250] Pointing out to Aurangzeb, he added: 'Did I not know that thou O faithless man, wert a worshipper of wealth and perjurer? Thou keepest no faith and observest no religion. Thou knowest not God never swerveth from his promise. Thou hast no idea of what an oath on the Quran is and canst have no belief in Divine providence.'

Guru Gobind Singh was of the view that public opinion on a particular matter must be considered as the pointer and the political authority must conform to the will of the people. It means that rulers must always be responsible to the ruled just as leaders must always personify the aspirations of the led. The Guru had mentioned that while the 'Guru's sovereignty is full of twenty measures, that of the *sangat*, as the mouth-piece of the people, is of twenty-one measures'.[251] He had also pointed out that 'God would always be present in the general body of the Khalsa, and that wherever even five Sikhs assembled, God would be with them'.[252] He also emphasized that the true service is the service of the common people.

> True service is the service of these people:
> I am not inclined to serve others of higher castes;
> Charity will bear fruit, in this and in the next world,
> If given to such worthy people as these.
> All other sacrifices and charities are profitless.
> From top to toe, whatever I call my own,
> All I possess or carry, I dedicate to these people![253]

The high esteem in which he held the Sikhs was witnessed when after selecting the 'five loved ones', he partook the sanctified water at their hands and thereby gave the Khalsa the pride of having selected their leader. So was it when Guru Nanak bowed before Bhai Lehna while appointing him the Guru in his place.

REBELLION AGAINST THE RULER

The martyrdom of Guru Arjan Dev and Guru Tegh Bahadur on the orders of Jahangir and Aurangzeb respectively confirmed the belief of the Tenth Guru that force must be met with force. Guru Gobind Singh favoured peaceful means in order to resolve the conflicts, but when the sovereign authority did not appreciate it and ignored them, then use of extreme means in order to vindicate one's own cause are necessary and justified.

> When all other means have proven ineffective
> It is right then to take up the sword.[254]

The peaceful approach can bear fruit only if the opponent has some scruples and is influenced by religious and ethical values. If he did not have any regard for such values, the only remedy would be to oppose him with all one's strength. Guru Gobind Singh considered the request of hill rajas to borrow his elephant as a pressure tactic and told his mother who had intervened on their behalf.[255] 'The hillmen have now come to beg with the humility of goats, but when they have received what they have asked for, they will assume the bravery of tigers. Mother dear, if we betray fear of them, they will soon be ready to devour us. They will only respect us when we show them the sword.'[256]

Guru Gobind Singh advocated the use of force only as a measure of last resort. He found that the Sikhs had suffered a lot at the hands of the Mughals. That is why he reached the conclusion that the time had come when they should prepare themselves for effective opposition to established authority. In order to achieve these goals, he substituted the old ideals of humility and surrender practised by Guru Arjan Dev and Guru Tegh Bahadur to one of self-assertion and self-reliance. The Guru was engaged for the whole of his life in active military operations, first against the Hindu rajas and later against the Mughal armed forces. He was convinced that force must be met with force. Guru Gobind Singh introduced in the Sikh prayer an invocation to the sword and the prayer starts with: 'Having first remembered the sword, meditate on Guru Nanak'. He firmly believed in combining spiritual achievements with physical prowess.

IDEAL PEOPLE

The Guru was not happy with the caste ridden Hindu society and the fanatical attitude of the *mullahs* and others who held non-Muslims as *kafirs*. He was of the view that human beings are essentially the same, whatever religion, race, colour, or creed they may belong to.[257] He was of the view that different customs and habits were the product of a different environment in which people lived and not because they were different from each other. In the eyes of God, everybody has an equal status.

> He is also in the temple as He is in the mosque;
> He is in the Hindu worship as He is in the Muslim prayer;
> Men are one though they appear different,
> The Hindus and the Muslims are all one.
> Each have the habits of a different environment,
> But all men have the same eyes, the same body,
> The same form compounded of the same four elements,
> Earth, air, fire, and water.
> Thus the Abhekh of the Hindus and the Allah of the Muslims are one,
> The Quran and the Puran praise the same Lord.
> They are all of one form,
> The One Lord made them all.[258]

Guru Gobind Singh laid a good deal of emphasis on honest living. A householder who lived honestly, earned his bread by the sweat of his own brow, gave charity and believed in God, helped in raising secular life to a higher pedestal. Guru wanted to have no truck with those who, under the garb of saintliness, exploited the people. This applied to *masands*, the brahmins and the *mullahs*. More than that it applied to the political rulers. An ideal ruler, whatever his station in the hierarchy, must be an embodiment of virtue, believer in the Almighty.[259]

Guru Gobind Singh believed that all authority, secular as well as spiritual, flows from God who is omnipotent and the final determinant of all things. But he did not concede the doctrine of divine right of authority as had been claimed by some of the despotic rulers. If a ruler strayed away from the divine mandate, if he engaged himself in the satisfaction of his own earthly pleasures and indulged in selfishness, greed and favouritism and if he alienates the sympathies of the people by resorting to acts of high-handedness, injustice and coercion, he loses the mandate of God and such a person must be thrown out even by the use of force. Moreover the rulers must always be responsible to the ruled because the God's will manifests itself through the will of the people. The Guru stressed the spiritual and physical improvement of the individuals. He was the first Indian leader who advocated equality, fraternity and democracy and stood for basing all human activity: political, economic and social, on ethical and spiritual foundations.[260]

The temporal sovereignty (the sovereignty of the Sikh state) was bequeathed by Guru Gobind Singh to the collective wisdom of the Khalsa Panth at the time of his demise in October 1708. Knowing fully well that as the need arose, it would throw up its own leaders. That Guru's hopes were not belied is shown by the crucial role that even such obscure men as Kapur Singh and Jassa Singh played in the Sikh war of independence. It was held as a sacred trust both in victory and in defeat. During the First Anglo-Sikh war in 1845 and the signing of the humiliating treaty in March 1846, the Sikh sardars had played a very dubious role. However, the Sikh soldiers, unlike the selfish and disloyal Sikh sardars who had allied with the British, continued to profess loyalty to their Gurus and fought bravely for the preservation of Sikh sovereignty. M.L. Ahluwalia states:

> As to a crore of rupees of the war indemnity imposed by the British on the Lahore government, an offer was mooted by the "Panches" representing the Darbar army to deduct one month's pay from the salaries of all the armed personnel of the Darbar for making up the amount of one crore of rupees which the British were accepting from Raja Gulab Singh . . . the British did not agree to the said proposal of the Darbar.[261]

This shows that even though the Sikh rulers of the Lahore Darbar had lost their respect for the principle of Sikh sovereignty in their self-serving pursuit of their personal gains, the dedication and reverence for Sikh sovereignty was still very dear to the Sikh soldiers, even in defeat.

NOTES

1. Louis E. Fenech, *The Darbar of Sikh Gurus*, New Delhi: Oxford University Press, p. 286.
2. *Selections from the Sacred Writings of the Sikhs*, London, 1960, pp. 115, 96.
3. Max Arthur Macauliffe, *The Sikh Religion*, Oxford, 1909, vol. I, p. XLIV.
4. J.S. Bains, *Indian Journal of Political Science*, vol. XXIII, 1962, p. 309.
5. Ibid., p. 311.
6. A.C. Banerjee, *Guru Nanak and his Times*, Patiala: Panjabi University, 1984, p. 1.
7. A.B. Panday, *The First Afghan Empire in India (1451-1562)*, Calcutta, 1956, pp. 243-4.
8. Banerjee, *Guru Nanak and his Times*, p. 2.
9. W.H. Moreland, *The Agrarian System of Muslim India*, Cambridge, 1921, p. 71.
10. *Sri Guru Granth Sahib* (Translation), Gopal Singh, Delhi: Gurdas Kapoor & Sons, 1960-2, vol. I, p. 350.
11. Macauliffe, *The Sikh Religion*, vol. 1, p. 232.
12. Radhakrishnan (ed.), *History of Philosophy Past & Present*, London, 1957, vol. 1, p. 522; Quoted by Jodh Singh in *Sikh Philosophy*.
13. Mohd. Latif, *History of Panjab*, Ludhiana: Kalyani Publishers, rpt, 1989, p. 15.
14. *Selections from the Sacred Writings of Sikhs*, Rag Asa, p. 93.
15. *Sri Guru Granth Sahib* (translation), vol. 1, p. 470.
16. G.C. Narang, *Transformation of Sikhism*, Lahore, 1945, p. 31.
17. Ibid., p. 25.
18. Sewaram Singh, *The Divine Master*, Lahore, 1930, p. 247.
    Also: There are lowest among the low castes
    Nanak, I shall go with them.
    What have I got to do with the great
    God's eye of mercy fall on those who
    Take care of the lowly.

It is mere nonsense to observe caste and
To feel proud over grand names.

'Sri Rag' quoted in Teja Singh, *Sikhism: Its Ideas and Institutions*, Lahore, 1928, p. 10.

19. *Selections from the Sacred Writings of Sikhs*, p. 45.
20. Macauliffe, *Sikh Religion*, p. 38.
21. *Bhai Gurdas Varan* (tr Jodh Singh), vol. 2, Patiala: Vision and Nature, Var 1, pauri 27.
22. J.D. Cunningham, *History of Sikhs*, New Delhi, 1972, pp. 36-8.
23. Banerjee, *Guru Nanak and his Times*, pp. 198-9.
24. (i) W.H. McLeod, *Guru Nanak and the Sikh Religion*, Oxford: Clarendon Press, 1968, pp. 277-8.
    (ii) J.S. Grewal, *Guru Nanak in History*, Chandigarh: Panjab University, 1969, pp. 168-9.
    (iii) A.C. Banerjee, *The Sikh Gurus and Sikh Religion*, New Delhi: Munshiram Manoharlal, 1983, pp. 92-3.
25. (i) Indu Bhushan Banerjee, *Evolution of Khalsa*, 2 vols., Calcutta: A. Mukherjee and Co., 1979, vol. 1, p. 94.
    (ii) Macauliffe, *Sikh Religion*, p. 278.
26. J.S. Ahluwalia, *Sovereignty of Sikh Doctrine*, New Delhi: Bahri Publications, 1983, p. 30.
27. Ibid., p. 43.
28. Ibid., p. 42.
29. Macauliffe, *The Sikh Religion*, vol. II, p. 26.
30. Ibid., vol. I, p. 382.
31. Banerjee, *Guru Nanak and his Times*, p. 161.
32. Archer, *The Sikhs,* NY, USA: Princeton, 1946, p. 109.
33. McLeod, *Guru Nanak and Sikh Religion*, p. 143.
34. Harbans Singh, *Guru Nanak*, Preet Larhi, p. 14.
35. *Bachittar Natik* (tr M.L. Peace), Jullundur, undated, p. 12.
36. G.C. Narang, *Transformation of Sikhism*, p. 34.
37. Cunningham, *History of Sikh*, p. 34.
38. Ernest Trumpp, *Adhi Granth* (tr), New Delhi: Munshiram Manoharlal, 1978, p. xxvii.
39. *Bhai Gurdas Varan*, Var 1, pauri 45.
40. Ibid., Var 7, pauri 8.
41. Ibid., Var 26, pauri 31-2.
42. Ibid., Var 39, pauri 3.
43. A.C. Banerjee, *Guru Nanak and his Times*, p. 182.
44. J.C. Archer, *The Sikhs*, p. 60.
45. Kapur Singh, 'Baisakhi of Guru Gobind Singh', in *Parasaraprasna*, Amritsar, 1989, p. 12.

46. Sher Singh, *Philosophy of Sikhism*, Lahore, 1944, p. 24.
47. Nihar Ranjan Ray, *Sikh Gurus and Sikh Society*, Delhi: Munshiram Manoharlal, 1975, p. 59.
48. *Bhai Bala's Janamsakhi*, Quoted by Sewaram Singh, *The Divine Master*, pp. 73-4.
49. *Selections from the Sacred Writings of Sikhs*, pp. 96-7.
50. Macauliffe, *The Sikh Religion*, pp. 58-9.
51. Ibid., p. 121.
52. *Selections from the Sacred Writings of Sikhs*, pp. 86-8.
53. Macauliffe, *The Sikh Religion*, p. 109.
54. Bains, *Indian Journal of Pol Sciences*, p. 5.
55. *Selections from the Sacred Writings of the Sikhs*, p. 96.
56. *The Sikh Review*, Calcutta, November 1961, p. 44.
57. Bains, *Indian Journal of Pol Sciences*, p. 16.
58. *The Sikh Review*, Calcutta, August 1962, p. 32.
59. *Selections from the Sacred Writings of Sikhs*, p. 118.
60. Macauliffe, *The Sikh Religion*, p. 60.
61. *Sri Guru Granth Sahib*, p. X, 'The seed of the testament of the Guru cannot germinate except in the field of ethical conduct constantly irrigated by the waters of truth. . . . A man of religion is ever characterized by ethical deeds, honest living, sincerity of heart, and a fearless passion for truth. . . . Nanak maketh this public declaration, let all men ponder over it: Ethical conduct is the only true foundation of human life on earth.'
62. Macauliffe, *The Sikh Religion*, p. 44.
63. Ibid., p. 72.

    Also: That man who calls himself a teacher of truth
    But lives by begging, do not pay him homage
    The man who earns his bread by the sweat of his brow
    And gives some of his gains in charity
    Knoweth, Nanak, the true way of life.

    Selections from the Sacred Writings of Sikhs, p. 116.
64. Bains, quoted from Jodh Singh, *Sikh Philosophy,* p. 515.
65. Macauliffe, *The Sikh Religion*, I, p. lxxix.
66. Gupta, *History of Sikh Gurus*, p. 55.
67. Macauliffe, *The Sikh Religion*, II, pp. 13-14.
68. Cunningham, *History of Sikhs*, p. 44.
69. Mohd. Latif, *History of Panjab*, p. 250.
70. (i) *Encyclopaedia of Sikhism*, p. 834.
    (ii) Kanhiyalal, *Tarikh-i-Panjab (Urdu)*, p. 15.
71. *Seletions from the Sacred Writings of the Sikhs*, p. 123.

72. Macauliffe, *The Sikh Religion*, II, pp. 64-6.
73. Banerjee, *The Sikh Gurus and Sikh Religion*, p. 162.
74. Ibid., p. 165.
75. Gupta, *Sikh Gurus*, p. 84.
76. Surinder Singh, *Sikh Coinage: Symbol of Sikh Sovereignty*, New Delhi: Manohar, 2004, p. 173.
77. Banerjee, *Sikh Guru and Sikh Religion*, p. 175.
78. Gupta, *Sikh Gurus*, pp. 84-5.
79. Ibid., p. 85.
80. Indu Bhushan Banerjee, *Evolution of Khalsa*, p. 167.
81. Ibid., p. 162.
82. Ibid., pp. 181-2.
83. *Sri Guru Granth*, *Rag Sohi*, pp. 767-8.
84. Cunningham, *History of Sikhs*, p. 44.
85. Gupta, *Sikh Gurus*, pp. 87-8.
86. Ibid., p. 88.
87. Banerjee, *Sikh Gurus and Sikh Religion*, p. 182.
88. Mohsin Fani, *Dabistan-i-Mazhab* (tr. Troyer and Shia), vol. 1, p. 271.
89. Gupta, *Sikh Gurus*, p. 90.
90. (i) Banerjee, *Sikh Gurus and Sikh Religion*, p. 182.
    (ii) Gupta, *Sikh Gurus*, p. 90.
    (iii) I.B. Banerjee, *Evolution of Khalsa*, p. 195.
91. Macauliffe, *The Sikh Religion*, vol. III, p. 85.
92. Ibid., p. 57.
93. Ibid., p. 64.
94. Banerjee, *Sikh Gurus and Sikh Religion*, p. 192.
95. Mohsin Fani, *Dabistan-i-Mazhab*, pp. 233-4.
96. Ibid., pp. 225 and 233.
97. Gupta, *Sikh Guru*, pp. 93, 98.
98. Ibid., p. 98.
99. I.B. Banerjee, *Evolution of Khalsa*, p. 254.
100. Narang, *Transformation of Sikhism*, p. 76.
101. Ibid.
102. *Tuzak-i-Jahangiri*, tr. Rodgers and Beveridge, 1996 edn., Delhi: Munshiram Manoharlal, p. 76.
103. Ibid., pp. 72-3.
104. Banerjee, *Sikh Gurus and Sikh Religion*, p. 205.
105. (i) Gupta, *History of Sikh Gurus*, p. 104.
     (ii) Mohd. Latif, *History of Panjab*, Kalyani Publishers (rpt. 1989), p. 254.

106. I.B. Banerjee, *Evolution of Khalsa*, vol. II, p. 6.
107. (i) Ibid., vol. II, p. 8.
    (ii) Mohd. Latif, *History of Panjab*, p. 25, III.
    (iii) Narang, *Transformation of Sikhism*, p.101.
    (iv) Ernest Trumpp, *Adi Granth*, p. LXXXII.
    (v) Macauliffe, *Sikh Religion*, vol. IV, p. 2.
    (vi) Cunningham, *History of Sikhs*, p. 50.
    (vii) Gupta, *History of Sikh Gurus*, p. 108.
108. Ibid., p. 92.
109. Macauliffe, *Sikh Religion*, vol. III, p. 50.
110. Ibid., p. 99.
111. Ahluwalia, *The Sovereignty of the Sikh Doctrine*, p. 91.
112. *Adi Granth*, Bani Bhagat Ravi Dass, p. 345.
113. Nihar Ranjan Ray, *The Sikh Gurus and Sikh Society*, New Delhi: Munshiram Manoharlal, 1975, p. 57.
114. Banerjee, *Sikh Gurus and Sikh Religion*, p. 235.
115. Ibid.
116. Gupta, *History of Sikh Gurus*, p. 100.
117. Ibid., p. 110.
118. Ibid.
119. Ahluwalia, *Sovereignty of Sikh Doctrine*, p. 1.
120. Gupta, *History of Sikh Gurus,* p. 110.
121. Surinder Singh, *Sikh Coinage*, p. 179.
122. Ahluwalia, *Sovereignty of Sikh Doctrine*, p. 227.
123. Gupta, *History of Sikh Gurus*, p. 116.
124. Ibid., p. 117.
125. Jadunath Sarkar, *Short History of Aurangzeb*, p. 156.
126. Ibid., Jadunath's date of 1628 is obviously wrong.
127. Macauliffe, *Sikh Religion,* vol. V, p. 96
128. Mohd. Latif, *History of Panjab*, p. 256.
129. Sarkar, *Short History of Aurangzeb*, p. 156.
130. Gupta, *History of Sikh Gurus*, p. 118.
131. Ibid.
132. Ibid., p. 119.
133. Ibid.
134. Mohsin Fani, *Dabistan*, p. 235.
135. Ibid.
136. Gupta, *History of Sikh Gurus*, p. 120.
137. Ibid., p. 125.
138. Mohsin Fani, *Dabistan*, p. 239.
139. Gupta, *History of Sikh Gurus*, p. 130.

140. I.B. Banerjee, *Evolution of Khalsa*, vol. II, p. 34.
141. Gupta, *History of Sikh Gurus*, p. 130.
142. Ibid.
143. Ibid., p. 132.
144. Ibid.
145. Ibid., pp. 132-3.
146. Ibid., p. 133.
147. Ibid., pp. 132-3.
148. Ibid., p. 137.
149. Ibid., p. 134.
150. Ibid., p. 137.
151. Ibid., p. 135.
152. Ibid.
153. Ibid., pp. 137-9.
154. Ibid., p. 140.
155. Ibid., pp. 142-3.
156. Ibid., p. 144.
157. Ibid., p. 148.
158. Ibid., p. 149.
159. Ibid., pp. 148-50.
160. Grewal and Bal, *Guru Gobind Singh*, p. 52.
161. Gupta, *History of Sikh Gurus*, p. 149.
162. Kirpal Singh Narang, 'Socio-Religious Ideals of Guru Gobind Singh', *Sikhisim and Indian Society, Transactions of the Indian Institute of Advanced Study*, vol. IV, Shimla 1967, p. 143.
163. Ibid., p. 144.
164. Ibid.
165. Ibid., p. 146.
166. Ibid., p. 147.
167. Gupta, *History of Sikh Gurus*, pp. 149-50.
168. Ibid., p. 150.
169. Ibid.
170. Louis E. Fenech, *The Darbar of the Sikh Gurus*, p. 26.
    There were 52 poets surrounding the Guru, everyone of whom brought bani to light. Within the Guru's court (in the presence of the Guru) there were 52 poets. They were right by his side. Several were of them came and went eulogizing the Guru. In return for which they were rewarded.
171. Gupta *History of Sikh Gurus*, p. 155.
172. Ibid.
173. Ibid.

174. Ibid.
175. Ibid.
176. Surinder Singh, *Baba Banda Singh Bahadur's Battle Strategy Against Mughal Forces*, New Delhi: Har-Anand Publication, 2009, p. 43.
177. Ibid.
178. Ibid.
179. Gupta, *History of Sikh Gurus*, p. 158.
180. Grewal and Bal, *Guru Gobind Singh*, pp. 82-3.
181. Ibid., p. 83.
182. Ibid., p. 86.
183. Ibid.
184. Gupta, *History of Sikh Gurus*, p. 158.
185. Ibid., p. 159.
186. Ibid., p. 160.
187. Grewal and Bal, *Guru Gobind Singh*, p. 96.
188. Ibid., p. 100.
189. Macauliffe, *The Sikh Religion,* vol. V, p. 301.
190. Ibid., p. 322.
191. Grewal and Bal, *Guru Gobind Singh*, pp. 113-14.
192. Ibid., p. 114.
193. Ibid., p. 115.
194. Ibid.
195. Gupta, *History of Sikh Gurus*, p. 185.
196. Kirpal Singh Narang, *Socio-Religious Ideals of Guru Gobind Singh*, p. 143.
197. (i) Gupta, *History of Sikh Gurus*, p. 189.
     (ii) Grewal and Bal, *Guru Gobind Singh*, p. 123.
198. Narang, *Socio-Religious Ideals of Guru Gobind Singh*, p. 150.
199. *The Sikh Review*, January 1963, Calcutta, p. 16.
200. Narain Singh, *Guru Gobind Singh*, Chandigarh, 1967, p. 16.
201. Macauliffe, *The Sikh Religion*, vol. V, pp. 124-6.
202. Sainapat, *Guru Soba*, Lahore, 1925, pp. 138-42.
203. Ibid.
204. Macauliffe, *The Sikh Religion,* pp. 153-4.
205. Ibid., pp. 156, 162-4.
206. *Bachittar Natik*, Sec. XII, Chaupai 10.
207. Gupta, *History of Sikh Gurus*, p. 202.
208. Ibid., p. 203.
209. Ibid.
210. Santokh Singh, *Sri Guru Pratap Suraj Granth*, pp. 5819-22.
211. Gupta, *History of Sikh Gurus*, p. 205.

212. Ibid., p. 207.
213. Grewal and Bal, *Guru Gobind Singh*, p. 126.
214. Ibid., p. 127.
215. Gupta, *History of Sikh Gurus*, pp. 198-202.
216. Grewal and Bal, *Guru Gobind Singh*, p. 136.
217. J.S. Grewal, *From Guru Nanak to Maharaja Ranjit Singh*, Amritsar: Guru Nanak Dev University, 1982, p. 109.
218. *Sarb Loh, Gursobha*, p. 183.
219. Grewal and Bal, *Guru Gobind Singh*, p. 138.
220. Gupta, *History of Sikh Gurus*, pp. 204-5.
221. Grewal and Bal, *Guru Gobind Singh*, p. 140.
222. Ibid., p. 143.
223. Ibid.
224. Ibid., p. 145.
225. Gupta, *History of Sikh Gurus*, p. 228.
226. Ganda Singh, *Hukamnamas* (Punjabi), Patiala: Punjabi University, 1985, p. 186. Hukamnama no. 63, dated 2 October 1701.
227. *Gurbilas Patshahi-6*, 20.575-6.
228. Guru Gobind Singh, *Bachhittar Natk*, VIII, 34.
229. Ganda Singh, *Banda Bahadur*, p. 154.
230. Santokh Singh, *Sri Guru Pratap Suraj Granth*, pp. 6. 20, 16-19.
231. Guru Gobind Singh, *Bachittar Natak*, Chapter XI.
232. Guru Gobind Singh, *Zafarnama*, V.53, 55, 18.
233. Ibid., V.106.
234. Guru Gobind Singh, *Akal Ustat* 16/86.
235. *Sri Guru Granth Sahib*, p. 544.
236. Harbans Singh, *Heritage of the Sikhs*, New Delhi: Manohar, 1994, p. 89.
237. Ganda Singh, *Life of Banda Bahadur*, Patiala: Punjabi University, 1990, rpt, p. 12.
238. Macauliffe, *The Sikh Religion*, vol. V, p. 245.
239. Giani Gian Singh, *Twarikh Guru Khalsa*, vol. I, 1981, Sialkot. pp. 355-6.
240. Gupta, *History of Sikh Gurus*.
241. Dharm Pal, 'Poetry of Dasam Granth' (Ph.D. thesis), Punjab University, Chandigarh, p. 26.
242. Ahluwalia, *Sovereignty of the Sikh Doctrine,* p. 48.
243. Surinder Singh, *Sikh Coinage: Symbol of Sikh Sovereignty*, p. 32.
244. J.S. Bains, *Political Ideas of Guru Gobind Singh, Sikhism and Sikh Society,* Shimla: Indian Institute of Advanced Studies, vol. IV, 1967, p. 122.
245. Macauliffe, *The Sikh Religion*, vol. V, p. 204.

246. Ibid., vol. II, p. 305.
247. Archer, *The Sikhs*, p. 210.
248. Ibid., p. 204.
249. Bains, *Political Ideas of Guru Gobind Singh,* p. 130.
250. Macauliffe, *The Sikh Religion*, vol. V, p. 205.
251. Kapur Singh in *Parasaraprasana*, op. cit., p. 325, F. No. 19.
252. Narang *Transformation of Sikhism*, p. 83.
253. *Selections from the Sacred Writings of the Sikhs,* p. 272.
254. *Zafarnama*, quoted in Archer, *The Sikhs*, p. 203.
255. Macauliffe, *The Sikh Religion*, vol. V, p. 11.
256. Ibid., p. 13.
257. *Akal Ustat*, 16, 86.
258. *Selections from the Sacred Writings of the Sikhs*, p. 269.
259. Bains, *Political Ideas of Guru Gobind Singh*, p. 141.
260. Ibid., p. 142.
261. M.L. Ahluwalia, *Landmarks in Sikh History* (A fully researched and documented history 1699-1947), New Delhi: Ashok International Publishers, 1996, p. 169.

    M.L. Ahluwalia has vide his letter dated 18 October 1999 intimated the authority for the Sikh Panches, offering one month salary for Kashmir to the British as Lahore Political Diaries, vol. III, p. 88, National Archives of India Secret Series.

CHAPTER 4

The Battle Strategy of Banda Bahadur

Mughal Forces no Match for Banda Bahadur's War Tactics

Banda Bahadur with his meagre resource of men and materials fought numerous battles against the Mughal forces having a much larger and a trained army with unending supply lines of soldiers, arms, ammunition food-stocks, etc. In spite of these disparities, Banda Bahadur won many battles against them. The Sikh Gurus had breathed, as if, an undying spirit of sacrifice in the Sikh volunteers. These soldiers fighting and dying for their faith had a greater edge over those who were fighting as mercenaries. Banda Bahadur combining his battle strategies to the valour of the Sikh volunteers guaranteed victory for them.

With the rise of the Muslim rulers in India, a large number of Muslim camp followers also came along with them to India and began looting and harassing the common public. To counter them, the Hindu *deras* and *maths* who were having ascetic warriors for their protection greatly increased their strength. Hindu ascetic warriors used certain military strategies even when their strength was much lesser than the armies against whom they were fighting. The guerrilla style of rapid attack-retreat-reattack had been used by them since ages. They also used the surprise element and would make lightning attacks on their opponents, especially in the night.

Banda Bahadur made extensive use of these strategies. It was the combined effect of the spirit of sacrifice in the sikh volunteers and the war strategies of Banda Bahadur that made Sikhs win many battles against the much larger Mughal forces. These battle

Plate 6: Banda Bahadur (sitting)

strategies had been used by the ascetic warriors of India, also by Banda Bahadur and thereafter by the Sikh Misls in their fight against the Mughals and Afghans. During the Misl period it was called *dhai phat*, i.e. two and a half steps.

Books written on Banda Bahadur have given accounts of various battles fought by him against the Mughal forces. But the strategies adopted by Banda Bahadur have not been explained in sufficient detail. The chronological account the battles fought by Banda Bahadur and the detailed description of these battles are portrayed well by Ganda Singh in his book *Life of Banda Singh Bahadur.* This author has taken the descriptive details of various battles from the above-said work of Ganda Singh, whereas the main stress has been author's contribution to the strategical appreciation of these battles. Almost every battle won by Banda Bahadur had a distinct strategy.

Banda Bahadur initially subdued small towns and large villages around the *faujdari* of Sirhind. This enabled his followers to pick-up the art of warfare and the strategies brought into play by Banda Bahadur. Banda Bahadur himself would generally occupy a central space with a small section and the rest of the army was deployed on either sides. He would let his commanders, both on the right and left, engage the Mughal/imperial forces or the forces of the local commanders in the fight. He would watch their fight on both sides and see if they were able to maintain their advance against their opponents or were they unable to withstand the might of the Mughal forces. Wherever the Sikh forces were not able to maintain their advance against the Mughal forces, Banda Bahadur would himself with his small force jump into the fray with such force that the Mughal forces invariably would lose initiative and the sikh forces emerge victorious. This strategy was used by Banda Bahadur in most of the battles and thereby the Sikh forces were able to win the fight for the day. The phenomenon of Banda Bahadur jumping in the thick of battle, and the winning enemy forces dispersing helter skelter and defeated in many battles, have been recorded. The factors leading to the enemy's defeat after Banda's entry requires further research as to how one man's entry at a particular stage, quite often changed the course of battle.

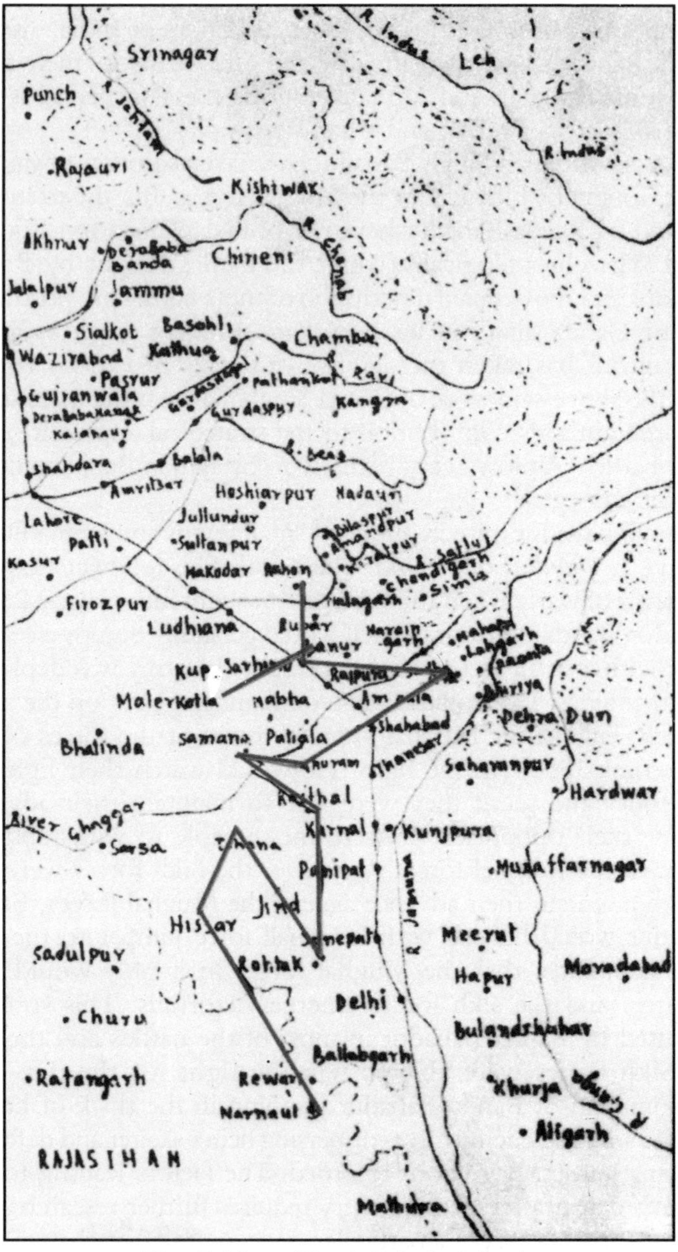

Plate 7: Map of Banda Bahadur's battles

FROM BANGAR (HISSAR) TO SIRHIND

Banda Bahadur, after becoming a disciple of Guru Gobind Singh, moved to the Guru's camp.[1] He was given an insight about the situation in Punjab *vis-à-vis* the Sikhs and the Mughals, and presumably some instructions deemed necessary by Guru Gobind Singh to be followed by Banda as and when situations so required. The directions given by the Guru to Banda Bahadur were only between the two and there was nobody else privy to it. Historians have given varying accounts as to what the Guru told Banda Bahadur. Since there is no contemporary record or even oral evidence of anybody privy to the instructions, though there are varying accounts of it but none can be credited with any historical authenticity.[2] Banda was given five advisors, who had been senior Sikhs with Guru Gobind Singh and about 20 soldiers. Shortly after Banda Bahadur left for the Punjab in October 1708, he got news of the sad demise of Guru Gobind Singh at the hands of a fanatic assassin from Sirhind.[3] Banda took extreme precautions to avoid contact with the Mughal espionage network and a distance of about 1,600 km was covered in a year's time, which ordinarily could have been covered easily in three months. He took circuitous routes and reached the town of Kharkhauda about 30 km away from Delhi, the Mughal capital.[4]

Banda Bahadur tried to settle down and study the various aspects of the situation regarding his resolve to teach a lesson to the rulers of Sirhind who had carried out large-scale atrocities on the Sikhs and executed the two younger sons of Guru Gobind Singh aged nine and seven. He became popular with the local people by giving them blessings of *Dudh Put* (Milk and Son) to the locals who came to seek his blessings.[5] He found that professional gangs of dacoits were in the habit of raiding and looting nearby prosperous villages of Bangar area (Hissar). These dacoits at times used to give warnings of their attack and rich people would generally vacate their houses leaving it to the mercy of the dacoits.[6]

On one such occasion, Banda Bahadur encouraged the elders of the village to stay back and face the dacoits, but the city fathers were not prepared to accept his advice. Banda Bahadur locked them up in a house on the night of the attack.[7]

Banda Bahadur found out that the dacoits assemble in a closeby mangrove and from there attacked the village after allotting positions to the various members of the gang. Before the arrival of the dacoits, Banda Bahadur put his men on tree tops, behind bushes, etc., at the place they used to assemble. The instructions given to his men were to jump down upon the dacoits just as they were preparing to attack the village. Banda Bahadur's attack was so sudden and bold that the dacoits were thrown into confusion, their leader was captured and those who had come to rescue him were either captured or killed.[8] Banda Bahadur released the city fathers now and ordered the hunting down of the robbers till they were eliminated.[9]

Banda Bahadur thus gained the sympathy and confidence of the villagers. He now publicly proclaimed that he would undertake to protect the poor and the helpless against all professional robbers and official tyrants, and for that he expected nothing, in lieu of the service rendered except some simple ration of life like milk, curd, etc.[10] He also invited people to join the Khalsa brotherhood and promised them a share in the booty and the conquered land.[11]

Banda Bahadur now dispatched the Guru's letters to the Sikhs in Malwa, Doaba and the Majha districts of the Punjab calling upon them to join him in the laudable object of uprooting the tyrannous Mughals.[12] His companions from Nanded as well wrote a large number of letters to the leading Sikhs all over the country telling them that Banda Bahadur had been appointed by the Guru himself as Jathedar of the Khalsa and called upon every true Sikh to join under his banner.[13]

The first town to be attacked was Sonepat by a small force of about 500 Sikhs. The *faujdar* of Sonepat was ill-prepared to oppose the advancing Sikhs and he was soon routed and made to flee from the field.[14]

Banda Bahadur received information that a small military detachment escorting a box of revenue collections from a number of districts was halting at village Bhuna, on their way to Delhi. He along with with his men immediately reached the village and overpowered the Mughal force guarding the treasure and took possession of it without any opposition.[15] The raid of Banda Bahadur on the imperial treasury was reported to the *amil* of

Kaithal, a Hindu commander, who at once hurried to the site with his troops. Banda Singh and his men had by then hid themselves behind some old walls, trees, etc. At the opportune moment when they found that the enemy could be successfully taken by surprise, they rushed out of the hiding places, leapt at their horses and threw many of them off horses. The *amil* was also captured. He was, however, released on the condition of handing over all his horses and weapons to the Sikhs to which he readily agreed.[16] He was allowed to retain his office on behalf of the Khalsa on payment of requisite tribute and a detachment of Sikh soldiers was detailed for collection of revenue.[17] The *amil* of Kaithal to pay tribute and a Khalsa detachment to help collection of revenue, was the first administrative measure in setting up of a Sikh State.

Banda Bahadur who was now running short of funds distributed liberally the entire booty amongst his followers.[18] The Sikhs were now preparing to attack Samana. This was a town occupied by a number of 'Sayyads' and 'Mughal *zamindars*'. Jalal-ud-din, the executioner of Guru Tegh Bahadur, Shashal Begh and Bashal Begh, the executioners of young sons of Guru Gobind Singh also resided here.[19]

The town of Samana was well fortified with a strong wall and every *haveli* (large house) was a fortress by itself. On the morning of 26 November 1709, Banda Bahadur and his men suddenly rushed into the town from a distance of about 10 miles and entered it from all sides with such suddenness that the gates could not be closed for them.[20] This strategy paid a rich dividend in the form of saving many a Sikhs' lives, which could have been lost had the gates been closed before the attack. In the attack of the Sikhs on the *havelis*, the desperate and infuriated peasants of the neighbouring villages also joined the Sikhs to wreak vengeance on the much hated Mughals, and set their houses on fire. Before nightfall, the beautiful town of Samana, with its lofty buildings, was converted into a heap of ruins never to regain its past glory.[21] About 10,000 lives are said to have been lost, majority of them being Mughals.

Banda Bahadur, greatly impressed by the bravery of Bhai Fateh Singh, appointed him the *faujdar* of Samana. Samana has generally been called by historians as the first regular conquest of Banda Bahadur.[22] Wazir Khan of Sirhind was greatly alarmed at the Sikh invasions and had sent some spies to Samana to gather information. These spies were caught and brought before Banda Bahadur. He ordered them to be given a good shoe-beating and then sent back to Wazir Khan.[23]

The contemporary historian Khafi Khan has written:

> In two or three months' time, four to five thousand pony-riders, and seven to eight thousand warlike footmen joined Banda Bahadur. Day by day their number increased, and abundant money and material by pillage fell into their hands. Soon eighteen to nineteen thousand men in arms under him raised aloft the standard of plunder and persecution.[24]

He goes on to say, 'Numerous villages were laid waste, and he appointed his own police officers (*thanedars*) and collectors of revenue (*tahsildar-e-mal*).'[25]

Next came the town of Ghuram, which was plundered and put under the charge of Bhai Fateh Singh, the *faujdar* of Samana.[26] Thaska surrendered without offering any resistance.[27] The next towns to be seized were Thanesar and Shahbad, inhabited by the Mughal Sayyads and Shaikhs, but none dared to oppose the Sikhs. After these, the town of Mustafabad came in the way of Sikh troops.

The local *faujdar* had 2,000 imperial troops and two large guns. On the appearance of artillery, many of the gangs of plunderers who had started following Banda Bahadur for the prospects of booty deserted him. Banda Bahadur encouraged and rallied his brave Sikhs and made so desperate an attack that the Mohammedan soldiers fled leaving their canons behind them.[28] After this victory, several of the deserters returned and joined Banda Bahadur's army.

Banda Bahadur was now moving towards the next bigger town of Sadhaura and the town of Kapuri which was ruled by Qadam-ud-din. There was hardly a pretty Hindu woman whose chastity had been spared by this depraved ruler.[29] He is also said to have forcibly carried away a Sikh woman from the city of Amritsar by entering her house in the disguise of a Sikh.[30]

The passions of the Sikh volunteer force having been greatly aroused by the misdeeds of Qadam-ud-din, they fell upon Kapuri, overpowered the resistance offered by its residents and set on fire the strongholds of Qadam-ud-din. Who is said to have perished in the general conflagration.[31]

Banda Bahadur's next expedition was against Sadhaura. Its ruler Usman Khan was notorious for the oppression of his subjects.[32] He was the same person who had tortured to death the great Muslim saint Sayyad Badr-ud-din Shah, popularly known as Sayyad Buddhu Shah, whose family members and followers were also given the same treatment and none was allowed to be buried and all were burnt, simply because he had helped Guru Gobind Singh in the battle of Bhangani against the Hindu hill rajas.[33] The Hindus were subjected to every kind of indignity, even their dead were not allowed to be burnt.[34] Sadhaura is a corrupted form of Sadhuwara, or the abode of *sadhus*, which in the days of Buddhist ascendancy was one of their holy places.[35] Macauliffe has stated that Sikh forces fought with great bravery, captured the fort and levelled it to the ground. This does not seem to be correct. Macauliffe has stated that 'Banda Bahadur attacked Sadhaura fort and the Imperial forces stationed there came forth to oppose them but were easily defeated. They fled and took shelter behind the city walls. Banda Bahadur's forces, with great bravery, captured the fort and levelled it to the ground.'[36] Had there been a fort he would have used it rather than wasting his time and energy in destroying it. The statement of Macauliffe seems to be incorrect. Ganda Singh, Sohan Singh, M.S. Ahluwalia, H.R. Gupta, Gokul Chand Narang and H.K. Sagoo have not mentioned the existence of any fort at Sadhaura while writing about the attack and occupation of Sadhaura by the Sikhs. M.S. Chandla quotes Sukhdial Singh that 'the *haveli* of Pir Buddhu Shah had become a *Qatal Garhi*. The fort and the *haveli* were reduced to a smoking rubble and the animals like horses and camels were captured by the Singhs.' This statement is incorrect, as no fort can be burnt down and the said *haveli* was standing till recently and the place is used as a Jain High School. The town of Sadhaura has been examined on a number of occasions. What seems to be the ground position is that there may have been a wall around the town for general security purposes, but no fort existed as no foundations, etc., thereof are visible.

After the occupation of the Sadhaura town, Banda Bahadur seems to have made some entrenchments close to the town for use of his troops from where the Sikhs fought the Mughal army in 1710 and 1711.

With the advance of Banda Bahadur's army on Sadhaura, the peasants all around who had been bullied and harassed by Usman Khan and his officials got an opportunity to seek revenge against them and they joined Banda Bahadur in great numbers to loot and destroy the properties of the rich Sayyads and Sheikhs. Bloody battles ensued between the masses and the Sayyads and Sheikhs to an extent that it was not possible for Banda Bahadur and his soldiers to stop the same.[37] They also located the rich Sayyads and Sheikhs who had hidden themselves in the *haveli* of Shah Badr-ud-din believing it to be a safe place, and put them to death. The *haveli* till today is called *Qatal Garhi* or slaughter house.[38]

Another story goes that a couple of Sikhs were having difficulty in taming their camel. They saw a fellow going with a strong *lathi*, took his *lathi* and gave a few blows to the camel. The *lathi* broke and lot of letters fell out of it. These letters had been written by all the important Muslim residents to Wazir Khan to come and attack the Sikhs and save them from disgrace and indignity.[39]

Banda Bahadur called a meeting of all the prominent Muslim leaders, showed them these letters, which made each one begging for mercy. Banda Bahadur is said to have told them to get into one house. All the rich Muslims went into the *haveli* of Badr-ud-din, which has an enclosed area of about an acre or so. Banda Bahadur then let the local populace to kill all the people assembled in the *haveli* and hence the place has been called Qatal Garhi till today.

The building has how been taken over by a Hindu organization which demolished to it build a school. The outer gate and walls all around alone are standing till date. The version of both Sukhdyal Singh and M.S. Chandla are not correct when they say that the Sikhs had burnt down the *haveli* of Pir Buddhu Shah.[40] These sites have been closely examined and the correct position stated. The allegation that Sikhs destroyed the old mausoleums and burnt the dead bodies is totally incorrect as the mausoleums of Ganj-i-Ilam and Qutab-ul-Aqtab stand intact to the present day in the same condition in which these were before Banda Bahadur's invasion.[41]

The Hindus of Chhat complained to Banda Bahadur that they were being greatly harassed by the Muslim rulers. Banda Bahadur sent a detachment which occupied the small town of Chhat and a Sikh *amil* was posted there.[42] Chhat is close to Banur. Banda was waiting for the Sikh troops from Majha to join him before he was to take the final plunge against Wazir Khan, the *faujdar* of Sirhind. The Sikhs had crossed the Sutlej and reached Kiratpur.

A large number of Sikhs from Doaba and Majha were soon expected to join Banda Singh.[43] Wazir Khan was greatly worried and he was devising ways and means of preventing the combination of the two forces. He sent Sher Mohammad Khan of Maler Kotla along with his brother and cousins with various other resources of warfare to go and stop the Sikhs at Ropar.[44] Majha troops which had reached Ropar were attacked by Sher Mohammad Khan with much greater force than that available with the Sikhs. The battle was going in favour of Pathans due to their better fire power. The Sikh commanders decided to keep their soldiers in the trenches to save themselves from artillery fire.[45] As the day was coming to a close, Sher Mohammad Khan was confident of a decisive victory on the following day.[46] During the night, a fresh batch of Sikh volunteers from north-east came to join them, which redoubled the courage of the Sikh forces. Guru Tegh Bahadur had spent a number of years in the north-east and had a large following of disciples. It was these disciples who had come as volunteers to fight for the Sikh cause. The Sikhs had spent the night in the trenches and early morning they were prepared for a hand to hand fight in which the enemy was no match for the Khalsa.[47] Khizar Khan, brother of Sher Mohammad Khan, was waiting for daybreak, when a bullet fired from the trenches struck him and he went rolling down dead to the ground.[48] The death of Khizar Khan created lot of confusion amongst the Afghan ranks and some of them started running away. Sher Mohammad Khan came out to face the Sikhs. The Sikhs rushed upon their enemy and drove away the Afghans and Ranghars before them. Nashtar Khan and Wali Mohammad Khan were both killed in the scuffle and Sher Mohammad Khan was severely wounded.[49] The Sikhs were now victors of the day. The strategy adopted by the Sikhs in this battle which was not going in their favour till evening, was to spend the night lying in the trenches and be able to take a lead on them in the early morning.

While the Mujhail Sikhs were fighting with the Afghans of Maler Kotla, Banda Bahadur marched upon Banur and occupied the same. The Sikhs were very jubilant and Banda Bahadur's army marched a few miles to receive the Sikh forces coming from the Ropar side. The memorable convergence of the two Sikh forces took place between Kharar and Banur on the Ambala-Ropar road.[50]

BATTLE OF CHHAPARH JHIRI (SIRHIND)

Historians have all along been writing incorrectly Chappar Chiri whereas the land in the area was then and still is full of ponds (*chaparhs*), small and big, and mangroves that had grown up on the banks of the ponds, which are called 'Jhiri' in the local dialect and the correct name for the place is 'Chhaparh Jhiri'.

Banda Bahadur seems to have made some sort of a plan in his mind to consolidate his hold on nearby Muslim towns and large villages around Sirhind, especially those where some executioners of the Gurus and their children were located (see map on p. 212). Banda Bahadur's smaller battles, viz., Banghar dacoits, Sonepat, Kaithal, Samana, Ghuram, Thaska, Thanesar, Shahbad, Kapuri and Sadhaura, etc., helped him to plan for bigger battles, the increase in the strength and field training of his volunteer force, collection of arms and ammunition, etc. The victory of Banda Bahadur in all these battles created a state of helplessness and depression in the ruling Mughal officials who had not experienced such defeats during the past few centuries of Mughal rule.

Wazir Khan had an army of about 20,000 men of all ranks—cavalry, musketeers, archers, artillery and a train of elephants to give battle to the Sikhs and check their advance towards Sirhind, besides the armies of local *mansabdars* and big *zamindars* and the large-scale Ghazi volunteer force of Muslim militants.[51] The Sikh army strength has not been assessed by any contemporary historian, but it was far smaller than the Mughal army. It was mainly a volunteer force assisted by an irregular force interested in booty and plunder only. They stayed on to loot when their side was winning and fled when the side was losing.[52]

Banda Bahadur had chosen a mound with mangroves on both sides and a pond in front with marshy land on the other end. He would generally watch the battle from the raised point and then personally enter the battle as and when it was so required. It was at Chhaparh Jhiri about 25 km outside Sirhind, that the Mughal army came out to face the Sikhs on 22 May 1710.[53] The mound and the mangroves and the *chhaparh* stand till today in memory of the historic fight between the Sikhs and Wazir Khan.

Wazir Khan had a large number of elephants, mounted gunnery, archers, lancers and swordsmen. Banda Bahadur had no elephants, no artillery; his soldiers had long spears, arrows, swords and unbounded courage to avenge the assassination of their Guru's younger sons. Sikh volunteers from Doaba and Majha joined Sikh forces in the evening before the battle. The artillery of Wazir Khan inflicted heavy casualties on the Sikhs. But the Sikhs were able to snatch one of their main guns and thereafter hand to hand fight ensued.[54]

Whenever the Sikhs were feeling the pressure of enemy attack, Banda Bahadur would rush to the forefront. In the words of Sohan Singh, 'Banda rose like a hungry lion and sprang on the enemy like a bolt from the blue, the irresistible Banda Bahadur with a single sally changed the whole scene'.[55] Khafi Khan says, 'Money, horses, elephants fell in the hands of infidels, horsemen and footmen in large numbers fell under the swords of infidels, who pursued them as far as Sirhind, Wazir Khan fell from his horse and was captured alive'.[56] 'Coming face to face with Banda Bahadur, Wazir Khan's head was struck off with one blow by Banda Bahadur', states Macauliffe.[57] The Mughal army ran for their lives leaving behind them a large number of arms and ammunition.

Wazir Khan indulged in a very petty war strategy by sending one mischievous Hindu leader with 1,000 paid men pretending that they had come over to him as they were fed up with the tyranny and injustice of the Nawab. They were actually hired to kill Banda Bahadur for which handsome rewards were to be made.

Banda Bahadur accepted them, allotted them a place amongst his troops knowing fully well that it was a trap laid out for him. They were warned that if they indulged in any treacherous activity they would be punished. Shortly after the start of the battle, these men were noticed to be shifting towards the enemy side. They were suitably punished along with the rest of the Mughal army.[58]

Banda Bahadur and his men carried out the last rites of the fallen Sikhs at the battle site before entering the city. The body of Wazir Khan was hung from a nearby tree upside down and later burnt.[59] The said tree still stands in the compound of a school built at that site.

The victorious Sikh army entered Sirhind on 24 May 1710 and large-scale plundering went on for three days.[60] The plundering was stopped on the fourth day when Banda Bahadur entered Sirhind. He established his own government.[61] Baj Singh was appointed governor of Sirhind. Baba Ali Singh was appointed his Naib (Assistant), Fateh Singh was confirmed in his post as *faujdar* of Samana. Binod Singh and Ram Singh were jointly appointed governors of Thanesar. Hindu officials were appointed in all other subordinate posts in the place of Muslim officials. The Khalsa flag was hoisted on the fort of Sirhind. The battle of Sirhind is considered the first major battle fought and won by the Sikhs against the Mughal forces.

It is a great irony that for Banda Bahadur, the tallest Indian warrior of his times, the Indian nation, the Punjab state and the Sikhs in particular have failed to give him his due place of honour. While monuments and memorials are raised every now and then for the big and the small, there is no memorial set-up so far for this brave son of the Motherland anywhere in India.

The place where the last rites of about 5,000 Sikh volunteer force were performed stands sanctified by the local population guarding the area of about 50 acres alongside the Chhaparh Jhiri, where no cultivation has since been done, nor even cattle allowed to graze; lest the mortal remains of the Sikh martyrs be disturbed. We are reminded of an Urdu couplet that used to be sung during the Independence movement.

Shaheedon ki chitaon par lagenge har bars mele,
watan par mitne walon ka yahi baaki nishan hoga.

INCURSIONS IN THE JAMUNA-GANGA DOAB

Banda Bahadur and his warriors marched on Saharanpur on their way to Jalalabad. Saharanpur was a principal stronghold of bigoted Mohammedans. Ali Hamid Khan was the *faujdar*. He, however, collected his family and valuables and fled to Delhi the same night.[62] The residents put up a stiff resistance but they were no match to the Sikh warriors and were subjected to slaughter and plunder. A large booty fell into the hands of the Sikh soldiers.[63]

The Peerzadas of nearby Behat were notorious fanatics, and it was on the request of the Hindu population, that the Peerzadas were put to the sword.[64]

Sikhs now moved towards Jalalabad and a message was sent to Jalal Khan to release the Sikh prisoners and tender his submission. Jalal Khan insulted the Sikh messengers and turned them out of the town. Since the Sikhs were to pass through Ambehta and Nanauta, they looted these villages. The Gujjar community of Nanauta had become the worshippers of Guru Nanak. The Shaikhzadas of Nanauta put up resistance but they were severely crushed. According to a contemporary writer, 300 Shaikhzadas fell dead in the Shaikh Afzal's courtyard. The prosperous town of Nanauta was a mass of smouldering ruins and the same has been popularly named afterwards as *phoota shahr*.[65] The Sikhs reached Jalalabad and besieged the fort. Since rains had set in and breach of the fort was not possible, the Sikh warriors made a tactical retreat and left Jalalabad.[66] Unfavourable weather and the shortage of resources were responsible for this retreat.

UPRISING IN MAJHA

Haidri Flag Crusade from Lahore

The Sikhs on their own part, were only waiting since the battle of Chamkaur in December 1704 for an opportunity to settle old scores with their persecutors. There was a sudden eruption and the Sikh volcanic lava flowed with such rapidity and force that it drove away all who came in its way, Muslims or Hindus, officials or non-officials.[67]

Sayyed Aslam Khan, the imperial governor of Lahore, was a weak person. He behaved in a most cowardly manner and dared not leave the city to oppose the Sikhs in an open fight.[68] The Muslim religious leaders disappointed with the behaviour of Aslam Khan met near the Idgah Mosque and proclaimed a *jehad* (crusade) against the Sikhs, and their green flag was named 'The Haidri Flag'. The Hindu traders and Muslim in general contributed liberally to this *jehad*. Governor Aslam Khan also deputed Mir Ataullah with a contingent of 500 horses and 1,000 foot-soldiers.[69] The Sikhs turned their attention at first to Batala and Kalanaur. They turned out Muslim government officials and established their own *thanas*. These were rich areas and conquest thereof added much to their resources. Some Sikhs went towards Lahore and ravaged the country up to Shalimar Gardens.[70] Others moved towards Pathankot and occupied the city and its surrounding areas.

The crusaders took the lead under the Haidri flag and proclaimed a *jehad* against the Sikhs. The Sikhs had occupied the small fort named Qila Bhagwant Rai. In a week's time a very large number of crusaders came and besieged the fort. There was immense bloodshed on both sides. As a tactical measure Sikhs moved out of the fort on a particular night cutting through the lines of crusaders and went out of their reach.[71] The *jehadis* were greatly disappointed and went back to Lahore.

The Sikhs once again collected at fort Kotla Begam, a few miles from Lahore, and began their customary ravages. The crusaders in order to cover up their shame at Qila Bhagwant Rai once again marched against fort Kotla Begam ravaging many poor villages all along the way. They came face to face with the Sikhs at the foot of fort Kotla Begam.[72]

The Sikhs came out of their enclosures and a fierce battle ensued. The Sikhs had an upper hand. Panic and confusion gripped the crusaders and everybody was running away and by evening the Mohammedan force melted away into nothingness.[73] On the way back, the crusaders stopped at fort Bhilowal for resting in the night. The regular troops were lodged in the fort and the *jehadis* were in the open all around the fort. The Sikhs were watching their enemy movement and following them. During the night they hid themselves in behind some bushes and trees. Early next morning, the Sikhs came out of their hiding places and attacked the crusaders who could not stand up to this unexpected attack and lost heavily in men and horses.[74] The Sikhs were now in possession of the whole of Majha and Rearki except Lahore city.[75]

BATTLE OF RAHON

The Doaba of Bist Jullundur comprising the present districts of Jullundur and Hoshiarpur, being on the border of the province of Sirhind, which had been conquered and occupied by Banda Bahadur, was the first to be electrified with the spirit of uprising and independence. In a few weeks many of the petty officials in the districts of the Jullundur Doab were turned out and Sikh *tahsildars* and *thanedars* were appointed in their places.[76] Shamas Khan was the *faujdar* of Doaba Bist Jullundur with his capital at Sultanpur. In accordance with the normal practice, Sikhs addressed a letter to Shamas Khan in the form of a *parvana* calling upon him to submit, to carry out certain reforms, and come out to receive them, bringing with him all the amount held in the treasury. Shamas Khan gave an evasive reply to the messenger that he would soon come to meet the Sikhs. Shamas Khan was a clever officer and he proclaimed by beat of drum a *jehad* against the Sikhs. Khafi Khan says that more than a 100,000 men were collected and they marched out of Sultanpur with great display and fanfare. (This number in a fairly small place appears to be exaggerated.) Shamas Khan proceeded against the Sikhs at the head of 4,000 to 5,000 horses and about 30,000 infantry armed with match-locks and other weapons.[77] On hearing of these proceedings and the advance of Shamas Khan with such a large army and equipment of war, the Sikhs moved with all their force numbering 40,000 to 50,000 horse and foot-soldiers.[78] As they came to the town of Rahon, about 7 km from Sultanpur, they occupied the mounds of some old brick kilns lying to the north-west. From here the Sikhs sent out patrols in all directions and issued threatening orders to the Chaudharies, revenue officials and qanungos, calling upon them to submit. When Shamas Khan and the crusaders came close to the Sikhs, about 10,000 to 12,000 balls and stones from slings came all at once rattling like hail upon the forces of Islam. The crusaders were swarming like locusts from all sides and rushing in with the cries of *Allah-u-Akbar*. Shamas Khan warned them against haste and ordered them a steady advance. After two volleys from the Sikhs, the Muslim regulars supported by 40,000 to 50,000 crusaders charged them. The Sikhs were heavily outnumbered therefore they thought it best to retire to the fort of Rahon, which they had previously occupied.[79]

The fort of Rahon was invested for several days. The Sikhs rushed out of it in small parties at night and attacked the besieging forces, inflicting heavy losses upon them in men and horses. But their number was too large to be thinned or affected by these sorties. The Sikhs, therefore, thought of tricking the enemy with tactics peculiar to themselves and in the darkness of the night, they slipped away from their entrenchments. Shamas Khan did not risk a pursuit of them beyond a few miles and was quite content with a gun and some loaded camels and oxen that fell into his hands. Apparently he felt tired and was looking for an opportunity to leave the Sikhs alone, especially since he thought of their being reinforced by the terrible Banda Bahadur, the conqueror of Sadhaura, Sirhind and Saharanpur. He, therefore, ordered the breaking up of the camp and marched away from Rahon before daybreak and returned in triumph to Sultanpur. The crusaders were demobilized and despatched to their homes.[80]

But the Sikhs had not quitted the neighbourhood of Rahon. They were only lurking in the neighbouring bushes. In the morning, only a few hours after the evacuation, a thousand of them rushed upon Rahon and attacked the garrison, placed by Shamas Khan in the *thana* (fort) of Rahon, drove them out, occupied the fort and established themselves therein.[81]

This tactic of war, which is peculiarly a Sikh tactic and has so often been used by them in their wars with the Mughals, the Durranis and the local officials, has generally been misunderstood and misinterpreted as a defeat. Their trick-flights were many a time mistaken for their actual flights and under this impression the enemy followed them up, but they were soon disillusioned on finding the Sikhs turning upon their heels, pouncing upon their pursuers and cutting them down to the last man. It was after such a practical experience that Qazi Noor Mohammad Gunjabavi, the author of the *Jangnamah* warns his co-religionists against this tactic of the Sikhs, and says:

> If defeat befalls their armies,
> take it not as a defeat, oh youth.
> Because it is a war-tactic of theirs.
> Beware beware, of it!
> Their tactic is such that in wreaking vengeance,
> their defeat is changed into victory.
> The army that pursues them is cut-off from reinforcement.
> Then they (the Sikhs) turn upon their heels, and,
> even if their pursuers be 'water', they set fire to it.[82]

Qazi Noor Mohammad usually addressed Sikhs as 'dogs', 'infidels', and even worse, yet his above exposition is an exemplary understanding of the oft-used battle tactics of the Sikhs.

The battle of Rahon was fought on 11 October 1710 and the news reached Emperor Bahadur Shah on 25 October 1710 while he was encamped near Sonepat. In a period of a little over one year, after the arrival of Banda Bahadur in Punjab as the commander of the Sikh forces, the situation had turned into a general Sikh uprising throughout eastern and south-eastern Punjab except the capital city of Lahore. After the occupation of Rahon, the Sikhs moved on to Jullundur. The Pathans of this place were so terrified that they found safety in running away and unwittingly fell into the hands of the Sikhs without any resistance at all from the officials and residents. Hoshiarpur followed suit and like all others of the neighbourhood, its rulers acknowledged the authority of the conquerors. Thus, before long, practically the whole of the Bist Jullundur Doab came under the sway of the Sikhs.

To summarize the whole situation at this stage, it stood thus: there was general Sikh uprising throughout the eastern and south-eastern Punjab, except the city of Lahore which was held by the Imperial Governor. The whole of Majha, the Rearki and Kandi as far as Pathankot lay prostrate at the feet of the Sikhs. Jamuna-Ganga plains had been overrun and to the south of Sutlej, Sikhs had complete mastery over the territory of Sirhind, from Machhiwara to Karnal. They penetrated into the province of Delhi proper and according to Iradat Khan there was no noble man daring enough to march from Delhi against them.

EMPEROR BAHADUR SHAH MARCHES AGAINST SIKHS

'If Bahadur Shah had not quitted the Deccan, which he did in AD 1710 and marched towards the Panjab with all his Imperial forces, there is every reason to think that the whole of Hindustan would have been subdued by these invaders (Sikhs)', says Malcolm in the *Sketch of Sikhs*.[83]

The news of Sikh outbreak under Banda Singh Bahadur was received by Emperor Bahadur Shah on 30 May 1710 while at Ajmer. He had come to Rajputana to reduce the refractory chiefs Raja Jai Singh Kachhwaha and Raja Ajit Singh Rathore. The alarming news from the Punjab changed the situation. Various reports of the newswriters and loud cries of Muslims of Sirhind, Peerzadas of Samana and Sadhaura who had waited on him at Ajmer on 22 June 1710 influenced him to attack the Sikhs.[84]

The popular rising of the Sikhs, very near to the capital, was considered more serious and of far-reaching consequences than the pending quarrel with the Rajputs, who even if left in quiet possession of their hereditary country were not likely to be encouraged to further aggression.

On receipt of the news of the Mughal emperor advancing to Punjab with large armies to crush the Sikh movement, Banda Bahadur became aware of the fact that with his meagre resources of men and materials he could not stand against the Mughal imperial armies led by their emperor. He, therefore, sought help from the Rajputs, who were closer to the Panjab and with whom he had some contacts. It is understood that he contacted Raja Jai Singh of Amber and Raja Ajit Singh of Jodhpur and the ruler of Jawalapur seeking their help. But unfortunately none of the Rajputs, who, though had and grouses against the Mughals were prepared to come to Banda Bahadur.[85]

Bahadur Shah ordered Asad Khan, governor of Delhi, to mobilize an army for immediate advance against the Sikhs. He ordered Khan Dauran of Oudh, Amin Khan, *faujdar* of Moradabad, Khan Jehan, Nazim of Allahabad and Abdullah Khan of Barha to join him in the projected expedition. The emperor also left Ajmer and moved towards Punjab. The imperial army that arrived on 7 August was dispatched against the Sikhs under the command of Feroz Khan Mewati.[86]

Such was the scare that no one in the imperial army was allowed to halt in Delhi, nor any relation allowed to come to the camp. Further, to eliminate any disguised Sikhs amongst the bearded Hindus in the royal camp, an order was issued on 8 September 1710, that all Hindus employed in the imperial offices were to shave off their beards. Hindu officials immediately obeyed the royal orders.[87] The emperor also ordered that an imperial army of 60,000 horsemen be kept ready for action against the Sikhs.

The Sikh forces at this time were distributed all over the country in garrisons and detachments for duties at Sirhind, Samana, Thanesar, Sadhaura, etc. Many were busy in their own areas in Majha, Rearki and Jullundur Doab. Banda Bahadur and his leading officers had moved only a few days earlier against Shamas Khan of Sultanpur. Thus Binod Singh and Ram Singh were to bear the brunt of the battle with the imperial forces.[88]

In the neighbourhood of Chhichhra, the Sikh army was able to drive back the Mughal army under Mahabat Khan. The Sikh forces were greatly outnumbered by the imperial forces commanded by Feroz Khan Mewati and were defeated. The dead and dying Sikhs were treated with every indignity. Carts loaded with 300 heads of Sikhs were sent to the emperor.[89] The Sikhs retired from Thanesar and retreated towards Sadhaura to fall back on Lohgarh if necessary.

Bayzid Khan with Shamas Khan and Umar Khan marched against the Sikhs in Sirhind. The Sikhs being greatly outnumbered retired to the fort of Sirhind. The emperor ordered the siege of the fort for which a force was dispatched. The fort then fell into the hands of Shamas Khan and he dispatched the heads of 300 Sikhs killed in the battle to the emperor, which were received at Sadhaura.[90]

THE BATTLES OF SADHAURA AND LOHGARH: JUNE 1710 TO DECEMBER 1711

Historians and newswriters now started calling Banda Bahadur a 'great magician'. This had a very depressing effect on the emperor and his commanders.

On 4 December 1710 Rustam Dil Khan and other commanders moved towards Sadhaura fort to face the Sikhs. They were faced with a shower of arrows, rockets and musket balls. According to Khafi Khan

> The Sikhs in their faqir dress struck terror in the royal troops. The number of dead and dying of imperial troops was so large that for a time it seemed that they were losing ground. The nephew of Feroze Khan Mewati was killed and his son wounded. Most of the Rustam Dil Khan's followers could not stand the on-rush and were scattered.[91]

But soon after rest of the imperial troops arrived and outnumbered the Sikhs. Kamwar Khan, the author of *Tazkirat-i-Salatin-i-Chughtaiya* was then present with the troops and saw that everyone of the cursed Sikhs came out of the entrenchment, challenged the imperial troops and after a great struggle and trial fell under the swords of the Ghazis. During the night, the Sikhs retreated towards the eastern mountains and fell back upon the fort of Lohgarh on 5 December 1710.[92]

The strength of the Mughal armies, both the Mughal Imperial Army and the armies of the various other governors and generals taken together were approximately 2 lakh combatants, horsemen, 1 lakh or so non-combatant camp followers, etc. As against this strength the fighting force of the Sikhs which could be collected at this short notice was less than 15,000 horsemen and footman.

The Mughal armies now moved on to the other bank of Som *nadi* (rainy season water stream) facing Lohgarh. The rivulet was running very low on water due to it being winter. The emperor also arrived at the site on 9 December 1710, and set-up his camp close to Lohgarh which was built atop a small hill.[93] The fort was filled up with over 60,000 imperial troops, horses and foot-soldiers, reinforced by a large number of plunderers and others. Lohgarh was considered so strong and inaccessible by the Mughals

Plate 8: Standing tower at Sadhaura.

that Bahadur Shah did not attack the Sikhs in their fortress and resolved to seem inactive for some time to tempt them to an engagement. When Munim Khan arrived within a shot of their entrenchments the Sikhs began a cannonade from their works while bodies of their infantries on various heights behind 4 ft high walls rained with rockets, musketry, and arrows. The *wazir* more out of jealousy of his military fame than fear of the emperor's displeasure ventured for once to disobey the imperial orders and ordered an attack. When some of the Mughal officials went close to the mud-fort, a cannonball from a tamarind tree on the top of a hillock threw the group in disorder.[94]

At the time of evening prayer, Munim Khan sure of having the Sikh chief in his power, ordered his troops to cease the attack and to lie upon their arms in their present position till morning should enable them to finish it with success. He left Rustam Dil Khan and his troops to surround the hill and the fort of Lohgarh and returned to the Royal Camp to report to the emperor the course of events. The besieged Sikhs had no stores of foods and fodder in the fort of Lohgarh and they feared to be reduced to great extremities in no time. From the top of their fort they bargained with signs of their hands and eyes with the grain dealers of the royal armies and bought what they could from them at Rs. 2-3 a seer of grain. They threw their sheets from above and pulled them up with ropes.[95]

Banda Bahadur decided to move out of the Lohgarh Fort on the night of 11 December 1710. An explosion of a cannon made out of a hollow tamarind tree trunk which was filled with gun powder and was blown to pieces as they were just about to retreat. The Mughal soldiers lying low for the morning to come did not obstruct the marching out of the Lohgarh Fort by Banda Bahadur and his troops in the middle of the night and escaping towards the mountains of the Barfi Raja of Nahan.[96]

In the morning when the Mughal commanders with their soldiers arrived at the fort, to their utter dismay, they found total silence and inside the fort were about a dozen injured persons and the alleged Gulab Singh besides some five elephants, three pieces of cannons and some silver pots, etc., The five elephants mentioned above also seem to be a fictional concoction as the Sikh armies in the period of Banda Bahadur never had elephants.

The area was extensively dug up to search out some hidden treasure and it is said that about Rs. 8 lakh were recovered. This assessment is an exaggeration as the amount realized at the time of each and every battle was distributed among the soldiers and only a very small amount was kept for contingencies. When this news was conveyed to the emperor, he was greatly displeased and disappointed with some of his commanders. He is said to have chastised his commanders thus: 'a pack of wild hounds could not catch a jackal?'. The emperor dismantled his camp and proceeded towards Lahore via Ropar, Hoshiarpur, etc.[97]

Note: The accounts of almost all historians suffer from factual inaccuracies with regard to the existing ground position of the fort and its surroundings. The story of the fall of Sadhaura and Lohgarh as narrated above taken primarily from Mughal news reports of Khafi Khan and Kamwar Khan said to be present with the troops, suffers from various inaccuracies and distortions. The Sadhaura and Lohgarh sites have been examined by the author a number of times during the last five years, in connection with the committee formed by Shiromani Gurdwara Parbandhak Committee, Amritsar, for the establishment of a memorial of Banda Bahadur at these sites. The author was appointed convenor of that committee and hence had to examine these two places from various aspects and the recorded historical accounts of the battles. The various inaccuracies and distortions are as under:

1. Macauliffe has stated that Banda Bahadur's forces fought with great bravery and captured the fort at Sadhaura and levelled it to the ground. However, besides a couple of historians who have mentioned about the fort, no other historian has shared the views of Macauliffe. If any fort existed it would have been put to use by the Sikh forces and the question of destroying it would amount to destroying a useful defence asset.
2. When Banda Bahadur occupied Sadhaura, there was no fort as such made by the Mughal authorities at Sadhaura. It could be that there was a wall around the city, but no signs of it remains. There are ruins of an old abandoned fort slightly

away from the town which obviously belonged to the early centuries of Hindu period. It is likely that Sikh forces had dug some trenches as it is recorded that they would come out of these trenches and fight bravely with the Mughals.

3. The statement that the emperor's camp had within its sight the Lohgarh Fort on a high summit, is incorrect. Even today, standing on the partly standing walls of the fort, the Som *nadi* and its opposite bank are not visible and the situation being talked of is 300 years old when the forests were very dense as compared to the present times when large-scale deforestation has taken place.
4. The Lohgarh Fort being called a mud-fort by the newswriters is incorrect as all the walls of this fort have been built with one side chiselled stone with the chiselled side facing the outside. There are absolutely no sign of any white building or ruins of a building that could be visible from the royal camp. In fact, even at present and in broad daylight, the remains of the fort are not visible from the bank of Som *nadi*.
5. There is no fort at Sitaragarh but only remains a thatched hut with stone walls from where Banda Bahadur used to survey the entire area and the position of the Mughal troops. The top of the Sitaragarh is 1 km away from the Lohgarh Fort as the crow flies, but to this date spoken words from Sitaragarh are heard at Lohgarh and likewise from Lohgarh to Sitaragarh owing to some acoustic phenomenon. This phenomenon has been explained by Christiaan Huyens (1629-95), a Dutch astronomer and founder of the wave theory of light. This phenomenon can be seen in sound waves also. The sound wave of our speech has a wavelength of 50 cm to 1 m. In case it meets an obstacle of the size of a few metres, it bends around it and reaches the point behind the obstacle. But when it comes across a large-sized obstacles few hundred metres high, it is reflected back and is heard as an echo. This phenomenon can be observed in some forts in Rajasthan also. [*Textbook of Physics*, NCERT, New Delhi, 2007, p. 353.]
6. The Mughal forces moved from Sadhaura to Lohgarh area from 7 December with the emperor reaching the bank of Som *nadi* near Lohgarh on 9 December 1710. There was no

difficulty in the way of Sikh forces to collect rations, etc., up to 6 December. The Sikhs left Lohgarh on the night of 10 December 1710. The stay of the main body of Sikh troops from Sadhaura was only for three days at Lohgarh. The statement that the besieged Sikhs had no stores of food and fodder in the fort of Lohgarh and they feared to be reduced to great extremities in no time is an incorrect and frivolous statement. There was no pressure on Sikh troops at Lohgarh and the lines of communication had remained open till 6 December 1710. Moreover, the Sikh troops always kept emergency ration of roasted grams which would be enough for them and their horses for a couple of days. The story that they bargained with the grain dealers of the royal army and bought what they could from them for Rs. 2 to 3 a seer of grain, is fictional in view of the existing situation.

7. The story of Gulab Singh, a trader, who volunteered to wear the clothes of Banda Bahadur and move on the ramparts so that Banda Bahadur and his troops could walk out of the fort in incognito is incorrect. In the month of December in a jungle it becomes dark by 5 p.m., hence Gulab Singh moving on the ramparts could not be visible to the Mughal emperor and his commanders. The story is a pure concoction. Banda Bahadur has nowhere in all the battles with Mughal forces ever used such a tactic of leaving behind another person to die imitating him, to facilitate his escape. In case he used Gulab Singh to escape from Lohgarh, he would as well have similarly escaped from Gurdas Nangal. Use of such a tactic was not at all in the nature of Banda Bahadur.
8. Sikh armies during Banda Bahadur's time had kept only horses or may be a few camels, but there has been no reference anywhere of elephants having been kept. As such finding, five elephants in Lohgarh is a fanciful reconstruction.

On the morning of 11 December 1710, the Mughal commanders went to the fort to arrest Banda Bahadur and his forces, but found to their dismay, that they had already left Lohgarh Fort the previous night and found only a few wounded Sikhs and some families of a nearby village who had taken shelter were there. Taking the wounded Sikhs as prisoners, the Mughal commanders and nobles with their heads hanging down in shame came to the emperor.[98] Orders were issued on the same day to the Rajas (zamindars of Srinagar and Nahan) calling upon them to seize the Sikh leader and dispatch him to the royal presence.[99] The emperor, his movement hampered by rains, reached Ropar on 30 April and Lahore on 11 August 1711.[100]

Banda Bahadur conquered and set-up a Sikh state over a vast area in over a year's time. The same was, however, taken back by the Mughals in three months' time. The Mughal Emperor Bahadur Shah reached Lahore in June 1711, but died due to some brain disorder in February 1712. The battle of succession amongst the claimants for the throne and the weak rule of Jahandar Shah gave another opportunity to Banda Bahadur to reoccupy Sadhaura and Lohgarh and its surrounding territories in the first half of 1712. Sadhaura and Lohgarh were made ready to face a second attack by the Mughal imperial forces in the first half of 1713.

SUBMISSION OF HILL CHIEFS TO BANDA BAHADUR

Battles of Bahrampur, Batala, etc.

The escape of Banda Bahadur and the Sikhs and the evacuation of the fort of Lohgarh cannot be considered a defeat for the Sikhs. Rather it was a defeat for the emperor and his marauding forces, whose every effort to capture or kill the Sikh leader had hopelessly failed. In fact, Banda Bahadur escaped, sword in hand, cutting through the lines of over 60,000 horse and foot.[101] He had, of course, conquered six districts of the Punjab from Panipat to Lahore, but it was purely a military occupation and not mastery over that area. Banda Bahadur was, however, not dejected by the loss of his stronghold and territories. These, he knew, were not the main sources of his strength.[102] His strength lay mainly in the indomitable spirit of the Khalsa, on whom, he knew, he could safely depend.[103] Within a fortnight of the departure from Lohgarh, he had issued *hukamnamas* to the Khalsa throughout the country calling them to join him at once.[104] Immediately on receipt of Banda Bahadur's letters, Sikhs from all parts of Punjab assembled at Kiratpur.

Raja Bhim Chand of Kahlur had been a source of great annoyance to Guru Gobind Singh. A *parvana* as usual was sent to him to submit to the Khalsa.[105] Bhim Chand started securing help from neighbouring leading zamindars and other hill rajas and strengthened the fortress of Bilaspur. His main force were the 1,300 *mians*. In the Sikh attack, most of the *mians* were killed.[106] They were buried in thirteen ditches. The town yielded an immense booty to the Sikhs. The defeat of Bhim Chand unnerved most of the Rajput chieftains of Shivalik hills and they readily came to the Sikhs, offered their allegiance and paid *nazrana* and tribute in the Sikh treasury.[107] The next to fall in line was Raja Sidh Sain of Mandi. Here Guru Gobind Singh had stayed for some time and a large gurdwara has been built on the river bank and some relics of the Guruji are preserved therein.

Raja Bhup Parkash was arrested by the Mughals and brought to the Royal camp on 22 December 1710. According to Khafi Khan, Bhup Parkash (Barfi Raja) was sent to Delhi in an iron cage for his not being able to catch Banda Bahadur. Mughal sappers excavated various places in the Lohgarh Fort for hidden treasure. It is alleged that they were able to locate a total wealth of Rs. 8 lakh and gold *mohars*. This seems to be a morale boosting exaggeration as most of the booty collected by Sikh forces was distributed among the Khalsas immediately on its receipt. Emperor Bahadur Shah reached Ropar on 17 March 1711 and reached Lahore on 11 August 1711.

From Mandi, Banda Bahadur proceeded towards Kullu and the story goes that he fell in the hands of Raja Man Singh of Kullu. The Raja imprisoned him in a cage, probably with a view to hand him over to the Mughal Emperor Bahadur Shah. Banda Bahadur in the meantime managed to escape and made his way to Mandi.[108] This story does not seem to be true as Banda Bahadur had his forces with him and when he went to Chamba from Mandi via Kullu, he had a sizeable number of Sikh force with him who were left behind at the Kotla Fort when Banda Bahadur went to Chamba with a few of his confidantes. The story that Banda's army stayed here for some months in Kotla Fort during a visit to Chamba, on top of a hill near Nurpur, is widely prevalent amongst the locals. Hence, the story of his having been arrested by the Raja of Kullu seems to be a fabrication. During his stay in Chamba, Banda Bahadur married a Chamba girl, and a son Ajit Singh was born to them towards end of year 1711 at Riasi where he was camping. In the beginning of February/March 1711, that is within three months of the fall of Lohgarh, Banda Bahadur came to Raipur and Bahrampur and began to extend his influence in the direction of Gurdaspur.[109] Bayzid Khan, *faujdar* of Jammu was near Raipur. His nephew Shamas Khan had also come there to him. On the news of the appearance of the Sikhs in the area, 1,500 horses were gathered in a haste for the protection of Raipur. Bayzid Khan and Shamas Khan moved out at the head of 900 horse, and having gone half-way they started indulging in hunting, etc., rather than preparing to fight with the Sikhs.[110]

Shamas Khan went out to meet the Sikhs, but was easily tricked by them with their old Rahon tactics. It seems that they pretended to flee at the sight of Shamas Khan, who, in spite of the warning of his uncle Bayzid Khan hastened to pursue them at close quarters. They had not gone very far when the Sikhs, all of a sudden, sharply turned upon their heels and pounced upon their pursuers.

In an instant a fierce battle ensued and the Mohammedans were driven back line by line, leaving heaps of them dead and wounded. When Bayzid Khan and Shamas Khan saw that scales were turning against them they rushed to oppose the advancing Sikhs under Baj Singh and others. Baj Singh and Fateh Singh came out to meet them. Shamas Khan was wounded and he rushed towards Baj Singh with a naked sword. Baj Singh received the sword upon his shield and gave him so heavy a blow that Shamas Khan's sword fell down from his hands. Pahar Singh fell upon Shamas Khan before he could attack Baj Singh a second time, and so strongly hit him that his head rolled on the ground. Bayzid Khan was also mortally wounded and died a few days later.[111]

With the fall of their leaders, confusion spread in the Muslim ranks and they took to their heels. With great difficulty they were able to get the bodies of Shamas Khan and Bayzid Khan. The whole of the camp equipage of *faujdar* of Jammu and Shamas Khan fell in the hands of the Sikhs who overran the town of Raipur and Bahrampur and advanced on the parganas of Kalanaur and Batala.[112]

Banda Bahadur arrived at the Tank of Achal, 2 *kos* to the east of Batala, and on the following day turned his attention to the city. The inhabitants shut the gates and prepared themselves for its defence. Shaikh-ul-Hind with his followers went out of Hathi Gate to meet Banda Bahadur. He put up a bold fight, but was overpowered and slain. The Sikh forces broke open the gates and entered the city. Part of the city including many palatial buildings perished in the fire.[113]

Banda Bahadur desired to advance towards Lahore, but having come to know that he was being followed by the Mughal army, he sacked Aurangabad and Pasrur.

Mohd. Amin Khan and Rustam Dil Khan combined their forces and encircled Banda Bahadur on three sides. Banda Bahadur, by his fertile mind in expedients, extricated himself without any loss. He kept moving on their outskirts and avoided direct confrontation. When he had given them a slip, he suddenly sailed forth from the opposite side near Parol and Kathua, and fell upon the troops of Rustam Dil Khan. All efforts of Rustam Dil Khan failed to stem the tide of the advancing Sikhs. They would cut through Mughal lines and escape unhurt massacring imperial troops and destroying everything that came their way.[114]

Rustam Dil Khan could not take his defeat and perpetuated extreme excesses against the civil population of Parol and Kathua giving them to his soldiers in lieu of pay, who would, in turn, sell them in the horse market of Lahore.[115]

An imperial order was issued for the wholesale massacre of Sikhs. This gave the mad fanatics an official encouragement for their excesses which now know no bounds. The oppression was carried out most indiscriminately and many people were murdered and persecuted on charges of being Sikhs or their supporters and sympathizers, as has been reported in *Tarikh-i-Muhammad Shahi*. The emperor re-published the royal *farman* calling upon all the Hindus in the royal camp to shave off their beards. The hair and the beard were considered to be the only visible distinction between the Sikhs and Hindus. The Sikhs would under no circumstances, even under pain of death, cut or shave off their beards.[116]

Bahadur Shah reached Lahore on 23 June 1711. He did not reside in the fort, but set-up his camp at Anwala near the bank of river Ravi.[117] He had developed some mental ailment and his health started failing and his decisions became more and more erratic. He expired on 28 February 1712.[118] The Bahadur Shah's death was followed by the usual struggle for the throne amongst his sons from 14 to 17 March 1712. Azim-us-Shan's elephant being wounded by a cannonball threw itself down into the Ravi where the prince and the animal were swallowed up by quicksand. Ultimately, Jahandar Shah having surprised and slain his remaining brothers, Jahan Shah and Rafi-us-Shan in a battle fought on 27-8 March 1712 ascended the Mughal throne on 29 March 1712.[119]

The period of struggle for the imperial throne and the disturbed state of affairs at Lahore and Delhi from February 1712 till the summer of 1713 when Abdul Samad Khan laid siege of Sadhaura was extremely favourable for the re-establishment of the power of the Khalsa.[120] Banda Bahadur had reappeared in the neighbourhood of Bahrampur, killing Shamas Khan and mortally wounding his uncle Bayzid Khan, the *faujdar* of Jammu. The Khalsa army overran the parganas of Kalanaur and Batala.[121]

After the death of Bahadur Shah, Mohd. Amin Khan returned to Lahore to take part in the struggle for succession. Banda Bahadur availed himself of the opportunity and occupied Sadhaura without any loss of time. After capturing Sadhaura, the fort of Lohgarh was repaired and made usable.[122] The agility with which he moved about in the craggy mountains was remarkable.

Siege of Sadhaura and Lohgarh

After Jahandar Shah took over as the Mughal emperor, Amin Khan and Zain-ud-din Khan, *faujdar* of Sirhind, were sent back to continue campaign against the Sikhs. Besides the imperial army, whatever troops that could be spared from the nearby area were also sent. For several months, these two commanders maintained a close siege of Sadhaura and Lohgarh Fort, but they failed to make any effect on the besieged Sikh troops and the half-hearted repeated attacks were repulsed by the Sikh forces. In December 1712, Jahandar Shah moved towards Agra to oppose the advance of Farrukh Siyar. Amin Khan and his troops were withdrawn and the expedition against the Sikhs remained virtually suspended.[123]

Jahandar Shah was defeated in January 1713 and murdered in February 1713.[124] The reign of Farrukh Siyar which began with a series of murders and famine in north India has been a notorious period for the most cruel policies adopted against the Sikhs.[125]

Banda Bahadur made use of the lull in fighting and to raise a fort of sufficiently large size close to the town of Sadhaura. Besides maintaining his position against the opposing *faujdar* of Sirhind, he had got a deep trench dug around the fort and a 10 ft high mud-wall raised from the dug-out earth and filled the trench with water from a nearby canal. He had also raised four 35 ft high towers at all the four corners to watch the movements of the Mughal forces. In the battle of Sadhaura in July 1713, three watchtowers were demolished, but the fourth escaped demolition and stands intact to this day.[126]

The fighting spirit of the Sikh garrison in the Sadhaura Fort was remarkable. They would continue to fire upon their enemy even while they were cooking and eating. Zain-ud-din brought a heavy gun in position and opened incessant fire on the Sikhs. The Sikh garrison, resolved to remove this gun. They dug out a tunnel exactly opposite the position where the gun stood. On a dark rainy night, where nothing could be seen, the Sikhs found their opportunity to drag away the gun. At midnight they pierced through the remaining wall before the earlier passage. Some Sikh soldiers swam across the moat, and reached the gun. They tied a rope firmly around the gun carriage and came back to their own positions. The cannon was getting pulled towards their side when unfortunately the ropes broke off and the gun carriage fell apart causing a large noise. The besiegers were really surprised as to where the gun had gone. After much search, the gun was located lying in the ditch. Zain-ud-din collected couple of hundred followers who were given Rs. 50 each to pull out the gun to a place of safety.[127] This example shows the spirit with which the

Khalsa volunteer force was fighting against the Mughal empire.

After securing himself on the throne of Delhi, Farrukh Siyar directed his attention to the affairs of Punjab. He appointed Samad Khan as governor of Punjab on 22 February 1713 and his son Zakaria Khan as *faujdar* of Jammu. The directions from the emperor to Samad Khan were 'to expel Banda from Sadhaura, or if possible, to destroy him altogether'.[128]

When Samad Khan arrived at Sadhaura, the siege laid by Zain-ud-din Khan had not made any progress. Banda himself was at Lohgarh and his main force at Sadhaura. The combined forces of Samad Khan and other Mughal commanders surrounded the fort of Sadhaura from all sides.[129]

To give support to the troops at Sadhaura, Banda Bahadur sent out three or four sections every other day or even on successive days. When the besieged Sikh army saw the arrival of Sikh troops from Lohgarh, they would rush out on all four sides and boldly strike the Mughal armies and cut down many a Mughal soldiers. But these attacks were not making any major effect on the Mughal armies. When the stores of ammunition and food stocks were getting depleted, Banda Bahadur, once again decided to withdraw his forces to Lohgarh. In the first week of October 1713, the Sikh forces, in the middle of a dark night, rushed out and made a determined sally upon the Zamindari militia. The hired levies could not stand against the death defying Sikh warriors. The desperate Khalsa cut through their lines and escaped with very little loss.[130]

During the long siege, when Banda Bahadur sent Sikh forces to relieve those at Sadhaura, a division of the imperial troops was sent to oppose them. The fight cost the life of imperial commander Baqa Beg Khan and large number of his troops.[131]

Abd-us-Samad Khan and Zain-ud-din Khan followed the Sikhs to Lohgarh and were surprised to see the elaborate preparations for resistance.

The Sikhs had made fifty-two defensive entrenchments all around the Lohgarh Fort. These entrenchments with small supporting walls were made in a manner that each supported the other. The forces moving up the hillock to the fort were to receive deadly fire throughout their advance from every entrenchment. The fear of Sikhs might turn back upon them from the fort was keeping the Mughal commanders and their forces ill at ease. After a few days, the Sikh forces moved away to the Haripur reserve forests. The fall of Sadhaura and the escape of Banda Bahadur was reported to the emperor on 9 October 1713.[132]

Kiri Pathan, Ropar and Batala

The decline of Sikh power and the official persecution of the Sikhs gave an impetus to the Mohammedans, officials and others all over the country to persecute them remorselessly. The oppression was felt most in Majha and Rearki where almost every Muslim considered it his duty to add to the miseries of the Sikhs. The parganas of Kalanaur, Batala and Kahnuwan in the present district of Gurdaspur had been the stronghold of Mohammedan power.[133] Most of the leading Muslims fanning Muslim bigotry against the Sikhs, belonged to the village of Kiri Pathan.

The Sikhs of the neighbourhood, who were greatly exasperated by the tyrannical attitude of the local Muslim population, collected under the leadership of Jagat Singh and on 27 March 1714 fell upon the village and entered the *garhi* of the Pathans. The resistance offered by the Pathans was overpowered and their leader was slain. Sufficient booty was also obtained.[134]

Banda Bahadur was awaiting his time in Jammu hills at a place now called Dera Baba Banda Singh Bahadur, waiting for a favourable opportunity to strike a blow for the independence of his people and for the re-establishment of his power. No details of his activities from October 1713 to February 1715 are available except that he solemnized a second marriage with Sahib Kaur, daughter of a Khatri of Wazirabad.

The allegations raised by Giani Gian Singh that Banda proclaimed himself a Guru, that he visited the Golden Temple, Amritsar and his disobedience of Mata Sundri who was prompted by Farrukh Siyar, are the allegations which lack authenticity. There is absolutely nothing in the contemporary or earliest available records, official diaries and chronologies, state and family histories, personal memoirs, etc., to show that any negotiations at that time were carried out between Farrukh Siyar and Mata Sundri. Banda Bahadur introduced a new and additional form of salutation 'Fateh Darshan' which is available on some of his *hukamnamas*.

Some later historians uncharitable towards Banda Bahadur have called it a war cry in replacement of '*Wahe Guru ji ka Khalsa Wahe Guru ji ki Fateh*' which also has been a form of salutation and not a war cry. The new salutation, however, appears to have been dropped for having not been appreciated by the Khalsa.[135]

There are other instances where the Sikhs did not like some new thing and the same was dropped, for instance the initial legend for the Sikh seal was dropped and a new legend selected. The Sikhs had lost their strongholds and their stores of food and fodder in the plains, hence it became difficult for them to subsist. Therefore, the Sikhs had no other course left but to retire to the hills.

The Sikhs under Banda Bahadur reappeared in the plains from the direction of Jammu and marched towards Kalanaur. The Faujdar Suhrab Khan of Kalanaur and others collected a large force of mercenaries, religious zealots and levies from the parganas of its neighbourhood, but with the very first blow of Sikhs they were scattered to the winds. Some fled from the field, others died in combat.[136]

Passing through Achal, Banda Singh marched towards Batala. The *faujdar* of Batala Shaikh Dayan, came out to encounter the Sikh force. A bloody battle was fought for about six hours, and there was great bloodshed on both sides. Many from among the nobility of Batala were killed. None of the zamindars and commanders could resist the Sikhs in the battlefield. Shaikh Dayan was defeated and he fled in dismay to his hometown of Bharowal. Batala and its neighbourhood were occupied.

Battle of Gurdas Nangal

The news of Sikh advances reaching the Mughal capital created great alarm. An expedition consisting of several Muslims and some Hindu commanders collected at Lahore to fight under the command of Abdul Samad Khan whose arrival was awaited. Banda Bahadur was not unaware of the above preparations by the Mughal government. He, therefore, decided to construct a mud-fort at Kot Mirza Jan, a small village between Kalanaur and Batala, as an escape route on the lines of Lohgarh into the forest area behind Kot Mirza Jan.[137]

But before a fort could be raised for his occupation, the combined Mughal forces under the command of Abdul Samad Khan and his deputy Arif Beg suddenly fell upon the Sikhs. It appears that the Mughal forces were keeping track of Banda Bahadur's movements when he reappeared from the Jammu side and was marching towards Kalanaur. Ghulam Hussain, the author of *Siyar-ul-Mutakhiran*, states that Banda Bahadur stood his ground to the amazement of all and in the first engagement fought so heroically that he very nearly defeated the imperial army. The Mughals were pursuing Banda Bahadur and his men vigorously. He escaped from post to post, losing endlessly his men and inflicting losses on his pursuers. According to Khafi Khan,

> The infidels fought so fiercely that the army of Islam was nearly overpowered and they over and over again showed the greatest daring but they had no place of defence and were, therefore, forced to evacuate their positions and fall back upon the village of Gurdas Nangal, now a heap of ruins, known as 'Bande Wali Theh' lying one mile to the west of the present village of Gurdas Nangal.[138]

The Sikhs took shelter in the *ihata* of Bhai Duni Chand's *haveli*. The enclosure had a fairly strong wall around it. Banda Bahadur made every effort to strengthen his defences and collect ration and ammunition to keep the enemy at a respectable distance from his fortification. He surrounded it with a moat filled with water from the neighbouring canal by cutting the imperial canal called the *shahi nahar* and other streams and allowing the water to spread and form a quagmire around the place so that the enemy could not easily come close to the enclosure.[139]

On 17 April 1715 Emperor Farrukh Siyar wrote to Abdul Samad Khan to follow the Sikhs to their new position. He asked Itmad-ud-daula to write to Abdul Samad Khan to kill or imprison the Sikh chief and his followers.[137] The enclosure containing the Sikhs was immediately surrounded and blockaded. The besiegers kept so watchful a guard that not a blade of grass nor a grain of corn could find its way in. Occasionally, Abdul Samad Khan and his son Zakariya Khan at the head of several thousand troops of their own and forces of their allies attempted to storm the Sikh positions, but their attempts were defeated by the comparatively small number of Sikhs who showed the greatest tenacity in their defence.[140] Mohammad Qasim, the author of *Ibratnama*, who was in the service of Arif Beg Khan writes:

> The brave and daring deeds of the infernal Sikhs were wonderful. Twice or thrice every day some forty or fifty of the black-faced Sikhs came out of their enclosure to gather grass for their cattle and when the combined forces of imperialists went to oppose them they (Sikhs) made an end of the Mughals with arrows, muskets and small swords and disappeared. Such was the terror of the Sikhs and fear of the sorceries of the Sikh chief that the commander of the army prayed that God might so ordain things that Banda Bahadur should seek his safety in his flight from the Garhi.[141]

Abdul Samad Khan utilized the reinforcement brought by Qamr-ud-din to further strengthen his reinforcements and to eliminate any chance of Sikhs breaking the siege. The area was divided into four sections commanded by three senior commanders: Abdul Samad Khan, Qamr-ud-din, Zakariya Khan, and the *faujdars* and *zamindars*. United efforts being necessary, the tents were pitched close together all round the fort and rope was joined to rope. Slowly and slowly, unnoticed by the Sikhs, they closed all the openings between each shelter, and before the Sikhs were aware of it, they were surrounded as if by a wall.[142] The Sikhs on several occasions showed the greatest boldness and daring to sweep the obstacles away and carried away from the besiegers camp whatever they could lay their hands on.

So bold and indomitable were the Guru's followers that they impressed their adversaries with the greatest respect for their fighting qualities. It was feared that the garrison might, by a sortie *en masse* and by sacrificing themselves, secure the escape of their leader Banda Bahadur.[143] Thus, the siege and the struggle continued for several months. There were considerable losses on both sides.[144] The losses of the Sikhs were irreplaceable whereas the losses of the Mughals were replenished by fresh supply of soldiers. With all these additions to the siege, Abdul Samad Khan had lost hope of success against so determined and valiant a foe. All his efforts to approach the gate and the walls of the Sikh enclosures had failed. The only alternative left to him was to approach it by underground means. He, therefore, ordered to drive subterranean passages towards the corners of the *ihata*.[145] This was comparatively successful. Before Abdul Samad Khan had reached the main gate, Qamr-ud-din Khan succeeded in capturing the ditch and a bastion, from which the musketery fire of the garrison had caused considerable damage. Zakariya Khan obtained possession of the second gate, the one chiefly used by the garrison. The Sikhs were hemmed in from all sides. The confinement of eight long months had exhausted their already small stock of provisions, not a grain being left in their storehouse. Famine now commenced its ravage among the besieged Sikhs and they were reduced to extremities.

At this stage, difference of opinion rose between Binod Singh and Banda Bahadur. It was decided that one of them should leave the place. Binod Singh accepted the decision and mounting his horse he rode out of the enclosure with sword in hand and cut his way through the besiegers.[146]

Samad Khan kept on the policy of strengthening the fortification around the fortress by raising tall towers and deep moats. He sealed all the outlets from the fortress. Yet he sought blessings from every *pir* and *wali*. He would not think of storming the fortress (a residential *garhi*) and was seeking some way, right or wrong, even by giving false promises, to make the Sikhs surrender and come out of the fortress.[147]

In fact, the entire Mughal history in India is replete with besiegements of forts. Almost all forts were taken by bribing some of the besieged soldiers and their commanders. In Gurdas Nangal, it was virtually impossible to purchase a section of the Sikhs. Hence, devious means such as false promises was taken up. He, therefore, adopted the only possible course of strengthening the siege and marking his time.[148]

Prolonged negotiations were carried out with the Sikhs and vague promises of their release after surrender were given, but even these did not come through. Banda Bahadur offered to surrender on the promise that the rest of the Sikhs would be released unharmed. But even this did not work. Baj Singh also offered to surrender, but it did not find approval. At one stage, Samad Khan wanted Banda Bahadur's son and a few important sardars to be sent to his court before giving any indication of what would be the final outcome.

These discussions have been summed up by Gurbaksh Singh as under:

1. Banda Bahadur would not surrender unconditionally and that the surrender would be preceded by a negotiated settlement.
2. According to the terms of the settlement, the nawab promised to spare the lives of the Sikhs if they relinquished their hold over the fortress, and that the nawab would recommend their case to the emperor and would mediate on their behalf.
3. The nawab offered these terms only 'out of expediency' and he was not sincere in keeping his promise.
4. The nawab deliberately broke his word because he knew the sanguinary nature of the emperor and he also wanted a further rise for himself in the imperial services.[149]

The Mughal commanders decided on cutting through subterranean passages close to the gate and in this manner they were able to surprise the Sikhs who were now hemmed in from all sides. The siege became so strong that it became impossible for Sikhs to bring anything from outside. Near famine conditions now prevailed. The survivors were reduced to mere skeletons. They were virtually half-dead and unable to use their muskets. It had become practically impossible for them to offer any resistance and continue defence any longer.[150] At last on Wednesday 17 December 1715, the Sikh enclosure at Gurdas Nangal, the so-called fortress of Gurdaspur, fell into the hands of the Mughal besiegers. The surviving Sikhs in the *ihata* had been physically incapacitated and disabled to continue the defence, but the imperialists were still benumbed with terror and they dared not enter their enclosure. Abdul Samad Khan had promised to intercede with the emperor for a free pardon for them, but when the gates were opened, the besieged, including Banda Bahadur, were made prisoners.[151] The imperialists fell upon the half-dead Sikhs like hungry wolves. Abdul Samad Khan had some 200 or 300 of them bound hand and foot and made over to Mughal and Tartar soldiers, who put them to sword. The dead bodies of the Sikhs were ripped open in search of gold coins supposed to have been swallowed by them and their heads were then stuffed with hay and mounted on spears.[152]

The news of the fall of the so-called fort was reported to the emperor at Delhi on 22 December 1715.[153] 'It was by grace of

God and not by wisdom or bravery', says Kamwar Khan, 'that this came to happen. Otherwise, it is known to everyone that the late Emperor Bahadur Shah with the four royal princes and numerous commanders had made efforts to repress this rebellion, but it had been all fruitless and now that the infidels (the Sikhs) and a few thousand companions had been starved into surrender.'[154]

SADHAURA-LOHGARH-SITARAGARH AXIS

Banda Bahadur had secured a large extent of territories in half a dozen districts of Punjab in about a year's time from his arrival in Punjab. The largest chunk thereof has been the *faujdari* of Sirhind which was won from the Mughals and its *faujdar*, Wazir Khan, captured and executed.

Bahadur Shah, the Mughal emperor, had correctly foreseen the situation, that a large Sikh rebellion near the capital city could become detrimental to the Mughal Empire. He, therefore, decided to personally move to the Punjab and crush the Sikh rebellion. He mustered a large number of smaller contingents of governors/ *faujdars* from the adjoining states beside the imperial forces. The entire strength of the Mughal army was around 2 lakh horse and foot-soldiers and almost the same extent of camp followers.

The Mughal forces advancing into the territory occupied by the Sikh forces did fight at a few places but from most of the places smaller detachments of Sikh army went back to either Sadhaura or Lohgarh. The entire operation took about three months.

Some entrenchments were made at Sadhaura from where the Sikh forces faced the Mughal imperial army. Khafi Khan writes: The Sikhs in their faqir dress struck terror among the royal troops. The number of dead and dying of imperial troops was so large that for a time it seemed that they were losing ground. Feroze Khan Mewati and Rustam Dil Khan's armies were literally mauled by the Sikhs, but before the close of day, a fresh army of about 50,000 Mughal troops reached and joined the battle and the Mughal army was saved of a disaster. Finding themselves in no condition to face the Mughal forces, the Sikh army retreated towards the Lohgarh Fort during the night. The distance between

Sadhaura and Lohgarh Fort is about 10 miles only. The Mughal armies also moved on to Lohgarh and after fighting for a couple of days with the besieging Mughal army, the Sikh army moved out of the Lohgarh Fort and got dispersed in the nearby Haripur reserve forests. This was a strategy which Banda Bahadur does not seem to have specifically planned, but was worked out as the Mughal forces with a much larger army were closing in on them.

Bahadur Shah moved his camp from Lohgarh to Ropar and then to Lahore where he reached on 11 August 1711 and set-up his camp on the bank of river Ravi. He developed some mental ailment and died on 27/8 February 1712.

The death of Bahadur Shah was followed by the usual struggle among his sons for the throne. Azim-us-Shan, the main contender, was riding an elephant when its trunk was hit by a cannonball and it became unmanageable. It threw itself in the river Ravi where the prince and the animal were swallowed by quicksand. Ultimately Jahandar Shah eliminated his remaining brother and ascended the throne on 29 March 1712. Ten months after ascending the throne, Jahandar Shah was defeated by Farrukh Siyar, son of Azim-us-Shan.

The period of struggle for the imperial throne and disturbed state of affairs at Lahore and Delhi from February 1712 to June 1713 was extremely favourable for the reestablishment of the power of the Khalsa. Banda Bahadur availed this period of disturbance and occupied Sadhaura without any loss of time. After capturing Sadhaura, Banda Bahadur raised a fairly strong fortress adjoining Sadhaura town. He dug out a trench around the fort, and used the dug-out earth to strengthen the walls of the fort and got water filled in the trench from a nearby canal. He also raised four towers at four corners inside the fort to be used as observation posts. The fort of Lohgarh was also occupied and repaired.

From the first ridge up to the walls of Lohgarh, Banda Bahadur got constructed fifty-two 3 to 4 ft high defensive ridges arranged in such a manner that each ridge lent protection to the next. In this manner any assailant who intended to reach the fort had to face hostile firing from every ridge that he crossed. Banda Bahadur also chose the adjoining Sitaragarh hill, about 400-500 ft higher than Lohgarh hill, from where he could observe the movements of the Mughal forces over the entire expanse. There is an acoustic phenomenon whereby anything spoken from here is clearly audible at Lohgarh fort and likewise the reply given from Lohgarh Fort is equally audible at Sitaragarh. Banda Bahadur used to stay at the top of Sitaragarh hill where a small stone-lined pond for collection of water still exists. However, there is no foundation of any building here, so probably he lived in a mud hut.

The Sadhaura-Lohgarh-Sitaragarh axis was used by Banda Bahadur in 1713-14 when a very large Mughal force under top commanders invaded the areas reoccupied by the Sikh forces with directions from Farrukh Siyar that they must wipe out completely the Sikh forces and their commanders.

After reoccupying the areas under Sikh operation, Mughal forces converged on Saḍhaura where the Sikhs gave them a stiff fight and in the middle of the night left for Lohgarh because of they had exhausted their logistic support. The Mughals were more than 2 lakh fighting men whereas the Sikh army comprised 20,000-30,000 only. The Mughal army pursued them to Lohgarh and here too after giving a stiff fight for a couple of days, the Sikh army disappeared during the night in the forests of Haripur.

The Sadhaura-Lohgarh axis was very effectively planned by Banda Bahadur to give a fight to a very large army and then get out of the same unscathed.

MASSACRE OF BANDA SINGH BAHADUR AND OTHER SIKHS AT DELHI

Banda Singh Bahadur and the other Sikh prisoners were initially taken to Lahore and then to Delhi for presentation to the Mughal emperor. Although Banda Bahadur had been captured, imprisoned and chained, yet the dread of his supernatural powers so haunted the minds of the Mughal commanders that at every moment they were afraid of his escape. A Mughal officer offered to be tied together with Banda Bahadur on the same elephant; the idea being that if he attempted to escape the Mughal officer would plunge a dagger into his body.[155] With fetters on his feet, a ring around his neck and a thick chain around his body, he was thrown into an iron cage, and chained from all sides. Two Mughal officers were tied to him on each side of the same elephant to prevent his escape.[156] His officers and principal men were put in iron chains and paraded, mounted upon lame, worn out, mangy asses and camels and with fools caps on their heads. They were preceded by drummers and bandsmen, and Mughals carrying the heads of Sikhs on spears. Behind the prisoners came the royal *amirs*, *faujdars* and Hindu rajas at the head of their respective troops. For miles, the *shahi sarak* was lined with eager spectators on both sides and the bazaars, the streets and the roofs of the adjoining houses, presented the spectacle of a surging sea of humanity. With such a cortege of half dead prisoners and gory heads, Abdul Samad Khan entered the city of Lahore.[157] What a disgraceful and abominable conduct of a victorious army of the so-called civilized Mughal Empire against the injured prisoners of war. Abdul Samad Khan requested for permission to present in person his great prisoner, but he was ordered to remain in his capital and send the prisoners in the charge of his son Zakariya Khan and Qamr-ud-din Khan.[158]

At the time of his departure from Lahore, Zakariya Khan considered the number of 200 prisoners to be too small to be presented to the emperor. He, therefore, ordered a general hunt for Sikhs throughout the country. The *faujdars* and *chaudharys* scoured the land for Sikhs. A number of innocent persons were arrested from villages and sent to Zakariya Khan to make up the required number of prisoners. In a few days, a large number of Sikhs having taken no part in the Sikh rebellion were arrested only because they were Sikhs, required to make a sizeable number of 740 to be butchered after the emperor's inspection at Delhi.[159]

According to Cunningham, Banda Bahadur and others were marched to Delhi with all the signs of ignominy usual with bigots and common among barbarous or uncivilized conquerors. Like their chief, they were fettered in chains from head to foot and loaded in twos and threes on bullock carts. At Sirhind they were paraded through the streets and exposed to the ridicule of the people who poured the filthiest of abuses on them. The Sikhs bore these indignities with the greatest patience singing the sacred hymns of their Gurus.[160]

On 25 February 1716, the arrival of the prisoners at Aghrabad was reported to the emperor. Mohammad Amin Khan was sent by the emperor to make necessary arrangements for bringing the Sikh chief and his followers in procession from Aghrabad to the imperial palace.

On 27 February 1716, Banda Singh and the other Sikh prisoners were paraded in a procession to the city of Delhi. The ceremonial on this occasion was copied from that observed after the capture of Maratha chief Sambhaji, son of Shivaji. First came the heads of 2,000 executed Sikhs, stuffed with straw and mounted on bamboo poles. Along with them was carried at the end of a pole the carcass of a cat to show that every living creature in the enclosure of Gurdas Nangal had been killed. Banda Singh himself came next imprisoned in an iron cage. The sides of the cage had a large number of embedded nails with the sharp ends facing the captive so that it would hurt him any time he moved. Behind him stood with a drawn sword in his hand, an officer from the Turani Mughals.[161] After his elephant came other Sikh prisoners, 740 in number, tied two and two on saddle-less camels. On their heads were placed foolscaps of ridiculous shapes. One of their hands was pinned to the neck between two pieces of wood, which were held together by iron pins. Some of the principal men, who rode near the chief's elephant were dressed in sheepskin with the wooly side turned outwards. At the end of the procession rode three Mughal commanders—Amin Khan representing the emperor Farrukh Siyar, Zakariya Khan and Qumr-ud-din Khan. The road from Aghrabad to Lahori Gate, a distance of several miles, was lined on both sides with troops and large crowds mocking Banda Bahadur.[162]

Mirza Mohammad Harisi, who witnessed the procession, has recorded the same as an eyewitness in his *Ibrat Namah*.

> On this day I had gone to see the *tamasha* and accompanied the procession to the *Qilah-i-Mubarik*. Almost the entire city population had come to see the prisoners. The Musalmans could not contain themselves for the joy. But those unfortunate Sikhs, who had been reduced to this last extremity, were quite happy and contented with their fate, and not the slightest sign of dejection or humility was to be seen on their faces. In fact, as they passed along on their camels, they seemed happy and cheerful, joyfully singing the sacred hymns of their Scriptures. If any one said: 'now, you will be killed', they shouted, 'kill

us, when were we afraid of death'. Sayyed Muhammad, author of the *Tabsirat-un-Nazirin*, who was present there has stated, 'Not all the insults that their enemies had inflicted could rob the brave disciples of Guru Gobind Singh of their natural dignity, without any sign of dejection or shame they rode on calm and cheerful even anxious to die the death of martyrs.[163]

Banda Singh Bahadur and other Sikh leaders were made over to Mir Atish to be imprisoned at Tripolia. The remaining 694 Sikhs were handed over to Sarbara Khan Kotwal for execution.[164] The Sikhs arms and valuables collected and brought by Mughal commanders for inspection of the emperor were as under:

Swords	1,000
Shields	278
Bows and Quivers	173
Matchlocks	180
Daggers	114
Long knives	217
Gold mohars	23
Rupees	a little over 600
Gold ornaments	a few

The list of arms taken and cash seized, remarks Irvine, does not give a very exalted notion of the military strength or the wealth of the Sikh leaders in the fortress of Gurdas Nangal. It is really astonishing that with such scanty resources, the Sikhs so determinedly resisted the greatest empire of the day for such a long time, says Kamwar Khan.[165]

The execution of the Sikhs began on 15 March 1716 opposite Chabutra Kotwali. One hundred Sikh prisoners were taken out of their prisons everyday and were seated in lines in the Qatalgah with blacksmiths kept ready in attendance to sharpen the swords of the executioners. Life was promised to anyone who would renounce his faith, but they would not betray their Gurus and to the last it has not been found that one apostatized from their newly embraced faith, write Surman and Stephenson. The Sikhs welcomed death with undaunted spirit and presented their heads to the executioners with cheerful faces, with the words *Waheguru*! *Waheguru*! on their lips, amidst the wondering praise of the populace. At the time of execution, 'My Deliverer! Kill me first!' was the joyful prayer that constantly reverberated in the ears of the executioners.

All observers, Indian and European, says William Irvine, unite in remarking on the wonderful forbearance and resolution with which these men met their fate. Their attachment and devotion to their leader were wonderful to behold. They had no fear of death and they called the executioner 'Mukta' or the Deliverer, but what is singular, writes Ghulam Hussain Khan, the author of *Siyar-ul-Muthakherin*, was that these people not only behaved firmly during the execution but they would dispute and wrangle with each other for priority in execution and they entreated the executioner for the purpose. For a whole week the swords of the executioners did butcher's work and in this manner all the Sikh prisoners were beheaded. After the heads had been severed from the body, the bodies were thrown into a heap and at nightfall they were loaded in carts, taken out of the city and hung upon trees.[166]

Many wonderful stories of the unshakable constancy and the wholehearted devotion of the Sikh prisoners to their faith and their leader were then current. Some of them were so wonderful that those who were not eyewitnesses to them were inclined to dismiss these as incredible, says Khafi Khan. But the following is recorded by him in his *Muntakhib-ul-Lubab* (pp. ii, 766) as what he saw with his own eyes.

Among the prisoners sentenced to death was a Sikh youth of tender age. He was the only son of a widowed mother. He had only recently been married and as yet had the *Kangan-i-Arusi*, the marriage thread, on his wrist. Hearing of the impending doom of her son with the other prisoners, the old mother approached Ratan Chand, diwan of the wazir, and through his influential support, pleaded the cause of her son with great feeling and earnestness before the Emperor Farrukh Siyar and Sayyed Abdullah Khan. To avail of the emperor's general offer to spare the lives of those who renounced the Sikh faith, the old woman, probably as tutored by Diwan Ratan Chand, represented that her son was only a prisoner in the hands of the Sikhs and was not a follower of the Gurus. He was brought here, she said, while in their captivity and now stood innocent among those condemned to death. Farrukh Siyar commiserated the old woman and sent an officer with orders to release the youth. The woman arrived with orders for the release just as the executioner was standing with the bloody sword over the young man's head. She presented the order for his release to the kotwal. He brought out the prisoner and told him he was free. But the boy refused to be released, says Khafi Khan, and loudly cried out: 'My mother is a liar. I am heart and soul a devoted follower of the Gurus. Send me quickly after my companions.' No bewailing cries and tearful entreaties of his old mother and no persuasion of the state officers, writes the author of the *Tarikh-i-Muhammad Shahi*, could shake the young Sikh in his devotion to his faith. The spectators were further dumbfounded when the heroic boy retraced his steps back to the place of execution and calmly bowed his head before the executioner to meet his death. In an instant the executioner's sword went aloft and descended on the frail neck of the youth, and he was enrolled as one of the truest of the martyrs produced by the Sikh religion.[167]

On 9 March 1716, Sarbrah Khan Kotwal conveyed, under the emperor's orders, seventeen of Banda Singh's principal men into the fort. For three months after the massacre there was a lull, and Banda Singh and his companions remained confined in the Imperial Fort. The object of this confinement and the three months' delay in the execution of the Sikh chief and his deputies is explained in a letter, dated 10 March 1716 from Messrs John Surman and Edward Stephenson, members of the English embassy to Emperor Farrukh Siyar, to the Honourable Robert Hedges, president and governor of Fort William. 'He at present', the ambassadors reported, 'has his life prolonged with most of his Mutsuddys in the hope to get an account of his treasure and of those that assisted him, when afterwards he will be executed. It was not till June 19 that he was let out to execution and subjected to a death of torture.'[168]

The fate reserved for Banda Singh is too excruciating to be described. On Sunday the 19 June 1716, 'when the sun had risen about three spears on the sky', Banda Singh, his son Ajai Singh, Sardar Baj Singh, Ram Singh, Bhai Fateh Singh, Ali Singh, Gulab Singh Bakhshi and others, who had been confined in the fort of

Plate 9: Banda Bahadur at his execution.

Plate 10: Banda Bahadur's child being snatched by executors.

Delhi, were led out of the fort. As on the day of his entry, the Sikh chief, laden with fetters, was dressed in a gold embroidered red turban and a robe of gold brocade. He was placed on an elephant and with twenty-six other Sikhs in chains marching behind him were taken through the streets of the old city to the shrine of Khwaja Qutab-ud-din Bakhtiyar Kaki, where the redstone Qutab Minar is located amidst white marble over the crumbling walls of the old Hindu fortress. Here he was paraded around the tomb of the late Emperor Bahadur Shah.[169]

After Banda Singh had been dismounted and seated on the ground, he was offered the usual choice between Islam and death. But the brave disciple of Guru Gobind Singh chose to lay down his life as a devoted follower than to abjure his faith for the sake of enjoying a few more years of life. His young son, Ajai Singh, about four years, was then placed in his arms and he was told to take the boy's life. Banda Singh refused to oblige. The executioner then hacked the child to pieces with a long knife, dragged out his quivering heart and thrust it into the mouth of his father, who stood unmoved like a statue, completely resigned to God's will.[170]

Amin Khan, having had the opportunity to look closely at Banda, was surprised at the nobleness of his features, and could not help exclaiming. 'It is surprising that one, who shows so much acuteness in his features and so much of nobility in his conduct, should have been guilty of such horrors.' With the greatest composure, Banda Singh replied:

> I will tell you. Whenever men become so corrupt and wicked as to relinquish the path of equity and to abandon themselves to all kinds of excesses, then the Providence never fails to raise up a scourge like me to chastise a race so depraved; but when the measure of punishment is full then he raises up men like you to bring him to punishment.

His own turn came next. First of all, his right eye was gauged out with a pointed butcher's knife and then his left. His left foot was cut-off next, and then his two hands were severed from his body. His flesh was then torn with red-hot pincers, and finally he was decapitated and hacked to pieces, limb by limb. Banda Singh remained calm and serene amidst these tortures, completely resigned to the will of God and the Guru, and died with unshaken constancy, 'glorying', says Elphinstone, 'in having been raised up by God to be a scourge to the iniquities and oppressions of the age'.[171] The other Sikh prisoners shared the same fate and were put to the sword.[172]

Farrukh Siyar ridiculed Baj Singh over his bravery and Baj Singh said, 'If you remove my fetters, I will show you some *tamasha*'. The emperor ordered his fetters to be removed. No sooner Baj Singh was free, he pounced like a hawk and killed two or three of the Mughal soldiers with his handcuffs before he could be apprehended and executed.

Tagore has written a highly touching poem *Bandi Bir* (Banda Bahadur) on Banda Bahadur's execution, whose last stanza is as follows:

All who watched were struck dumb,
Banda's body was torn to pieces,
With pincers and burning tongs,
Bit by bit, he was scorched and burnt
With unshakable courage Banda faced
A martyr's death that day,
Uttering not a single cry of pain,
All who watched stood dumb
With horror their sight was numbed.[173]

NOTES

1. Hari Ram Gupta, *History of the Sikhs*, vol. II, 1978, p. 7.
2. Ganda Singh, *Banda Singh Bahadur*, Amritsar, 1935, p. 25.
3. Gupta, op. cit., p. 6.
4. Ibid., p. 7.
   'Banda seems to have travelled in disguise and by circuitous routes to avoid detection. Generally he adopted the same route across Maharashtra and Rajasthan as was followed by Guru Gobind Singh. The distance between Nander and Hissar in Haryana by that route was 1,600 km. At the rate of 16 km or 10 miles a day on an average, Banda should not have taken more than 100 days during his journey, but he actually took about a year. It means that he might have frequently been in hiding. The Mughal spy system was most elaborate during Aurangzeb's period. Had Banda and his party come to their notice, it would have been eliminated. That is

why Banda travelled right across Maharashtra and Rajasthan, both of which were in revolt against the Mughals.'

5. Ganda Singh, *Banda Singh Bahadur*, p. 27.
6. Ibid., p. 29.
7. Ibid.
8. Ibid.
9. Ibid., p. 30.
10. Ibid.
11. Ibid.
12. Ibid., p. 31.
13. Ibid.
14. Gupta, op. cit., pp. 9-10.
15. G.S. Deol, *Banda Bahadur*, Jullandhar: New Academic Publishing Co., 1972, p. 33.
16. Ganda Singh, op. cit., p. 36.
17. Ibid., p. 37.
18. Gokul Chand Narang, *Transformation of Sikhism*, Lahore: New Book Society, 1945.
19. Deol , op. cit., p. 35.
20. Ganda Singh, op. cit., p. 39.
21. Ibid., p. 40. Thus, before nightfall, the beautiful town of Samana, with its palatial buildings, was converted into a heap of ruins, never to regain its past glory.
22. Ibid., p. 41.
23. Ibid., pp. 41-2.
24. Khafi Khan, *Muntakhab-ul-Lubab*, quoted by Hari Ram Gupta, op. cit., p. 10.
25. Gupta, op. cit., p. 10.
26. Deol, op. cit., p. 36.
27. Ibid.
28. Ibid., p. 37.
29. Ganda Singh, op. cit., p. 45.
30. Ibid.
31. Ibid., p. 46.
32. Ibid.
33. Ibid., p. 47.
34. Ibid.
35. Ibid.
36. M.A. Macauliffe, *The Sikh Religion*, New Delhi: S. Chand & Co., (1st published in 1909), p. 247.
37. Ganda Singh, op. cit., p. 49.

38. Ibid.
39. Sohan Singh, *Life and Exploits of Banda Singh Bahadur*, Patiala: Punjabi University (1st published in 1915), pp. 45-6.
40. M.S. Chandla, *Banda Bahadur*, Chandigarh: Aurva Publications, 2006, p. 122.
41. Ganda Singh, op. cit., p. 49.
42. Deol, op. cit., p. 39.
43. Ibid., p. 41.
44. Ibid.
45. Ibid.
46. Ibid., p. 42.
47. Ibid.
48. Ibid.; Ganda Singh, op. cit., p. 53.
49. Ibid.
50. Ibid., p. 43.
51. Ganda Singh, op. cit., pp. 59-60.
52. Ibid., pp. 61-2.
53. Ibid., p. 63.
54. Deol, op. cit., p. 47.
55. Sohan Singh, op. cit., p. 59. 'Banda Bahadur rose like a famished lion from his cave and sprang upon the enemy like a bolt from the blue. His appearance encouraged the Khalsa by far the most, while it struck terror amongst the enemy.'
56. Deol, op. cit., p. 47.
57. Ibid., p. 48.
58. Ibid., pp. 44-5.
59. Ibid., p. 49.
60. Ibid., p. 51.
61. Ganda Singh, op. cit., p. 72.
62. Ibid., p. 91.
63. Ibid., pp. 91-2.
64. G.R.C. William, 'The Sikhs in Upper Doab', *Calcutta Review*, LX, p. 23.
    'These victims were solemnly executed after conviction on the capital charge of cow slaughter, an offence easily proved against them.'
65. Ganda Singh, op. cit., p. 95.
66. Ibid., p. 98.
67. Ibid., p. 101.
68. Ibid., p. 102.
69. Ibid., p. 103.

70. Ibid., p. 102.
71. Ibid., p. 105.
72. Ibid., p. 107.
73. Ibid., p. 109.
74. Ibid., p. 110.
75. Ibid.
76. Ibid., p. 112.
77. Ibid., p. 115.
78. Ibid., p. 116.
79. Ibid., p. 117.
80. Ibid., p. 118.
81. Ibid., pp. 118-19.
82. Ibid., pp. 119-20.
83. Malcolm, *Sketch of Sikhs*, London, 1812, p. 79.
84. Ganda Singh, op. cit., p. 125.
85. H.K. Sagoo, *Banda Bahadur*, p. 83.
86. Ganda Singh, op. cit., p. 127.
87. Ibid., p. 128.
88. Ibid., p. 131.
89. Ibid., p. 132.
90. Ibid., p. 134.
91. Ibid., p. 136.
92. Ibid., p. 137.
93. Ibid., p. 138.
94. Ibid., p. 140.
95. Ibid., pp. 143-4.
96. Ibid., pp. 144-5.
97. Ibid., pp. 145-6.
98. Ibid.
99. Ibid., p. 147.
100. Ibid., p. 150.
101. Ibid., p. 151.
102. Ibid.
103. Ibid.
104. Ibid., p. 152.
105. Ibid., p. 154.
106. Ibid., p. 155.
107. Ibid.
108. Ibid., p. 159.
109. Ibid., p. 160.
110. Ibid., p. 161.

111. Ibid., p. 163.
112. Ibid., p. 164.
113. Ibid., p. 165.
114. Ibid., p. 167.
115. Ibid., p. 168.
116. Ibid., p. 169.
117. Ibid., p. 174.
118. Ibid., p. 179.
119. Ibid., p. 180.
120. Ibid.
121. Ibid.
122. Ibid., p. 181.
123. Ibid., p. 183.
124. Ibid.
125. Miss Corner, *History of India and China*, p. 296.
126. (i) Ganda Singh, op. cit., p. 183.
     (ii) *Akhabarat-i-Darbar-i-Mualla*, 25 November 1710, *Panjab Past and Present*, *1707-18*, vol. xviii-II,October 1984, p. 44.
127. Ibid., p. 184.
128. Ibid., p. 186.
129. Ibid., p. 187.
130. Ibid., p. 188-9.
131. Ibid., p. 189.
132. Ibid., p. 190.
133. Ibid., p. 192.
134. Ibid., p. 193.
135. Ibid., p. 195.
136. Ibid., pp. 195-6.
137. Ibid., p. 199.
138. Ibid., p. 201.
139. Ibid., p. 202.
140. Ibid., p. 203.
141. Ibid., p. 204.
142. Ibid., p. 205.
143. Ibid., p. 206.
144. Ibid.
145. Ibid.
146. Ibid.
147. *Panjab History Conference Proceedings*, Patiala: Punjabi University, (Seventh Session) 1972, p. 47.
148. Ibid., p. 48.

149. Ibid., Gurbux Singh assessment, p. 59.
150. Ganda Singh, op. cit., p. 210.
151. Ibid., pp. 211-12.
152. Ibid., p. 212.
153. Ibid.
154. Ibid., p. 213.
155. Ibid., p. 214.
156. Ibid.
157. Ibid., p. 215.
158. Ibid., p. 216.
159. Ibid., p. 217.
160. Ibid., p. 217-18.
161. Ibid., p. 219.
162. Ibid., p. 221.
163. Ibid., p. 223.
164. Ibid.
165. Ibid., p. 224.
166. Ibid., p. 226.
167. Ibid., p. 228.
168. Ibid., p. 230.
169. Ibid., p. 232.
170. Ibid.
171. Ibid., p. 234.
172. Ibid., p. 235.
173. Ibid., p. 236.

CHAPTER 5

Establishment of Initial Sikh State

In Accordance with the Concept of Sikh Sovereignty

Guru Nanak was a social and religious thinker and not a political philosopher, but his experience and reactions to the organized political authority find sufficient place in his teachings. The degeneration in the body politic had brought about revulsion not only against the ruling Islamic authorities but even against the servility of the people at large. Hindus had become docile prey to atrocities of the Islamic conquerors and exploitation by their own selfish priests. Guru Nanak's teachings awakened the individual from this lethargy and helped rekindle in him the failing religious and divine fire and to guide him to lead a useful life for the realization of his self and enjoyment of divine bliss.[1]

Hindu society suffered from despondency and stagnation as a result of rigid casteism and the ritualistic tyranny of the deeply entrenched brahminhood. The springs of true religion had been choked by the weeds of meaningless rites, rituals and superstition, the selfishness of the priests and indifference of the people. The true spirituality of Hinduism lay buried under the ostentation and sectarianism.[2]

Guru Nanak taught that the one who inflicts torture and the one who submits to it are both equally guilty in the eyes of God. He preached the vision of a self-reliant society devoid of fear whose members worship one God with absolute devotion.[3] His teachings laid the foundations of a society of people who would not like to be cowed down by the tyranny of any organized authority.[4] This was the first step, like planting a seedling, towards an independent political organization with the strength to protect its faith and its followers.

Guru Nanak adopted a novel method of choosing his successor in his own lifetime and himself becoming the first disciple. Although a great amount of tolerance has been exercised by the Sikh Gurus against the descendants of their predecessors as compared to the Mughal system of virtually eliminating every other claimant, yet almost on every succession the descendants of the deceased Gurus created at times serious problems for the successor Gurus. Guru Arjan's share of these problems was, however, much larger than the earlier Gurus. At the time of Guru Arjan's succession, the Sikh Panth was rapidly coming of age and its consolidation was to be carried out urgently. Guru Arjan faced many difficulties including the lifelong hostility of his disinherited and embittered elder brother Prithia. The latter founded his own sect called the Minas and indulged in intrigues and conspiracies against Guru Arjan, his younger brother. Guru Tegh Bahadur was attacked by Dhir Mal and his armed followers. The bullet fired on the Guru just grazed past his shoulder.[5]

In the consolidation of Sikh religion, the successors of Guru Nanak made their own contributions in the improvement of the institutions of *sangat*, *pangat* and *langar* (free food served in a gurdwara). Guru Angad created a separate language called Gurmukhi, devised from the existing rough and crude *lande mahajani* and he prepared a refined version of it with the help of Devanagari script, resulting in a separate script called Gurmukhi, literally meaning 'having come from the Guru's mouth'. The Gurus verses here onwards were written in this language.[6] Guru Amar Das laid down the *anand*, the song of joy sung at marriages and other social occasions. He also laid down many simple ceremonies cutting down the role of brahmin priests in the Sikh way of life.[7] Guru Ramdas set-up the site and the holy temple at Amritsar in the midst of a tank.[8]

Guru Arjan's first task was the completion of the city of Ramdaspur, the tank of nectar (Amritsar) and Harimandir located in the centre of the tank with four doors opening on each side, the implication being that God is accessible from every direction.[9] The foundation stone of the holy temple, as the tradition goes, was laid by the Qadri Sufi Saint Mian Mir of Lahore.[10] The tank, the temple and the Guru fostered psychological integration among the Sikhs as a continuous process.[11] Before the fifth Guru, no tribute was exacted from the Sikhs. Contributions were, however, made to the Guru by the disciples according to their own discretion. However, the donations were proving to be insufficient and hence each Sikh was asked to donate one-tenth of his income (*daswandh*)[12] every year and the Guru's agents called *masands* were called upon to bring this tribute to the Guru in the month of Baisakh.[13] Thus developed a voluntary system of tax collection which in later times resembled to a system of parallel government. The Guru came to be looked upon by his Sikhs as exercising temporal authority in addition to providing spiritual guidance.[14] Thus the seedling planted by Guru Nanak became a tree shooting out its branches.

The most notable achievement of Guru Arjan was the compilation of the *Adi Granth*, the holy book of the Sikhs. Sikh worship consisted of singing the hymns composed by their Gurus. Guru Ram Das had collected the hymns of the Gurus from the time of Guru Nanak to his own time, which he had left with his son Mohan. Guru Arjan personally went to Mohan and collected from him the *pothis* containing the hymns of the previous Gurus.[15] When the collection of hymns was completed Guru Arjan dictated them to Bhai Gurdas in a tent set-up on a selected spot near Amritsar. The great task was finished in August 1604 and the sacred volume was deposited in the Harimandir.[16] The *lok bhasha* (Gurmukhi) thus permanently replaced the *devabhaṣha* and religion was brought to the heart of the masses. The role of the brahmin priest to guide or misguide the illiterate and ill-educated Sikh disciples was thus eliminated to a great extent.

Guru Arjan lived in style for the inspiration of his disciples. He considered the spiritual life and the worldly life as two aspects of a single reality.[17] He erected many buildings in Amritsar, kept horses and had retainers in attendance. His personal life was otherwise very simple. The Sikhs venerated their Guru and called him *Sacha Padshah*.[18] Guru Arjan encouraged his disciples to take to trade and commerce and with the settling down of traders in Amritsar, it soon grew into a prosperous city. The number of Sikhs also increased greatly and according to Mohsin Fani, in almost all parts of the country a few Sikhs were to be found.[19] In accordance with the *Akbarnama* by Abul Fazl, Emperor Akbar visited the Sikh shrine in November 1598 and on Guru's suggestion reduced the land revenues for that year.[20] Sikh religion prospered during half-a-century reign of Akbar.

The important measures taken by the earlier Gurus especially Guru Arjan, consolidated the Sikh community, completely separating from them the Udasis and the orthodox Hindu community; development of Amritsar into a sacred place and the centre of the Panth's authority; compilation of the holy Granth and the compulsory contribution of one-tenth of their income as *daswandh* through the authorized agents called *masands*. These were more or less revolutionary measures with far-reaching consequences.[21] The Guru's *daswandh* was paid by his Sikhs more regularly and readily than the Mughal revenues. The large *sangat*, increased resources and the splendour and magnificence of the *darbar*, gave it the appearance of a princely court.[22] 'A state, peaceful and unobtrusive, had been slowly evolved and the Guru as its head was called *Sacha Padshah* of the Panth. The Sikhs had already become accustomed to a form of self-government within the empire.'[23] The growing tree of social order started flowering. But after the death of Akbar in 1605, the peaceful existence of the Sikhs with the Mughal government came to an end.

The martyrdom of Guru Arjan Dev in 1606 and Guru Tegh Bahadur's martyrdom in 1675 were great setbacks to the Sikh community but every setback gave them added strength in their resolve to stand against the tyranny of the Mughals. It has been like the rise of the phoenix after every misfortune instead of after every 500 years. Despite these major blows, the tree of the Sikh order kept growing in strength.

Guru Hargobind became Guru at the age of 11 years. Some historians argue that Guru Hargobind brought about the transformation of the Sikh community from a non-violent religious organization to a military organization.[24] This is an ill-conceived and incorrect assessment as it was Guru Arjan who had quite clearly foreseen the difficult times ahead. During the half century long reign of Akbar, the orthodox Islamic fanatics had been kept under control, but their re-emergence after the death of Akbar and under the rule of Jahangir who was a religious bigot, was foreseen by Guru Arjan. He changed the style of his *darbar* from a princely court to a more modest one. He arranged for horses and armed retainers and instructed Baba Buddha to train his young son Hargobind in horse-riding and the use of all defensive and offensive weapons, as well as languages, arts and sciences.[25] Shortly before his death he sent word through his Sikhs that his son Hargobind should sit fully armed on the throne and maintain his army to the best of his ability.[26] Guru Hargobind's actions had been in accordance with the directions of his predecessor and father Guru Arjan and his teacher Bhai Buddha, hence were merely the continuation of the direction given by Guru Arjan due to the changed political situation and not a serious innovation by Guru Hargobind.

According to Bhai Mani Singh, the concept of *miri* and *piri* was also introduced by Guru Arjan, when he conceived the spiritual life and worldly living as two aspects of a single reality. Guru Arjan had conceived Sikhism essentially as a State with Halemi Raj right from the very beginning. Halemi Raj placed great value on equality among human beings, liberty to all and ready justice without any discrimination on grounds of caste, creed, race, religion and social position.[27] Nihar Ranjan Ray has correctly concluded that Guru Nanak laid the main foundation on which the edifice of Sikh political order was to be built. The later Gurus walked on these foundations and a few of them—Guru Arjan, Guru Hargobind and Guru Gobind Singh—strengthened them by buttressing and expanding them.[28] Guru Hargobind at his succession wore two swords, one on either side—one symbolizing *miri*, or temporal power, and the other *piri*, or spiritual power.[29] He inherited 52 bodyguards, 700 horses, 300 horsemen and 60 gunners.[30] In front of the Harimandir, he built a 12-feet high platform in 1606, called the *Akal Takht* or the God's throne, on which he sat in a princely attire. Harimandir was the seat of spiritual authority from where he provided spiritual solace to his disciples and the Akal Takht was the seat of temporal authority from where he administered justice like a king in court, accepted gifts, awarded honours and meted out punishments. Court bards used to sing songs in praise of the great Indian heroes.[31] Thus the Sikhs came to occupy a kind of separate state within the

Mughal state, the position of which was established by the independent fiscal policy of Guru Amar Das and Guru Arjan and his system of armed self-protection.[32] Hostility between Mughal troops and the Guru broke out in the early years of Shah Jahan's reign, based on rather flimsy grounds of a disputed hawk. The Guru decided to defy Mughal authority and fought six engagements against them from 1633 to 1638, the first being the battle of Jallo over a disputed hawk in 1633.

> I will not give the hawk to them,
> I will get the crown and the hawk from them.
> I will wrest from them the sovereignty of the country,
> I will bestow all this on the poor and the helpless.[33]

Thus the tree of Sikh order got a protector from poachers. He shifted his headquarters from Amritsar to Hargobindpur, then to Kartarpur, then to Phagwara and finally to Kiratpur, in order to get away from the plains where more military engagements, even a major attack by Mughal imperial forces, was quite likely.

Guru Tegh Bahadur, at the age of 43, became the ninth Guru. He worked for the physical and spiritual needs of the poor people of Malwa, where fields were barren and dry he got wells dug, where there was scarcity of milk he procured cows and distributed them free of cost to the people. For the landless peasants, he procured some land and urged them to live courageously as free people. In barren areas he got trees planted.[34]

Distorted and exaggerated reports about the activities of Guru Tegh Bahadur were sent to the Mughal court and the guru was summoned.[35] Near Gwalior, he was arrested along with his five companions and put in an iron cage on way to Delhi. The governor and the *qazi* tried their best to persuade the Guru to embrace Islam but he resolutely rejected their overtures. The companions of the Guru were tortured to death in his presence and the next day he was beheaded outside the *kotwali* in Chandni Chowk on 11 November 1675.[36] In the confusion, a low caste Sikh by the name Jaita carried away the Guru's head to Anandpur, 340 km away, and placed it before Gobind, a nine-year old child, who bestowed all affection and love on this hero and remarked, *Rangrete Guru ke bete*, meaning that all the low caste Sikhs were Guru's own children. A Labana Sikh, Lakhi Shah, stole the decapitated body of the Guru in a cart laden with cotton/straw and carried it into his house in his village named Rakab Ganj (near the present Parliament House) and set fire to his house. The ashes of the body were collected and placed in a vessel and buried under ground on that very spot.[37]

Guru Gobind Singh became the tenth Guru in 1675 on the execution of his father Guru Tegh Bahadur when he was only nine years old. A small army grew around the Guru and at a nearby strategic place a settlement was established in 1678 and the place was named Anandpur. The Guru would meet his daily congregation in an expensive tent with a trained elephant and horses as part of his retinue. Guru Gobind Singh sat on a raised platform wearing princely attire, the Sikhs called him *Sacha Padshah* and princes from distant places visited him; the whole setting was that of a royal court.[38]

The life of Guru Gobind Singh is a story of unparalleled sacrifice, which begins at the age of nine, and traversing a flaming course which involved martyrdom of his father and all his four sons, ends at the age of 42. Guru Gobind Singh (1675 to 1708) had to fight 20 battles in 23 years, i.e. 1682 to 1705 against the Hindu hill rajas and Mughal forces. A sufficiently detailed account of these battles has been given in an earlier chapter on Sikh sovereignty. None of these wars was to secure any territory or subdue any people. All these wars were forced on him to defend his young faith and equally young community by the established Hindu and Islamic rulers. In a short but crowded span of life he changed the character and destiny of a whole people. The meek, lowly and cowardly serfs were transformed into invincible warriors and invested with dignity and dream of an independent state of their own. The Guru taught his followers to translate the cardinal principles of the religion into their day-to-day life and the religion thus became a way of life. Religion according to him was the noble life lived amongst one's fellow beings. A life enlivened by religion with purity, love, service and sacrifice, as it goes, was real life; rest was all unreal. Guru Gobind Singh created such a religious revolution in the social set-up of those days that the dry bones of an oppressed peasantry were stirred into life. It aroused a new sense of purpose and gave a new direction to faith.[39] He impressed upon his disciples that it was irreligious to submit to oppression and tyranny and it was religious 'to lift the sword to fight the tyrant provided all other means had been exhausted'. In this one sentence Guru laid down the principle under which the oppressed people can rightfully rise in rebellion against an oppressive ruler, in early eighteenth century in India, much earlier than the questioning of the Divine right of the kings and rise of the people in rebellion against their autocratic rulers in European countries.

> Hear Khalsaji, with all attention
> You are dearest of the dear to me.
> The Brahmins were proud that God had given the sovereignty of the world to them,
> There was no ruler (Raja) like them in the world.
> The Rajputs felt that they had been created from God's arms.
> But, Vaishya, Shudras and Jats in large numbers I have incorporated in the Panth.
> The sovereignty of the whole world is given to you, the Khalsa.
> I have made you leaders of the Khalsa,
> The way you received Amrit (baptism) from the Guru,
> I wish to receive it the same way from you.
> The Guru and the Sikhs are interwoven with one another,
> It had been so recognized by the nine Gurus.
> The Sikhs and the Guru are related to each other as head is to the body.[40]

Bhim Chand could not withstand the way of life adopted by Guru Gobind Singh in his territory and a quarrel thus became inevitable. He twice attacked the Guru with the help of some other hill rajas in 1682 and 1685 and on both occasions was defeated with huge losses. To avoid further deterioration in relations with Bhim Chand, Guruji was persuaded by his well-wishers and Raja Medhni Prakash of Sirmaur to come to his area and Guruji moved his camp with about 500 soldiers and a large number of animals in April 1685 to settle down at Paonta, a place on the bank of river Jamuna, about 50 km equidistant from Nahan and Dehradun.[41] Hari Ram Gupta and some more historians have stated that Guru built a fort at Paonta.[42] The site has been visited a number of times, but no sign of the existence of the fort, or of any wall, foundation, etc., of a fort has been found in the vicinity of the Guru's camp at Paonta. In the northern corner there is a raised ground by the side of the river. It has been called '*Tekrin*' which at one time was used for defense purpose and perhaps the same is being referred as 'fort' by those historians who have not personally visited the site. Guru's literary and martial activities flourished during his stay of about three years at Paonta. Sikh disciples brought money, arms and horses, and plenty of war games and martial exercises were carried out. On the literary front, the Guru had 52 poets in his *darbar* who recited their martial compositions. The Guru himself composed *Var Sri Bhagwati*, *Chandi di Var*, *Krishan Avtar* and other martial hymns. The Guru soon realized that there is a long standing feud between Garhwal and Sirmaur for the last few generations. Medhni Parkash chose Paonta for Guru's camp mid-way between the two states, which situation of having his headquarters being sandwiched between two rival states was not liked by Guru Gobind Singh.

The first major battle was fought by the Guru with the Garhwalis who came down to push out the Guru from Paonta. The battle of Bhangani was fought between the Garhwalis and the Sikhs for the whole day and by evening the Garhwalis were defeated.[43] After the battle Guru Gobind Singh decided to raise his camp and go back to Anandpur. The Rani of Raipur and some other friendly people patched up the differences with Raja Bhim Chand. The *masands* had deserted the Guru in this battle and he abolished the very institution of *masand*, gave punishment to some of them and issued *hukamnamas* to his Sikhs that they should bring the offerings personally or through selected persons and not through the *masands*. Guru Gobind Singh was aware of his own limitations as well as the limitations of his disciples. On the Baisakhi of 1699 the Guru created the Khalsa, a set of disciples whose initiation ceremony was called the 'baptism of the sword'[44] (*khande ki pahul*). All the baptized Sikhs were to take four principal vows:

1. that they will have no pride of their occupation or position (called the *kritnash* vow);
2. that they will have no pride of high birth, etc. (called the *kulnash* vow);

3. that they will discard all superstitions, beliefs and rituals (called the *dharmnash* vow);
4. that they will discard all old social customs and practices (called the *ritinash karmnash* vow).

After he had baptized his chosen five, Guru Gobind Singh asked his five 'beloved ones' to initiate him in the same manner and the Guru was also administered *khande ki pahul*. The Guru, thus, stood merged in the Khalsa and the Khalsa in the Guru.[45] The creation of the Khalsa gave added strength to the Sikhs to protect their faith and themselves.

The hill rajas gradually realized the futility of continuing hostility with Guru Gobind Singh. They made peace and invited him to attend the fair at Riwalsar, a holy place of Hindus and Buddhists. It is famous for a couple of floating islands and lies 16 km from Mandi. The Guru visited Riwalsar with all his family members and was very well received by the hill rajas. The Guru addressed the hill rajas thus:

> You adopt the ways of the Khalsa;
> You have agreed to pay tribute to the Turks (Mughals);
> And regard yourselves as subordinates of the Turks.
> Come under the protection of the Khanda, the banner of the Khalsa;
> Overturn the Mughal authority.
> Lest you should complain afterwards that
> I have discriminated against you,
> I have sent for you so that you may follow the leadership of the Khalsa.[46]

The reaction of the hill rajas to the Guru's proposal was not satisfactory and was not acceptable. Their reply has been:

> You have welded four castes into one;
> How can we dine together with the four castes?
> How can your Panth get Raj?
> How can goats kill tiger?
> Some do agriculture;
> Some deal in merchandise;
> Some are the despised castes of the foothills plains.
> How can these wrest from us our Raj? People will laugh at this idea.
> It is a preposterous idea that the twelve high castes should join the low castes.[47]

The Guru was anticipating a major battle with the Hindu hill rajas and the Mughal forces. He had fortified Anandpur Fort and placed two cannons named *Baghan* and *Vijay Ghosh* on its walls. About four small fortresses were also raised around his territory. A formidable combination was formed of a number of hill rajas and the governor of Lahore and *faujdar* of Sirhind against Guru Gobind Singh. Fierce fighting continued for several days and thereafter a long siege was laid at Anandpur. The Guru was asked to vacate Anandpur for which sworn pledges for safe passage were given by Mughal authorities and Hindu hill rajas. Guru's own people were pressing him to vacate as living conditions under the long siege had become unbearable. The Guru Gobind Singh left Anandpur on 21 December 1704 and a ruthless pursuit was carried out by the Mughal forces. The Guru with great difficulty was able to reach Talwandi Saboo. In this battle Guru Gobind Singh lost everything that was so painfully established by him and the earlier Gurus. He lost all his four sons, his mother and most of his Sikh Khalsas.

For several years Guru Gobind Singh was in possession of Anandpur Sahib. He was not paying any rent or tribute to any temporal authority, i.e. the hill raja of Bilaspur or the Mughal authorities. His Khalsa at times laid contributions on the neighbouring villages. He got constructed fortresses at Anandpur and introduced the use of small cannons and muskets. He enjoined upon all his followers to wear arms. Short of the combined strength of the hill rajas and the Mughal forces, he was able to hold his own individually against the various hill rajas and some attempts by Mughal commanders sent individually against him. He was virtually a master of the small principality. He did not strike any coin in his own name, but then most of the smaller states all over India were only using the Mughal coinage and did not have their own coinage. He had under his control about 100 sq. mile area around Anandpur Sahib.[48] Some historians have said that Guru Gobind Singh did not intend to create a Sikh state of his own and for his followers. This statement, which is without any analytical examination, cannot be sustained.[49] Guru Gobind Singh is said to have addressed Bhai Nand Lal to the following effect:

Listen, Nand Lal, to this plan;
I will bring into being our Raj.
I shall weld four castes into one;
I shall make people remember God.
The Khalsa under this plan, will ride horses and support hawks;
The Turks will run away on seeing them.
It will make one man fight a lakh and a quarter;
He who dies (fighting) will be liberated. . . .
The drum will beat at every door step. . . .
The Khalsa will be victorious from one end to the other,
The Khalsa will rule; no one will remain unsubdued,
Every one will join the Khalsa.
For they along would be saved who submitted to the Khalsa.[50]

R.S. Bhangoo, author of the *Prachin Panth Prakash*, further states:

Sovereignty cannot be had without armed struggle;
The Guru initiated the armed struggle. . . .
The Guru gave sovereignty to the poor, and the seven Sanat (lowest castes) and twelve low castes, who knew nothing of politics.
The world calls them rustic Jats, Bawas, Kirars, Khatris, Iron smiths and carpenters of the low castes.

The Guru showed the benevolence to the despised calico printers, Kalas and the low castes Gujars, Ahirs, Kambohs and Soods whom no one took into any account.

The Guru thought that the water-carriers, barbers, Aroras, potters, Sainis, goldsmiths, sweepers, leather-workers, Bhatts, Brahmins, beggars, Bahoroopias, Labanas and potters—all downtrodden—should be given sovereignty;

They would remember the gift of the Guru.

The creation and growth of the Sikh state, right from the time of Guru Nanak to Guru Gobind Singh, has been likened to the planting of a sapling and its growth being strengthened and protected by successive Gurus against poachers and by the Mughal authorities. The tree of Sikh state had blossomed and borne fruit in the time of Guru Gobind Singh and the battle of Anandpur Sahib in 1704 could not make serious damage thereto. The Sikhs were in a sort of depression, when Banda Bahadur was sent to the Punjab to reclaim the lost territories and he took up the task of setting up a full-fledged independent Sikh state, with the tree of

Khalsa bearing fruit. In late 1708, Guru Gobind Singh took two major decisions, viz. (1) sending of Banda Bahadur to the Punjab to reclaim the lost territories and re-establish Sikh hegemony. The second decision was to abolish personal guruship by placing his spiritual authority in the Granth hereafter called *Guru Granth Sahib* and his temporal sovereignty with the Khalsa. The Khalsa had matured to throw up its own leadership. The tree of Sikh sovereignty had also matured and a sovereign Sikh state came into existence after a century of turmoil.

Banda Bahadur left Nanded with his five advisers and a small contingent of soldiers in October 1708 and reached Kharkhoda, the border of Punjab, in late 1709. His primary plan was to punish the nawab of Sirhind for his role in making the Guru leave Anandpur and thereafter pursuing him. Banda Bahadur was awaiting the arrival of the Sikh volunteers from all over Punjab to join him. The first to be subdued were the dacoit groups of which the local population was greatly scared.[51] He publicly proclaimed by waving a scarf that hereafter he undertook to protect the poor and the helpless against robbers and official tyrants, and expected no reward from the people in lieu of the service rendered except the simple necessities of life, such as some rations, milk and curd. He further invited people into the fold of Khalsa brotherhood and promised them a share in the conquered land.[52]

Banda Bahadur came to know that a small detachment escorting a treasure of revenue collection of various districts was halting at village Bhuna on their way to imperial capital. Banda, deeply in need of funds, fell upon the escort party and took hold of the treasure without much opposition.[53] The matter was reported to *amil* of Kaithal, a Hindu commander, who at once hurried to the spot with his troops. Banda and his men were, however, able to subdue them and *amil* was captured. He was released on the condition of making over all his guns and horses to the Sikhs, which he agreed. He was further allowed to retain his office on behalf of the Khalsa on payment of tribute and a detachment was detailed with him for the collection of revenue.[54] This was the first act of Banda Bahadur in the collection of revenue by appointing his own revenue collection staff and setting up the Sikh state. The booty was freely distributed by Banda Bahadur among his followers who were thus convinced of the unselfishness of their heroic leader.[55] Banda Bahadur started subduing smaller centres of Mughal power around Sirhind before actually taking on Wazir Khan. He subdued and occupied Samana, Ghuram, Thaska, Thanesar, Shahbad, Kunjpura, Mustafabad, Kapuri and Sadhaura. Bhai Fateh Singh had greatly contributed in the subjugation of Samana and as a reward he was appointed *faujdar* of Samana with its nine dependent parganas.[56] In fact, the battle of Samana is said to be Banda Bahadur's first regular battle. While moving towards Sadhaura, Banda Bahadur came to know of the activities of Qadam-ud-din, the ruler of Kapuri.

> There was hardly any beautiful Hindu woman whose chastity had not been violated by this depraved ruler by his force of arms. His men prowled over the territory waylaying the Hindu marriage parties and snatching away the new brides for the midnight revelries of their lustful masters. In his woman-hunting expeditions he was said to have forcibly carried away a Sikh woman from the city of Amritsar entering her house in the disguise of a Sikh.[57]

Banda Bahadur decided to attend to the chastisement of the ruler of Kapuri before going to Sadhaura. Early in the morning, on the next day, the Sikhs fell upon Kapuri, overpowered the resistance offered and set fire to the strongholds of Qadam-ud-din's debaucheries. Qadam-ud-din is also said to have perished in this onslaught.

The ruler of Sadhaura, Usman Khan, was notorious of his oppression of his subjects. He was responsible for the torture to death of the great Muslim saint Sayyid Badr-ud-din Shah, popularly known as Buddhu Shah, simply because he had helped Guru Gobind Singh in the battle of Bhangani.[58] Hindus complained to Banda Bahadur that Muslims slaughtered cows in their streets before their very houses and leave the blood and entrails of the animals there. They were not allowed to perform their religious ceremonies. Banda Bahadur was greatly enraged at this high-handedness and ordered the attack on Sadhaura. With the advance of the Sikh soldiers on Sadhaura, the aggrieved peasantry and many others of the neighbourhood who were only waiting for a favourable chance for rising, swelled the number of the invaders and rushed into the town.[59] The angry mobs set fire to the *havelis* and the houses of the Muslims. Most of the Sayyeds and Shaikhs took shelter in the *haveli* of Pir Buddhu Shah, but such was the anger of the local public that all the people inside the *haveli* were put to sword. The place got the name of *Qatalgarhi* or slaughter house after this incident.[60] The name still persists but the building has been demolished and a Jain Public School has been built in its place. The Malwa Sikhs had joined them, but they were waiting for the Majha Sikhs who were able to join Banda Bahadur's troops by defeating the Maler Kotla ruler Khizar Khan at the battle of Ropar.

His next target was Sirhind, by which time the Sikh volunteers from Malwa and Majha had also arrived. The battle of Sirhind was fought on 22 May 1710 at Chappar Jhiri, about 25 km away from Sirhind proper in accordance with the plan of Banda Bahadur.[61] The Mughal army was defeated and Wazir Khan killed.[62] The city was put to collection of booty and other resources, a sum of Rs. 2 crore was collected from the house of Wazir Khan alone.[63] Banda Bahadur was now the undisputed master of the territory from Sadhaura to Raikot and from Machhiwara and Ludhiana to Karnal.

The subdued territories were put under the charge of various sardars as a measure of distribution of authority and work in accordance with the democratic spirit of the Khalsa. Since no regular method of paying fixed salaries had been adopted, every member of the Sikh army received as his share of booty sufficient money and the surplus added to the general resources for purchase of equipment and foodstuff. After the occupation of Sirhind, Banda Bahadur appointed Baj Singh, his adviser from Nander, as the governor of Sirhind.[64] Ali Singh was appointed his deputy. Bhai Fateh Singh was confirmed in his appointment as *faujdar* of Samana and Ram Singh was appointed *faujdar* of Thanesar jointly with Baba Binod Singh. Sirhind was made the base depot for supply of stores and detachments were detailed to occupy the country at strategic places to the south, east and west. Such was the terror of the Khalsa army that deputies appointed by the imperial authorities, both Mohammedan as well as Hindus, found safety in acknowledging and submitting to their authority. All the subordinate parganas yielding a revenue of Rs. 36 lakh per annum fell into the hands of the Sikhs.[65] The Hindu revenue officials who were earlier removed in the time of Aurangzeb were posted back to their offices. Khalsa *thanas* were also set-up at strategic places in the whole territory. In this process, the administration of the entire occupied area was taken up in a formal way.

Guru Tegh Bahadur had worked for the physical and spiritual needs of the poor people of Malwa, where fields were barren and dry he got wells dug, where there was scarcity of milk he procured cows and distributed them free of cost to the people. For the landless peasants, he procured bits of land and urged them to live courageously as free people. In barren plots he got trees planted.[66] This aspect of the Guru's service to the poor people before his arrest and execution by the Mughal authorities, had greatly touched Banda Bahadur. He took the task of helping the poor peasants as the first item of civil administration immediately after the appointment of governors and other administrative officers, for example, incharge of *thanas* and civil administration at various levels. The common peasant had groaned under the inequitable revenue system during the Mughal period. In the times of Mughal emperor, any person who was holding a sizeable chunk of land, was designated as a *zamindar*, who employed or turned out the cultivators upon his sweet will and pleasure. These *zamindars* or landlords, who in most cases were high government officials, were more autocratic than the kings themselves and they were not responsible to any higher authority. The higher authorities in themselves did not interfere in their internal management as long as they paid in their fixed contribution in the government treasury. The ways and means through which they exacted money from the actual cultivators of land was not the concern of the Mughal government and in most cases peasants were practically reduced to the position of slaves. The cultivators by and large were non-Muslims and hence their emancipation was not a subject matter for the gvernment or its officials to take into consideration, except when some serious rebellion took place and the revenue collection got seriously affected. Besides the *zamindars*, the government officials too were indulged in extortions and wide scale corruption.

The Sikhs being mostly from the agricultural class had suffered these extortions at the hands of the *zamindars* and local officials. The first thing that Banda planned to carry out was to eliminate the tyranny suffered by the poor peasants and cultivators. To achieve this object Banda Bahadur asked his officers to take over all the lands which are not self-cultivated and were held by landlords, *zamindars*, government officials, etc. Every complaint from the oppressed people, therefore, excited them against the local officials and aristocrats. They considered it their religious duty to help their suffering brethren and this could only be accomplished by the removal of Mughal deputies. Sikhs all over the occupied lands, embarked on large-scale change of revenue officials. Their religious instinct drove them to those gallant deeds which alone could reverse the centuries old order of things in about two months.[67] Thus, the land grants made by the Mughal government to *zamindars* and government officials were now given to the peasants who were actually cultivating those lands. Thus, the peasant who was cultivating a particular piece of land became the owner of that land. In the villages the produce was divided between them and the tillers, one part to them and two parts to the tiller.[68]

The egalitarian character of the Sikh social order as preached by the Sikh Gurus got a real boost when the cultivator became the proprietor of the land. The equality of individual in the Sikh society being a cardinal feature of Sikh ethos was achieved when the poor peasant became the proprietor of the land he tilled. The abolition of *zamindari* which had to take place for the achievement of this egalitarian character, was a by-product of the Sikh movement. The attitude of Banda Bahadur being extremely communicative with the local public, the people for the redress of their grievances, howsoever insignificant these might be, used to come to him and he would listen to their complaints and carry out corrective measures. One Bulaqa Singh, a Sikh musician, complained to him that the Ram Rayias of Ghudani had treated him very badly. After the evening service of *Rahiras* in the gurdwara of Guru Hargobind where he repeated the words *khalsa sab bolo ji wahe guru* after the name of Guru Gobind Singh in the prayer, the Ram Rayias got enraged, they abused and assaulted him and broke his harp and even used abusive language towards Guru Gobind Singh. This account greatly enraged Banda Bahadur. He could not withstand any discourtesy to Guru Gobind Singh. He at once marched out of Sirhind to Ghudani. The Ram Rayia *masands* were arrested, punished and driven out of their village. A Sikh *thana* was established at Payal and Bulaqa Singh was appointed as *thanedar* of the circle.[69] The neighbouring villages presented *nazar* to Banda Bahadur and offered their allegiance. Banda Bahadur now proceeded to Maler Kotla.

In the confusion that had followed the attack upon Guru Gobind Singh after he crossed the Sirsa, Bibi Anup Kaur, a Sikh maidservant of the house of the Guru, fell in the hands of Sher Muhammad Khan of Maler Kotla and was carried away by him. The brave woman, however, sacrificed her life at the altar of her faith and chastity by thrusting a dagger in her heart to save her honour. Sher Muhammad Khan quietly buried her in a grave. Bibi Anup Kaur had not embraced the faith of Islam and had died a Sikh. She should therefore have been cremated according to Sikh rites. Banda Bahadur was moved to hear this pathetic story and said that the last remains of the brave Sikh woman should no longer be allowed to rot in a grave. He therefore marched upon the town of Maler Kotla.[70] There was no one to oppose his advance. The sons of Sher Muhammad Khan with all their family and belongings had fled from the place. Banda Bahadur was recognized at Maler Kotla by one, Kishan Das Bania, a Hindu merchant with whom Banda had spent some time. Kishan Das collected money from the local *shahukars* and shopkeepers and presented a purse to Banda Bahadur as an offering and begged him to spare the town. Banda Bahadur left the town unmolested. He directed his attention exclusively to the last rites of Bibi Anup Kaur. Her body was exhumed and cremated according to the Sikh rites.[71]

The propagation of Sikh religion was also in the mind of Banda Bahadur and while at Sirhind, instances of both Hindus and Mohammedans converting to the Sikh faith were quite striking. Amin-ud-Daulah in June 1710 states that many Hindus and Mohammedans finding no alternative to obedience and submission adopted the faith and rituals of the Sikhs. Banda

Bahadur virtually captivated the hearts of all towards his inclinations and whether a Hindu or a Mohammedan who came in contact with him was addressed by him as *Singhjee*.[72] Dindar Khan, a powerful ruler of the neighbourhood was named Dindar Singh and Mir Nasir-ud-din, the newswriter of Sirhind, became Mir Nasir Singh. In this manner, a large number of Mohammedans abandoned Islam and followed the path of Sikhism and took solemn oath and pledges to stand by Banda Bahadur.[73]

The terror at the very name of the Sikhs was so completely established that even the sight of a single Sikh horseman would unnerve a multitude of the erstwhile unbending officials and their followers. In the *parganas* occupied by the Sikhs, the reversal of the previous customs was striking and complete. A low scavenger or leather dresser, the lowest of the low in Indian estimation, had only to leave home and join the Guru (Banda Bahadur) when in a short time he would return to his birth place as its ruler with his order of appointment in his hand. As soon as he set foot within the boundaries, the well-born and wealthy went out to greet him and escort him home. They stood before him with enjoined palms, awaiting his orders. . . . Not a soul dared to disobey an order, and men who had often risked themselves in battlefields, became so cowed down that they were afraid even to remonstrate. Hindus who had not joined the sect were not exempt from these.[74]

The entire territories from Sadhaura to Raikot and from Machhiwara and Ludhiana to Karnal came under the control of Banda Bahadur. Ganda Singh states that all the subordinate parganas yielded a revenue of Rs. 36 lakh per annum. Karam Singh, historian, states that the 28 parganas of Sirhind during those times yielded a revenue of Rs. 52 lakh per annum. Hari Ram Gupta also states that the 28 parganas under the control of Sirhind yielded a revenue of Rs. 52 lakh per annum.[75]

It appears that search for a town which could be the capital of the conquered territories was undertaken. Sirhind was the largest city in the entire conquered territory but the same was rejected mainly for the two reasons. Sirhind was deemed as a cursed city due to the execution of the two younger sons of Guru Gobind Singh and this was not forgotten by the Sikhs for a long time to come. Secondly, it was in the plains and on the Grand Trunk

Road and any consolidated attack by the imperial army may become difficult to oppose and repulse by the Sikh forces. It was mainly used as a base camp for storage, etc., of defence stores and food-stuff. The second largest town was Sadhaura. It too was located in the plains and would become difficult to retain in the event of a major attack by the Mughal emperor. The historians are all of the view that choice of capital of the Sikh state fell on the fortress of Mukhlispur. The latter was actually a *shikargah* built by Mukhlis Khan, the governor of Sirhind, for the Mughal rulers to be used for their hunting expeditions. In some accounts it is named as *quilchi*, meaning a small fortress. The said Mukhlispur fortress is located at a distance of about 10 miles from Sadhaura on a small hilltop only about 500 ft from the ground level and two *choes* (rain water rivulets) running on both the open sides. Banda Bahadur made this area as a part of the Sadhaura-Lohgarh-Sitaragarh axis so that in case of an attack by imperial forces, the Sikh forces could retreat from Sadhaura to Lohgarh, and then disappear in the Haripur reserve forests around the fortress.[76]

Banda Bahadur carried out the repairs to the Mukhlispur fortress and renamed it as Lohgarh. He also fortified it by laying 3 to 4 ft high and 50 to 100 ft long stone walls, 52 in number. Sikh soldiers could stay behind these walls and the Mughal forces trying to reach the fortress had to face their gunshots and arrows about 15 times before they could reach the top. Large-scale troops could not climb and on two occasions when they were able to follow Banda Bahadur and his troops up to Lohgarh, the imperial forces lost a large number of soldiers but were not able to catch Banda Bahadur and his men. This small defensive arrangement has been deemed as a capital by large number of historians from Punjab when the site was hardly about 100 to 200 km from major parts of Punjab and could be easily visited and examined.

The author had the occasion to visit and examine this—the Sadhaura-Lohgarh-Sitaragarh axis—a large number of times in his capacity as convenor for the raising of a suitable memorial by the Shiromani Gurdwara Parbandhak Committee. This author is of the opinion that half-an-acre of land on which Lohgarh has been raised is generally occupied by medium-sized *havelis* (large houses). He is also of the opinion that Lohgarh was not declared as the capital of the nascent Sikh state because three series of the coins issued by Banda Bahadur from 1710-12 does not carry any name of the city or town after the word *zarb* meaning 'minted at'. Had it been fixed as a capital, the name of Lohgarh would have certainly come on the coin. The legend after the word *zarb*, is 'place of perfect peace, picture of a beautiful city where the fortunate throne of Khalsa is to be located'.

Ganda Singh writes:

> With the establishment of his power, Banda Singh assumed regal state. He fixed the fort of Mukhlispur as his capital and a base depot for his future military operations. Banda Bahadur was now a King all but in name. He had conquered many territories and was governing them through his deputies. He commanded a large army and had a capital and palaces to live in.[77]

The entire para, although very pleasing to the eye, is totally incorrect and gives an altogether different and incorrect impression than what existed on the ground. The so-called capital could not even provide a sitting space to a few thousand soldiers. There are no buildings near this fort even now, where people could take shelter nor any place to set-up a base depot. To state that he had palaces to live in is the highest travesty of the reality. Researches have shown that Banda Bahadur used to live on a nearby hilltop which was named Sitaragarh where he had a thatched hut and a small dug up pit lined with stones and mortar to store water. From Sitaragarh he could have a view of the entire valley in front from where the Mughal forces came on both the occasions. Local inhabitants state that he had put up a *nigarkhana*, a small stone hut, in the side of a hill in which two large-sized war drums were kept and when the dust raised by the Mughal army became visible to the watchmen sitting there, they would start beating the drums whereby Banda Bahadur could get some time to prepare himself to face the Mughal armies.

Christiaan Huyens (1629-95), a Dutch astronomer, is the founder of the wave theory of light. This is a property of a wave in general, and can be seen in sound waves too. The sound wave of our speech has a wavelength of about 50 cm to 1 m. In case it meets with an obstacle of the size of a few metres, it bends around it and reaches the points behind the obstacle. But when the obstacle is very large, i.e. about a few hundred metres, such as a hillock, most of it is reflected back and heard as an echo. It was possible to converse between these forts without going out. There are quite a number of such forts in Rajasthan.[78]

After the establishment of a rudimentary structure for the administration of the conquered territories, Banda Bahadur gave his attention to some of the finer aspects of a proper administrative set-up. He seemed to have a flair for preparation of legends perfectly befitting to the ideas of Sikh sovereignty. His seal, coins have been one of the finest specimens of literary compositions, of course, on the lines of Mughal system of coinage, etc., and a simple legend for greetings.

The earliest account of a Sikh seal and Sikh coins pertains to the period of Guru Gobind Singh. Khushwaqt Rai, a Persian chronicler and an official newswriter of the East India company stated in *Tarikh-i-Sikhan* in AD 1811 that Guru Gobind Singh had issued a coin with the legend *Deg Teg Fateh Nusrat O Baidrang, Yaft uz Nanak Guru Gobind Singh* on it, but he has not been able to provide any source reference for his claim.[79] Khushwaqt Rai's statement is not supported by any other historian nor has any such coin been located. He gives a similar account about Ranjit Singh having struck coins in his own name on the day of his coronation and having distributed these among the poor; but the statement is apparently incorrect as no historian or numismatist has shared his views nor has any such coin been located anywhere in the Punjab or elsewhere. Similarly, Muhammad Latif in his *History of Panjab* has stated that Guru Gobind Singh had a personal seal inscribed which the *pujaris* used to affix on his *hukamnamas*.[80] We have quite a few *hukamnamas* issued by Guru Gobind Singh, but none of them bears the imprint of any seal, even the *zafarnama* written by Guru Gobind Singh to Emperor Aurangzeb does not bear any seal imprint. These facts make it highly likely that both the accounts of Khushwaqt Rai and Muhammad Latif are imaginary and hence unreliable. Contemporary historians and newswriters mention about the striking of Sikh coins with the establishment of the first Sikh state after the fall of Sirhind in

AD 1710 to the Sikh forces under the leadership of Banda Bahadur, the commander of the Khalsa army. For a long time, these historical accounts either remained unnoticed or were not given any credibility by numismatists presumably on account of the non-availability of such coins. The proper research of the contents on the obverse and reverse of the coin starts only after the location of a particular coin. The problem with the historians regarding Sikh coins has been that they have been writing about the Sikh coins without actually having seen any coin. The author had approached Ganda Singh and Hari Ram Gupta, two major historians of this subject, during the course of his research on Sikh coinage. During discussion, it came out that both the historians had not actually seen the coins and had written about the same on the basis of whatever they could make out from the record of the earlier historians who too do not seem to have given their accounts after observing the same from the actual coins. Hence all sorts of inaccurate and distorted accounts of the Sikh coins have appeared in the history books. Since 1967 a couple of such coins have been located and it appears reasonable and logical to assume that the initial Sikh coinage was struck during 1710-12 with the formation of Sikh state over the province of Sirhind and its surrounding territories under Sikh occupation.[81] The first Sikh coin pertaining to third year of its striking of Banda Bahadur's period was thus located by Charles Panish in 1967.

Before we take up the numismatic investigation that commenced from 1967, we examine the historical backdrop against which these coins were struck. The first account of such coins occurs in the account of newswriters of January 1710 in the *Akhbar-i-Darbar-i-Mualla*.

> The Khalsa Sikhs have strange practices among themselves. They call one person as an army. In their dispatches, they write that an army of Sikhs has arrived. Some say they have struck coins and in their *hukamnamas*, the year '*Ahad*' is written. In the villages the produce is divided between them and the tillers of the land, two parts to the tiller and one part to them. The land has been given to the tillers. They want all this to be made known to the emperor. Elephants, cash and grain of Wazir Khan of Sirhind have fallen in their hands in large quantities. They have made their own '*mohar*' (seal).

Azmat-i-Nanak Guru ham zahir O Ham Ghaib ast
Badshah din O duniya aap sachcha sahib ast.

[The greatness of Guru Nanak is both patent and latent and the true lord himself is the king of both the spiritual and the temporal worlds.]

There is a great cry amongst the people (the ruling class). They are astonished at the decree of God.[82]

The word *ghaib* is a distortion of the correct word *batin,* meaning 'inner' and the same word is given in the newsletter dated 6 July 1710.[83] Hidayat Kesh, the chief newswriter, presented to the emperor the following verse of the rebel Guru—*Azmat-i-Nanak Guru, ham zahib o ham batin ast, Padshah-i-din-o-duniya aap sachcha sahib ast.* This is corroborated by the recordings of the same couplet by another contemporary historian in *Hadiqat-i-aqalim.*[84] The use of this legend on the state seal is not authenticated by the availability of its imprint on any state document. These reports clearly bring out the abolition of the existing feudal society and its replacement by landholding peasants free from feudal domination as preached by the Sikh Gurus. The above seal may have been a specimen one and there are no such imprints on any *hukamnama*, etc.

The seal impression of the Khalsa seal that has been located is:

Degh Tegh Fateh O Nusrat Baidrang,
Yaft Uz Nanak Guru Gobind Singh.

The cauldron to feed, sword to defend and the resultant victory have been achieved with the unrestrained help received from Guru Nanak to Guru Gobind Singh.[85]

The Arabic word *nusrat* means 'help'. It has also been shown as 'victory' in some Persian dictionaries. The legend appears as a seal imprint on the *hukamnamas* issued by Banda Bahadur, for instance, on 12 December 1710 to the *sangat* at Jaunpur and another (undated) to Bhai Dharam Singh.[86]

The author visited the *dera* of Banda Bahadur on the bank of the river Chenab near Riasi and close to the Pakistan border. While Banda Bahadur's family (wife and son) were taken as prisoners to the Mughal court at Delhi, his second wife escaped since she had gone to her parents house in Jammu for her confinement. Her son was the first *Gaddi Nashin* of the *dera* and the present Baba Jatinder Pal Singh is the 10th descendant of Banda Bahadur. I was shown a seal at the *dera*, which is said to belong to Banda Bahadur's period and the impression of that seal matches the seal impression on the *hukamnamas* of Banda Bahadur. This seal is used by the present *Gaddi Nashin* Baba Jatinder Pal Singh on *hukamnamas* issued by him to the *Bandai sangathan*. This seal remained operative in Banda Bahadur's time and imprints thereof are available on the *hukamnamas* issued by Banda Bahadur. The Sikhs occupied the capital city of Lahore in 1765 and were in a position to issue a Sikh coin and used the legend of the Banda Bahadur's seal on the obverse of the coin. As the seal has no reverse, Sikhs used the prevalent reverse of the Mughal coinage, i.e. *Darul Sultanat Lahore, Maiminat Manoos Jaloos* with 'S 1822', i.e. AD 1765. It is a matter of great irony that a proper seal of the Sikh state came into existence and was used only for the available short period of Banda Bahadur and thereafter during the period of Misls and further thereafter during the period of Maharaja Ranjit Singh, but nobody in the authority thought of having a state seal when even lower officials of the Mughals had their seals for use on official documents. It is understood that some sardars had their seals with the legend *Akal Sahai* and their name underneath. During the quarter century long period of Jassa Singh Ahluwalia, no attempt was made to have a seal of the Sikh state. Maharaja Ranjit Singh also used his personal seal *Akal Sahai Ranjit Singh* on state papers and never thought of getting a proper seal made out for the Khalsa state. Although the phrases *Raj Khalsa* and *Sarkar Khalsa* were frequently used in the corridors of power, the seal of *Sarkar Khalsa* never came into existence. A doubt comes to one's mind that it was deliberate on the part of Ranjit Singh to install his incompetent sons on his *gaddi* rather than *Sarkar Khalsa* selecting the most competent leader as his successor.

Half a century later, this legend was being widely used by the Sikhs on the obverse of their coins struck regularly from Lahore, Amritsar, Multan, Kashmir, Peshawar and some other towns as well.[87] William Irvine in *Later Mughals* writes, 'At Lohgarh Banda Bahadur tried to assume something of a regal state. He was *Sacha*

Padshah, the veritable sovereign; the coin was struck in the new sovereign's name.' It bore the following legends:

Obverse *Sikka Zad Bar Har Do Alam, Tegh-i-Nanak Wahib Ast.*
Fateh Gobind Singh Shah-i-Shahan, Fazal Sacha Sahib Ast.

Reverse *Zarb Ba aman-al-Dahar, Masawwarat Shahr-i-Zinat*
Al-Takhat Khalsa Mubarak Bakht.

Fateh Gobind, King of Kings, struck coin in the two worlds, the sword of Nanak is the granter of desires, by grace of God he is the veritable Lord. Coin at refuge of the world, the walled city, ornament of the fortunate throne.[88]

The legend is given in a faulty manner.

William Irvine has not given any reference in the form of footnotes, etc., as to from where he has taken these facts and the legends on the obverse and reverse of the coin. Unfortunately, this statement of William Irvine has been taken up by later historians, some having quoted the above account of Irvine and some not giving any reference to it at all. Ganda Singh also seems to have taken this legend from Irvine's account. The statement that Banda tried to assume something of a regal status is totally incorrect. The statement of Ganda Singh that Banda Bahadur had palaces to live in at Lohgarh is also totally incorrect as already explained above. The last line of the legend has one word 'Khalsa' missing and it is placed as *Altakhat Khalsa Mubarak Bakht* on the reverse of the coin itself. The meaning has been drawn in an incorrect manner. The legend in the Mughal style which was adopted by Banda Bahadur, starts from the bottom and the last part of the legend is on the top line. The transcription in English as done by William Irvine from top to bottom is absolutely incorrect. The proper meaning in this case is:

Obverse: 'Coin has been struck for both the worlds, herein and hereafter. Double-edged sword of Guru Nanak is the guarantor for the same' (like the Reserve Bank of India who guarantees the payment of the amount written on the paper currency) the double-edged sword of Guru Nanak is the guarantor of the coin. 'Victory of Guru

Second Year's Coin

Obverse *Sikka Zad Bar Har Do Alam Tegh-i-Nanak Wahib Ast*
Fateh Gobind Shah-i-Shahan Fazal Sachcha Sahib Ast
Reverse *Zarb Ba-Aman-ul-Dahar Masawarat Shahr Zinat*
Al-Takht Khalsa Mubarak Bakht

Third Year's Coin

The word Gobind is changed as Gobind Singh on the Obverse.
The word *Aman-ul-dahar* is written as *Aman-al-din* on the Reverse.

Plate 11: Initial Sikh Coinage

Gobind Singh, King of Kings, has been achieved with the grace of God Almighty'.

Reverse: *Zarb* 'Place of minting', which in this case is not shown by the name of any town or city, but what sort of a capital town it would be from where the coin deemed to be struck till such time the capital comes into existence, is described as *Ba aman-al-dahr*, i.e. most protected place, safe and peaceful, *Masawarat Shahr Zinat*, picture of a beautiful city, *Altakhat Khalsa Mubarak Bakht* where the fortunate throne of the Khalsa is located.

It is also equally incorrect that the coin was struck in the new sovereign's name and Banda Bahadur was called *Sacha Padshah*. William Irvine seems to be totally unaware of the concept of Sikh sovereignty which was vested in their Gurus, both spiritual and temporal. The tenth Guru abolished the temporal Guruship by abolishing the office of the Guru and he vested the spiritual sovereignty in the Granth hereinafter called *Guru Granth Sahib*. The coin has been struck in the name of the 'Guru Nanak Guru Gobind Singh' which is deemed as an idea and God Almighty and not in the name of any individual howsoever strong and important he may be. Banda Bahadur was only the commander of the Sikh forces and he had no other surname or position or any regal position attached to him. As explained above, the coin was struck in the name of Sikh Gurus as sovereignty with all its symbols rested with them.

Irvine is known for giving copious references from original manuscripts, of which he had a very large collection, to establish the authenticity of the factual portion of his accounts. There are, however, no footnotes giving the primary or contemporary accounts from which Irvine took the above legends and drew his impressions quoted above. *Later Mughals* could not be completed due to Irvine's ill-health, and the manuscript was entrusted to Jadunath Sarkar for editing and completion by Irvine's daughter. Jadunath Sarkar is stated to have carried out a severe compression of the copious footnotes and the references made by Irvine.[89] In the biographical note on William Irvine, Jadunath Sarkar who edited this book has stated:

The editor has considered it advisable to subject Mr. Irvine's copious footnotes to a severe compression. These notes were written by him more for his own satisfaction—i.e. as a means of verifying his statements and giving an outlet to his overflowing miscellaneous but extremely accurate information, the garnered harvest of a long and studious life,—than as a means of instructing the reader. His notes as he left them would have buried his narrative under their ponderous load. To have printed them in full would have had the effect of exhibiting the *Later Mughals* hidden by its scaffoldings. The notes, therefore, have been given here in an abbreviated form, as a guide to sources for students, but many interesting sidelights and Persian verses and proverbs have been left out.

It is a great irony that neither William Irvine nor Jadunath Sarkar has given any source reference from where these legends on the Sikh coins have been taken.

A doubt arose as to whether footnotes/references, if any, about the legends may have been struck down under the editor's pen and the opportunity to compare the recorded legends with the imprinted legends on the coins was lost for ever, especially when there are certain discrepancies between the two versions.

Fortunately, some earlier portions of *Later Mughals* had been published in various magazines and journals. The portion pertaining to the striking of the Sikh coin was reproduced in the *Journal of the Asiatic Society of Bengal* in 1894,[90] but even therein no footnotes or references have been given regarding these coins. Irvine, however, appears to have taken the material on the coins from an 'anonymous fragment' of a manuscript folio no. 141 (from his own collection). This seemed to be a part of Mohammed Ihsan Ijad's manuscript of which another fragment is in the British Museum Library, MS OR 25; Ijad's manuscript not being available in the important centres in India, I requested a friend in London to locate it from the British Museum. The curator of the Persian Section at the British Museum reported that a careful checking of folio nos. 14 to 16 of Ijad's manuscript did not reveal any mention of Sikh coins.[91] A long search was needed to identify the library which held Irvine's manuscript. With the availability of the second year's and third year's coins, search for Irvine's manuscript no longer remains that essential. On the reverse of the legend, the missing word 'Khalsa' after *Altakhat* has been incorporated on the basis of the same appearing on both the coins.

Almost the entire portion on the Sikhs given in *Later Mughals* was published by Irvine in the *Journal of the Asiatic Society of Bengal* [No. 3 (1984), pp. 112-43] under the heading 'Guru Gobind Singh and Banda', and the two accounts are identical in every way without any editing done by Jadunath Sarkar. The account regarding Sikhs written in the *Later Mughals* and that published in the *Journal of Asiatic Society* being exactly similar throws serious doubt on Jadunath Sarkar's statement of having carried out a severe compression of the copious footnotes of Irvine or else the subject matter would have remained submerged under the load of copious footnotes. Since Jadunath Sarkar has not carried out any editing of the period on Sikhs as dealt with by Irvine, his comments are certainly a very sad note on his benefactor and friend William Irvine whereas William Irvine had been responsible in giving various important documents collected by him to Jadunath Sarkar for his use.

In the book *Life and Letters of Sir Jadunath Sarkar* edited by H.R. Gupta, Panjab University, Chandigarh, 1958, it has been brought out by Hari Ram Gupta,

> A man without the fine sense of literary proportions possessed by Jadunath would have been lost in the woods in the attempt to edit such a book (*Later Mughals* of William Irvine). Once Sir Jadunath humorously remarked that if he had not used his discretion in omitting much of what Irvine had written against the Sikh community, he would have been by that time become a martyr. *The History of the Later Mughals* came out in 1922 in two thick royal octavo volumes covering only thirty-two years' history of the Mughal Empire after Aurangzeb's death. It was admitted that no more competent an authority than Professor Jadunath Sarkar could have been found to edit it (Irvine's life's work).

In all these laudatory words collected by Hari Ram Gupta and showered on Sir Jadunath Sarkar, a very sad note remains buried under them. Jadunath had whether humorously or seriously made the statement that 'had he not used his discretion in omitting much of what Irvine had written against the Sikh community he would have been by that time become a martyr'. This statement is not justified from the recorded facts. The Sikh period which was published by William Irvine in the last decade of the nineteenth century stands incorporated in the *Later Mughals* without any editing thereto. This establishes that Jadunath Sarkar had no occasion to use his discretion in omitting much of what Irvine had written against the Sikh community and hence his statement is totally false and a malicious comment on the character of the Sikh community. His comments against William Irvine, a benefactor of his, also shows pettiness on the part of Jadunath Sarkar.

Hence Jadunath Sarkar's remark that 'if he had not used his discretion in omitting much of what Irvine had written against the Sikh community he would have by that time become a martyr' is an apparent distortion of facts and is totally unwarranted.[92] Similar misinterpretations of the history of nations and events detract from the stature of Jadunath Sarkar as an unbiased historian.

Around this period, Karam Singh, a scholar in the employ of the Patiala State, wrote a couple of books on Banda Bahadur. He was fully conversant with the Persian language. His first book on Banda Bahadur written in 1907, makes no reference to the coins having been struck by the Sikhs, nor is there any reference to *Farrukh-Siyar-Nama* by Ihsan Ijad in the bibliographical notes. His second book *Banda Kaun Se* (1929) has details about *Farrukh-Siyar-Nama* by Ihsan Ijad and the special features of his work in the bibliographical notes.[93] Based on Ijad's authority, he had recorded the striking of coins by Banda Bahadur and the obverse legend on these coins (no specific page is cited for this claim). Ijad was a court chronicler who wrote *Farrukh-Siyar-Nama* under the orders of Farrukh Siyar in 1131 Hijri, i.e. AD 1715. Some of his accounts of the period of Banda Bahadur are not available in any other Persian manuscript.[94] Karam Singh also gives a second reference *Hadiqat-i-Aqalim* for these Sikh coins, but this statement is incorrect as the legend mentioned therein is a different one.[95] Both writers were contemporaries but apparently never met or exchanged views. The complete manuscript of Ihsan Ijad, located at the Aligarh Muslim University, unfortunately also does not mention these coins, and the volume ends much before the reign of Farrukh Siyar. The legend mentioned by Karam Singh is exactly the same as that mentioned by Irvine, giving the impression that both these scholars might have taken the above legends from some other account of Ihsan Ijad.

In his book on Banda Bahadur (1935), Ganda Singh states that Banda Bahadur struck a coin in the name of his saviours Guru Nanak and Guru Gobind Singh. The legends mentioned by Ganda Singh are the same as those noted by Irvine except that he has inserted the word 'Singh' after 'Gobind'[96] (Ganda Singh has not cited any reference for the addition of the word 'Singh'). Ganda Singh's rendering of the Persian legends into English is slightly different. In fact, he changed his rendering in his next piece of writing on Banda Bahadur. However, the Roman English rendering of the legends is exactly the same as that done by Irvine and some minor mistakes committed by Irvine are also repeated by Ganda Singh, viz., the word *al* between *aman* and *dahar* and before *takht* has been written as *ud*. Ganda Singh quotes Persian extracts and references at great lengths but does not give any source reference on the coin and its legends. He wrote another booklet on Banda Bahadur in 1976 in which he mentions the coin and its legends as in the earlier footnotes, viz., Ijad's *Farrukh-Siyar-Nama* and *Hadiqat-ul-Aqalim*.[97] He does not give the page number of Ijad's work nor its location.

Hadiqat-ul-Aqalim is available at the Aligarh Muslim University, besides other places, and it is recorded that the successors of the sect of Nanak Shah have struck a coin in their own name with the legend exactly as mentioned in *Akhbar-i-Darbar-i-Mualla*,[98] but not the one recorded by Ganda Singh and thus this is an incorrect reference. A similar mistake has been made by Karam Singh and it is quite likely that Ganda Singh reproduced the error from Karam Singh's account. The author contacted Ganda Singh twice at his Patiala residence in 1982-3 to enquire about the source reference for the said legends but he could not cite any specific reference for them. In another long article, 'Banda Singh Bahadur, His Achievements and the Place of His Execution', Ganda Singh gives the same legends and the same incomplete and incorrect references as in the case of his earlier booklet.[99]

Hari Ram Gupta merely states that Banda Bahadur struck coins and issued orders under his own seal,[100] without giving any source reference for this claim, although he has otherwise been as meticulous as Irvine in giving references and footnotes. In fact,

Banda Bahadur did not use any seal in his own name and therefore Hari Ram Gupta's contention is incorrect. Khushwant Singh notes in this context:

> Thus Banda the bairagi-hermit who as a military commander had become Banda Bahadur—the brave, assumed his third incarnation as Banda Padshah, the emperor. He introduced a new calendar year dating from his capture of Sirhind. He had also got new coins struck to mark his reign bearing the names of Guru Nanak and Gobind.[101]

Khuswant Singh's above statement is totally incorrect. Banda Bahadur never called himself 'Padshah' or emperor. The new calendar year introduced by him was in the name of the Gurus and not in his own name. Khushwant Singh has not given any reference as to from which source he has got the above facts. In fact, when an acclaimed historian makes such incorrect statements which are not based on any facts, they do a great disservice to Sikh history.

The legends mentioned by Hari Ram Gupta in the footnotes are those mentioned by Ganda Singh, without giving his source reference or acknowledging Ganda Singh's accounts. Gupta's comments are apparently incorrect.

G.S. Deol, a fairly recent biographer of Banda Bahadur, acknowledges that the coins and their legends have been taken from Ganda Singh's account.[102] Giani Gian Singh in his book *Shamsher Khalsa Alharof Guru Khalsa* gives a fairly detailed account of Banda Bahadur but here again there is no mention about the coin or its legends.[103]

J.S. Grewal has stated that Banda Bahadur adopted Mukhlispur, an imperial fort now called Lohgarh, as his capital and struck a new coin in the name of Guru Nanak and Guru Gobind Singh. Mukhlispur was a *shikargah*, spread over less than an acre in area. It could not have been used as a state capital. With a similar inscription he started using a seal on his *hukamnamas*.[104] (The inscription on the seal was totally different from that on the coins.) Although Grewal cites Ganda Singh on the matter of the seal on the *hukamnamas*, he does not give any reference/footnote about the coin or the legend inscribed on it.

From the above accounts, it emerges that the legends on the

coins said to have been struck by Banda Bahadur were apparently recorded by Ihsan Ijad in a manuscript of his which appears to have been scrutinized by Irvine and Karam Singh. Karam Singh carried out most of his research in Lahore libraries and hence Ijad's manuscript is likely to be available in some library in Lahore. I have not been able to secure any access to these archives so far in spite of repeated requests to various authorities in Lahore. The manuscript examined by Irvine was his own copy; I have not been able to determine the library in Britain to which this manuscript was donated. Ganda Singh seems to have taken the account of the legends from the works of Irvine and Karam Singh without acknowledging them; nor does he appear to have examined any original source reference. The historians who wrote on the initial Sikh coinage apparently did so without any examination of the actual coins; hence their analyses are based on inadequate evidence, especially when the most important and reliable source of evidence, i.e. the actual coins which were available, were not located and taken into account.

Repeated reading of Ijad's *Farrukh-Siyar-Nama* seems to indicate that the author included the description of the coins in some other of his works or in that of some other chronicler, as the available volume in the British Museum and the photocopy with the Aligarh Muslim University virtually close before the Sikh period and hence is not the pertinent document. About half a century after the fall of the first Sikh state, it arose again in AD 1765 and the legend adopted on the coins issued from Lahore in Samvat 1822 was the same one as on the state seal of Banda Bahadur.

The available Sikh coins are as under:

1. The first year's coin has on the reverse the word *ahad* in place of 'one', but this coin has not been located so far.
2. *John Dyell's Coin:* The details of this coin along with a photograph thereof are given by John Dyell in his article published in *Numismatic Digest*.[105] On the reverse, the year of the coinage is '2' in Arabic numeral, being the second year's coin. The drawings and photograph of this coin also appear in Hans Herrli's catalogue of Sikh coins and in the *Standard Guide to South Asian Coins*.

3. *Charles Panish's Coin:* In addition to the information given by Panish, the drawings are given by Hans Herrli in the *Standard Guide to South Asian Coins*. On the reverse, the year of issue is shown as '3' in Arabic numeral. I have also received a tin-foil of the coin with its details from Panish (see Plate 11).
4. One such third year's coin is in possession of Norma J. Pudderster.

The meaning of the legends, according to our understanding, keeping in view the Sikh ethos, should be as follows:

Obverse: The coin has been struck in both the worlds herein and hereafter. With the guarantee of Guru Nanak's double-edged sword or guaranteed by Guru Nanak under the strength of his sword. The victory of Guru Gobind Singh, King of Kings, has been achieved with the grace of Sachcha Sahib, the God Almighty. Sikhs have a firm belief in the absolute supremacy of God and their ten Gurus as having one identity and all these saviours, God and Nanak to Gobind Singh, stand encompassed in this couplet on the obverse of the coin as the sovereign of the Sikh state.

Reverse: Differing literal meanings have been given by various historians. To our understanding it should be *Zarb-ba-aman-Ul-dahar*, coined at the refuge of the world, the most protected place, safe and peaceful, the emphasis being primarily on the security of the place; *Masawarat-Shahr-Zinat*, the picture of a beautiful city; the word *Zinat* should appropriately be linked with *Shahr* and not with *altakht* (*Altakht Khalsa Mubarak Bakkt*), where is the auspicious throne of the Khalsa. With the addition of the word *Khalsa* this would mean, where the auspicious throne of the Khalsa is located. Thus, the meaning is: coined at the place of peace and security, picture of a beautiful city, where the auspicious throne of the Khalsa is located.

It now stands firmly established that the initial Sikh coinage was started by Banda Bahadur in AD 1710 on the basis of the historical accounts and numismatic investigation of the coins located so far. This also throws light on a very important feature of the Sikh concept of sovereignty shortly after the demise of Guru Gobind Singh and the institution of the first Sikh state. The two legends, both on the coin and the seal, give a true depiction of the concept of temporal sovereignty as bequeathed by the tenth master to the Khalsa Panth. It is noteworthy that Banda Bahadur although belonging to a different religion became a staunch disciple of Guru Gobind Singh and within a short span of only a month or so was selected as the commander of the Khalsa army and was sent to the Punjab where all his energies and time were spent in creating and defending the infant Sikh state. Yet in this short time he understood and expressed the Sikh concept of sovereignty in such simple, lucid, and meaningful words that no Sikh authority has ever suggested any modification or any improvement on his original description. He certainly had a profound insight into the Sikh ethos and traditions, and was an extraordinary commander of the army.

The development of the initial Sikh coin very lucidly depicts the democratic spirit of Sikh society as laid down by their Gurus in the midst of the feudal age. The legend on the initial coin was composed in praise of Guru Nanak only. It is presumed that some Sikh would have desired the inclusion of the name of the tenth Guru also. Hence the above legend with the names of both the first and the tenth Gurus was decided upon. Hereto the name of Guru Gobind Singh was written as Gobind only and some Sikhs would have desired the recording of his full name and hence in the third year's coin the name given is Gobind Singh. This shows the use of democratic measures even in the most sensitive state issues.

FATEH DARSHAN: A NEW SALUTATION

Guru Gobind Singh was somewhat free from armed conflicts in the closing years of the seventeenth century. He spent his spare time in literary activities. It was during this outwardly peaceful interval that he instituted the Khalsa on the Baisakhi day of 30 March 1699.[106] The five Sikhs who came to be known as the 'five beloveds' (*panj pyare*) were given the baptism of double-edged sword (*khande ki pahul*). After serving *pahul* to the five selected Sikhs, hereafter called the 'five beloved ones', the Guru himself took *pahul* from them, thereby merging himself with the Khalsa.

In Guru Nanak's time, Sikhs greeted one another by saying *Satnam*, *Sat Kartar*, *Sat Sri Akal* meaning that God, the creator, or the immortal one is ever lasting.[107] Whereas *Sat Sri Akal* still exists as a very common greeting among Sikhs, the other forms of greeting, viz., *Satnam*, and *Sat Kartar* are no longer in common use. A salutation *Wahe Guru ji ka Khalsa, Wahe Guru ji ki Fateh* came to existence around the period of the creation of the Khalsa. It means that the Khalsa belongs to the Wahe Guru and so do the victories of the Khalsa belong to the Wahe Guru. Some historians contend that this salutation was issued by Guru Gobind Singh himself.[108] The language and the meaning of the salutation does not give the impression that Guru Gobind Singh would have made such a salutation. In his *vani*, the Guru has been proclaiming all that he possesses belong to the Khalsa and all his achievements are due to the Khalsa. The legend in the salutations obviously seems to be out of place. It is very likely that the salutation has been spelt out by some poet of the Guru's court, who put the entire Khalsa as belonging to the Guru placing their absolute loyalty at the feet of the Guru and when the Khalsa belonged to the Guru, all the victories of the Khalsa also stand to the credit of the Guru. This was a salutation among the Khalsa and could not be deemed to be a war cry. With the passage of time, this salutation, which appeared to be fairly long, was conveniently reduced to *Wahe Guru ji ki Fateh* only.[109] This abridged salutation now stands further abridged to *Guru Fateh* in the corridors of the Shiromani Gurdwara Parbandhak Committee, Amritsar.

Banda Bahadur designed a small salutation *Fateh Darshan* meaning that 'victory be yours' in those turbulent times. He had mentioned this in his *hukamnamas* after the establishment of the Sikh state as *Ek Onkar Fateh Darshan* below the seal impression of the Khalsa state. May be he had been addressing people with this salutation. Banda Bahadur had been addressing every Hindu and Muslim as 'Singhjee' who came to meet him. Salutation and war cry are meant for two different situations and cannot be exchanged with each another. This has never been a war cry and it is wrong to label it as thus by some historians as war cry in replacement of the initial salutation of the Sikhs. The mutual regard, consideration and devotion between the Guru and his Khalsa have been expressed by historians that henceforth Guru was the Khalsa and Khalsa was the Guru.

The Sikhs when in greater power in mid-nineteenth century had made an addition to the *Raj Karega Khalsa* couplet as

Dilli takht par bahegi aap Guru ki fauj,
Chhatter phirega sis paar; barhi karegi mauj,
Raj Karega Khalsa, baaqi rahe na koe,
Khwar hoye sab milenge, bache saran jo hoye.

Armies of the Guru shall rule Delhi, and only those will survive who seek the protection of the Khalsa. The frustrated shall submit and the enemies be vanquished.

After the British conquered Punjab they did not quite like the idea of any one (especially the Sikhs) ruling Delhi, except themselves, and so they banned this verse. The Sikh leaders compromised by removing the first two lines from the popular recitation and also rationalized the last two by explaining that the pure would rule, only in the spiritual and not the temporal sense. It was an old trick to preserve a dream by calling it an illusion. The British let it pass.[110]

All these changes carried out under the orders of British government have not been questioned by the Sikhs at any stage.

Guru Gobind Singh had mounted two heavy guns on the front walls of the fort at Anandpur Sahib. These guns were named *Baghan* meaning tigress and the *Vijay Ghosh* meaning 'declaration of victory'. During the first day of the last battle of Anandpur, 1704, these guns wrought havoc in the enemy ranks. In the first day's fight Wazir Khan lost 900 men.[111] It appears that Banda Bahadur in a very short time had picked up a lot from Guru Gobind Singh. The first few words on the seal of the Sikh state, that is, *Degh Tegh Fateh* were already appearing on the *hukamnamas* and he took these words and elaborated them into proper blessings of the Gurus to the Sikh nation. He had a flair for creating new terminologies, viz., that on the seal and the coins, but, of course, within the framework of the Sikh concept of sovereignty. His salutation *Fateh Darshan* is very much akin to the name of the second gun mounted by Guru Gobind Singh on the fort of the Anandpur Sahib, viz., *Vijay Ghosh*.

It hardly seems reasonable that Sikhs should have taken offence to the use of this legend of salutation. If a long salutation *Wahe Guru ji ka Khalsa*, *Wahe Guru ji ki Fateh* in use, could be cut into half and further cut for the convenience of the Sikhs, why has this small legend *Fateh Darshan* been alleged to have been objected by the Sikhs that it is a replacement of *Wahe Guru ji ka Khalsa*, *Wahe Guru ji ki Fateh* and hence was desired to be dropped as stated by Ganda Singh?[112]

We have no authentic record of the directions given by Guru Gobind Singh to Banda Bahadur after his denouncing *bairag* and becoming a disciple of the Guru. From the manner in which Banda Bahadur took up his assignment it appears that he was given the instructions to re-establish Sikh presence on the areas vacated by Guru Gobind Singh after the battle of Anandpur in 1705. He worked to this purpose with absolute devotion. His use of the advisers given to him and various other duties of a ruler as well as a Sikh as laid down in the concept of Sikh sovereignty have been carried out with total devotion and sincerity of purpose by Banda Bahadur. His actions show his humility towards every Sikh, howsoever lowly he may be placed, for instance his distribution of the booty among Sikhs without keeping any special share for himself. At the slightest complaint of a Sikh against the conduct of Muslim rulers or *masands* and other disgruntled elements, he would immediately take corrective action. These are summed up as under:

1. After the successful battle of Sirhind and in the process of consolidation of the conquered territories, he placed most of his advisers and other commanders as governors/naib governors/*faujdar* and other revenue and police assignments.
2. Banda Bahadur did not adopt any regal title for himself and lived a totally simple life of an ordinary soldier, totally divorced from the style of commanders and rulers in those times.

3. Every person, howsoever lowly he may be, who came in contact with him, he would address him as *Singhjee* and attend to his problems. A few examples are as under:

   (i) When Balaqa Singh, who used to play *rubab* in an area peopled by *masands*, when spoke highly of his Gurus was assaulted by the *masands* and came with a complaint to Banda Bahadur. The Sikh force went and punished the *masands* and Banda Bahadur posted Balaqa Singh as *thanedar* of the place;

   (ii) One Bibi Anup Kaur, a maidservant in the house of the Guru, was abducted by one of the Afghans of Maler Kotla. The lady sacrificed her life instead of succumbing to the lust of the Afghan. She was quietly buried so that it did not come to the notice of the Sikh forces who had obtained victory over Sirhind. But somehow it came to the notice of Banda Bahadur. He got the body of the girl exhumed and gave her a proper cremation as a Sikh. Suitable punishment was given to people involved in this crime.

   There are a number of occasions when such complaints came to Banda Bahadur and his justice was most appropriate and prompt.

4. His attitude towards the Muslim population was also very liberal and he would address them also as *Singhjees*. It has been reported that 4,000 to 5,000 Muslims of Kalanaur got themselves converted to Sikhism. Those who remained as Muslim but joined the army of Banda Bahadur were given proper salary and they had the liberty to do their *namaz*, etc., at their public places. Dindar Khan became Dindar Singh and Naseer Muhammad, a newswriter became Naseer Singh. This was his contribution to the propagation of the Sikh religion.

5. All landholdings which were primarily with the Muslim officials and *zamindars* were taken over and distributed among the peasants and cultivators. Hindu revenue officials who were removed and their place given to Muslim officials were restored

to their original places. In the entire area under the Sikh control, the *zamindari* system stood totally abolished and peasants and cultivators became the owners of all those lands. It is the first attempt at *zamindari* abolition in India.

6. A very concessional and simple system of revenue collection was brought into practice. Besides the imperial revenue, *zamindars* used to carry great atrocities on the cultivators who were reduced to a state of slavery by the exactions of the *zamindars* over and above the land revenue. Banda Bahadur arranged that twice a year after the collection of the crop, the cultivator was to get two-third thereof and one-third was the land revenue for the Sikh state. The revenue officials were to sell that grain to the *bania* present there at the market rate and deposit the amount realized with the Sikh treasury.
7. Banda Bahadur issued a state seal in praise of Guru Nanak. It is apparent that when this was put before the Sikhs somebody pointed out that along with Guru Nanak's name, the name of Guru Gobind Singh must also be included which was appreciated and the seal was redesigned with the legend: *Degh Tegh Fateh, Oh Nusrat Baidrang, Yaft uz Nanak Guru Gobind Singh*. This seal remained operative in Banda Bahadur's time and imprint thereof are available on the *hukamnamas* issued by Banda Bahadur. In 1765, when the Sikhs occupied the capital city of Lahore and were in a position to issue a Sikh coin they used the legend of the Banda Bahadur's seal on the obverse of the coin and for the reverse they wrote *Darul Sultanate Lahore, Maiminat Manoos Jaloos* with 'S 1822'. It is a matter of great irony that a proper seal of the Sikh state came into existence and was used only for the very little period of Banda Bahadur and thereafter during the period of Misls and thereafter the period of great Maharaja Ranjit Singh, who called his government *Sarkar Khalsa*, there has been no state seal for the state papers whereas every Mughal official used a proper seal of his office. Maharaja Ranjit Singh used his personal seal *Akal Sahai* on state papers and did go in for a state seal.

NOTES

1. J.S. Bains, *Indian Journal of Political Science*, vol. XXIII, 1962, p. 311.
2. G.C. Narang, *Transformation of Sikhism*, Lahore, 1945, p. 31.
3. Ibid., p. 25.
4. *Sacred Writings of the Sikhs*, London, 1960, p. 45.
5. Hari Ram Gupta, *History of the Sikhs*, vol. I, New Delhi: Munshiram Manoharlal, 1994, p. 191.
6. Ibid., p. 114.
7. Ibid., pp. 117-18.
8. Ibid., p. 127.
9. Ibid., p. 132.
10. A.C. Banerjee, *Sikh Gurus and Sikh Religion*, New Delhi: Munshiram Manoharlal, 1983, p. 182.
11. Mohsin Fani, *Dabistan-i-Mazhab*, tr. Troyer and Shia, vol. 1, p. 271.
12. Gupta, op. cit., p. 131.
13. Ibid.
14. Hari Ram Gupta, *Sikh Gurus*, New Delhi: U.C. Kapoor, 1994, p. 90.
15. M.A. Macauliffe, *Sikh Religion*, Oxford, 1909, vol. III, p. 57.
16. Ibid., p. 64.
17. Gupta, *History of the Sikhs*, p. 133.
18. Fani, *Dabistan-i-Mazhab*, pp. 233-4.
19. Ibid., pp. 225, 233.
20. Gupta, *Sikh Gurus*, pp. 93, 98.
21. I.B. Banerjee, *Evolution of Khalsa*, Calcutta: A. Mukherjee & Co., 1979, p. 254.
22. Narang, *Transformation of Sikhism*, p. 76.
23. Ibid.
24. Macauliffe, *Sikh Religion*, p. 50.
25. Ibid.
26. Ibid., p. 99.
27. *Adi Granth*, Bani Bhagat Ravi Dass, p. 345.
28. Nihar Ranjan Ray, *The Sikh Gurus and Sikh Society*, New Delhi: Munshiram Manoharlal, 1975, p. 57.
29. A.C. Banerjee, *Sikh Gurus and Sikh Religion*, p. 235.
30. Gupta, *History of Sikh Gurus*, p. 100.
31. Ibid., p. 110.

32. Ibid.
33. *Guru Hargobind in Gurbilas Patshahi 6*, p. 293.
34. Tarlochan Singh, *Guru Tegh Bahadur*, Patiala: Punjabi University, 1967, p. ix.
35. A.C. Banerjee, *The Sikh Gurus and Sikh Religion*, p. 264.
36. Gupta, *History of Sikh Gurus*, p. 143.
37. Surinder Singh, *Sikh Coinage*, New Delhi: Manohar, 2004, p. 183.
38. J.S. Grewal and S.S. Bal, *Guru Gobind Singh*, Chandigarh: Panjab University, 1967, p. 53.
39. Ibid., p. 144.
40. Koer Singh, *Gurbilas Patshahi 10*, p. 131.
41. Gupta, *History of the Sikhs*, p. 231.
42. Ibid.
43. Ibid., pp. 234-6.
44. Ibid., pp. 266-7.
45. Kapur Singh, 'The Baisakhi of Guru Gobind Singh', in *Parasara-prasna*, Amritsar: Guru Nanak Dev University, 1981, p. 1.
46. (i) Koer Singh, *Gurbilas Patshahi 10*, p. 137.
    (ii) Macauliffe, *The Sikh Religion*, vol. V, pp. 99-100.
47. Ibid., Macauliffe.
48. J.S. Grewal, *From Guru Nanak to Ranjit Singh*, Amritsar: Guru Nanak Dev University, 1982, p. 109.
    Ahmad Shah Batalvi in his *Tarikh-i-Hind* (p. 7) has stated 'as a result of Guru Gobind's conflict with the hill chiefs, he occupied about a hundred miles of territory around Anandpur. He was in fact bent upon creating a dominion for himself and his Sikhs.'
49. (i) A.C. Banerjee, *The Khalsa Raj*, New Delhi: Abhinav Publications, 1985, p. 19.
    (ii) G.S. Nayyar, *Sikh Polity and Political Institutions*, New Delhi, Oriental Publishers and Distributors, 1979, pp. 81-2.
50. *Rehatname*, Piara Singh Padam, p. 47.
51. Ganda Singh, *Life of Banda Singh Bahadur*, Amritsar: Khalsa College, 1935, pp. 29-30.
52. Ibid., p. 30.
53. Ibid., p. 36.
54. Ibid., p. 37.
55. Narang, *Transformation of Sikhism*, p. 105.
56. Ganda Singh, *Life of Banda Singh Bahadur*, p. 40.
57. Ibid., p. 45.
58. Ibid., pp. 46-7.
59. Ibid., p. 48.

60. Ibid., p. 49.
61. Ibid., p. 63.
62. Ibid., p. 65.
63. Ibid., p. 69.
54. Ibid., p. 72.
65. Ibid., p. 73.
66. Tarlochan Singh, *Guru Tegh Bahadur*, Patiala: Punjabi University, 1967, p. ix.
67. Ganda Singh, *Life of Banda Singh Bahadur*, pp. 87-8.
68. Surinder Singh, *Sikh Coinage*, p. 31.
69. Ganda Singh, *Banda Singh Bahadur*, pp. 75-6.
70. Ibid., p. 77.
71. Ibid., p. 79.
72. Ibid., p. 73.
73. Ibid.
74. William Irvine, *Later Mughals*, pp. 98-9.
75. Gupta, *History of the Sikhs*, vol. II, p. 14.
76. For details, see Sadhaura-Lohgarh-Sitaragarh axis, Chapter 4.
77. Ganda Singh, *Life of Banda Singh Bahadur*, p. 82.
78. Christiaan Huyens, *Wave Theory of Light*, mentioned in *Text Book of Physics*, Class XII, New Delhi: NCERT, 2007, p. 353.
79. Khushwaqt Rai, *Tarikh-i-Sikhan*, MS SHR, 1274, Amritsar: Khalsa College, p. 46.
80. Muhammad Latif, *History of Panjab*, Ludhiana: Kalyani Publishers, 1989, p. 270.
81. Charles K. Panish, 'First Sikh Trans-Sutlej Coinage', *Journal of the Numismatic Society*, Banaras, vol. XXIX, part II, 1967, pp. 88-90.
82. *Akhbar-i-Darbar-i-Mualla*, Old Historical Records, Jaipur, Newsletter, dated 9 January 1711, photocopy received from Ganda Singh, translated and edited version available in *Panjab Past and Present*, vol. XVIII, no. 2, October 1984, Patiala: Punjabi University p. 51.
83. Ibid., p. 39 and p. 30 of the above-quoted *Punjab Past and Present*.
84. *Hadiqat-i-aqalim*, MS, Murtaza Hussain, Aligarh Muslim University, p. 148.
85. Ganda Singh, *Banda Singh Bahadur*, p. 83.
86. Idem, *Hukamnamas*, dated 12 December 1710 and another addressed to Bhai Dharam Singh (undated) reproduced in *Hukamnama* by Ganda Singh, Patiala: Punjabi University, 1985, pp. 184-5.

87. Hans Herrli, *The Coins of the Sikhs*, Nagpur: Indian Coin Society, 1993, pp. 31-3.
88. Irvine, *Later Mughals*, p. 110.
89. Ibid., p. xxviii.
90. William Irvine, 'Guru Gobind Singh and Banda', *Journal of the Asiatic Society of Bengal*, part I, no. 3, 1894, p. 134. The name of the journal is incorrectly given as *Calcutta Review* on p. xxx of *Later Mughals*.
91. Letter dated 25 October 1990, from M.I. Walay, Persian and Turkish Section, British Library, London to Dr. B.S. Bagga: 'Your inquiry regarding a reference in Ijad's *Farukhsiyar Nama* to Banda Bahadur's coins of 1710 to 1712. I have to report that in checking carefully through folios 14 to 16 of our MS OR 25 I found no word at all on that subject—possibly a MS in some other library was intended'.
92. H.R. Gupta, *Life and Letters of Sir Jadunath Sarkar*, Chandigarh: Panjab University, 1958, p. 62.
93. Karam Singh, *Banda Bahadur Kaun See* (Punjabi), Amritsar, undated, p. 34.
94. Ibid., p. 35.
95. Ibid., p. 36, see note 21.
96. Ganda Singh, *Life of Banda Singh Bahadur*, pp. 82-3.
97. Idem, *Baba Banda Bahadur*, Sirhind: Sirhind Historical Research Society, 1997, p. 9.
98. *Hadiqad-ul-Aqalim* (MS), Aligarh: Aligarh Muslim University, p. 148.
99. Ganda Singh, 'Banda Singh Bahadur', *Panjab Past and Present*, Patiala: Punjabi University, vol. XXII, part II, October 1988, p. 123.
100. Gupta, *History of Sikh Gurus*, p. 10.
101. Khushwant Singh, *History of Sikhs*, vol. I, New Delhi: Oxford University Press, 1987, p. 107.
102. G.S. Deol, *Banda Bahadur*, Jullundur: New Academic Publishing House, 1972, pp. 57, 58.
103. Gian Singh Giani, *Shamsher Khalsa Alharof: Twarikh Guru Khalsa* (Urdu), published from Sialkot, 1892, Sec. 2, pp. 1 to 23 deal with Banda Bahadur but there is no mention of Sikh coins.
104. J.S. Grewal, *The Sikhs of Punjab,* The Cambridge History of India, vol. II, no. 3, New Delhi: Orient Longman, 1990, p. 83.
105. John S. Dyell, 'Banda Bahadur and the First Sikh Coinage', *Numismatic Digest*, vol. IV, pt. I, June 1980, Bombay, pp. 59-67.

106. Gupta, *History of Sikh Gurus*, pp. 181-6.
107. Ibid., p. 60.
108. Ibid., p. 186. With a view to giving the Singhs an optimistic view of life in the midst of trials and tribulations which lay ahead of them, the Guru gave them a unique form of salutation: *Wah Guru ji ka Khalsa, Wah Guru ji ki Fateh* (The Khalsa is thine, O Lord! So does the victory belong to you).
109. R.S. Bhangoo, *Sri Guru Panth Parkash*, tr. Kulwant Singh, vol. I, 2008, p. 219.
110. M.J. Akbar, *India: The Siege Within*, Harmondsworth: Penguin Books Ltd., 1985, p. 121.
111. Gupta, op. cit., p. 203.
112. Ganda Singh, *Banda Singh Bahadur*, p. 85.

CHAPTER 6

The Egalitarian Revolution of the Sikhs

The Plebeian Aspect of the Revolution

The Sikh revolution was not only an egalitarian social revolution, it was also a plebeian political revolution against the religious and political domination of the Mughal rulers, threatening to undermine the basic religious and moral fabric of Indian society. The Sikh Gurus, Guru Nanak to Guru Gobind Singh, raised a new religion, outside the caste framework, based on human values and maintained and protected those values against Mughal interference. The Sikhs carried out a long-drawn armed revolution during first three quarters of the eighteenth century, till they were able to throw out the decadent Mughal rule from Punjab and set-up their own egalitarian rule with large-scale plebeian participation. This democratic revolution against the decaying feudalism was more radical than the French Revolution.[1]

Some historians of the medieval India, not fully conversant with Sikh revolutionary history, have clubbed the same with agrarian disturbances in the Mughal period, mismanaged by the decaying *zamindari*, an assignment system. Irfan Habib, a noted historian of medieval period, while elaborately explaining the agrarian crisis of the Mughal Empire, has described the Sikh revolution as an agrarian revolt against the Mughal emperor.[2] The agrarian aspects of the Sikh egalitarian revolution was, however, merely a by-product of the same and the Sikh revolution cannot be treated as a mere agrarian revolt by any stretch of imagination.

In the Western world, the French Revolution began in 1789. In India, Guru Gobind Singh commenced it over a century earlier when he created the Khalsa in 1699, with the deliberate plan of the downtrodden to capture political power. Whereas in its initial thrust the French Revolution was for the middle class, but when the Khalsa wielded political power for the first time, the lowest of the low in Indian estimation were co-sharers of that authority.[3] There is not a single other movement of Indian origin, which owned, let alone having given the shape to, the ideal that the sovereignty of the land has to be vested in the common people. No other movement with a plebeian base succeeded in the medieval period.[4]

The Sikh movement established the Sikh Panth outside the caste society and successfully used it as a base to challenge political and religious dominance. It even captured political power for a plebeian cause, and what the radical Bhagats failed to achieve, the Gurus achieved the same. It was because of the Sikh Gurus' view of religion which regards all problems, social or political thrown up by life as a part and parcel of one's religious duty. The political orientation and development was only a projection of the Sikh view of their religion.[5]

As pointed out by Max Weber, there were only two alternatives before the Sikhs—either to abolish the caste system or be engulfed in the same. As abolition of the caste system at one stroke was not possible even in the distant future, the only practical way was to create a social order outside the caste system and resist any interference therein and to protect the same from outside. None of the medieval Bhagats or their successors made a serious attempt to establish a social order outside the caste system and defend it. These Bhagati sects either got wholly absorbed in the caste system or remained attached as an appendage of one kind or the other. With the passage of time these Bhagati sects got merged into brahminism and caste society. Chaitanya's Ramanandis and Kabirpanthis slowly got merged with brahminhood.

The conversion of Hindus mostly from the low castes to Islam were, by and large, voluntary. If large sections of low caste could embrace Islam, and in the process cut themselves off completely from the Hindu fold, socio-religious community could also be organized outside the caste society and used to break the shakles of the caste system. But there is no evidence that Bhagats ever aspired to do so. They made no attempt to change the caste society or build a new one outside the caste structure. By omitting to take any organizational steps and by confining their battle against the caste system only to the ideological pursuit of their social ideology, their ultimate failure in the social field were inevitable.

THE SIKH IDEOLOGY

The Sikh Gurus created an egalitarian society (the Sikh social order) outside the caste system and developed it in the shape of a revolutionary movement. Brahminism being a medley of various creeds and cults, with conflicting and contradictory systems and exponents of this system deemed Sikhism as an offshoot of Hindu religion. But the growth of Sikhism has been so exceptional that there is hardly any common essential between Sikhism and the traditional Hindu religions.

The dominant feature of Indian religions has been that the world was unreal and a place of suffering. A release from its bondage is to be obtained by resorting to meditational and ascetic practices. The Sikh movement built-up a society outside of the caste society. It was the only people's movement that originated in India and strove to capture political power for humanistic objective. This needed a new and original ideology, a clear-cut direction and hard and rigid alignments and a committed organization with determined leadership. For them, all problems of life were an integral part of religion itself and the entire field of life as contemplated was covered and moulded by religious precepts.

The Sikh Gurus regarded the world as real and meaningful. 'True is He, True is his creation.' 'By despising the world, one gets not to God.'[6] Thus Sikh religion broke away from the traditional Indian religious thought. The world being real, the object is not to secure a release from life but to strive for a moral and spiritual living and the so-called *mukti* or salvation from life, was not considered important as 'He who is fond of God, what has he to do with Mukti or Heaven.'[7] Guru Gobind Singh changed the title of Bhai Nand Lal's *rehat nama* from *bandgi nama* (meditational path) to *zindagi nama*, the way of life.[8] The idea of *mukti* was given a new meaning as release from self-centredness and selfishness and not from the world. *Mukti* was linked to the service of humanity. It is aptly described as 'By service in the world alone one finds a place in God's court.'[9]

Guru Nanak's utterance immediate after his enlightenment, 'there is no Hindu, no Musalman' was an announcement of great significance. It showed clear interest in man and his life only and not in any metaphysical doctrine. Guru Nanak told Shah Sharaf that those men who love their fellow beings always succeed in life.[10] In consequence of the above ideology, Guru Nanak advocated the primacy of the householder's life. It was so great a departure from established religious traditions that the Naths accused Guru Nanak of putting acid in the pure milk of religious life.[11] Thus normal life of the Sikh became the medium of spiritual training and expressions. The Sikh Gurus insisted on earning one's bread by honest work. He knows the right way who earns his living by hard work and shares his earnings with others.[12]

The Sikh Gurus made social service (*sewa*) a prerequisite to spiritual development. Without service there cannot be any *bhakti*. Social service is an essential component of the Sikh way of life even after the highest spiritual attainment. After his world tours, Guru Nanak himself took to cultivation of land. The produce therefrom went to the common kitchen to feed the needy and those who came to visit him. All the Sikh Gurus in their own way served the needy and in suffering. Sikh Gurus and Sikh society insisted on disinterested service of others. 'He who performs disinterested service meets God.'[13]

The Sikh Gurus had revolutionary aims, which necessitated employment of revolutionary means. To wean away people from caste values was an uphill task and to lead the downtrodden and despondent masses a still more difficult objective. The Gurus revolutionized *mukti* as social service for the emancipation of mankind, with freedom from fear of death, fear of insecurity, fear of oppression and injustice and fear of want. 'He who meditates on the fearless one, loses all his fear. When thou O God, art on my side, I cannot then be for another. Yea, when I become thine, thou blesseth me with all I seek, inexhaustible is my treasure howsoever I expend it.'[14]

The issues before the Gurus were very grave. It was either to accept or resist religious and political tyranny. The Hindus had suffered great humiliation under Mughal rule after Emperor Akbar's death. The Muslim mystic Bulleh Shah has recorded, 'Had there been no Guru Gobind Singh, everybody would have been circumcised, i.e. forced to embrace Islam.'[15] Guru Arjan and Guru Tegh Bahadur embraced martyrdom, though these created cohesion and strength among the Sikhs, the attitude of the Mughal rulers did not relent in their barbaric policies. The Sikh Gurus never considered it moral or spiritual to let the entire populations suffer humiliation and degradation. As such according to the Sikh ideology, armed resistance to tyranny was the religious duty of every Sikh.

Guru Gobind Singh, in his famous letter *Zafarnama* addressed to Emperor Aurangzeb has stated

> *Chon kar az hama healtey dar guzasht*
> *Halal ast, buzden ba Shamsher dast*
>
> When all efforts to make the ruler realize his duties fail, it is (*halal*) admissible to take up the sword against him.

Guru Nanak gave a clarion call to his disciples 'Those who want to play the game of love should be willing to sacrifice their lives.'[16] He condemns both Hindu and Muslim exploiters. He says, 'Riches cannot be gathered without resort to sinful means.'[17] About the rulers of his times, he states, 'Greed and sin are the ruler and the accountant, falsehood is the master of the mint. Lust his minister summoneth and examineth men and sitteth in judgment on them. The subjects are blind and without divine knowledge, and satisfy the judges greed with bribes.'[18] The kings are like leopards, the courtiers like dogs, they awaken those that sleep in God's peace. The kings servants tear the docile subject with their nails and like curs lick up all the blood that they spilt. But, hark, when these men are to be judged at the lord's court, their noses will be chopped off for God will trust them not.[19]

SIKH PANTH

The Sikh Gurus gave an entirely different meaning to 'Dharam'. The Sikh *dharam* meant to be the creation of the kingdom of God on earth. For all practical means a just order had to be established, social and political inquity including injustice had to be combated and eliminated. Power had to be captured for the poor and downtrodden.[20] Guru Gobind Singh institutionalized his ideal of defending *dharam* by the creation of Khalsa. Sikh history is a tale of sacrifices, persecutions and martyrdoms invited by the Sikhs in the service of their mission. It is for this mission the Gurus had inspired, prepared and led them.

The Sikh Gurus carried out various activities to strengthen the Sikh social and political order. Guru Nanak's greatest contribution is his *vani* which lays down the basic principles of a casteless social order. High and low sat in the same *sangat* side by side listening to the eternal *vani*. The same high and low sat in *pangat* to partake the food prepared in the Guru's kitchen. The Guru created *dharamsalas* where his disciples congregated morning and evening singing songs in the praise of the God Almighty. The single greatest steps that the Gurus took to prevent religious authority becoming the source of sectarianism was to detach ideology from the person of the ideologue. It was the doctrine, the principle that was made supreme over and above the person of the Guru or the Prophet. Guru Nanak nominated Angad as his successor and he laid his head at the feet of Angad as a mark of homage, because Angad had become the head and represented the spirit of the mission. Bhai Gurdas has stated, the light was the same, the system was the same, the only change was the change of bodies. Guru Gobind Singh emphasized the same as: First the Guruship was not embodied in any person but in the principle and the spirit be enshrined. Secondly it was the ideology that mattered and its source.[21] Guru Angad invented Gurmukhi (coming from the Gurus' mouth) from Lande Mahajani and wrote down all the verses of Guru Nanak and his own in Gurmukhi. The Sikhs thus got a simple language and a script called Lokbhasha in place of difficult Sanskrit called Devabhasha. Guru Amar Dass systematized the institution of *manjis* and created 22 centres for the extension of the Khalsa mission in response to 22 provinces of the Mughal Empire. The offerings were colleted and passed on to the central treasury. Guru Ram Dass started the centre at Amritsar and Tarn Taran. In later time Amritsar became the centre of Sikhs as Mecca is for the Muslims. Guru Arjan completed the Sikh Temple named Amritsar. He compiled all the hymns of the Gurus from Nanak to his own in a *pothi* called *Adi Granth*, so that no interpolations could be done by dissidents, etc. After the martyrdom of Guru Arjan by Jahangir, Guru Hargobind raised his own small army of volunteers, fought six battles against Mughal local commanders and thereafter moved in the relative security of the Shiwalik hills to avoid an attack by imperial Mughal forces. Guru Har Rai went further in the hills of Nahan. Guru Tegh Bahadur who succeeded child Guru Harkrishan, was helping small farmers with water wells, oxen for ploughing and other implements to make them self-reliant which was not liked by the Muslim *zamindars*. They sent disturbing reports to the Mughal court and the Emperor Aurangzeb called him to the capital Delhi. Even under the pressure of torturous persuasions, the Guru stoutly refused to embrace Islam and was executed in Chandni Chowk Kotwali in Delhi in 1675.

Guru Gobind Singh succeeded as the tenth and last Guru at the age of 9 years. During the next 30 years, he had to fight 20 battles, nine before the creation of the Khalsa in 1699 and eleven battles afterwards. In the battle of Anandpur (1704), after a prolonged seige of over eight months, the position of rations and ammunitions had become very critical. With repeated promises of safe passage by Hindu hill rajas and the Mughal forces, Guru Gobind Singh moved out of Anandpur on 20 December 1704. The period of 1705 to 1708 has been quite checkered in which destiny took him to Nanded in the south. Here he selected Banda Bahadur, a *bairagi*, whom the Guru converted into a *karamyogi*, advised him over the situation in the Punjab and sent him there to take back the lost territories and set-up an independent Sikh administration. This one act of Guru Gobind Singh to locate, convert and send Banda Bahadur to the Punjab strengthened the Sikhs to an extent that the Mughals with all their might were not able to subdue them and eventually lost the north-western areas of their empire to the Sikhs.

EGALITARIAN SOCIETY

The Sikh Gurus had developed the growth of Sikhs: (1) towards the establishment of an egalitarian society where all people belonged to one class and were equal in all respects, (2) to use this new society to wage an armed struggle against religious and political aggression and (3) to capture political power by the Khalsa. All these aims were integral part of the Sikh ideology.

The existing caste system was the greatest obstacle in the way of the Sikhs in developing an egalitarian society. Caste was essentially a social rank but it was given an added status of religious and linguistic significance. The ties of caste are stronger than that of religion.[22] When a king and a brahmin pass along the same road, the road belongs to the brahmin and not the king.[23] The king must show himself first in the morning to the brahmin and salute him.[24] Sikhism is opposed to any *status quo* in all forms and regards it as the greatest hurdle in the way of man's moral and spiritual progress. It declares: 'O foolish man, do not take pride in caste status, this pride leads to many an evil.[25] Religion does not consist in mere words, he who looks upon all men as equal, is religious.[26] Guru Nanak aligned himself with the lowest of the low castes. There are lower castes even among the low castes and some are absolutely low. It is their company that Nanak seeked. What has he to do with the higher ones? For where the lowly are cared for there is thine (God's) benevolence and grace.[27] Bhai Gurdas in his *vars* state that, 'the four castes were made into one and castes (*varn*) and outcastes (*avarn*) regarded as noble. . . . The twelve sects were obliterated and the noble glorious Panth created.'[28]

The very first and the constant companion of Guru Nanak during his tours was Mardana. He was unacceptable as he was a Muslim of a very low caste.[29] There was no place in his congregation for any one observing caste. All castes were treated as equal. At the *langar* (free kitchen) all sat on the same platform and ate the same food. Guru Gobind Singh chose five beloved ones (*panj piaras*) as leaders of the Khalsa. They were a kshatriya, a jat, a barber, a calico printer and a water carrier respectively. Guru Gobind Singh addressed them as follows: Let all embrace one creed and obliterate the differences of religion. Let the four Hindu castes who have different rules for their guidance abandon them all, adopt one form of adoration and become brothers. Let no one deem himself superior to others, let men of four castes receive my baptism, eat out of one dish and feel no disgust or contempt for one another.[30] Many belonging to the lower castes rose to the position of commanders. Such was the spirit of equality and democracy, that the collective wisdom of the congregation of the Sikhs was higher in value than that of the Guru alone (Guru 20 visve and *sangat* 21 visve).[31]

The prevalence of the spirit of democracy amongst the Sikhs is confirmed from evidence of non-Sikh sources:

1. Ghulam Mohy-ud-din, a contemporary of Banda Bahadur mentioned that low caste Hindus termed the 'dregs' of society of the hellish Hindus joined the ranks of Banda Bahadur in great numbers, and everyone in the army, would address the other as the adopted son of the oppressed Guru Gobind Singh.[32]
2. Sujan Rai Bhandari, a contemporary of Aurangzeb writes, 'If a stranger knocks at their door (the Sikhs) at midnight and utters the name of Nanak, though he may be a thief or a robber, he is considered a friend and brother and is properly looked after.'[33]
3. The Persian author Ghulam Hussain Khan writes, 'When a person is once admitted into their fraternity, they make no scruple of associating with him of whichever tribe, clan or race he may have been hitherto, nor do they betray any of those scruples deeply rooted in the Hindu mind.'[34]
4. The author of *Haqiqat* writes, that at the same time the Sikhs were told 'Whoever might join you from whichever tribe, do not have any prejudice against him and without any hesitation eat together with him. Now this is their custom.[35] Khatris, Jats, carpenters, blacksmiths and grain selling Lubanas all joined the Khalsa.

In 1780 Polier has stated that Sikhs begun to increase in number, and all who came from the lowest and abject classes were received, contrary to the Hindu custom, which admits no change of caste even Muslims were in the number of converts.[36] In 1794, Griffin, stated that the Sikh received proselytes of almost every caste, a point which differs most materially from the Hindus.[37] Hugel describes the Sikhs of the times as descendants of all the lowest caste of Hindus, from which they have been proselytized.[38] The participation of the people derived from all caste in the revolutionary struggle further cemented amongst them the spirit of comradeship and fraternization. It was a cohesion sealed with blood. Moreover Sikhs were inspired by a common cause—the cause of capturing power for the Khalsa.[39]

The raising of the status of the women formed an essential part of its progamme. The caste ideology had assigned to women, including those of the upper caste, a low social position. Guru Nanak declared, 'why call her bad from whom are born kings'.[40] Guru Amar Dass abolished the custom of *pardah* and *sati.*[41] Of the 22 *manjis*, i.e. preaching districts set-up by him, some were headed by women. Many Sikh women became preachers and some even led battles, e.g. Mai Bhago led Sikhs in the battle of Mukatsar.[42]

Revolutionary changes in the social, political or economic system can rarely, if ever, be brought about without using force. Power in the final analysis means political and military power. The Gurus planned to bring about revolutionary changes and it was for this purpose that Guru Gobind Singh created the Khalsa in order to capture political power for a plebeian mission. He did not depend on the privileged castes or classes to bring about the same. He wanted the downtrodden, degraded and despised section of the society to carve out their own destiny.[43] Samarth Ram Dass, Shivaji's mentor, met Guru Hargobind and questioned him, 'You are wearing arms, keeping an army and calling yourself *sacha padshah*, what sort of sadhu are you?' The Guru replied, 'I am internally a hermit and externally a prince. The arms are meant for protection of the poor and destruction of tyrants.'[44]

In the words of Koer Singh, Guru Gobind Singh addressed his five beloved ones thus:

> Hear, Khalsaji, with all attention,
> You are the dearest of dear to me.
> The Brahmins were proud that God had given the sovereignty of the world to them,
> There was no ruler (Raja) like them in the world.
> The Rajputs felt that they had been created from God's arms,
> But, Vaishya, Shudras and Jats in large numbers I have

Incorporated in the Panth.
The sovereignty of the whole world is given to you, the Khalsa.
I have made you leaders of the Khalsa,
The way you received Amrit (baptism) from the Guru,
I wish to receive it the same way from you.
The Guru and the Sikh are interwoven with one another,
It had been so recognized by the nine Gurus.
The Sikh and Guru are related to each other as head is to the body.[45]

Guru Gobind Singh is said to have spoken to Bhai Nand Lal as under:

Listen, Nand Lal, to this plan:
It will bring into being our Raj.
I shall weld four castes into one;
I shall make people remember God.
The Khalsa under this plan, will ride horses and support hawks;
The Turks will run away on seeing them.
It will make one man fight a lakh and a quarter;
He who dies (fighting) will be liberated. . . .
The drums will beat at every doorstep. . . .
The Khalsa will be victorious from one end to the other.
The Khalsa will rule; no one will remain unsubdued.
Everyone will join the Khalsa. For, they alone would be
Saved, who submit to the Khalsa.[46]

Ratan Singh Bhangoo in his introduction to *Shri Panth Prakash* explains the situation of the Sikh struggle for sovereignty as under:

Sovereignty cannot be had without armed struggle;
The Guru initiated the armed struggle. . . .
The Guru gave sovereignty to the poor . . . , and
The seven Sanat (lowest castes) and twelve low castes,
Who know nothing of politics.
The world calls them rustic Jats, Bawas, Kirars, Khatris,
Iron-smiths and carpenters of the low castes.
The Guru showed benevolence to the despised calico-Printers, Kalals and the low-caste Gujars, Ahirs,
Kambohs and Soods whom no one took into any account.
The Guru thought that water-carriers, barbers, Aroras, potters, Sainis, goldsmiths, sweepers (Chuhras), leather-workers,

> Bhats, Brahmins, beggars, Bahoroopias, Labanas and potters—all down-trodden should be given sovereignty; they would remember the gift of the Guru.[47]

THE PLEBEIAN BASE

The Sikh movement had not been only a plebeian political mission but it had also a plebeian base. It was necessary that the down-trodden castes and classes should be the architect as well as the master of their own destiny. When Guru Hargobind decided to raise an army of four hundred men, the volunteers came from the strata of calico-printers, water-carriers, carpenters, barbers, etc.[48] Mohammedan survivors of the battle of Lohgarh reported, 'although the Sikhs were of all castes and trades, they proved brave in the battles and the imperial army was not to be blamed for its defeat.'[49] Bhikam Khan has stated that the army of Guru Gobind Singh consisted of rustic jats, oil pressers, barbers, bhatis, Lubanas, leather dressers, banias, Aroras, Bhats, shudras, calico printers, carpenters, twelve caste and low caste had joined and were trained in the use of arrows.[50]

The plebeian composition of the Khalsa army is corroborated also by non-Sikh sources. Banda Bahadur's forces recruited chiefly from lower caste Hindus, scavengers, eobblers? and such like person were numerous amongst them.[51] Muslim historians have called them the 'dregs' of society of hellish Hindus. Khafi Khan says, 'these infidels have set up a new rule, and were forbidden shaving of the head and beard'.[52] The Sikh movement was not a sectarian one nor based on clannish, tribal, feudal or dynastic loyalties. Unlike the Marathas, the Sikhs were not held together by a regional nationalism. They were people from all castes and creeds and even some Muslims also joined Sikh armies by virtue of its egalitarian character. The majority of them came from the lower castes which formed the base of the Sikh army.

In the Indian society, the vast majority of the population was precluded from all political and military activity. This was not an accidental development but a well thought out plan of caste ideologues. The Brahmin made the ruling class, namely, the kshatriyas and later on the Rajputs to have the sole prerogative in the use of arms. The outcome of the conflicts within the ruling classes did not effect the brahmin community as such. Hence, from the time the brahmin supremacy got established, majority of the people were reduced to idle spectators to the military and political supremacy that raged around them. Megasthenes has noted that peasants went about their work unconcerned to the battlefield. This pacifism and caste system blocked the development of the military power of the common citizens. With the eclipse of kshatriyas, a few petty Rajput princess springing from the desert of Jaisalmer, were able to usurp political power throughout northern India.

The above phenomenon again happened when the Muslim invaders conquered the country. It has been a very painful experience when at times a handful of foreigners overran vast tracts of the country without countering any resistance. Nadia was occupied by the advance party of mere 18 horsemen.[53] This opened the way to the establishment of Muslim rule in Bengal. In the west the people of Maharashtra were conquered, oppressed and humiliated, to which they meekly submitted as dumb driven cattle.[54] The very constitution of caste system is the antithesis of social cohesion. Caste grown by fission, and in this process, goes on creating new mutually exclusive and antagonistic social groups. It was an irony of this system that it deprives its constituents of unity of purpose and rendered them incapable of unity of action, when caste system was the only social framework which held them together.[55] The failure of the Hindus to stand up against the Muslim domination was not so much a failure of the Indian people as, it was the failure of the caste system.[56]

In the lower caste, there were many sub-castes and divisions. It was these elements which the Sikh movement had to weld together into a new society on the basis of a new ideology. As such, the egalitarian society and the Sikh Panth which the Gurus had been building up was a part and parcel of the plan to provide a plebeian base to a militant revolutionary movement.[57]

As the movement gathered momentum, the opposition got transformed into open defiance. For this purpose, the ideal of *sacha padshah* was setup. *Sacha padshah* as the name implies was to be a combination of spiritual and temporal authority in one and was to be the embodiment of Sikh values, as opposed to all political authority based on injustice, oppression and exploitation. This idea soon got institutionalized. Guru Arjan used to hold assemblies which gave them the look of a royal *darbar*. Henceforth the Guru was looked upon by his followers as a worldly lord and a ruling sovereign.[58] The very idea of *sacha padshah* belittled the image of the Mughal emperor. The loyalty of the Sikhs to the Guru was absolute. The Guru was supreme in both fields and the foundation for creating and carrying out an independent political state was clearly laid.[59]

Toynbee notes that the predecessors of Guru Hargobind had already transformed the Sikh community from an embryonic church into an embryonic state.[60] Hari Ram Gupta calls the Sikh organization in Guru Arjan's time as a state within a state.[61] Guru Arjan entertained Khusrau, the rebel prince, which was not liked by Emperor Jahangir. Guru Arjan was summoned to Lahore, and he knew what was in store for him. He sent instruction that let Guru Hargobind sit fully armed on his throne and maintain an army to the best of his ability.[62] Guru Hargobind girded himself with two swords—one for the *miri* and the other for the *piri* and laid the foundation stone of the Akal Takht close to the Harimandir and called it the throne of God.[63] Four hundred Sikh volunteers offered their services at the disposal of the Guru.[64] In a short time, he possessed a stable of 700 horses, 300 horsemen and 60 gunners. Guru Hargobind successfully fought six battles against the Mughals. Anticipating an attack by the Mughal imperial army he shifted to the relative security of Shiwalik hills. Guru Hargobind certainly inaugurated a policy which was to lead the most down-trodden people slowly but assuredly towards political and military advancement. The Guru created a revolution in the lives of Sikhs.[65]

The third objective of the Sikh movement was to capture political power for a plebeian mission. Khalsa was the instrument created and used both to overthrow the Mughals and to capture political power for achieving plebeian objectives. The role of the Khalsa in the revolutionary struggle was of the highest importance.

When the severed head of Guru Tegh Bahadur was brought to Guru Gobind Singh, he asked how many Sikhs had sacrificed themselves along with Guru Tegh Bahadur. He was told that only two Sikhs had sacrificed themselves. The Guru remarked, 'but the Sikhs were many in number'. The answer given was that they turned their backs to the faith. There was no distinguishing mark for a Sikh to prevent that happening. This provoked the Guru to remark, 'I shall assign such a distinguishing mark to the Sikhs that a Sikh would be recognized even among thousands'.[66] Each and every Sikh was made not only an instrument of the declared revolution, but also its standard bearer.[67] The Guru had planned giving distinguishing marks to the Sikhs in 1675 but he carried out the same in 1699 on the creation of the Khalsa, 24 years later. He started creating a large force of revolutionaries. The Guru invited Rajput hill rajas to join him but they declined and instead joined the Mughals. On the creation of the Khalsa, the Guru is stated to have said:

> They would destroy the (established) rule and establish their own everywhere.
> Khalsa would become the image of God with his own attributes.
> They would acknowledge no authority other than that of the True Lord.

It not known as to who and how Guru Gobind Singh was given the title of 'Padshah Darwesh", the plebeian section of Sikh society used this title with love and admiration for their Guru.

Gurusobha testifies that the Khalsa is created to destroy the evil-doer. Koer Singh writes that after the baptism ceremony, the Guru gave instructions to the following effect: Destroy the Mughal forces. . . . And you rule for ever. The later Sikh literatures record the same tradition. Khalsa is one who fights in the frontline. Khalsa is one who protects the poor, Khalsa is one who crushes the tyrant.[68]

The Sikh movement was virtually crushed a number of times. It suffered many serious reverses, but each time, like the proverbial phoenix, it rose from its ashes. The first setback took place when Guru Gobind Singh had to leave Anandpur, Chamkaur and finally Muktasar. But within a year and half of the Guru's death, the Khalsa under Banda Bahadur conquered Sirhind and humbled the Lahore government. The Mughal power was so great that the Sikhs could not hold on to their territories and thereafter the persecution was so acute that Sikhs could not face the same. Prizes were fixed—Rs. 10 for the supply of information about the presence of a Sikh, Rs. 20 for actually showing a Sikh, Rs. 40 for helping in his capture and Rs. 80 for bringing every Sikh head.

Forester states, such was the keen spirit that animated the persecution, such was the success of the exertions, that the name of a Sikh no longer existed in the Mughal dominion. Those who still adhered to the tenets of Guru Nanak, either fled to the mountains at the head of the Punjab, or cut-off their hair, and exteriorly renounced their religion.[69]

It has been estimated that the number of Sikh guerrillas had come down to about 2,000 men.[70] But they grew from strength to strength and not only challenged the Mughal Empire, but became the master of the country right up to the bank of the Yamuna. Hari Ram Gupta states,

> thus had the Sikhs emerged triumphant from their deadly struggle of the past thirty years; and the long drawn agony of their subjection came to an end, and the dream of their independence was realized. They had admirably succeeded in holding their own and in steadily pursuing their course, notwithstanding the hosts of terrors and disasters that gathered themselves together not only to check their ardour and to intercept their progress, but also to bring them to the verge of annihilation. The internal vigour consisting of their dogged faith in themselves and in the prophecy of Guru Gobind Singh that they would one day become a nation, not only sustained them against the bloody persecution of the great government determined to suppress them, but also raised them again with greater strength after every attempt to annihilate them.[71]

The Khalsa guerrillas were dispersed into very small bands, sometimes of twos and fours, and in widely separated areas like those of the Siwalik hills, Lakhi jungle and the desert wastes bordering Rajputana. They had no common centre and no common leader. Contacts among the guerrilla bands were rare. The only sentiment that held them together and made them converge for collective action was attachment to a common cause and the deepest commitment to their faith. Arjan Das Malik writes that sustained guerrilla warfare was not possible without an ideological inspiration. 'As early as the very origin of the term guerrilla, Napoleon had observed that "in Spain moral considerations made up three quarters of the game and the relative balance of military power accounted only for the remaining quarter".'

Next to Guru Gobind Singh's contribution to the egalitarian revolution with large-scale plebeian participation, Banda Bahadur's contribution is greater than any other Sikh commander in the successful completion of the revolution. Banda Bahadur waylaid a large amount revenue treasure going to the Mughal capital at Bhuna. The *amil* of Kaithal under whose jurisdiction Bhuna village fell came to dispose the Sikhs of the treasure. Banda Bahadur with a strategic move arrested the *amil*, took possession of his horses and arms, and appointed the *amil* of Kaithal as a Sikh representative for the collection of revenue—thus creating the first nucleus of a Sikh state. In his further battles, Banda Bahadur would appoint his own governors/administrators including the revenue officials/*thanedars* in the occupied territories. He would take up all the *zamindaris* and assignment estates and distribute them to the tillers of those lands, following the principle that land belongs to the tillers and not the *zamindars*/assignment holders. He simplified the revenue collection by splitting the half-yearly crop into three parts—one part to be given to the government and remaining two parts to the tillers. Whatever booty was collected from the occupied territories was equally divided among the Sikh soldiers. Whoever came to see him was warmly received by him as 'Singhji' and his problem attended to immediately. William Irvine says,

> In all the parganas occupied by the Sikhs the reversal of the previous customs was striking and complete. A low scavenger or leather dresser, the lowest of the low in Indian estimation had only to leave home and join the Guru (meaning Banda) when in a short time he would return to his birth-place as its ruler with his order of appointment in his hand. As soon as he set foot within the boundaries the well-born and wealthy went out to greet him and escort him home. Arriving there,

they stood before him with joined palms, awaiting his orders. Not a soul dared to disobey an order and men who had often risked themselves in battlefield became so cowed down that they were afraid even to remonstrate.[72]

NOTES

1. Jagjit Singh, *The Sikh Revolutions*, New Delhi: Bahri Publications Ltd., 1981, p. vi.
2. Irfan Habib, *Agrarian Systems of Mughal India* New Delhi: Oxford University Press 2002, pp. 370-99.
3. William Irvine, *Later Mughals*, New Delhi, 1971, pp. 98-9.
4. Jagjit Singh, *The Sikh Revolutions*, pp. 1-2.
5. Ibid., p. 3.
6. *Guru Granth Sahib*, tr. Gopal Singh, Delhi, 1964, pp. 294, 962.
7. Ibid., p. 360.
8. Macauliffe, vol. V, p. 103.
9. *Guru Granth Sahib*, p. 26.
10. *Janamsakhi*, Bhai Mani Singhwali, p. 344.
11. Bhai Gurdas, Var 1, pauri 40.
12. *Guru Granth Sahib*, p. 1245.
13. Ibid., pp. 286-7.
14. *Janamsakhi Param Pera Antka*, pp. 44, 48.
15. *Janamsakhi Bhai Bala*, p. 279.
16. Macauliffe, op. cit., p. 300.
17. *Guru Granth Sahib*, p. 966.
18. Bhai Gurdas, Var 1, pauri 45.
19. *Gurbilas chevin Padshahi*, p. 341.
20. Jagjit Singh, *The Sikh Revolutions*, p. 99.
21. Mehma Parkash, op. cit., pp. 95, 103, 233.
22. M.A. Shirring, *The Tribes and Castes of Rajasthan*, Delhi: Cosmo Publications, 1975, p. 120.
23. G.S. Ghurye, *Caste and Races in India*, Bombay, 1969, p. 57.
24. Ibid., pp. 90-1.
25. *Guru Granth Sahib*, p. 266.
26. Macauliffe, op. cit., p. 60.
27. *Guru Granth Sahib*, p. 15.
28. Bhai Gurdas, Var 23, pauri 19.
29. Mehma Parkash, *Sarup Das Bhalla*, 1978, Bhasha Vibhag Punjab, 1978, p. 37.

30. Macauliffe op. cit., vol. V, pp. 93-4.
31. Bhai Gurdas, Var 3, pauri 11.
32. Gurbux Singh, *Punjab History Conference Proceedings*, 1973, pp. 55-6.
33. Sujan Rai Bhandari, *Khulasat-ut-Twarikh*, p. 81.
34. *Siyar-ul-Mutakharin,* tr. *John Briggs*, p. 73.
35. Haqiqat, *Indian Historical Quarterly*, March 1942, p. 5.
36. Ganda Singh, *Early European Account of the Sikhs*, Polier, p. 192.
37. Ibid., Griffin, p. 228.
38. Ibid., Hugel, p. 281.
39. Jagjit Singh, *The Sikh Revolutions*, p. 127.
40. Macauliffe, op. cit., vol. I, p. 244.
41. Hari Ram Gupta, *History of Sikh Gurus*, p. 84.
42. Mehma Parkash, op. cit., pp. 829-31.
43. Jagjit Singh, *The Sikh Revolutions*, p. 137.
44. Ibid.
45. Koer Singh, *Gurbilas Patshai Das*, p. 131.
46. *Rehat Nama*, ed. Piara Singh Padam, p. 47.
47. R.S. Bhangoo, *Panth Prakash*, p. 41.
48. *Gurbilas Cheven Padshahi*, p. 143.
49. Macauliffe, op. cit., vol. V, pp. 95-6.
50. Koer Singh, *Gurbilas Patshai Das*, p. 90.
51. William Irvine, *Later Mughals*, pp. 94, 96 & 98.
52. Khafi Khan, Elliot & Dawson, *History of India as Told by Its Own Historians*, vol. VII, pp. 419-20.
53. *The Cambridge History of India*, vol. III, p. 46.
54. S.R. Sharma, *The Founding of Maratha Freedom*, p. 48.
55. Jagjit Singh, *The Sikh Revolutions*, p. 150.
56. Ibid., p. 152.
57. Ibid., p. 153.
58. M.G. Ranade, *Rise of Maratha Power*, vol. 1, p. 40.
59. Jagjit Singh, *The Sikh Revolutions*, p. 155.
60. Arnold J. Toynbee, *A Study of History*, London, 1971 vol. V, p. 665.
61. Gupta, *History of Sikh Gurus*, p. 93.
62. Macauliffe, op. cit., vol. III, p. 99.
63. Ibid., vol. IV, p. 3.
64. Ibid., p. 4.
65. Gupta, *History of Sikh Gurus*, p. 125.
66. Malcom, op. cit., p. 22 and Hugel, op. cit., p. 263.
67. Jagjit Singh, *The Sikh Revolutions*, p. 176.

68. Ibid.
69. Forester, vol. I, pp. 312-13.
70. *Haqiqat*, March 1942, p. 17.
71. Hari Ram Gupta, *History of Sikh Gurus*, p. 281.
72. William Irvine, *Later Mughals*, pp. 98-9.

CHAPTER 7

Banda Bahadur and the Rajputs

> If Bahadur Shah had not quitted the Deccan, which he did in AD 1710, and marched towards the Punjab with all his Imperial forces, there is every reason to think, the whole of Hindustan would have been subdued by these invaders (Sikhs).[1]
>
> MALCOLM, *The Sketch of the Sikhs*

Emperor Aurangzeb died on 3 March 1707,[2] while still engaged in the quarter century-long Deccan war, in subduing the southern Pathan states. Being well aware of the inevitability of war of succession to the emperorship, he still had drawn a will, left under his pillow, earmarking 12 subahs of north-west to Mauzzam (Bahadur Shah) with its capital at Delhi, 6 subahs of central India to Azim Shah with its capital at Agra and 2 subahs in the south to Kam Bakhsh.[3] The inevitable war of succession did take place between Bahadur Shah and Azim Shah, who had also declared himself as emperor, at Jaiju (near Dhaulpur) on 8 June 1707, which was won over by Bahadur Shah.[4] On Bhai Nand Lal's recommendations, Guru Gobind Singh sent a detachment of 300 Sikh horsemen under the command of Bhai Dharam Singh to assist Bahadur Shah. They gave very good account of their valour.[5] After victory over Azim Shah, Bahadur Shah moved to Agra and invited Guru Gobind Singh to his court at Agra. Guru Gobind Singh and his followers were allowed to appear fully armed in the emperor's court, and costly gifts were exchanged between the two.[6]

Guru Gobind Singh, pleased with the attitude of Bahadur Shah, had raised the issue of punishment to Wazir Khan and some of his officers over atrocities committed on the Sikhs and execution of his younger sons. At this juncture, Kam Bakhsh, the youngest prince, declared himself as emperor and had raised the banner of revolt in Hyderabad. Bahadur Shah moved towards Hyderabad and took Guru Gobind Singh along with him.[7] The entire court of Bahadur Shah was against Guru Gobind Singh and the emperor was in no condition to punish Wazir Khan and had only kept a helpful façade with the Guru.[8] At Nanded, Guru Gobind Singh comprehended the real situation. He decided to stay back at Nanded and did not accompany Bahadur Shah any further. Kam Bakhsh was defeated and he died of wounds in an unequal battle and that too fought in a very clumsy manner by him.[9] In January 1709, Bahadur Shah pitched his tents in Hyderabad where he stayed for the better part of the year, attending to the setting up of administrative machinery for the southern subahs.[10]

In the meantime, Guru Gobind Singh, had selected a *bairagi* named Banda Bahadur and sent him to Punjab in September 1708 to reclaim the lost territories.[11] Guru Gobind Singh was attacked by some hired assassins from Sirhind and he expired on 30 October, 1708.[12] Emperor Bahadur Shah, after subduing Kam Bakhsh started back for Ajmer and crossed the Narmada on 25 December 1709.[13]

The detailed assessment of the conduct and ability of Bahadur Shah, Azim Shah and Kam Bakhsh (sons of Aurangzeb) gives clear indication of the downward slide and the disintegration of the once mighty Mughal Empire. During this period, after the demise of Guru Gobind Singh, the Sikhs under the command of Banda Bahadur raised the banner of revolt in 1709 against the Mughal government. Having captured the territories of Karnal, Talwandi, Hissar, Hansi, Tarawari, Kaithal, Jind, Sirsa, Ferozepur, Kasur, Jullundur, Pathankot, etc., they blocked the way between Lahore and Delhi and were considered a real threat to the Mughal capital.[14]

Guru Gobind Singh while on his way to the South, at Naraina, met Jait Ram Mahant. In the course of conversation, Guru asked the Mahant if he could secure help from Rajput princes to eliminate the Mughal Government. He replied that it.was almost impossible. The war between the Rathors and the Mughals was in full swing in Marwar and hence Ajit Singh could give no help. Jai Singh of Mewar had made peace with Aurangzeb. Mohkam Singh of Nagor was openly on the Emperor's side. Jai Singh, the young Raja of Jaipur was in the Mughal camp and was fighting under Aurangzeb against the Marathas, hence they were too busy with their own affairs for or against the Mughals and were not in a position to come to the help of the Sikhs at that juncture.[15]

Raja Ajit Singh and Raja Jai Singh had slipped back to Rajputana from Deccan. The letters of the Guru (Banda Singh) had reached them and the Rajas' replies had been dispatched to the emperor.[16] It has further been stated by Askar Rao Harkara in his report to the emperor on 30 November 1711, that:

> Banda Bahadur (rebel Guru) wrote to Raja Ajit Singh and Raja Jai Singh that they should come to his territory. They (the Sikhs) should be considered to have reached their territory. The Raja killed the spies of the rebels and told that they (the Rajas) were the servants of the Emperor. The rebels would be captured or killed soon. It was ordered that whosoever of the associates of the rebels was found should be murdered. Rai Singh, zamindar of Badnoor has written letters to the Rajas that Sikhs have carried out great devastation in the country. The Rajas wrote back that these people could not enter the hills without the knowledge of the zamindars. Jalal Khan, faujdar of Saharanpur wrote to the Rajas that Sikhs have entered the hills. The Rajas told Jalal Khan that the matter be reported to the Emperor. Raja Ajit Singh and Raja Jai Singh told Bakhshis that they should be ready to ride their horses against the rebel Sikhs. Muhammad Amin Khan Bahadur wrote to Raja Ajit Singh and Raja Jai Singh that they should jointly march against the rebel leader, that they should capture or kill him soon. The rajas stated in reply that the matter be reported to the Emperor.[17]

These reports are greatly exaggerated and the nonchalant attitude of the rajas in instructing over every matter, small or big, that the same be reported to the emperor, clearly shows their indifference towards taking any action against the Sikhs.

Bahadur Shah was able to establish peace in the south, but it was wanting in Rajputana. Sawai Jai Singh and Maharaja Ajit Singh had recaptured their territories Amber and Jodhpur respectively and destroyed the imperial military posts. Emperor Bahadur Shah was then awfully busy with the suppression of the rebellion of his brother Kam Bakhsh in the Deccan. When the emperor returned from Deccan to Ajmer, he had all the intentions to subdue the recalcitrant rulers of Rajputana, but, in the meantime, the emperor got the news of rebellion raised by the Sikhs in the Punjab.[18]

When Bahadur Shah was marching into the Deccan against his brother Kam Bakhsh, Raja Jai Singh Kachhwaha and Ajit Singh

Rathor had escaped from his camp near Mandeshwar and had entered into an alliance with Raja Amar Singh of Udaipur to resist the Mughal authority in Rajputana. The Imperialists sustained heavy losses in the bloody contest that followed and was driven to the necessity of adopting conciliatory measures to pacify the disturbances in the neighbourhood of the capital at a time when greater portion of the imperial forces were employed in the far south. On his return from expedition he thought of availing himself of the opportunity to reduce these insurrectionary chiefs.[19] With this object in view he marched into Rajputana and on 15 May 1710 his army was encamped at Daudwa serai on the banks of the Banas, 30 km from Ajmer. The negotiations began and the letters of the 'Chiefmen' of the rajas were presented to him.

Bahadur Shah, the Mughal emperor, on his way back from Deccan, was at Ajmer in mid-1710, where he was planning to subdue the refractory Rajput Rajas Jai Singh and Ajit Singh. At this juncture, the uprooted Muslim *umrahs* and *peerzadas* from Sirhind, Thanesar, Sumana, Sadhaura, etc., met the emperor and portrayed a very dark and gloomy picture of atrocities on them by the Sikhs.[20] Bahadur Shah, who was earlier governor of Punjab and Afghanistan in the late seventeenth and early eighteenth centuries, appreciated the gravity of the Sikh rebellion better than his ministers, who were against the emperor going against a petty Sikh leader. The emperor in haste patched up with the Rajputs who were left in quiet possession of their hereditary country and confirmed them in their allegiance to the empire. He resolved to lay aside, for the present, the design of subduing the Rajputs.[21]

The emperor insisted on going straight to Sadhaura without entering Delhi, the imperial capital.[22] He issued instructions to all the important generals to mobilize forces and reach Sadhaura where Banda's main army was located. In retrospect, Bahadur Shah for once took a very right decision. His appreciation of the Sikh struggle was very correct unlike some of his ministers who thought very poorly of the Sikh struggle and their leaders and took it below the dignity of a glorious monarch to fight with such insignificant people.[23]

Muzaffar Alam states that Banda's attempt to give his struggle against the Mughals the colour of a *dharmayuddha* (holy war) to protect the Hindu interest against Muslim tyranny was yet another weakness of the Sikh movement, which, even in the prevailing state of religious consciousness could not give him enough support.[24] The idea of said *dharmayuddha* does not appear in any account of Banda Bahadur and seems to be an impression of Muzaffar Alam.

Muzaffar Alam has given the following account from the Sitamau transcripts:[25]

> The Raja, however, did exactly the opposite of what Banda wanted them to do. Subsequently, Jai Singh along with Raja Ajit Singh marched towards Lohgarh, not in response to the Sikhs' invitation but in compliance with the imperial order to chastise the Sikhs. Also when after their arrival at Lohgarh, Banda wrote them a letter threatening them with the consequence of Sikh inroads into their territories, the rajas killed the Sikh messengers and issued orders to kill all the followers and associates of Banda in their camps.

The language written in the ultimate part of the script is typical of the Mughal mindset where brutality was exercised even on a messenger, not of the Rajput mindset, howsoever tyrant he may have been. There is no evidence, whatsoever, of the Rajput rajas having participated in any military action against the Sikhs. They did go to Sadhaura on repeated requests of the emperor to get their pending demands cleared from him. They returned back without participating in any action against the Sikhs in spite of the repeated requests of the emperor as is evident from the Vakil's reports given in Appendix.

It was with his tactfulness and statesmanship and use of force that Banda made the hill chiefs his allies. He also aspired to capitalize upon the discontent of Jai Singh and Ajit Singh over their fortunes under Bahadur Shah. The letter that some Sikh *sardars* namely, Bakht Singh, Bhagwan Singh, Jai Singh and Gaur Singh wrote to Raja Jai Singh allegedly in reply to the latter's note to them shows how the Sikh leaders endeavoured to mobilize the Rajput chiefs to their support.

Muzaffar Alam has correctly expressed the situation as under:

As the Mughals had failed to contain the Sikhs, their uprisings succeeded, to a very large extent, in dispelling the fear of the Mughal sword. They demolished the impenetrable wall that represented the majestic awe of the Mughals. In consequence the whole province became disturbed and the hill chiefs now showed scant regard for the Mughal crown.[26]

The Sikhs had been feeling very sour about Wazir Khan's role in the harassment of Guru Gobind Singh and the execution of the very young sons of Guru Gobind Singh. Their action at Sirhind was evidently instigated by a spirit of revenge. For two centuries, the Sikhs passing Sirhind used to pick-up-couple of bricks from the site and threw these in the river as an expression of their contribution to the destruction of Sirhind. This will give the reader the extent of hard feelings which Sikhs had against Wazir Khan and his officers. But the Muslim writers have given exaggerated accounts of the Sikhs. The *Siyar-ul-Mutakhrin* and also the *Muntakhab-ul-lubab* contain terrible details of the atrocious deeds of the Sikhs, but a Muslim writer is not to be implicitly trusted upon such a point.[27] Later writers like Muhammad Latif have blindly followed the statements of Ghulam Husain Khan and Khafi Khan. The remarks of Thornton apply to the distorted version of the Rajput-Sikh relations given in the Mughal government records.

Since the newspaper of the Royal Mughal Court (*Akhbar-i-Darbar-i-Mualla*) was the government mouthpiece, their giving fair account of the Sikh struggle had not been the order of the day and doubts arose as to what extent these are genuine statements of the help sought by Banda Bahadur and refused by the Rajput rajas. Perhaps to please their rulers, the newspaper accounts appear to be as much biased in favour of the Mughals as possible and likewise as much biased against the enemies of the state, the Sikhs, to the extent it could be.

In December 1710 the imperial forces were all set to attack the Sikh forces and destroy them. Banda Bahadur with his tactfulness and statesmanship and demonstration and use of force had made the hill chiefs his allies.[28] Banda is said to have received some useful intelligence from *bairagis* and *sannyasis* moving in the area and also Banjaras who led the Sikhs through difficult jungle routes.[29]

Banda Bahadur was able to give tough fight to the Mughal armies both at Sadhaura and Lohgarh. He was also able to take out most of his army into the Shivalik hills where Mughal forces were loathe to follow him fearing his alleged occult powers.[30] Bahadur Shah's comment to his ministers on Banda's escape were, 'The hawk had flown and an owl had been caught'.

Another set of records dealing with the period of Banda Bahadur's struggle are available with Rajasthan Archives, Bikaner where the Vakils reports addressed to the Rajput rulers pertaining to the above-said period are maintained. These reports are written by the Vakils (the loyal officials of various states) with the Mughal court, whose duty was to apprise their rulers of whatever things were happening in and around the Mughal court, which could be of interest to their rulers. There are instances where the Vakil, very loyal, devoted and understanding servant of the ruler, had to inform something which may not be very palatable to the Mughal administration and lest it may be intercepted by the Mughal authorities, such portions were written in coded language which his counterpart at the raja's court alone could interpret correctly. There are quite a few examples of this nature, wherein these coded portions of the reports have not been deciphered so far by research scholars, for example, reports of Bhikhari Das dated 26.4.1711 and 14.6.1711 have the last portions of the documents is in coded language. In a report dated 22.6.1711 by Bhikhari Das, he has informed the raja of Jaipur that Rathors (rulers of Jodhpur) have told Bhandari that the emperor is losing prestige. He further adds that they do not like Sawai Jai Singh and Raja Ajit Singh to join the emperor who is running himself in pursuit of a *fakir* (Banda Bahadur). Therefore, one is inclined to consider such record far more accurate and reliable as compared to those given in the *Akhbarat* by the agents of the state spread all over the country belonging to the Mughal court where the *Akhbarat* was compiled and distributed.

During the period from 22.2.1707 to 16.6.1713 there are about 63 reports which deal, in some form or the other, with the Sikh struggle against the Mughal Empire. In more than half of these reports, the Vakils carry on explaining to their rajas the desire of the Mughal emperor for them to come with their troops and participate in the crushing of the Sikh movement. Repeated directions and intimidating tactics, even requests were adopted but the rajas did not agree to take their troops to Sadhaura to fight against the Sikhs. The emperor who had ordered posting of Raja Jaisingh to Kabul had agreed to cancel the same in case he joined at Sadhaura. He further gave other concessions but the rajas did not move with their armies to Sadhaura. In fact, the Rajput held the view that it was most undesirable for Bahadur Shah to fight against a *fakir* (Banda Bahadur). The rajas in lieu offered to go with their troops in the Deccan area but were unwilling to fight against the Sikhs. When assured of their posting in Deccan area the two rajas ultimately moved with their troops to Sadhaura in October 1711. When they were given the *subedari* in the east and the south, they marched back with their troops. Bahadur Shah could not persuade or force these rajas to fight against the Sikhs or even leave their troops with him. A summarized account of the important reports dealing primarily with this subject is given in Appendix.

The situation as it existed in the early eighteenth century was the Mughal state, after the death of Aurangzeb, seemed to be in a disintegrating stage *vis-à-vis* the ruler as well as the result of the quarter century fruitless war in the south which virtually drained off the Mughal treasury as well as the fighting capabilities of their armies. The second power was the Rajputs in northern and central India. They had set-up some sort of a relationship with the Mughal forces by giving their daughters in marriage to the Mughal princes, by which some sort of a existential relationship of mutual existence. How comfortable or unbearable must have been the life of the Rajput princesses adjusting themselves to the Islamic way of life. The rajas of Rajputana had been at loggerheads with the Mughals right from Akbar's time till the time of the later Mughals. Aurangzeb and the later Mughals were in no condition to suppress them.

A third power which came into existence was the Sikh rebellion against the Mughal government in the Punjab. The rise of the Sikh state under Banda Bahadur was meteoric. He had the vision of defeating the Mughals and pushing them out of India but the time was not ripe at that stage. He desired to join hands with the

Rajputs to push out the Mughals from north-western India, but he was not in a position of military might to persuade the Rajputs to join him in that venture nor were the Rajput kingdoms in a state to join other Indians to push out the Mughals from their country, though the rajas of Rajputana area scrupulously rejected the requests of the Mughal emperor to join the Mughal forces to suppress the Sikh rebellion.

A second situation arose in the time of the Misl sardars when the power of the Afghan invaders and the Mughal government was somewhat weak. But the vision which Banda Bahadur had of defeating the Mughals was 'not' shared by the Misl sardars. The Sikhs were far more powerful but they had no leader of the vision of Banda Bahadur. Had Maharana Pratap been there in the eighteenth century, the Sikhs and Rajputs could have joined hands to throw out the Mughal government from India but then it is only a speculation.

Besides the decaying Mughal government, there were three more power centres in India—the Rajput kingdoms in the north, the rising Sikh power in the Punjab and its surroundings areas and the Marathas in the south. When the Muslims invaded India, Rajput states were ruling from north-west India to the Vindhya mountain ranges and these Rajput kingdoms bore the brunt of the invaders' attacks. Farishta tells us that at one time, the rajas of Ujjain, Gwalior, Kalunjar, Kanauj, Delhi and Ajmer entered into a confederacy for the expulsion of Mohammedans from India and considered it a sacred duty of theirs.[31] The Hindu women on this occasion sold their jewels and even melted down their gold ornaments (which they sent from distant parts) to furnish resources for the war.[32] These preparations of war give an indication of a Hindu national upsurge. But it was not so. First, it was confined to Rajputs only. Second, the history of Rajputs and the constitution of their polity both show that they were more concerned about their feudal or dynastic interest than with the Hindu religious or national sentiments as such. Most of the leading Rajput families gave their daughters in marriage to the Mughal princes at a time when an ordinary Hindu thought that his food was polluted if even touched by a Muslim.[33] To give in marriage their women to the males of another society which was despised, was to cross or violate the strongest hurdle of social exclusiveness not only in the caste society but in class society as well. The Rajputs became the pillars of the Mughal administration and military establishment. They were constantly employed in reducing into submission the enemies of the Mughal Empire. Of the 416 military commanders of Akbar's Empire, 47 were Rajputs. The aggregate of their quotas of armed assistance amounted to 53,000 horses, that was one-tenth of the Empire's total strength.[34] The Rajput rulers of Marwar, Amber, Bikaner and Bundi sided with Akbar against Rana Pratap.[35] It was Man Singh who led the Mughal army against Rana Pratap in the crucial battle of Haldighati. Again, it was Raja Jaisingh, who was in-charge of Aurangzeb's campaign against Shivaji. The exploitative and dominating polity left no scope for the Rajputs becoming the rallying point of Hindus in resisting Mughal domination. That their feudal system became the overriding consideration with them is revealed by their readiness to collaborate with the Mughals against all Hindu norms. The very military-cum-patriarchal-cum-feudal structure which bound them together created an unbridgeable gap between them and the non-Rajput people as a whole. When Nadir Shah invaded India, a pact was made between the three great kingdoms of the Sisodiyas, Rathors and Kachhwahas, which would have had an important result politically. But this compact broke down simply on a question of social precedence.[36] The Rajputs lacked even the perspective of forming a Rajput national state. As a consequence, all the virtues of the Rajputs, viz., their gallantry, their spirit of self-sacrifice, their fidelity continued to move within narrow grooves. The Rajputs who had one of the richest martial traditions in the world, not only submitted to their enemies, but became the pillars of their power. They became the instruments in defeating the one high-minded spirit among them—Rana Pratap—who defied the Mughals.

Taking away of the women of the defeated opponents had been a common practice among the Celtic races of Europe, and was taken up by Akbar in India. By this institution he sought to degrade those whom the chances of war had made him his vassals, by conduct so nefarious and repugnant to the keenly cherished feelings of a Rajput. Yet there is not a shadow of doubt that many of the noblest of the race were dishonoured on the Nauroza, and the chivalrous Prithvi Raj was only preserved from being the number by the high courage and the virtue of his wife, a princess of Mewar and daughter of the founder of the Saktawats. On one of the celebrations of *Khushroz*, the Mughal monarch was struck by the beauty of the princess of Mewar and he singled her out from amidst the united fair of Hind as the object of his passion. It is not improbable that an ungenerous feeling united with that already impure, to despoil the Sisodiyas of their honour through a princess of their house under the protection of the sovereign. On retiring from the fair, she found herself entangled amidst the labyrinth of apartments by which egress was purposely ordained, when Akbar stood before her; but instead of acquiescence, she drew a poniard from her corset and held it to his breast, dictating and making him repeat the oath of renunciation of the infamy of all her race. The anecdote is accompanied in the original with many dramatic circumstances. The guardian goddess of Mewar, the terrible Mata, it is believed appeared on her tiger in the subterranean passage of the palace to strengthen her mind and provide her with a weapon to protect her honour.[37] In the declining days of the Mughal Empire, Farrukh Siyar took Raja Jaisingh's daughter into his *harem* at the time of patching up with the Raja in 1715.

The Sikhs had no martial traditions worth the name. The shudras, who joined the movement, had been debarred by the caste system to the use of arms for centuries on end. The Jats, who joined the movement, had fighting qualities, but as Jats they had throughout remained subservient to the Rajputs, although they were equal in number to that of the Rajputs in Rajasthan, and in a majority in Sindh.[38] The Khalsas fought the Mughals to the bitter end till the latter were finally vanquished. This contrast in the attitudes of the Rajputs and the Khalsa towards Mughal authority arose because of the difference between their value patterns. The Rajputs were motivated by their feudal interests and prestige. The Khalsas were struggling to fight religious and political domination for a revolutionary cause. Hence, there was no room for a compromise for them. They spurned Abdali's several offers of peace[39] and fined Alha Singh for having compromised with him.[40]

The Rajputs who were bound to the person of their leader and not to a cause. Hence, they were at sea when the Mughal Empire was tottering. At that time, many upstart aspirants to political power cropped up. The Rajputs were not able to retain the principalities they were already holding and became the plaything of the Marathas.[41]

A large number of Rajput families moved into Punjab, Haryana, Himachal and Jammu area and a number of small Rajput principalities were set-up in these northern states. The Khalsa, on the other hand, owed its loyalty not to persons but to a cause. The Gurus had been emphasizing this point of view from the very beginning. Guru Gobind Singh had bestowed his sovereignty to the Khalsa as a whole.

NOTES

1. Malcolm, *Sketch of Sikhs*, London, 1812, p. 79.
2. William Irvine, *Later Mughals*, Delhi: Taj Publications, 1989 (1st published in 1922), p. 1.
3. Ibid., p. 6. Aurangzeb's will in an attempt to avoid the war of succession in the princes. The will was found by Hamid-ud-din Khan, head of the household, under the emperor's pillow. As the terms of the will accord with the measures taken by the emperor giving his three sons the provinces that he had assigned to them in his lifetime, it may be assumed to be authentic. Its terms were also appealed to afterwards by Muazzam (Bahadur Shah) when he wrote to his brother Azam Shah offering him a compromise. . . . It entreats his successors to leave Kam Bakhsh unmolested should he content himself with the two new provinces, i.e. Bijapur and Hyderabad. Of the two capitals, Agra and Delhi, one should be taken by each son. Bahadur Shah suggested Azam Shah to accept the contents of the will made by their father. Azam Shah stated that his answer was that a kingdom was not a thing which could be divided like an inheritance. His brother although a learned and well read man seems to have forgotten the verses in Shaikh Sadi Shirazi's *Gulistan* which every school boy knows.

   'Ten poor men can sleep comfortably under one blanket, while two kings cannot be contained within one kingdom. How could two swords be kept in one scabbard. Further if a division was to be made it should be an equal one. He has further suggested a division on the basis of that his share is from floor to the roof of the house.' Yours (Bahadur Shah) share is from the floor to the roof of the house, yours (Bahadur Shah) from the roof up to the firmament.

4. Ibid., pp. 34-5.
5. Hari Ram Gupta, *History of the Sikhs*, New Delhi: Munshiram Manoharlal, 1994, vol. I, p. 314.
6. (i) Sainapat, *Sri Guru Sobha*, p. 122.
   (ii) Gupta, *History of the Sikhs*, p. 315.
   A newsletter of the court of Bahadur Shah dated 24 July 1707 says: 'Guru Nanak, according to orders, fully armed, interviewed the Emperor and offered one hundred gold coins. He was granted a robe of honour and a jeweled padak and was given congee.'
7. Gupta, *History of the Sikhs*, p. 316.
8. Ibid., p. 317.
9. Irvine, *Later Mughals*, p. 64.
10. Ibid., pp. 65-7.
11. Gupta, *History of the Sikhs*, p. 323.
12. Ibid., p. 329.
13. Irvine, *Later Mughals*, p. 64.
14. Jugal Kishore Gupta, *Punjab History Conference*, Seventeenth Session, October 1982, p. 87.
15. Gupta, *History of the Sikhs*, p. 312.
16. *News of the Royal Mughal Court, 1707-1718*, tr. Bhagat Singh and published in the *Panjab Past and Present*, vol. XVIII-II, October 1984, p. 27.
17. Ibid., pp. 94-5.
18. Irvine, *Later Mughals*, p. 105.
19. Ganda Singh, *Life of Banda Singh Bahadur*, pp. 124-5.
20. Irvine, *Later Mughals*, p. 105.
21. Ibid.
22. Ibid.
23. Ibid., p. 106.
24. Muzaffar Alam, *The Crisis of Empire in Mughal North India*, New Delhi: Oxford University Press, 1997, p. 153.
25. Ibid.
26. Ibid., p. 185.
27. Thornton, *History of the Panjab*, Allen and Company, 1846, vol. I, p. 176.
28. Alam, *The Crisis of Empire in Mughal North India*, p. 161.
29. Ibid., p. 162.
30. Gupta, *History of the Sikhs*, vol. II, p. 20.

31. J. Briggs, *History of the Rise of Mohammadan Power in India*, vol. I, p. 26.
32. Ibid., p. 27.
33. Jagjit Singh, *The Sikh Revolution*, p. 213.
34. James Tod, *Annals and Antiquities of Rajasthan*, vol. I, p. 125.
35. C.H. Payne, *Tod's Annals of Rajasthan*, p. 74.
36. M.A. Sherring, *The Tribes and Castes of Rajasthan*, Delhi: Cosmo Publications, 1975, p. 4.
37. James Tod, *Annals and Antiquities of Rajasthan*, pp. 401-2.
38. H.A. Rose, *Glossary of the Tribes and Castes of Punjab and North West Provinces*, vol. II, 1970, Patiala: Language Department, p. 369.
39. Gupta, *History of Sikhs*, vol. I, p. 264.
40. Ibid., p. 143.
41. Payne, op. cit., p. 152; Sherring, op. cit., pp. 5, 40.

APPENDIX

The Vakil Reports

Addressed to the Rulers of Jaipur during 1707 to 1711

During this period Mughal emperors insisted on Rajput participation against the Sikhs and the Rajputs persistently avoided fighting against the Sikhs. Brief references in this regard are placed as under:

No.	Date	Vakil		Brief description
1.	22.2.1707	Pancholi Jag Jivan Das	Maharaja Sawai Jai Singh	Informing that Emperor Aurangzeb died in the morning but the news of his death has been disclosed at night by the Begum of Azam Shah and Azam Shah will be reaching there. The vakil of Kam Bakhsh has been interned.
2.	26.6.1710	Bhandari Khivsi	-do-	Informing that the news regarding the arrest of Guru (Banda) is wrong. Banda, after giving a fight to Mohd. Amind Khan and Rustam Dil Khan fled, but, when opposed by the Raja of Jammu, inflicted a serious injury on him. It is said that he has reached Dabar.
3.	1.1.1711	Dewan Bhikhari Das	-do-	Informing that he has submitted his letter and a copy of the Arzdasht to Nawab Khan Khanan. The nawab is much annoyed for the delay on his part (Maharaja) in attending the Royal Court. Requests to attend the Royal Court soon.
4.	10.1.1711	-do-		Emperor has ordered the arrest of raja of Nahan, so that he might produce the Guru (Banda).
5.	19.1.1711	-do-		It has been decided by the emperor that maharaja will not be sent to

				Kabul provided he attends the Court soon.
6.	27.1.1711	-do-	-do-	Informing that it has been reported that the mother of the raja of Nahan is bringing the Guru to the Royal Court. Adds that the emperor has ordered Mahabat Khan to put the Guru in a cage and to produce before him.
7.	8.2.1711	-do-	-do-	The Rathors of Jodhpur have expressed their mind that Raja Ajit Singh will never attend the Mughal Court; and in case an army is sent, both the rajas (Ajit Singh and Jai Singh) would combine and defeat it at Narnaul.
8.	8.2.1711	-do-	-do-	Reporting the rumour that the Guru after giving a fight to the army of the Raja of Nahan, has gone into the hills.
9.	8.2.1711	Pancholi Jag Jiwan Das	-do-	Informing that the Guru is reported to have gone into the hills and a cage has been got constructed for him (Guru). Adds that the cage is such that its nails will prick his body from all sides. Emperor has given strict orders regarding maharaja's attendance in the Court soon.
10.	9.2.1711	Dewan Bhikhari Das	-do-	Shahzada has promised to get the orders of maharaja's posting to Kabul cancelled and vakil shall send the *Nishan* to him.
11.	19.2.1711	Pancholi Jag Jiwan Das	-do-	Informing that the dewan and the bhandari have executed a *muchalka* to the effect that he (maharaja) would attend the court within two months.
12.	1.3.1711	Dewan Bhikhari Das	-do-	Shahzada desires that the maharaja to attend the Court very soon. Reports that the Guru and the Sikhs have become very powerful in Lahore area and it is also rumoured

				that Decannis have crossed over Narbada and are creating disturbances there.
13.	13.3.1711	Dewan Bhikhari Das	-do-	Informing that the Emperor has ordered the advance guard to move towards Lahore on hearing that the followers of the Guru have killed Shams Khan and Bazid Khan along with 1,500 horsemen. Maharaja to hasten to attend the Court.
14.	17.3.1711	-do-	-do-	Informing that Jahandar Shah has been ordered to proceed towards Lahore for suppressing the followers of Guru who have killed Shams Khan. Adds that Bhup Prakash (Bhupati Prakash) the raja of Nahan who was a prisoner of Mahabat Khan has been thrown into the iron-cage meant for the Guru.
15.	20.3.1711	-do-	-do-	Informing that the followers of Guru have become so powerful that the people of Batala have fled leaving behind property worth crores of rupees. Adds that the emperor has moved towards Lahore and his third stoppage will be at Ambala.
16.	21.3.1711	Pancholi Jag Jiwan Das	-do-	Maharajas Ajit Singh and Jai Singh have been appointed in the army of Shahzada Azz-ud-din and should come to Delhi to attend on the Shahzada.
17.	23.3.1711	Dewan Bhikhari Das	-do-	Emperor has ordered the imprisonment of the raja of Nahan and he is personally proceeding towards Lahore to suppress the Guru. Emperor considers it high time for the Maharaja to attend Royal Court and earn the emperor's favour.
18.	4.4.1711	-do-	-do-	Rustam Dil Khan has reported that Sikhs have been creating great trouble and the Emperor is personally going

				there. Rumours are prevalent that Deccanis have besieged Ujjain fort.
19.	-	-do-		These reports mention Banda Bahadur's large-scale aggressive activities and the Mughal repulses.
20.	-	-do-		
21.	-	-do-		
22.	-	-do-		
23.	26.4.1711	-do-	-do-	Informing that the emperor has told the princes and the Umaraos that they will encamp at Rupar as it is close both to Shahjahanabad and Lahore, and that the Guru will not escape towards the hills. Informs that Rustam Dil Khan's request to send him against the Guru has also been granted by the Emperor. (*Note:* The last page of the document is in code language.)
24.	9.5.1711	-do-	-do-	Emperor is marching towards Kalanaur against the Guru.
25.	17.5.1711	-do-	-do-	Informing that the Guru invaded the village Basi, killed some 2,000 persons and plundered it. Adds that he (Guru) has also an encounter with the Faujdar of Shahzada Muizz-ud-din. It is heard that either he (Guru) has been arrested or he has escaped.
26.	28.5.1711	-do-	-do-	Informing that the men and cattle have been killed or captured of the villages which have assisted the Guru. Adds that the Guru has come back to Kalanaur and has sent an army against Hamid Khan. Reports that Hamid Khan could not stand against the Guru in the absence of the Royal artillery. Adds that the emperor has marched towards river Bias (Behath). Also informs that the emperor has ordered to issue a

				farman to Maharaja Sangram Singh for Saropao, two horses, an elephant and a garland of pearls in Tikka.
27.	4.6.1711	-do-	-do-	Banda Bahadur's aggressive activities are detailed. Requests the maharaja to come soon as further delay is not desirable.
28.	4.6.1711	-do-	-do-	Nawab Mahabat Khan considers the delay on the part of the two rajas has harmed the imperial cause against the Sikhs. Further requests the Maharaja to attend the royal court soon.
29.	14.6.1711	Dewan Bhikhari Das	-do-	Half the report is in coded language which could not be deciphered.
30.	22.6.1711	-do-	-do-	Rathors have informed bhandari that the emperor is losing prestige. They do not like the two rajas to join the emperor who is ruining himself in pursuit of a *fakir* (Guru).
31.	22.6.1711	Pancholi Jag Jiwan Das	-do-	Informing that the Guru has fled towards Bareilly and is being hotly pursued by the Royal army. Adds that the Deccanis are still at Malwa.
32.	2.7.1711	Dewan Bhikhari Das	-do-	Emperor has ordered the shahzada to write to both the maharajas to reach river Sutlej soon and to encamp near the royal Camp, and punish the Guru in case he comes there.
33.	25.7.1711	Pancholi Jag Jiwan Dass	-do-	Informing that an advance party of the emperor has come and was staying at Chamari, a town 15 miles away from Lahore. Reports that the Guru is still in the mountains of Jammu and is being chased by Rustam Dil Khan.
34.	19.8.1711	Dewan Bhikhari Das	-do-	Maharaja has been advised that he should reach Sadhaura soon to punish the Guru. Emperor has also ordered Mahabat Khan to send a

			Hasb-ul-Hukm to both the Maharajas desiring to reach Sadhaura soon.
35. 22.8.1711	-do-	-do-	Bhandari has requested the Shahzada and Nawab Mahabat Khan to grant Subah Gujarat and Malwa to both the maharajas, but they have replied that nothing could be done until these rajas reach Sadhaura.
36. 26.8.1711	-do-	-do	Over some differences regarding the conduct of operations, Rustam Dil Khan instead of pursuing the Guru has gone to Lahore and taken shelter in his *haveli*. Emperor has ordered Rustam Dil Khan to be arrested and a *tokh* put around his neck.
37. 26.8.1711	-do-	-do-	The Shahzada and Nawab Mahabat Khan have told that both the maharajas must first proceed to Sadhaura soon.
38. 28.8.1711	Pancholi Jag Jiwan Das	-do-	Requesting the Maharaja Ajit Singh to reach Dabar and to kill Guru so that all their demands could be considered.
39. 30.8.1711	-do-	-do-	Shahzada has ordered Bhandari to go and bring both the maharajas to Sadhaura. Requests Maharaja Jai Singh to proceed to Dabar alone if Maharaja Ajit Singh is unwilling to accompany him for punishing the Guru.
40. 31.8.1711	Dewan Bhikhari Das	-do-	Informing that bhandari who has been sent to bring the maharajas to Sadhaura would give him details.
41. 23.9.1711	-do-	-do-	The prince has been told that due to rain the two rajas could not proceed. They have encamped near Narela.
42. 24.9.1711	Pancholi Jag Jiwan Das	-do-	Shahzada has written that both the maharajas would be relieved after their arrival at Sadhaura. Further asks to reach and to bring Maharaja Ajit Singh along with him.

43.	27.9.1711	-do-	-do-	Requests not to delay any more in reaching Sadhaura.
44.	27.9.1711	Bhandari Khivsi	-do-	Requests to reach Sadhaura soon as his *Mutalibs* will be considered on maharaja's arrival there.
45.	6.10.1711	Dewan Bhikhari Das	-do-	Qudrat-ullah Khan has agreed to request Shahzada for granting Subah Malwa and Gujarat to both the maharajas. If the maharajas are willing to offer *peshkash* to the emperor then both of them could be appointed in the Deccan and leave could be granted to them for going to their *Watan*.
46.	7.10.1711	-do-	-do-	Informing that Shah Qudrat-ullah Khan has told that on the arrival of both the maharajas at Sadhaura all their *Mutalibs* would be accepted as desired.
47.	24.10.1711	Pancholi Jag Jiwan Das	-do-	Mahabat Khan has told the emperor that the two rajas have reached Sadhaura and are awaiting their posting orders.
48.	27.10.1711	-do-	-do-	The vakil informs that the emperor has decided to appoint Maharaja in the Deccan. He adds that Mahabat Khan has requested the Emperor to grant *subedari* of Prayag to Maharaja Jai Singh and that of Sorath to Maharaja Ajit Singh.
49.	31.10.1711	-do-	-do-	Informing that *faujdari* of Ahmedabad-Guhara has been granted to Maharaja Jai Singh and *faujdari* of Sorath has been granted to Maharaja Ajit Singh.
50.	3.11.1711	Dewan Bhikhari Das	-do-	Requests for a permission of the payment of *peshkash* and suggests that maharaja should remain at the royal court. Emperor desires that one of them should remain at his court.
51.	7.12.1711	-do-	-do-	Emperor has ordered Mahabat Khan to send *Hasb-ul-Hukm* to both the

				maharajas directing them to stay at Lahore for some time due to the disturbance created by the Guru.
52.	2.1.1712	-do-	-do-	Shahzada desires that two maharajas must remain with Hoshdar Khan at Sadhaura.
53.	17.2.1712	Bhandari Khivsi	-do-	Emperor is ill and the three Princes have been preparing for a war against Prince Azim-ush-Shan who has mobilized his army.
54.	24.2.1712	-do-	-do-	Azim-ush-Shan has ordered a *farman* to be sent to the maharaja to attend the court with his army soon. The text of the document is in coded language.
55.	10.3.1712	-do-	-do-	Informing that it is rumoured that the Guru has reached Dabar and the *faujdar* of Ambala has collected an army of 1200-1300 sawars. Further adds that Sher Afgan Khan, the *faujdar* of Ujjain has come to Panipat. Sarbuland Khan has reached Agra and Prince Farrukh Siyar is also expected there soon.
56.	6.4.1712	Pancholi Jag Jiwan Das	-do-	Informed that he is sending the seal after getting inserted the title of 'Sawai' in it.
57.	20.5.1712	-do-	-do-	Informed that the emperor has reached Sarhind and nawab has called the vakil in his presence and told that it would be better if the maharaja attends the court at Jahanabad.
58.	3.7.1712	-do-	-do-	Reporting that the emperor took his seat on the throne which was constructed at a cost of Rs. 9 crore by Shahjahan and held a Jashn on 4th Jamadi-ul-awwal. Adds that Amir-ul-Umara and other *umraos* have presented *nazars* to him. Further informs that some trouble-some persons have spread a rumour

				that the emperor has ordered for plundering Jai Singhpura and people have fled away from there.
59.	8.12.1713	Bakht Mal	-do-	Informed that the queen has requested the emperor to keep good terms with Rajputs and Iranis.
60.	19.6.1713	Pancholi Jag Jiwan Das	-do-	Emperor has granted the title of 'Mirza Raja Sawai' to the maharaja.

Author's assessment of these reports *vis-a-vis* the recorded history of Mughal historians. In early eighteenth century the demise of Guru Gobind Singh, the Sikhs under the command and control of Banda Bahadur raised the banner of revolt against the Mughal Empire. It was in fact a religious-cum-egalitarian movement in which they overran entire Punjab and surrounding areas in a few months time and could not be contained by the Mughals for almost 5 years. The Sikhs requested the Rajputs to join hands which the Rajputs did not accept for various reasons either they felt that the Sikhs from the lowest strata of society could not be their equals or the Sikh struggle may fizzle out very soon. It can also be said that the Rajputs were so much used to be the subordinates of the Mughal Empire that they could not break away from that bondage; they did not have either the strength or courage to do so. The fact remains that at that juncture the spirit of Maharana Partap did not vibrate in the blood of any Rajput king otherwise the combined forces of the Sikhs and Rajputs would have not only hastened the fall of Mughal Empire, but also would have set up the first Indian State ruled by Indians. This aspect has not been touched by any of the historians and after study of the Vakil reports I have felt that it was the most opportune time for the Rajputs to enter the fray.

Bahadur Shah, the Mughal emperor, on return from Deccan after subduing his brother Mohammad Kam Bakhsh in Deccan, he was moving towards the Mughal capital. It was at Ajmer when he was planning to subdue the refractory Raja Jaisingh and Raja Ajit Singh that he hastily patched up with these rajas and gave all of his attention to the Sikh movement, news of which first came to him in May 1710. Bahadur Shah rightly assessed the Sikh movement as a popular uprising in part of the empire very close to the capital, which might have much more serious and far reaching consequences. He lay aside the desire to subdue Rajputs and gave all his attention to the Sikh uprising. He decided to march in person against the Sikhs. Iradat Khan states that Bahadur Shah thought it his duty to lead a *jehad* against the Sikhs in person like Aurangzeb who in later part of his reign appeared almost at the seizure of every fort belonging to the non-Muslims.

It has been recorded that the Sikh armies under Banda Bahadur, after conquering almost the entire Punjab, were knocking at the border of Rajasthan. Banda Bahadur is said to have made an overture to Maharaja Jai Singh and to some of the rulers of the states of Rajasthan to join him in his campaign against the Mughal government to put an end to their atrocities on the non-Muslim population, in a letter sent through courier addressed to some of the rajas. The reactions of the rajas have been very strong and they are said to have spurned the suggestion in a very unbecoming manner.

During the study of the records pertaining to rulers of Jaipur with Rajasthan State Archives, Government of Rajasthan, Bikaner, the accounts of the vakil reports issued by the vakils of the Jaipur rulers give a wildly different account. The vakils of the raja of Jaipur based with the Mughal Court sent correct accounts to their rulers and wherever they were writing something very confidential to their maharaja they would write it in coded language lest the secret statements if intercepted by authorities inimical to the raja, these could not be deciphered.

CHAPTER 8

A Critique on Rattan Singh Bhangoo's *Sri Gur Panth Parkash*

Sri Gur Panth Parkash is a poetic composition about the Sikh struggle for a homeland, against the Mughal and Afghan conquerors of India. This epic has been likened by some historians of the Sikhs to Tulsi Das' *Ramayana*, Ved Vyas's *Mahabharata*, Homer's *Illiad*, *Odyssey,* Virgil's *Aenid*, Milton's *Paradise Lost* and *Paradise Regained*.[1] The composition of *Panth Parkash*, consisting of 169 episodes, took Rattan Singh over 30 years to complete. The same has been translated into English by Prof. Kulwant Singh very creditably and the first volume (episodes 1-81) was published by the Institute of Sikh Studies, Chandigarh in 2006.[2] The present critique is confined to episodes 27-69 dealing with the life and times of Banda Bahadur, the greatest commander not only of the Sikhs, but of the medieval India, who with his virtually bare handed volunteer force, blunted the teeth of the Mughals, the mightiest empires of the world. Praise be to Guru Gobind Singh who selected him and to Banda Bahadur who breathed a death defying spirit in the newly raised plebeian social order of the Sikhs.

Gurdev Singh, president of the Institute of Sikh Studies, has remarked in the Foreword to *Sri Gur Panth Parkash:*

> Rattan Singh learnt the truth of the incidents in proper perspective from his ancestors who had borne the hardships and were actively involved in organizing and executing the plans of the Khalsa. They made supreme sacrifices for claiming what was their birthright. The historians and the Sikh people will remain ever indebted to Rattan Singh for bringing to limelight the efforts of the Khalsa to remain committed to their faith under excruciatingly trying circumstances.

Prof. Kulwant Singh with his rich experience and command of

Punjabi and English has carried out the translation with a missionary zeal.[3]

Prof. Kharak Singh states that 'Rattan Singh's account of the origin and rise of Khalsa is original and fairly comprehensive'. In fact, there is no other original and reliable source for this period. The accounts given by the Mughal rulers were highly biased and derogatory and showed the Sikhs as outlaws and criminals interested only in trouble-making. Far from showing them as saint-soldiers fighting for their freedom and the defense of the weak and downtrodden, they painted them as devils with no legitimate claim to power and authority. The English translation of this work gives an account of the happening of the eighteenth century. Rattan Singh Bhangoo, a well-to-do landlord, developed acquaintance with Capt. Murray at the time, the British were trying to have a correct version of the rise of the Sikhs to power. Murray brought out the dilemma as to how did the Sikhs establish their rule and who gave them sovereignty. Rattan Singh's reply was that it was Guru Nanak who had conferred the sovereignty to the Khalsa.[4] Murray has also been asking the Mughal emperor the same question how and from whom the Sikhs got sovereignty and statehood. The Mughal emperor held the view that no authority had bestowed any sovereignty or statehood on the Sikhs. They had neither accomplished any deed worthy of praise nor had they routed any powerful rival in war. This has been elaborately dealt with in the earlier part of this book. It's a ridiculous question raised by the British and has been explained by Rattan Singh at length. The British had conquered half the world without anybody willingly parting with their sovereignty to the British. The question itself is meaningless, with which Bhangoo has been bothering unnecessarily. He being conversant with the Sikh ethos, should have been aware of the views of Guru Gobind Singh given in his composition *Krishan Avtar*. Guru Gobind Singh has given a most befitting answer to this question:

koi kise raj na de hai. Jo le hai nij bal sit lai hai.

No people can have self-rule as a gift from another. It is to be seized through their own strength.[5]

Bhangoo has explained the same as:

The perfect Guru, the tenth master created the Khalsa Panth in this manner,
So that they must wage a war against oppression.
Since nobody achieves sovereignty without waging a war,
The tenth Guru had decided this strategy from the very beginning.[6]

Bhangoo should have in turn questioned Murray as to who gave the British the right to rule and hold sovereignty over India and half of the world, instead of bothering about the sovereignty of the Sikhs.

Rattan Singh Bhangoo was a prosperous landlord having a poetic flair and was interested in writing the history of his ancestors who had participated in the Sikh wars during the eighteenth century against the Mughal authorities. He had come in contact with Murray stationed at Ludhiana who was trying to get an authentic record of the origin and rise of the Sikhs. The version of Sikh history prepared by Khushwaqt Rai and Maulvi Bootey Shah of Batala were not considered sufficiently authentic and deemed to be biased accounts. The association of Murray with Rattan Singh Bhangoo led to his writing a comprehensive account of the Sikh Gurus and the Sikh struggle to rule their country for which they had a long drawn fight with the Mughal authorities. The recording of major episodes of Sikh history by Rattan Singh Bhangoo, author of *Gur Panth Parkash*, for more than three decades was finally completed in 1841.[7] Prof. Kulwant Singh states that for recording historical events he travelled extensively to collect information. Being a scholar of Persian and conversant with Sikh and Hindu scriptures, he was fully qualified to record an authentic version of Sikh history. How reliable has been the version of Bhangoo's Sikh history is a fairly debatable question and cannot be accepted on its face value. Bhangoo's paternal grandfather Mehtab Singh of Mirankot and maternal grandfather Sham Singh of Karor Singhia misl were notable Sikh warriors. Bhangoo has used sources of oral history as well as written sources for writing this epic which took three to four decades to complete.

With the object of both guarding against the projection of a biased view about the Sikh religion and history being passed on to the Western world, Rattan Singh Bhangoo developed acquaintance with Murray. Kulwant Singh says that it was out of this twofold objective of protecting the rich Sikh heritage and history and projecting almost an eyewitness account of the saga of Sikh struggle and revolution that he undertook the writing of this monumental epic. Though Kulwant Singh has shown appreciation of Bhangoo's laudable accounts of his elders, he, however, along with a number of other historians, has turned a blind eye to the numerous derogatory and unauthenticated remarks against Banda Bahadur. For instance, Bhangoo has stated:

> Now I undertake to write the account of Sikhs,
> As it was narrated by our ancestors and forefathers.
> And as heard from still earlier and ancient elders,
> Who had heard from their own talented peers.[8]

The 50 episodes or so dealing with Banda Bahadur are in fact about 50 stories and each episode is virtually a story by itself dealing with a Banda Bahadur in some way or the other. Most of the stories are fables with a certain admixture of the supernatural. These stories are, however, bereft of authentic historical material. In most of these episodes, a deliberate attempt has been made to belittle or degrade Banda Bahadur with fanciful stories.

Guru Gobind Singh on his way to the south had halted at Daduduar of Saint Dadu along with his 5,000 Sikh followers. Mahant Jait Ram had mentioned to Guru Gobind Singh that Narayan Das, a *bairagi* at Nanded, initially made saints and *sadhus* sit on his special bed and thereafter topples the bed upside down and felt delighted at the discomfiture of his guests. He played this prank on *sadhus* and saints who came to his *dera* and had practised it on Mahant Jait Ram too. Almost all historians of Sikhs have mentioned these incidents in their accounts.

In the early eighteenth century, a large-scale of degeneration had taken place amongst the *sadhus*, *bairagis* and ascetic warriors who were indulging in all kinds of vices and fighting battles for mercenary purposes. Banda Bahadur had left his home in search of eternal bliss and spent almost 20 years amongst *bairagis* and ascetic warriors before settling down in Nanded as a disappointed person where he had set-up a *dera*. He used to give blessings of *Dudh Put* to the visiting people.[9] The tradition of the blessing of *Dudh Put* is still current at Lohgarh, where Banda Bahadur had camped for a while. A plausible view of why he had settled at Nanded was that Banda Bahadur who could not fit in anymore with the *bairagis* and ascetic warriors after about 20 years in search of truth, had at last settled down, as a disappointed person, in Nanded. He used his tantric power to assess a spiritual strength of saints and *sadhus* coming to his *dera*. He would seat them on a special bed and then topple it upside down to assess the spiritual power of his visitors. When Guru Gobind Singh, who had the spiritual strength to match Banda Bahadur's tantric tricks, went there. Banda Bahadur immediately accepted him as his guru and became his disciple in right earnest. A *karam-yogi* becoming a *bairagi* is fairly common, but a *bairagi* becoming a *karam-yogi* is very rare, which happened in this case.

Guru Gobind Singh then gave five arrows from his quiver to Banda Bahadur as it was a normal practice those days for the seniors to give some of their own weapons to the juniors going to a war.

> Whatever condition the Guru laid down before the supplicating Banda,
> The Banda accepted those stipulations in complete humility.
> The Guru, then, named him as Banda Singh from his earlier name,
> Which the Guru's new disciple accepted in all humility and reverence.
> . . . .
> Satguru remarked that if Banda Singh was really worthy of a great task,
> He must set out and destroy the murderers of Guru's Sahibzadas,
> The Guru directed him to destroy the hill principalities after destroying Sirhind,
> As that was the task assigned by the Guru to him.
> . . . .
> News spread far and wide in the whole world,
> That the Guru had invested and appointed Banda Singh with his spiritual powers.
>
> The Guru then handed over his double edged dagger to Banda Singh,
> Which he accepted and wore around his person as an armour.
> Feeling enraged at the loss of their legitimate right of being the Guru's heirs,
> The Khalsa Singhs stripped Banda Singh of the Guru's armour.

As a stripped Banda Singh complained to the Guru (about the Singh's act)
The Guru went into peals of laughter,
The Guru remarked that with Singh's forcible possession is deemed as their legitimate right,
His mission of empowering the Khalsa Panth has been fulfilled.[10]

The above story concocted by Bhangoo himself or by some of his ancestor shows the existence of the total lack of discipline in the Guru's camp. The commander of the Guru's forces being stripped of the weapon given to him by the Guru, by the alleged contestants for the same post, further shows the existence of the wide range of rancour and anarchy abounding during that time. Knowing Banda Bahadur, he should have dealt with the situation personally rather than complaining to the Guru. Such a situation never existed in Guru's camp or under the leadership of Banda Bahadur. The entire story is a concoction of a biased and unbalanced mind, unknowingly damaging the greatness of the Guru while attempting to damn Banda Bahadur, the Guru's selected commander.

Rattan Singh Bhangoo states that the five arrows given by the Guru were invested with miraculous powers. These arrows had the power to create dust-laden storms to impair the visibility and eyesight of the enemy force. The blinding storm would force the enemy to turn on their backs and help the user in vanquishing the enemy and winning victory over them.[11] Guru Gobind Singh had fought over 20 battles with the Mughal forces and Hindu hill rajas but after the last battle of Anandpur Sahib (1704) and the battle of Chamkaur the Guru had to withdraw from Anandpur Sahib and leave Chamkaur incognito. The Guru had, however, not used any such powers to change the course of the battles. He did not use these supernatural powerladen arrows to help his two sons fighting against the mighty Mughal forces and so the supernatural power of these arrows appear to be doubtful. In fact, the Guru had been giving his blessings to the needy people but had not used any supernatural powers to change the course of a battle and had faced every difficulty with the force of his arms and strength of his character. This is true of all the Gurus. Whereas the truth was that the Guru had directed Banda to work in league with the Sikhs, and Banda had willingly accepted the same, Bhangoo has said that Banda Bahadur had requested to the Guru to bestow him with certain miraculous powers to which the Guru replied that he has handed over all his powers to the Khalsa.[12]

After the creation of the Khalsa Panth, Guru Gobind Singh called for more volunteers and created a sizeable army. The army was trained by engaging them in fighting mock battles. The Guru encouraged them to think of acquiring more and more territories and material assets. The Sikhs, however, could not grasp the far-sighted wisdom of the Guru and aspired to possess territories in Punjab alone. The Guru tempted them to aspire for territories in the south as well as the mountainous territories of east and west. The Sikhs represented that they did not want to leave for far off regions and were keen to live in their homeland in Punjab and repeatedly asked for the sovereignty over Punjab alone.[13] The Mujhail Sikhs having a major bias amongst the Singhs lacked imagination to aspire to rule over the larger areas and stuck only to Punjab. In case they had the vision and imagination they would have perhaps ruled over a large area of India, especially the adjoining areas of Punjab. A similar attempt was made by Banda Bahadur to persuade Rajputs to join the Sikhs in pushing out the Mughal authorities from the Indian soil and have the entire Indian homeland under their sovereign rule. But the Rajputs could not appreciate Banda Bahadur's aspirations and were content in remaining under the protection of the Mughal emperors by giving their daughters to Mughal princes, an old Celtic custom of humiliating defeated rivals.[14]

The Mujhail Sikhs were the most hard hitting fighters and were somewhat superior to the other Khalsa volunteers, an aspect about which they were proud. With the selection of Banda Bahadur as the commander of the Sikh forces, by hindsight, an undercurrent of some Mujhail discontentment does seem to have appeared here and there, but no distinct observation of it was expressed during the lifetime of Banda Bahadur. Perhaps they were appreciative of the battle strategies and other capabilities of Banda Bahadur at the battlefield, which converted every losing battle into a success for the Khalsa. With the death of Banda Bahadur in 1716, the Mujhail dislike of Banda Bahadur became more and more aggressive especially, at the time of story-telling in their villages. It is an old saying that all the faults of a person are forgotten after his death, but in this case the enumeration of his drawbacks if any became more and more expressive, especially when narrators of the stories and the story writer (R.S. Bhangoo) were both Mujhails.

Rattan Singh Bhangoo writes:

> Banda Singh entered into the precincts of the city of Sirhind,
> And took possession of the whole treasure of Wazir Khan,
> He occupied but he did not ransack the city of Sirhind,
> For which lapse he had to repent later on.
> The Guru had instructed him to demolish the whole city,
> And raze it to dust after thoroughly ransacking it.
> Banda Singh had forgotten the mandate of the Guru,
> With which he had been sent by the Guru,
> He had to bear the consequences for his disobedience,
> For preserving the cursed city of Sirhind.[15]

The above account of Bhangoo is incorrect and not in accordance with the Guru's instruction laid down from time to time. Guru Gobind Singh had laid down various principles to be observed in wars, viz., not to attack the unarmed or the weak, not to plunder the private property of peaceful citizens, fair treatment be accorded to women and children, no general massacre, or damage to places of worship, no harm to the persons who had surrendered and treatment of the injured after the battle. Under these rules laid down by the Guru himself, he would not have given instructions to demolish or ransack the whole city. The mausoleums of Muslim saints built in the fourteenth century are still intact without any damage done by the Sikhs. This is a concoction made by Rattan Singh Bhangoo or any ancestor of his and is far from being a true account of the instructions given by Guru Gobind Singh to Banda Bahadur.

The account of the Sikh struggle given by Bhangoo has a definite bias for the Mujhail Sikhs. There are numerous places where special place is given to Mujhails *vis-à-vis* the rest of the Sikh army. For example,

1. Whatever instructions were issued by the tenth Guru,
   These were accepted and followed by the Mujhail Sikhs.

All others who accepted and followed Guru's instructions,
Also became worthy recipient of Guru's blessings.[16]

2. The Guru proclaimed his decree,
Instructing the initiated Singhs from the Majha region,
They should first expand the strength of the Khalsa,
And then raise fearful strife against the Mughals.[17]
3. Whenever a Singh was spotted and captured,
He was beheaded there and then by the Muslims,
Even then the Sikhs did not cease their initiation into the Khalsa Panth,
The brave Sikhs of Majha were not scared of death.[18]
4. The Guru directed him (Banda) to invite the Mujhail Singhs to join him,
And instruct them to lead his forces from the front.
These Mujhail Singhs were the bravest of the brave and so much committed
That the Mughals would flee from the field scared of them.
They being committed followers and disciples of their Guru,
Had been invested with all the spiritual powers of their Guru,
The Guru had passed on his sovereignty to these Singhs,
Which they had preserved and imbibed in true spirit.
The Mujhail Singhs and the Guru were images of each other,
As the Guru and these Singhs were part of the state of Punjab.[19]

The above excerpts are from Bhangoo's accounts in which a definite bias for Mujhail Singhs is evident and the rest of the Sikh soldiers are deemed to be a secondary force or what we call non-combatants in the modern armies. A certain amount of bias is quite natural in the writing of a Mujhail writer but the altogether superiority shown to the Mujhails over the rest cannot be appreciated. This alleged strain of superiority of the Mujhails runs throughout the *Panth Parkash*. Very often there are attempts to achieve superiority for some by denigrating others, a most unbecoming characteristic in a historian working on an authentic historical account for posterity.

When Aali Singh and Mali Singh from Sailodi near Sirhind came, Banda Bahadur received them with the traditional Khalsa greetings *Wahe Gur ji ki Fateh*. Aali Singh and Mali Singh expected to see a miracle performed by him but Banda Bahadur told the Singhs that all the miracles belonged to the Guru, who would stand by those whom he had sent.[20] People from various areas of Punjab were coming and joining Banda Bahadur. Banda Bahadur attacked Samana and demolished the town. He had now come close to Sirhind and the people of the city were greatly scared of the imminent attack. The Royal Mughal force was equipped with all provisions. The Singhs did not have provisions even for their next meal. While the Mughal army possessed bags full of coins, the Singhs arranged everyday's provision through loot and plunder. It was indeed a miracle of the Supreme Divine, that a mendicant stole a victory over a powerful sovereign. Sikh forces were under great pressure by the Mughal forces who were well equipped with guns. Banda Bahadur was watching the fight from a mound. The Sikh warriors were pleading with Banda Bahadur to join the battle but Banda Bahadur was telling them to go on for some more time. He was waiting for an opportune moment when he would plunge into the battle. Rattan Singh Bhangoo has introduced a *chaupai* at this stage:

> But the bravest Mujhail Singhs assured Banda Singh
> That they would fight with the Mughals even without his participation.
> So as Banda Singh's own followers started deserting him
> The Mujhail Singhs kept on fighting with the Mughals fighting from the front.[21]

At the opportune moment of his choice, 'Banda rose like a hungry lion and sprang on the enemy like a bolt from the blue—the irresistible Banda Bahadur with a single sally changed the whole scene.'[22] Khafi Khan says,

> Money, horses, elephants fell in the hands of infidels; horsemen and footmen fell under the swords of infidels who pursued them as far as Sirhind. Wazir Khan fell from his horse and was captured alive. Coming face to face with Banda Bahadur, Wazir Khan's head was struck off with one blow by Banda Bahadur.[23] The Mughal army ran away leaving behind vast quantities of arms and ammunition.

The *chaupai* introduced by Bhangoo is a totally unwarranted attempt to praise Mujhails who had actually become jittery in opposing the Mughals and were pleading with Banda Bahadur to join the battle, while he was waiting for a strategic moment to jump into the battle. After defeating the Mughal forces at Chhappar Chiri (the real name is Jhiri, a thick mangrove of trees), Baj Singh was appointed as the custodian of Sirhind by Banda Bahadur, and handed over all the captured treasure from Sirhind.[24] Rattan Singh Bhangoo in the initial episodes was somewhat fair to Banda Bahadur, but as time passed, his attitude got hardened towards Banda Bahadur and became hostile from episode no. 54 onwards until Banda Bahadur's death. It became much worse in describing the alleged differences between the Bandhayees and the Tat Khalsa.

A controversy rose amongst the Sikhs over a greeting (*Fateh Darshan*) made out by Banda Bahadur and it was feared that it was going to replace the existing salutation *Wahe Guru ji ka Khalsa, Wahe Guru ji ki Fateh* issued by Guru Gobind Singh after the creation of the Khalsa. In Guru Nanak's time, the Sikhs greeted one another by saying *Satnam*, *Sat Kartar*, *Sat Sri Akal* meaning that God, the creator is ever lasting. Whereas *Sat Sri Akal* still exists as a very common greeting among Sikhs, but the other two are no longer in common use. A salutation *Wahe Guru ji ka Khalsa, Wahe Guru ji ki Fateh* came out in existence around the period of the creation of the Khalsa. It means that the Khalsa belongs to the Wahe Guru and so the victories of the Khalsa also belong to the Wahe Guru. Some historians contend that this salutation was issued by Guru Gobind Singh himself.[25] However, the language and meaning of the salutation does not give the impression that Guru Gobind Singh is the author of it. In his *vanis*, the Guru has been proclaiming that all he possesses belong to the Khalsa and all his achievements are due to the Khalsa. The legend in the salutation obviously seems to be out of place. It is very likely that the salutation has been spelt out by some poet of the Guru's court, who put the entire Khalsa as belonging to the Guru placing their absolute loyalty at the feet of the Guru and when the Khalsa belonged to the Guru, all the victories of the Khalsa also stand to the credit of the Guru. This was a salutation among the Khalsa and could not be deemed to be a war cry. Bhangoo has on the first page of his *Sri Gur Panth Parkash* given a new salutation, *Ik Onkar Satguru Prasad*, *Sri Wahe Guruji ki Fateh* which appears to be a rather poor composition, changing the first half of the salutation with his own construction and keeping the second half as it is. At various places in the book where this greeting has been used, it had been reduced to the second part only, *Wahe Guruji ki Fateh* and the first part *Wahe Guru ji ka Khalsa* stands eliminated.[26] Nowhere have these distortions have been criticized by Bhangoo.

Fateh Darshan was made popular by Banda Bahadur as a salutation, and meant that you should have vision of the victory, which is very appropriate to say to a person you should see victory in those turbulent times of incessant warfare. Perhaps it is the most suitable wishful salutation as compared with the earlier ones. Ganda Singh has stated, 'There is no denying the fact, however, that he (Banda Bahadur) introduced a new war cry *Fateh Darshan* and that as it came to be used for and to replace the old Sikh salutation—*Wahe Gur ji ka Khalsa, Wahe Gur ji ki Fateh*—it was rejected by the Khalsa.'[27] Ganda Singh is very wrong to call it as a war cry. It is a salutation and salutation alone between individuals and thus cannot be deemed as a war cry. *Fateh Darshan* appears on the *hukamnamas* issued by Banda Bahadur on 12 December 1710 to the *sangat* at Jaunpur. The legend *Fateh Darshan* appears under the seal of Khalsa made out by Banda Bahadur. The second *hukamnama* also bears the seal and the legend *Fateh Darshan* but there is no date.[28] According to Ganda Singh, *Fateh Darshan* was dropped when it was rejected by the Khalsa. The entire antipathy against *Fateh Darshan* after Banda Bahadur's death, is a malicious tirade and nothing else. Salutations have been cut short as well as dropped with no objections raised from any side.

While evacuating Lohgarh after a last ditch fight, the Sikhs blew up a hollow trunk of tamarind tree with gunpowder as a signal to the Mughal emperor camping on the other side of the *choe* that the Khalsa was leaving Lohgarh and moving into the reserved forest of Haripur where no Mughal commander was willing to follow them. Whereas the Mughals had displaced Banda Bahadur from his occupied territories, they miserably failed in catching him or killing him. The Mughal Emperor Bahadur Shah was the one who really lost the battle and went back disappointed. Banda Bahadur in no time reassembled the Khalsas and took back the territories lost to the Mughal forces.

Raja Bhim Chand of Kahlur had always been a source of great annoyance to Guru Gobind Singh and had played a leading part in the expeditions led against the Guru by the hill chiefs or by the imperial troops. Banda Bahadur sent a *parwana* calling upon him to submit to the Sikhs but Bhim Chand was preparing to meet the Sikh forces. He had 1,300 *mians* (trained soldiers). However, even then, Bhim Chand and his men and his *mians* could not stand against the Sikh forces and were badly defeated. The town of Bilaspur yielded a large booty to the Sikhs. The defeat of Raja of Kahlur and his allies unnerved most of the Rajput rajas of the Shivalik hills and many of them readily joined the Sikh camp to greet the conquerors, to offer their allegiance and to pay *nazrana* or tribute to the Sikh treasury.[29] The first to submit was Sidh Sain of Mandi. From Mandi, Banda Bahadur proceeded to Kullu. Rattan Singh Bhangoo has woven long story of tantric powers which sounds like a grandmother's story to young kids with ample use of supernatural powers, etc., to put the kids to sleep. These cannot be taken as a piece of authentic history based on facts.[30] Some of the unlikely things mentioned by Bhangoo in these episodes are as under:

1. 'Bhim Chand who procured a written permission for his own assistance
   To be rendered by the ten lakh Mughal forces stationed at Kandahar.'
   (It may be noted that the entire Mughal regular force never reached ten lakh).[31]
   . . . .
   He (Banda Bahadur) would be harassed as Guru Gobind Singh was harassed
   With the assistance of ten lakh Mughal forces (which came from Kandahar)
   . . . .
   As their (Sikhs) Guru also claimed that he possessed miraculous powers,
   Banda Singh was also reputed to know an alchemist's formula.
   The gathering of all Hill Chiefs passed a unanimous resolution
   That they must device a strategy to capture Banda Singh alive.[32]
2. As a trial of strength between Hill Rajas and the Sikh forces, Banda Bahadur was to fix a flag post of the Khalsa which the Hill chiefs were to remove if they could.
   Thus, arriving at the flag post at night, these wicked Hill chiefs, tried their utmost to dismantle Banda Singh's flag post.

> After trying every technique to uproot, pullout, lift it, bury it under ground, they tried every other method to dismantle and mutilate it.
> When a soldier tried to cut the supporting rope with sword, the sword, instead of cutting the rope, attempted to slit his own throat,
> Putting the sword into its sheath after this vain attempt,
> The soldiers stood away scared and fled after saluting the flag post.[33]
> (Leaving aside the authenticity of Bhangoo's account, it is a ridiculous to say that they tried every technique to uproot, pull out, lift, and bury it under ground. If a pole cannot be uprooted, pulled out, lifted then how can it be buried under ground.)
> Exposing their conspiracy Banda Singh challenged each one of them,
> That the mightiest among them should try their utmost might,
> Feeling extremely ashamed and crestfallen at their duplicity
> They left humbled like veiled gentle women.[34]

Rattan Singh Bhangoo has brought out a story. According to him a lady in the service of Banda Singh somehow got hold of a book on necromancy. She later rose to be Banda Bahadur's wife. The queens of king of Jaiswal of the dynasty at Jajowal, were unable to have male issue and were deep in great agony about it. Somebody approached the king and told him that a woman claiming to be Banda Singh's wife had the power that whatever she uttered, never remained unfulfilled. So, the Jaiswal queens in great desperation and hope came to her who blessed the queens and both of them had male issues.[35]

Another story propagated by Rattan Singh Bhangoo was that when Banda Singh entered the Kullu territory the hill chief put Banda Singh under arrest. Banda Singh is stated to be bragging his powers and in the meantime the Kullu chief kept on tightening the security ring around him. He also got manufactured an iron cage and put Banda Singh in it. Banda Singh somehow escaped and started to have a plan to teach a lesson to the Kullu chief. Banda Bahadur commanded the Birs at his command to lift the iron cage and take it to the boundary of Mandi state. Banda Singh had prophesied that Khalsa would arrive and commit arson in the state of Kullu. When Banda Singh arrived in Mandi, the Mandi chief was greatly delighted. Banda Singh put up his camp at Mandi palace and people started making offerings and seeking his blessings. (There is no mention in history books that Banda Bahadur ever raised or lived in a palace. He always stayed in a thatched hut.)

> After this, Banda Singh came to be called as a Guru,
> And established his shrine at Gurukot in the midst of hills,
> While the worship of all the Sidhas came to an end,
> All the people started worshipping Banda Singh.[36]

The author had spent a year, 1972-3 at Bias Sutlej Link Project and visited all the places in Kullu, Mandi and Sundernagar areas. There is no village by the name Gurukot and that too associated with Banda Bahadur. The latter moved in the hill states with his army to subdue the hill states who had taken a very hostile attitude, under the leadership of Bhim Chand of Kahlur, towards Guru Gobind Singh. After the subduing of Bhim Chand the rest of the rulers realized that it was futile to fight with Banda Bahadur and they submitted to him, paid *nazrana* and annual tribute. Under these circumstances the story concocted by Rattan Singh Bhangoo seems to be totally baseless and unrealistic.

Rattan Singh now describes Banda's visit to Chamba. In this area the three major forts are the fort of Kangra, the fort of Noorpur and fort of Kotla. Banda Bahadur left most of his army at Kotla Fort and went with a small force to Chamba. While taking photographs of these forts, the author came to know that Banda Bahadur left the bulk of his army at Kotla Fort. The installation of a stone horse carved by the local artisans alleged to have been installed by Banda Bahadur is another fabricated story of Bhangoo. It is true that Banda Bahadur married a Chamba lady, but it is doubtful if he had made two marriages at Chamba. Banda Bahadur did not stay in Chamba for three years as stated by Rattan Singh Bhangoo.[37] The major part of these three years was spent in Riasi district of Rajouri in Jammu, where a *dera* of Bandheyee Sangathan stands established.

Another story of Rattan Singh Bhangoo is a letter of appreciation sent through a Sikh messenger by Emperor Bahadur Shah to Banda Bahadur.

So the emperor sent a Sikh messenger (with a letter of appreciation),
That Banda Singh had performed a noble deed by killing Wazir Khan,
And that the hill chiefs whom Banda Singh had also chastised,
Were also the most wicked enemies of Guru Gobind Singh.

Although the emperor himself keen to kill all those hill chiefs,
Yet it was better that Guru's own disciple had dealt with them.
The emperor reiterated that he was a humble servant of the Guru,
Since it was with the Guru's grace that he had become a sovereign.[38]

He would visit Banda Singh before his pilgrimage if the latter so desired,
Otherwise he would pay his obeisance on his return from Lahore.
He requested for a right of passage through the Sirhind province,
And sought Banda Singh's permission for a passage up to Lahore.

He further proposed that half of Punjab territory be handed over to him,
While Banda Singh kept his custody over the entire hill states.
He would pay a visit to Banda Singh if the latter permitted,
Otherwise he would go to Lahore through the outer fringe of Punjab.[39]

Finally he pleaded for permission for a passage up to Lahore,
Which should run through the territory of the Sirhind province.
With these proposals, he sent a Sikh messenger (to Banda Singh),
Who conveyed the emperor's message with folded hands.[40]

The above alleged letter was issued with the consent of Emperor Bahadur Shah in which the emperor virtually begs Banda Bahadur for peace in the Punjab and security of his throne. This letter obviously is a figment of imagination of Rattan Singh Bhangoo and discredits Bhangoo for treating the same as a historical document. The Mughal government had not become so weak as portrayed by Bhangoo to be scared of facing Banda Bahadur. Where Bhangoo says that besides writing the account of the Sikhs as narrated by his ancestors and forefather and their ancestors; he also states that he has used his own understanding and faith in writing the same. Wherever Bhangoo enters into a tricky situation and had gone too far in blaming Banda Bahadur, he would repeatedly state that he was writing what he had heard from his ancestors and what they had heard from their ancestors.[41] This becomes an apology by Bhangoo for his incompetence to weave a somewhat plausible story.

In one of the episodes there is mention of alleged interference by Mata Sundari (Guru's wife) in the affairs of the Sikhs with the Mughal government. Banda Bahadur, in a decisive move killed Shamas Khan, Baizid Khan and Jaly Khan. It became a talking point in the large cities that Banda Bahadur would next attack Lahore and thereafter Delhi.[42] No Mughal warrior had the guts and daring to confront and look squarely in his face. The emperor at Delhi called a meeting of his commanders and asked from among them as to who could challenge and kill Banda Bahadur. Nobody volunteered.[43]

The emperor's ministers suggested that as Banda Bahadur was the creation of Guru Gobind Singh, the guru's wife Mata Sundari should stop Banda Bahadur from advancing further on to major cities of the Mughals, otherwise she would be put under arrest.[44] Bhai Nand Lal was called to the Mughal court and the emperor pleaded with him to seek Mata Sundari's help in restraining Banda Bahadur from further warfare. Although Mata Sundari was of the opinion that Banda Bahadur would not agree with any such advice to stop his further occupation of Mughal territories. However, she was persuaded to issue suitable instructions to Banda Bahadur under Guru Gobind Singh's seal. These instructions were sent to Banda Bahadur and whatever reply he gave was sent to the Mughal emperor. (Guru Gobind Singh never used any seal on his *hukamnamas* or on any other document.) Bhai Nand Lal had expired in 1705 in accordance with the *Mahakosh* written by Bhai Kahan Singh. Bhangoo gives his year of death as 1711-12. However, this date cannot be relied upon as he was in the habit of fabricating fables and fictions.[45]

Banda Singh had written that he was, no longer a guru's follower,
As he had been a follower of *Bairagi Vaishno* seat.
He remarked that his collaboration with the Guru was over,
As he would become a sovereign with his own powers.

Henceforth, he would introduce his own slogan of *Darshan Fateh*,
In place of the guru's slogan of *Wahe Guruji ki Fateh*

He would harass and torture the Sikhs as brutally
As the Singhs had slaughtered his goats (at his monastery).

So Banda Singh kept on eliminating the Mughals,
Who failed to put any stop to their slaughter by Banda Singh.
After all the Mughals admitted defeat at the hands of Banda Singh,
He started harassing and torturing all the people of Punjab.

Ganda Singh in his account of Banda Bahadur has stated, that the allegation of Bhai Gian Singh and Rattan Singh Bhangoo, that Banda Bahadur at this time proclaimed himself as the Guru of the Sikhs does not stand the test of historical scrutiny based on original authentic accounts of better informed contemporary writers, official as well as private. Nor is there any evidence available of Banda Bahadur's visit to Amritsar where he is alleged to have assumed the mannerisms of a Guru. There is absolutely nothing the contemporary, or the earliest available record—official diaries and chronologies, state and family histories, personal memories, etc.—to show that any negotiation were, at that time or at any other time, carried on between the Emperor Farrukh Siyar and Mata Sundari, the widow of Guru Gobind Singh. No conflict ever took place between Banda Bahadur and Mata Sundari, or the Khalsa. All these allegations appeared to have given rise to idle gossips about Banda Bahadur lapses and excommunication, which have of late been used as history by ill-informed writers.[46]

A dispute arose between the Bhandeyees and the Tat Khalsa over the distribution of the offerings by the general public. The Bhandeyees tempted the Mughal administrator by offering him a larger amount of taxation than already fixed. In this process the Tat Khalsa was likely to be defeated. Since half the Sikh congregation consisted of Bhandeyee followers, the Singhs alleged that since the Guru's shrines belonged to the Singhs, the Bhandeyee Singhs had no business to make such a claim. They also claimed that Bhandeyees should join the mainstream by giving up *Fateh Darshan*. They also should get initiated with *khande ki pahul* and other conditions. Ganda Singh states that *Fateh Darshan* greeting was dropped under the protest of the Khalsa. The strife between the two factions reached such a pitch, as though they would be at each other's throat in a moment. There were certain descendants of Bhai Buddha and Bhai Salo, Bhai Bhagtu and Bhai Bahlo among the Sikhs, besides some *masands* and *mewras* who suggested a compromise situation to a free fight among the Sikhs.

The wise on both sides of the Khalsa factions remarked,
That they must find a solution acceptable to both the factions.
If both the factions were willing to accede to their advice,
Both the parties should sit together in a peaceful manner.

They advised that both the parties should leave the issue to Divine God,
And accept gracefully whatever the Divine will revealed.
Since everything happens according to the Divine Will,
Why should they ruin themselves by fighting each other?

Either they should lay down both the written claim before the *Guru Granth Sahib*,
Or immerse both the versions in the waters of the sacred tank.
Out of the two written captions of *Wahe Gurji ki fateh* and *Fateh Darshan*,
Whichever version floated above should be accepted as the valid religion.

Whichever bundled version got drowned should be rejected,
And nobody should ever follow and propagate that religion.
The Mughals fondly wished for the drowning of both the versions,
So that they might get benefited (by the extinction of Khalsa Panth).

Both the Bhandeyee and Tat Khalsa Singhs accepted the proposal,
And left the whole controversy to be resolved by God's will.
Since the Khalsa Panth was destined to be the sovereign,
How could it ever come to be defeated (by anybody).

. . . .

A cotton thread, got prepared by an innocent girl,
Was wrapped around both the packets containing the two versions.
Summoning a boy, both the packets were placed on the water's surface.
Near *Har-ki-Puari* adjacent to the back entrance of the sanctum sanctorum.

Once both the packets went down under the water for a while,
Both the factions felt extremely concerned (about their future).
If, perchance, both the packets sank down in the water,
There would not remain a trace of the Hindu (the Sikhs) on earth.

. . . .

Instantly, one of the packets came afloat after going down,
Containing the written version of one of the factions.
The (Tat Khalsa) Singhs felt somewhat relieved at this scene,
And felt as if the Guru had responded to the prayer.

Immediately after the police officials handed over the letter,
The arbitrators handed it over to the Tat Khalsa after reading it,
Disclosing that the version with *Wahe Gurji ki Fateh* had floated,
The arbitrator pronounced the judgment to both the factions.

While the Tat Khalsa Singhs felt delighted at the declaration,
The Bhandeyee Singhs were crestfallen after this decision.
They were shocked after hearing the decision,
As if a monarch had been deprived of his sovereignty.

So crestfallen, desperate and frustrated felt the Bhandeyee Singhs,
As if both the elements (earth and sky) were refusing to shelter them.
Wringing their hands and shaking their heads in desperation,
They felt as if they had no place to hide their shameful faces.

It is a scientific phenomenon that paper when submerged in water becomes heavier than water and it cannot rise to the surface again. There cannot be any Guru's interference to make the *chit* of Tat Khalsa to float and the *chit* of Bhandeyees to sink. Either this story is the imagination of Bhangoo or some trick had been played to make the Tat Khalsa *chit* rise to the surface.

Rattan Singh Bhangoo designed a sort of charge-sheet against Banda Bahadur so false and vicious that in contrast a false charge-sheet issued by the worst police station of Punjab would appear to be the work of a novice. Rattan Singh Bhangoo raises the issue in the form of question and answer:

(A question): If anybody posed this question (to the author),
That Banda Singh, being an omniscient person,
How could he not see through the game,
That the Mughals were playing a fraud on him?

(Author's Answer): Banda had made the following lapses;
First, he had offended the Guru mother,
Second, he had compromised his moral character,
Through his sexual indulgence with so many women.

> Third, he had lost command over his Birs (Captive spirits),
> Which incapacitated him from flying at his own will,
> Fourth, he had left his book of necromancy in Mandi,
> By handing it over to Mandi chief Sudh Sain.
>
> Fifth, he indulged in talking ill of the great Guru,
> Sixth, he got estranged from the Khalsa Panth.
> Seventh, he founded his own (separate religious order)
> Eighth, he (committed the sin) of burying alive his own infant daughter.
>
> Ninth, he had received powers of miracles gratuitously,
> Tenth, he had abandoned meditation (on Guru's words)
> A rare gift acquired gratuitously soon gets lost,
> While a craft acquired with hard work always lasts longer.

The above-mentioned allegations made up by Bhangoo are totally false and malicious. There is no historical evidence in the form of any correspondence, record, etc., between Mata Sundari and Banda Bahadur. Calling her Guru Mother has no sanctity in Sikh religion. In fact, she had moved to Mathura from Delhi in a house provided by the Raja of Jaipur during the Sikh-Mughal hostilities. The *hukamnamas* by Mata Sundari are available and the first *hukamnama* dated 1717 was issued after the death of Banda Bahadur. The story is a creation of Bhangoo, and to levy such allegations against the most ablest and bravest of Sikh commanders is not only disgraceful but also unpardonable for the Sikh nation to have accepted the same all along.

The allegation of Bhai Gian Singh, the author of *Twarikh Guru Khalsa* and the author of *Panth Parkash*, that Banda Singh at this time proclaimed himself as the Guru of the Sikhs does not stand the test of historical scrutiny based on authentic accounts of better informed contemporary writers, official and private. Nor is any evidence available of his visit to Amritsar where he is alleged to have assumed the mannerisms of a Guru. It may also be mentioned here that there is nothing in the contemporary or the earliest available records-official diaries and chronologies, state and family history, personal memoirs, etc., to show that any negotiations, at this time or at any other time, were carried on between Farrukh

Siyar and Mata Sundari, the widow of Guru Gobind Singh, or that any conflict took place between Banda Singh and Mata Sundari or the Khalsa (Ganda Singh, pp. 195-6). The alleged correspondence between Farrukh Siyar and Mata Sundari stated to have been carried out in 1714-15 is totally incorrect as during the said period Banda Bahadur and his forces were besieged in Gurdas Nangal. Bhai Nand Lal during his last year was running a school in Multan and the date of his death is given as 1705 in *Mahan Kosh*.

The first charge against Banda Bahadur of having offended Mata Sundari is totally false. There has been no contact ever between Banda Bahadur and Mata Sundari. Nand Lal was no longer alive at the time and alleging to be the messenger between Farrukh Siyar and Mata Sundari is again totally false.

The second charge that he had compromised his moral character is totally baseless and unbecoming of a historian making these charges without the slightest proof thereof.

The allegation that he had lost command over the captive Birs is also false and frivolous. Although people had been saying, especially the Mughal historians, of Banda Bahadur possessing supernatural powers but since Banda Bahadur's becoming a disciple of Guru Gobind Singh, he did not practice any such miracle to gain any benefit for him or his men. When Aali Singh and Mali Singh from Bhasor expected to see a miracle from Banda Bahadur, Rattan Singh Bhangoo states that Banda told the Singhs that all miracles belong to the Guru who will stand by those who are his Khalsa. Therefore, time and again the stories woven about miracles alleged to have been carried out by Banda Bahadur are totally false and malicious. If he could fly at will, would he not have flown out of Gurdas Nangal?

The fifth allegation that Banda Bahadur indulged in talking ill of the great Guru is not supported by the any evidence howsoever. Bhangoo's concocting of such stories is certainly unbecoming of him as a historian.

About the sixth allegation that he got estranged from the Khalsa Panth, there is no evidence that the Khalsa soldiers had at any time abandoned him, in fact uptil the last battle the Sikhs came in large number to fight whenever Banda called them. There is only a single solitary case of Baba Binod Singh leaving the Khalsa and riding out of Gurdas Nangal after some difference of opinion had occurred over the conduct of operations. The democracy in the Khalsa was of such level that even in the time of Guru Gobind Singh forty Sikhs left Anandpur Sahib and went back to their villages. The allegation is baseless and incorrect.

The seventh allegation is that he founded a separate religious order and called himself the Guru. Among the Sikh community, there are Babas who called themselves Gurus and some are called Sat Gurus. If Banda had called himself a Guru and set-up a new religious order, his successors should also have used the surname as Gurus. This author has visited their *dera* at Riasi and has observed that there is no infringement, howsoever minor, of the religious tradition of the Sikhs. Of course, they seem to have great devotion to the person of Guru Gobind Singh.

The eighth allegation, that Banda Bahadur had buried alive his own infant daughter is without an iota of evidence and the creation of an unbalanced mind.

The ninth and tenth allegations are similar to the third and fourth allegations. If Banda Bahadur had stopped using supernatural powers on becoming the disciple of Guru Gobind Singh, Bhangoo's harping on the use or non-use of supernatural powers is the job of a mind devoid of positive thinking. Never has a historical account been fudged in such blatant manner and still proclaimed to be a great historical work. The entire portion dealing with Banda Bahadur needs to be further research in greater detail to restore his honour and valour as well as to redeem the beauty of the epic *Sri Gur Panth Parkash*.

Some of the books (*pothies*) written about Sikh history (seventeenth and eighteenth century) had leanings towards Brahmanism. These books have been edited by Sikh scholars, from time to time, led by Bhai Veer Singh. The *Sri Gur Panth Parkash* by R.S. Bhangoo has also been edited. The first two chapters which traced Guru Nanak's genealogy from Ram Chander have been dropped. Further editing has been done of the portions not in conformity with the Sikh ethos. Where editing has been done of *Panth Parkash* to bring it in line with Sikh ethos, there has been virtually no editing thereof with regard to malicious and unauthenticated charges levied against Banda Bahadur by Bhangoo.

It is high time that SGPC undertake the editing of *Panth Parkash* and make it an authentic and unbiased history of the early eighteenth-century struggle of the Sikhs under command of Banda Bahadur. The frivolous charges and character assassination carried out by Bhangoo without the slightest authenticity have been in existence for the last about 200 years. The *Panth Parkash* is called a great epic of the struggle of the Sikh nation for the last 200 years for which credit has gone to Rattan Singh Bhangoo. The memory of Banda Bahadur has been kept virtually in cold storage and no large scale functions or setting up of memorials have been carried out during this period.

During this year (2010), from March onwards large scale functions have been held by various organizations of the Sikhs, by Punjab government and SGPC. Large number of pictures, sculptures and replicas of coins issued by Banda Bahadur has been distributed and 20 acres of land where the battle of Sirhind was fought has been earmarked by Punjab government for a suitable memorial in memory of Banda Bahadur. The character assassination and vilification carried out by Rattan Singh Bhangoo of Banda Bahadur stays in the *Panth Parkash* as such. It is a great irony that where all over Punjab and its organizations are celebrating Banda Bahadurs' victory over Mughal Forces of Sirhind, the vilification and character assassination stares in our face when we study *Panth Parkash*. The continuation of the combination of these two aspects side by side is not compatible. It is high time that SGPC undertake the editing of 50 episodes on Banda Bahadur in *Panth Parkash* and make it an authentic and unbiased history of early eighteenth century under the command of Banda Singh Bahadur. It is understood that a regular task force of scholars under Professor Kirpal Singh has been engaged by SGPC, for quite some time for editing these historical books on Sikh History. It is desirable that the editing of episodes on Banda Bahadur be taken up on a priority basis.

NOTES

1. Rattan Singh Bhangoo, *Sri Gur Panth Parkash*, vol. I, Chandigarh: Institute of Sikh Studies, 2006, p. iii.
2. Ibid. (Episodes 1-81).
3. Ibid., p. viii.
4. Ibid., p. xxiii.
5. Guru Gobind Singh's composition *Krishan Avtar*.
6. *Panth Parkash*, p. 77.
7. R.S. Bhangoo, *Panth Parkash*, p. xviii.
8. Ibid., Episode 1, p. 3.
9. Ibid., Episode 31, p. 203.
10. Ibid., p. 195.
11. Ibid.
12. Ibid., *Chaupai*, p. 201.
13. Ibid., p. 93.
14. See chapter on Sikh-Rajput Relations.
15. Bhangoo, *Panth Parkash*, p. 245.
16. Ibid., p. 91.
17. Ibid., p. 95.
18. Ibid., p. 99.
19. Ibid., p. 197.
20. Ibid., p. 219.
21. Ibid., p. 243.
22. Sohan Singh, *Banda the Brave*, Faridkot, 1915, p. 59.
23. G.S. Deol, *Banda Bahadur*, Jalandhar, 1972, p. 47.
24. Bhangoo, *Panth Parkash*, p. 245.
25. Hari Ram Gupta, *History of Sikh Gurus*, p. 186.
26. *Panth Parkash*, p. 219 line 10, p. 273 3rd line of dohra, p. 435 Chaupai para 3, pp. 443, 445.
27. Ganda Singh, *Life of Banda Singh Bahadur*, Amritsar: Khalsa College, 1935 p. 85.
28. Ganda Singh, *Hukamname*, Patiala: Punjabi University, pp. 182, 184.
29. Ganda Singh, *Life of Banda Singh Bahadur*, p. 155.
30. Bhangoo, *Panth Parkash*, Episodes 48-51, pp. 265-99.
31. Ibid., p. 265.
32. Ibid., p. 269.
33. Ibid., p. 275.
34. Ibid., p. 277.
35. Ibid., Episode 50, 293.
36. Ibid., p. 299.

37. Ibid., p. 305.
38. Ibid., p. 315.
39. Ibid., p. 315.
40. Ibid., p. 316.
41. Ibid., p. 321.
42. Ibid., p. 335/2.
43. Ibid., p. 335/4.
44. Ibid., p. 335/6.
45. Bhai Kahan Singh, *Mahakosh*.
46. Ganda Singh, *Banda Bahadur*, pp. 195-6.

CHAPTER 9

Banda Singh Bahadur

An Assessment

Banda Bahadur was born on 27 October 1670 in the house of Ram Dev, an ordinary Rajput farmer at Rajouri, Poonch district, western part of the state of Jammu & Kashmir. He was named Lachhman Dev and is said to have developed into a youth of very active habits, full of energy and fond of shooting and hunting. In those times there were no schooling facilities and growing children would help in the fields and enjoy hunting, riding, etc. It is said, that in one of his hunting excursions, he killed a doe and while cleaning its stomach, two young ones fell out from the womb and died in a few minutes. The pitiable sight of the dying doe and its young ones touched a very tender and sensitive cord in his heart and affected him to such a great extent that his mind took an ascetic turn. He left his home and his family at the age of around 15 years and took to the role of an ascetic. His first preceptor was Sadhu Janaki Prasad, who could not measure up to his expectations. At Ram Thaman near Kasur, he came under the patronage of the Bairagi Ram Das. Banda Bahadur did not stay long with him as well and started wandering as a *bairagi*, in search of a true guide.

With the advent of Islamic invaders since twelfth century onwards, a large number of free-booters had also come and were carrying large-scale harassment and looting of pilgrims going to and fro to Hindu pilgrimage centres. To counter these Islamic free-booters, large-scale volunteers were taken in the ranks of *bairagis* and ascetic warriors. With the entry of untrained and indisciplined volunteers came all sorts of vices and lax livelihood. The use of drugs, alcohol, meat and to some extent keeping women mellowed down the extreme form of discipline and ascetic way of life.

How Banda Bahadur spent almost 20 years in their midst is not historically known and is deemed to be a dark period of Banda Bahadur's life. His criss-crossing the length and breadth of the Indian subcontinent from north to south came to a halt in Panchvati (south India) where he joined Aughar Nath, an occult *yogi*. After the death of Aughar Nath he came to Nanded (which was in earlier time a place of holy men). Here he set-up his own *dera* at the bank of the river Godavari, on a small mound and said to be giving blessings of *Dudh Putt* to the visiting pilgrims and devotees. Banda Bahadur had wandered away from his home in search of a true precept to imbibe in him the fundamental principles of asceticism. Its seems that his search was not rewarding enough and he ultimately settled down at Nanded, a disappointed person. A number of *sadhus* used to visit his *dera* for staying purposes while going down south or while returning to the north. With the experiences which Banda Bahadur had with the *sadhus* and *bairagis* from all over India he seems to have developed a sort of cynicism against the selfish *bairagis* and *sadhus*. A story is prevalent that he had a couch on which if any *sadhu/bairagi* sat down he would topple them over with his tantric powers and laugh at their discomfiture.

During this period Guru Gobind Singh was attacked by the Mughal forces and Hindu hill rajas in 1704 at Anandpur and after a prolonged siege of eight months, he had to leave Anandpur due to exhaustion of food and ammunition stocks. He was promised safe passage by the Mughal forces, but in spite of their pledges the Mughal forces attacked him, and during the course of it he got separated from his family, lost his mother and all his four sons and a large number of his soldiers/disciples besides a huge amount of religious literature maintained by him. In Delhi, Guru Gobind Singh helped Bahadur Shah in his war against his younger brother Azim Shah for succession to the Mughal throne after Aurangzeb's death in 1707 and in return he requested Bahadur Shah for award of suitable punishment to Wazir Khan and some of his officials for the brutal execution of his two younger sons and atrocities on the Sikhs. Bahadur Shah was moving to the south where his youngest brother had raised the standard of rebellion. On the suggestion of Bahadur Shah, the Guru accompanied him up to Nanded. During this period the Guru realized that Bahadur Shah was not sincere in his promise, and so he settled down at Nanded and did not accompany Bahadur Shah any further.

Guru Gobind Singh and Banda Bahadur's meeting under normal circumstances would never have happened. It was perhaps destined that they should meet in 1708 in Nanded. The said meeting took place at the Guru's initiative. What transpired between them in a short time was known only to them as nobody else was privy thereto. Various accounts of the meeting between the Guru and Banda Bahadur have been written by almost all the historians who have written about the early period of Sikh history. However, all these accounts give fanciful reconstructions and are not authentic historical accounts. Some of them contradict each other and even to the extent of questioning the selection by the Guru of the Banda Bahadur over his tried commanders. What is historically true is that in the meeting with the Guru, Banda Bahadur seems to have found his true mentor. Banda Bahadur forgot to attempt any trick on the Guru and became his disciple instantaneously. Banda Bahadur spent a few days or a couple of weeks with the Guru, stored all the Guru's instructions in his mind and left for Punjab to recapture the lost territories back to the Khalsa. The greatness of the meeting between the Guru and Banda Bahadur can be assessed from his becoming a *karma-yogi* from a *bairagi* at the desire of the Guru and going to Punjab and making the Sikh movement a living rebellion getting beyond the control of the mighty Mughal Empire.

Historically we have no knowledge of how Banda Bahadur spent about 20 years of his *bairag*, which sects he had joined, and how high he rose in their cadre. It deems to be a dark period of his life. Banda Bahadur had a very sharp mind. In his mixing with the *bairagis* and ascetic warriors, he seems to have picked up the essential of ascetic life, viz., mental training and self-control in the laid down procedure of exercise, control of diet and treatment of their victims. Secondly, he learnt the art of battle strategy of fighting with a small army against a much larger one. The process of *Dhai Phut*, the popular battle strategy used by the *misl* sardars, was prevalent among the ascetic warriors. It was due to these superior qualities of the ascetic warriors and *bairagis* that the

Mughal emperors employed some battalions composed only of ascetic warriors and *bairagis*. It may be mentioned here that Akbar had some battalions of Naga ascetic warriors who were paid double the salaries than that of the trained Mughal soldiers. Aurangzeb also employed ascetic warriors at exorbitant salaries and permitted them to move anywhere within the Mughal territories. It was these qualities of the ascetic warriors and *bairagis* which made them far superior soldiers, that had been imbibed by Banda Bahadur which singled him out as a great warrior in his seven-year long fight with the Mughal authorities. The fact of his possessing a sharp mind can be observed from the fact that in his stay for only a couple of weeks with Guru Gobind Singh, he assimilated all the instructions given by the Guru and acted upon them both in war and peace with acute precision.

When Muslim newswriter's praise of Banda Bahadur's qualities both in war and peace has become quite authentic observation that the unlettered and untrained boy who entered the world of *bairag* and asceticism as a novice, came out fully accomplished with principles of ascetic life as well as battle strategies. His display of these qualities immediately after his entering Punjab and leading the Khalsa revolution established the authenticity of our assessment of his basic qualities.

In the next seven years, Banda Bahadur had to fight ceaseless battles against Mughal forces, some successful and some not. The important battles he fought were at Sumana, Kapuri Sadhaura in 1709; Sirhind in 1710; Behrampur, Batala and Kalanaur in 1711; Sadhaura and Lohgarh in 1712; and Batala and Kalanaur again in 1715. His most important battles were at Sirhind (1710), Lohgarh (1711 and 1712) and Gurdas Nangal in 1715. Banda Bahadur's plan was to establish an independent Khalsa state in Punjab. However, his attempt to carve a Khalsa state was rather premature and did not succeed. However, he was able to shake the mighty Mughal Empire with such terrible force that it could not establish its authority firmly again.

Some peculiar and special aspects of Banda Bahadur's battles are given as under:

1. Banda Bahadur received information that a treasure of revenue

collections from a number of districts was halting at Bhuna village on way to Delhi under protection of a military escorting detachment. Banda Bahadur reached Bhuna and in a surprise attack defeated the Mughal force and took possession of the treasure. The report of loot of the treasury was made to *amil* of Kaithal, a Hindu commander, who rushed to the site with his cavalry force. Banda Bahadur and his men hid behind old walls, bushes and in trees and when found the enemy relaxing on the site, they in a surprise attack defeated the Mughal force and captured the *amil*. Banda Bahadur took away all the horses and guns from the Mughal force and the *amil* was allowed to retain his office on behalf of the Khalsa and carry out collection of revenue for the Khalsa. A Khalsa detachment was posted at Kaithal. This was the first step taken by Banda Bahadur in acquiring Mughal territory and placing his own administrative set-up in the setting up of a Sikh state. Khafi Khan states that in two or three month's time, 4,000 to 5,000 pony riders and 7,000 to 8,000 footmen joined Banda Bahadur and day by day their number increased and abundant money and material came to their hands. In many villages he appointed his own police officers (*thanedars*), and revenue collectors.

2. Banda Bahadur now moved to the towns of Kapuri and Sadhaura. The depraved ruler Qadam-ud-din of Kapuri, had hardly left a Hindu women whose chastity was unspared. The Sikh forces attacked Kapuri, overpowered the local resistance and set fire to the strongholds of Qadam-ud-din, who also perished in the general conflagrations.

   Sadhaura was ruled by Usman Khan, notorious for oppression of his subjects. He had also tortured to death the Muslim saint Sayyad Badar-ud-din, popularly called Buddhu Shah. His family members and disciples was killed and burnt and not allowed to be buried, their fault being that Buddhu Shah and his men had helped Guru Gobind Singh in the battle of Bhanghani against Garhwal raja and his Rajput friends.

   The Mughal force could not stand against the Sikh forces and was defeated. A story goes that Mughal zamindars wrote letters to Wazir Khan, *faujdar* of Sirhind, to come to their help against the Sikhs. These letters somehow fell into the hands of the Sikhs. Banda Bahadur called a meeting and exposed the guilty ones, who had to apologize. Banda Bahadur suggested that all those who get into a particular house will be spared and the rest will be punished. Most of the recalcitrant persons went into the deserted *haveli* of Buddhu Shah and under orders of Banda Bahadur were slain and the *haveli* to this day is called 'Qatal Garhi'. Today a Hindu school is run therein.

The Hindus of Chhat (a town on way to Sirhind) complained of great harassment by the Muslim ruler. A detachment was send, the Mughal ruler was eliminated and a Sikh *amil* was posted there.

3. *The Battle of Chapparh Chiri (Sirhind):* Banda Bahadur had his mindset on punishing Wazir Khan, the *faujdar* of Sirhind who was responsible for the execution of the two young sons of Guru Gobind Singh. He subdued and occupied the surrounding areas, increased the strength of his army and also the joining of volunteers from Malwa and Majha areas was accomplished. He took position on a raised mound behind a large pond of water about 15 miles from Sirhind.

   Wazir Khan's forces were larger in number, well trained, with heavy guns and foot-soldiers with rifles whereas the Sikh volunteers had mainly swords and spears besides unbounded courage and resolve. In the first couple of hours about 5,000 Sikhs were killed. Thereafter Banda Bahadur with his chosen band leapt in the battle and soon the course of the battle changed. Wazir Khan was captured and killed, the Mughal forces started running away and by evening the Sikhs had won the battle. Banda Bahadur carried out the last rites of the fallen Sikhs for two days and thereafter entered Sirhind. The battle of Sirhind is the first major battle won by the Sikhs and lost by the Mughals.

After the victory at Sirhind, Banda Bahadur appointed Baj Singh as governor of Sirhind with Aali Singh as his deputy. All the booty was given to Baj Singh for distribution. Binod Singh and

Ram Singh were appointed in the Thanesar area. Fateh Singh was confirmed as the governor of Sumana. Hindu and Sikh officers were posted in all important revenue and administrative posts in place of Muslim officers. This was Banda Bahadur's method of distributing military and administrative powers amongst his men. Banda Bahadur had secured large territories in over half a dozen larger districts of Punjab and was aware of the emperor's attack with his imperial forces any time in the near future.

Banda Bahadur, in response to such a contingency, had planned a 'Sadhaura-Lohgarh-Sitaragarh axis'. He had planned for a major battle with the imperial troops at Sadhaura.

Bahadur Shah, the Mughal emperor, had correctly foreseen the situation, that a large Sikh rebellion near the capital city could prove detrimental to the Mughal Empire. He, therefore, decided to personally move to Punjab and crush the Sikh rebellion. He mustered a large number of smaller contingents of governors and *faujdars* from the adjoining states besides the imperial forces. The entire strength of the Mughal army comprised around 2 lakh horse and foot-soldiers and almost the same extent of camp followers.

The Mughal forces advanced into the territory occupied by the Sikh forces. They did fight at a few places but from most of the places smaller detachments of Sikh army went back to either Sadhaura or Lohgarh. The entire operation took about three months.

Some entrenchments were made at Sadhaura from where the Sikh forces faced the Mughal imperial army. Khafi Khan says that, The Sikhs in their *faqir* dress struck great terror among the royal troops. The number of dead and dying of imperial troops was so large that for a time it seemed that they were losing ground. Feroze Khan Mewati and Rustam Dil Khan' s armies were literally mauled by the Sikhs, but before the close of the day, a fresh army of about 50,000 Mughal troops reached and joined the battle and the Mughal army was saved of a disaster. Finding themselves in no condition to face the Mughal forces, the Sikh army retreated towards the Lohgarh Fort during the night. The distance between Sadhaura and Lohgarh Fort is about 10 miles (16 km) only. The Mughal armies also moved on to Lohgarh and after fighting for a couple of days with the besieging Mughal army, the Sikh army moved out of Lohgarh Fort and got dispersed in the nearby Haripur reserve forests. This was a strategy which worked out as the Mughal forces with much larger manpower were closing in on them.

Bahadur Shah moved his camp from Lohgarh to Ropar and then to Lahore where he reached on 11 August 1711 and set-up his camp on the bank of river Ravi. He developed some mental ailment and died on 27/8 February 1712.

The death of Bahadur Shah was followed by the usual struggle among his sons for the throne. Azim-uz-Shan, the main contender, was riding an elephant when its trunk was hit by a cannonball and became unmanageable. It threw itself in the river Ravi along with the prince atop and both were swallowed by quicksand. Ultimately Jahandar Shah eliminated his remaining brother and ascended the throne on 29 March 1712. Ten months after ascending the throne, Jahandar Shah was defeated by Farrukh Siyar, son of Azim-us-Shan.

The period of struggle for the imperial throne and disturbed state of affairs in Lahore and Delhi from February 1712 to June 1713 was very favourable to the reestablishment of the power of the Khalsa. Banda Bahadur availed this period of disturbance and occupied Sadhaura without any loss of time. After capturing Sadhaura, Banda Bahadur raised a fairly strong fortress adjoining Sadhaura town. He dug out a ditch around the fort and used the dug out earth to strengthen the walls of the fort and got water filled in the ditch from a nearby canal. He also raised four towers at four corners inside the fort to be used as observation posts. The small fort of Lohgarh was also occupied and repaired.

From the first ridge up to the walls of Lohgarh, Banda Bahadur got constructed fifty-two 3 to 4 ft high defensive ridges arranged in such a manner as each ridge lent protection to the next. In this manner any assailant who intended to reach the fort had to face hostile firing from every ridge that he crossed. Banda Bahadur also chose the adjoining hill, another 400-500 ft higher than Lohgarh hill, from where he could observe the movements of the Mughal forces over the entire expanse. There is an acoustic phenomenon in that hill named Sitaragarh *vis-à-vis* Lohgarh Fort. The spoken orders from Sitaragarh are clearly audible at Lohgarh

Fort and likewise the reply given from Lohgarh Fort is equally audible at Sitaragarh. This phenomenon still exists at the site and it is a joy to converse with a person standing more than 1 km away. Banda Bahadur used to stay at the top of Sitaragarh hill where a small stone-lined pond for collection of water exists. There is no foundation of any building raised there. Probably he stayed there in a mud hut.

This Sadhaura-Lohgarh-Sitaragarh axis was used by Banda Bahadur in 1713-14 also when a very large Mughal force under top commanders invaded the areas reoccupied by the Sikh forces with directions from Farrukh Siyar that they must finish the Sikh forces and their commanders once for all.

After reoccupying the areas under Sikh operation, Mughal forces converged on Sadhaura where the Sikhs gave them a good fight and during the middle of the night left for Lohgarh because of the logistics being totally against them. The Mughal armies were more than 2 lakh fighting men whereas the Sikh army was about 20,000-30,000 only. The Mughal armies followed them to Lohgarh and there again, after giving a good fight for a couple of days, the Sikh army dispersed during the night in the reserve forests of Haripur.

The Sadhaura-Lohgarh axis was very effectively planned by Banda Bahadur to give a befitting fight to a very large army and then get out of the same unscathed. The Punjab government has recently agreed to put up a memorial at the heritage site of the battle of Chhaparh Chiri in the memory of Banda Bahadur. The Punjab government should mark the entire land on which the Chhaparh Chiri battle was fought and not a smaller piece in order to accommodate a golf course and an NRI housing colony. The area where 5,000 Sikh soldiers were cremated must be treated as a heritage site to be preserved in the memory of the sikh martyrs of 1710.

The Mughal revenue system was designed for collecting much revenue as possible without caring for the well-being of the farmers, the tillers of the land. They had a system of giving assignments to Mughal officers and other landowners, who would after collecting the revenue required to be paid to the Mughal government, would grab as much as they could for themselves and this resulted at times into agrarian rebellions. Bernier points out the attitude of the *jagirdars* as:

> Why should the neglected state of this land create uneasiness in our mind? And why should I expend our money and time to render it fruitful? We may be deprived of it in a single moment, and our exertions would benefit neither ourselves nor our children. Let us draw from the soil all the money we can though the peasant should starve or abscond. We should leave it, when commanded to quit, a dreary wilderness.

Guru Tegh Bahadur on his arrival in the Punjab, used to visit nearby villages and help the needy farmers by providing them with milch animals, oxen for ploughing, land for tilling, provision for water, etc. This action of the Guru was not liked by the Muslim landowners and exaggerated reports were sent to the Mughal government. Guru Tegh Bahadur was called to Delhi and all torturous persuasions were used to make him agree to embrace Islam, which he stoutly refused and was finally executed in Chandni Chowk at Delhi. Banda Bahadur had this issue in his mind and he divided all the lands held by landowning *zamindars* and distributed it among the tillers of the land, the basic principle being that the land belongs to the person who tills it. The land revenue was calculated twice a year at the time of ripening of crops. The entire produce was divided in three parts, one part was as state revenue and two part for the tillers. The village *bania* used to be present and if the state did not need the crops the *bania* would take over the government share and pay its price to a government. This was a most liberal deal, with the government in power taking only one-third of the crop with no intermediates taking their own share from the tillers. This action of Banda Bahadur was the most revolutionary step taken by his government when it came to power.

Karam Singh has stated that Banda Bahadur was largely responsible for the liquidation of the *zamindari* system in the Punjab. On his suggestion, the tillers of the soil ejected the landlords and the peasants themselves became the masters of land. Large estates were broken into smaller holdings in the hands of Sikh or Hindu peasants. These agrarian changes, to a great extent, ameliorated the lot of the poor peasantry. He ousted the Mughal officers from the various parganas of Sirhind division and put his own men in their places. Hindu *qanungos* and *amils* who had been replaced by Muslims under Aurangzeb were dismissed and the jobs of the displaced Hindus were restored to them.

While at Sirhind and other places, Banda Bahadur converted many a Hindu and Muslim to the faith of Sikhism. 'The authority of that sect (of the Sikhs) extended to such an extent,' wrote Yar Muhammad Qalander, the then *subedar* of Shahjahanabad, in June 1710, that many Hindus and Muslims, finding no alternative other than obedience and submission to them, adopted their faith and manners and their chief Banda captivated the hearts of all towards his inclinations, and whether a Hindu or a Muslim, whosoever came in contact with him, he (Banda Bahadur) conferred upon him the title of Singh – baptized him into the Sikh faith.' Accordingly, Dindar Khan, a powerful ruler of the neighbourhood, became Dindar Singh, and Mir Nasir-ud-Din, the newswriter of Sirhind, became Mir Nasir Singh. In the same way, a large number of Muslims abandoned Islam and 'followed the misguided path (of Sikhism), and took solemn oaths and firms pledges to stand by him'.

An edict for an indiscriminate wholesale massacre of the Sikhs was repeated by Emperor Farrukh Siyar when he came to power (1713-19) and was acted upon for over forty-four years with more or less rigour. It may be stated here that the royal anti-Sikh edict brought about no change in Banda Bahadur's attitude and policy towards the Muslims. His was a political struggle for the emancipation of the people—Hindus, Muslims and Sikhs alike—from the tyranny of the Mughal government. He, therefore, allowed the fullest religious liberty to them and they in turn flocked to him in large numbers. It was reported to the Mughal emperor on his way to Lahore in April-May 1711 that as many as 5,000 Muslims of the neighbourhood of Kalanaur and Batala had joined Banda Bahadur and that they were at liberty to shout their 'Azam' the call for the prayer and recite their prayers and *khutba* in the army of the Sikhs. This speaks volumes for the religious tolerance of the Sikh leader.

Banda Bahadur issue a seal for the initial Sikh state after due deliberations and it was decided to fear the inscription:

> *Deg Tegh Fateh O Nusrat Baidrang*
> *Yaft Uz Nanak Guru Gobind Singh*
>
> Deg meaning, economic power, *Tegh* being sword arm, *Fateh* meaning the resultant victory, *Nusrat Baidrang* meaning unrestrained help, *Yaft Uz* meaning received from Guru Nanak to Guru Gobind Singh, and Nanak Guru Gobind Singh denotes the idea of the collectiveness of the Gurudom.

The imprints of the seal are available on some of the *hukamnamas* issued by Banda Bahadur. It is a matter of great irony that the much more stable and larger organization of the Sikhs *misls* and even the large Sikh state under Maharaja Ranjeet Singh did not have a state seal. Although the Sikh government was called Sarkar Khalsa and Raj Khalsa but the all the *sardars* had their seal with *Akal Sahai* and their names underneath. A doubt lurks, unlike Banda Bahadur, that the Sikh *sardars* did not make the seal in the name of the state and used their personal seals on state matters, in order to keep those lands under their powers rather than with the Sikhs state.

Banda Bahadur also issued a coin for the initial Sikh state in the name of the Sikh Gurus:

> Obverse: *Sikka Zad Bar Har Do Alam Tegh-i-Nanak Wahib Ast,*
> *Fateh Gobind Singh Shah-i-Shahan Fazal Sacha Sahib Ast.*
>
> Meaning, coin has been struck with both the words herein, and hereafter, the double-edged sword of Guru Nanak is the guarantor of the same (like Reserve of Bank of India is the guarantor of all the paper money issued by the government). The victory of Guru Gobind Singh, the King of Kings, has been grace of the Lord Almighty.
>
> Reverse: *Zarb Ba Aman-ud-Dahar, Masawwarat Shahr-i-Zinat,*
> *Al Takht Khalsa Mubarak Bakht*
>
> *Zarb* meaning coined at, *Baa Aman-ud-Dahar*, meaning a place of perfect peace, *Masawwarat Shahr-i-Zinat*, picture of a beautiful city, *Ultakht Khalsa Mubarak bakht*, where the fortunate throne after Khalsa is to be located.

Note : In writing the full legends of the seal and the coin and in explaining the meaning thereof almost all historians of Sikh history from Ganda Singh including William Irvine onwards have made some or the other mistake.

Plate 12: Banda Bahadur's coin.

Like the Sann-i-Jalus or the regnal year of the Mughal emperors, Banda Bahadur introduced the Sammat as the year commencing with the Baisakhi of 1710.

During the short span of Banda Bahadur's rule and struggle against the Mughal government, there was both a political as well as a social revolution in the Punjab which has been well described by William Irvine:

In all the parganas occupied by the Sikhs the reversal of the previous customs was striking and complete. A low scavenger or leather dresser, the lowest of the low in the Indian estimation has only to leave home and join the Guru (Banda Bahadur) when in a short time he would return to his birth place as its ruler with his order of appointment in hand. As soon as he set foot within the boundaries the well born and wealthy went out to greet him and escort him home. Arrived there they stood before him with joined palms, awaiting his orders. . . . Not a soul dared to disobey his order and men who had often risked themselves in battlefield, became so cowed down that they were afraid even to remonstrate.

It has been beautifully summed up by Teja Singh and Ganda Singh:

There was a revolution effected in the minds of the people, which history often fails to take note. A will was created in the ordinary masses to resist tyranny and to live and die for a national cause. The example set by Banda Bahadur and his companions in this respect was to serve them as a beacon light in the days to come. The idea of a national state, long dead, once again became a living aspiration and although suppressed for the time being by relentless persecution, it went on working underground like a smouldering fire and came out forty years later with a fuller effulgence, never to be suppressed again.

Bibliography

I. PRIMARY SOURCES

A. Collections of Sikh Coins

Government Museum, Chandigarh.
Government Museum, Lahore.
Personal collection and some private collections.
Sheesh Mahal Museum, Patiala.
Sri Pratap Museum, Srinagar

B. Catalogues of Coins and Gazetteers

Gupta, Parmeshwari Lal and Sanjay Garg, *The Coins of Dal Khalsa and Lahore Darbar*, Patiala, 1989.

Hans, Herrli, *The Coins of the Sikh*, Nagpur: Indiana Coins Society, 1993.

Odgers, C.J., *Catalogue of Coins,* Lahore Museum, 1985.

Standard Guide to South Asian Coins and Paper Money Since 1556 AD, Wisconsin: Krause Publications, US.

Whitehead, R.D., *Catalogues of the Coins of the Punjab Museum*, Lahore: Oxford, 1843.

World Coins Standard Catalogues, Wisconsin, 1994.

C. Travelogues and Accounts by Newswriters

Ali, Shahamat, *Sikhs and Afghans*, Patiala: Language Department, rpt., 1970.

Barr, William, *Journal of March from Delhi to Kabul*, Patiala: Language Department, rpt., 1970.

Forster, George, *A Journey form Bengal to England*, Patiala: Language Department, rpt., 1980.

Hornigberger, John Martin, *Thirty Five Years in the East Calcutta*, 1852, Patiala: Language Department, rpt., 1970.

Leach, Major, *Survey 1837*, Foreign Department, Secret Consultation, No. 22, New Delhi: National Archives of India, 1943.

Vigne, G.T., *Travels in Kashmir, Ladakh and Skardu* (2 vols.), London: Henry Galburn Publishers, 1842.

D. Persian Manuscripts and Documents

Akhbari-Darbar-i-Mualla, The News of The Royal Mughal Court, 1707-18, tr. Bhagat Singh, *Punjab Past & Present*, vol. XVIII, no. II, October 1984, Patiala: Punjabi University.

Ali-ud-din, Mufti, *Ibratnama* (2 vols.), Lahore: The Punjabi Adabi Academy, 1854.

Elliot, H.M. and John Dawson, *The History of India as Told by its Owm Historians*, 8 vols., New Delhi: Low Price Publications, rpt., 1990.

Fain, Mohsin, *Dabistan-i-Mazhab*, tr. David Shea and Anthony Troyar, Paris, 1843. Portion on Sikhs, tr. Ganda Singh, in *Punjab Past* & *Present*, Patiala: Punjabi University, April 1967.

Hadiqat-al-aqalim (MS), Murtza Hussian, Aligarh Muslim University, Aligarh.

Ijad, Mir Muhamad Ahsan, *Farukhsiyar Nama*, OR 25, BM, London (copy with Aligarh Muslim University, Aligarh).

Karim, Abdul, *Tarikh-i-Punjab*, Amritsar: History Research Department, Khalsa College.

Khan, Mohammed Hadi Kamwar, *Tazkirat-i-Salatin-i-Chughtaiya*, ed. Muzaffar Alam, New Delhi: Asia Publishing House, 1980.

Khan, Khafi, *Muntakbad-ul-Lubab* (2 vols.), Calcutta: Mohamad Hashim, 1874.

Lal, Kanehiya, *Tarikh-i-Punjab*, tr. Jeet Singh Seetal, Patiala: Punjabi University, 1960.

Vakil Reports Addressed to the Rulers of Japur During 1710-1711, Rajasthan State Archives, Bikaner.

Mohyi-ud-din, Gholam (Bute Shah), *History of Punjab*, SHR 1288, Amritsar: History Research Department, Khalsa College.

Rai, Khushwaqt, *Twarikh-i-Sikhan,* Ms SHR 1275, Amritsar: History Research Department, Khalsa College.

Shah, Ahmad (of Batala), *Tarikh-i-Hind*, SHR 1291, Amritsar: Khalsa College.

Shah, Gulam Hussain, *Siyar-ul-Matakherin*, Kanpur: Newal Kishore Press, 1897.

Steingass, F., *Comprehensive Persian English Dictionary*, New Delhi: Munshiram Manoharlal, 1996.

Suri, Sohan Lal, *Umadat-ut-Tawrikh* (5 vols.), Lahore: Arya Press, 1885 (with Punjab States Archives, Patiala).

Tuzak-i-Jahangiri, tr. Rodgers and Beveridge, New Delhi: Munshiram Manoharlal, 1996.

E. URDU MANUSCRIPTS AND DOCUMENTS

Faiz-ul-Haq, *Tawrikh-Darbar Sahib*, SHR 93, Amritsar: Sikh History Department Khalsa College, 1896.

F. PUNJABI MANUSCRIPTS AND DOCUMENTS

Bachittar Natik, tr. Ujjagar Singh Bawa, Washington, USA: Sikh Youth Forum, 1999.

Bachittar Natik, Guru Gobind Singh, tr. and published by M.L. Peace, Jullundur (undated).

Bhangoo, Rattan Singh, *Parchin Panth Parkash*, ed. Bhai Vir Singh, Amritsar: Wazir Hind Press, 1962. Translated in English by Kulwant Singh, 2006.

Giani, Gian Singh, *Panth Prakash*, Patiala: Language Department, rpt., 1970.

———, *Tarikh Guru Khalsa* (2 vols.), Patiala: Language Department, rpt., 1970.

Gurdas, Bhai, *Varan* (2 vols.), tr. into English by Dr Jodh Singh, Patiala: Vision and Venture, 1998.

Nabha, Kahn Singh, *Encyclopedia of Sikh Literature (Mahankosh)*, Patiala: Language Department, rpt., 1981.

Sena Pat, *Sri Gur Sohha*, ed. Ganda Singh, Patiala: Punjabi University,

Singh, Harbans (ed.), *Encyclopedia of Sikhism* (4 vols.), Patiala: Punjabi University, 1995-8.

Singh, Karam, *Banda Bahadur*, Amritsar: Chief Khalsa Diwan, 1907.

———, *Banda Kaun See*, Amritsar: Amrit Agency, undated.

Sri Guru Granth Sahib, tr. Gopal Singh (4 vols.), New Delhi: Gurdas Kapoor & Sons, 1962-2.

Sri Guru Granth Sahib, tr. Gurubachan Singh Talib, Patiala: Punjabi University, 1988.

Sri Guru Sahib, tr. Manmohan Singh, Amritsar: SGPC, 1983.

II. SECONDARY SOURCES

A. ENGLISH BOOKS AND PRINTED WORKS

Ahluwalia, J.S., *The Sovereignty of Sikh Doctrine*, New Delhi: Bahri Publications, 1983.

Alam, Muzaffar, *The Crises of Empire in Mughal North Indian*, New Delhi: Oxford University Press, 1986.

Anand, Balwant Singh, *Guru Nanak*, New Delhi: Guru Nanak Foundation, 1983.

Archer, J.C., *The Sikhs*, Princeton NJ, 1946.

Ạshta, Dharam Pal, 'Poetry of Dasam Granth', Ph.D. thesis, Chandigarh: Panjab University.

Banerjee, Anil Chandra, *Guru Nanak and His Times*, Patiala: Punjabi University, 1984.

———, *Guru Nanak to Guru Gobind Singh*, New Delhi: Rajesh Publications, 1978.

———, *Sikh Gurus and the Sikh Religion*, New Delhi: Munshiram Manoharlal, 1983.

———, *The Khalsa Raj*, New Delhi: Abhinav Publication, 1985.

Banerjee, Indu Bhushan, *Evolution of Khalsa* (2 vols.), Calcutta: A. Mukherjee & Co., 1997.

Banga, Indu, *Agrarian System of the Sikhs*, New Delhi: Manohar, 1978.

Bhagat, Lakshman Singh, *Guru Gobind Singh*, Patiala: Language Department, rpt., 1970.

Browne, James, *History of the Origin and Progress of the Sikhs* (*India Tracts*), London: East India Company, 1788.

Chandra, Satish, *Medieval India*, New Delhi: Har Anand Publication, 1999.

Chhabra, G.S., *Advanced History of Punjab* (2 vols.), Jullundur: Parkash Brothers, 1976.

Court, Major Henry, *History of Sikhs*, Lahore: CMG Press, 1888.

Cunningham, J.D., *A History of Sikhs*, New Delhi: S. Chand & Co., 1972 (original edn. 1948, Chandigarh: Panjab University).

Deol, G.S., *Banda Bahadur*, Jullandhar: New Academic Publishing House, 1972.

Devahuti, *Problems and Indian Historiography*, New Delhi: D.K. Publication, 1979.

Dhillon, Dalbir Singh, *Sikhism, Origin and Development*, New Delhi: Atlantic Publishers & Distributors, 1988.

Duggal, D.S., *Zafar Nama*, Jullundur: Institute of Sikh Studies, 1980.

Elliot, A.C., *The Chronicles of Gujrat*, Patiala: Language Department, rpt., 1970.

Fane, H.E., *Five Years in India*, Patiala: Language Department, 1970.

Fenich, L.E., *The Darbar of the Sikh Gurus*, New Delhi: Oxford University Press, 2008.

Forster, George, *A Journey from Bengal to England*, Patiala: Language Department, rpt., 1970.

Gill, Pritam Singh, *History of the Sikh Nation*, Jullundur: New Academic Publishers, 1978.

Gordon, John, *Sikh*, Patiala: Language Department, rpt., 1970.
———, *The Sikhs*, Patiala: Language Department, rpt., 1970.
Gregor, M. William, *History of Sikhs*, Patiala: Language Department, rpt., 1970.
Grewal, J.S. and Indu Banga, *Civil and Military Affairs of Ranjit Singh*, Amritsar: GNDU, 1987.
———, *Early 19th Century Punjab*, Amritsar: GNDU, 1975.
———, *Maharaja Ranjit Singh and His Times,* Amritsar: GNDU, 1980.
Grewal, J.S. and S.S. Bal, *Guru Gobind Singh*, Chandigarh: Panjab University, 1967.
Grewal, J.S., *Guru Nanak in History*, Chandigarh: Panjab University, 1969.
———, *From Guru Nanak to Maharaja Ranjit Singh*, Amritsar: GNDU, 1982.
———, *Guru Tegh Bahadur and Persian Chroniclers*, Amritsar: GNDU, 1976.
———, *Historians of Punjab*, Amritsar: GNDU, 1974.
———, *Ideology, Polity and Social Order*, New Delhi: Manohar, 1996.
———, *In the By-lanes of History: Some Persian Documents from a Punjab Town*, Shimla: Indian Institute of Advanced Studies, 1975.
———, *Medieval India: History and Historians*, Amritsar: GNDU, 1975.
———, *The Sikhs of Punjab*, The Cambridge History of India, New Delhi: Orient Longman, 1990.
Gupta, Hari Ram, *History of Sikh Gurus*, New Delhi: U.C. Kapoor & Sons, 1973.
———, *History of Sikhs*, vol. II, New Delhi: Munshiram Manoharlal, 1978.
———, *History of Sikhs*, vol. III, New Delhi: Munshiram Manoharlal 1980.
———, *History of Sikhs*, vol. IV, New Delhi: Munshiram Manoharlal 1982.
———, *History of Sikhs*, vol. V, New Delhi: Munshiram Manoharlal 1991.
———, *Jadu Nath Sarkar*, *Essays*, Chandigarh: Panjab University, 1958.
———, *Jadu Nath Sarkar, Life and Letters*, Chandigarh: Panjab University, 1958.
———, *Marathas and Panipat*, Chandigarh: Panjab University, 1961.
———, *Punjab on the Eve of the First Sikh War*, Chandigarh: Panjab University 1975.

Gurdas, Bhai, *Varan* (2 vols.), tr. Dr. Jodh Singh, Patiala, 1998.

Habib, Irfan, *Agrarian System of Mughal India*, New Delhi: Tulika, 2000.

Hans, Surjit, *A Reconstruction of Sikh History form Sikh Literature*, Jalandhar: ABS Publications, 1988.

Hutchison, J. and P. Vogel, *History of Punjab Hill States* (2 vols.), New Delhi: Low Price Publications, 1999.

Irvine, William, *Later Mughals*, New Delhi: Taj Publications, 1989.

Khilnani, N.M., *Rise of Sikh Power in Punjab*, New Delhi: Independent Publishing Co., 1990.

Lawrence, H.M.L., *Adventures of an Officer in Punjab* (2 vols.), Patiala: Language Department, rpt., 1970.

Loehlin, G.H., *The Sikhs and Their Scriptures*, Lucknow: Lucknow Publishing House.

Macauliffe, Max Arthur, *The Sikh Religion, Its Gurus, Sacred Writings and Authors* (6 vols.), New Delhi: S. Chand & Co., 1985.

Macauliffe, R.K. and A.N. Srivastava, *Historiography*, New Delhi: SBD Enterprises, 1988.

Malik Arjan Das, *An Indian Guerilla Warfare*, London: John Wiley & Sons, 1975.

Mansukhani, Gobind Singh, *The Quintessence of Sikhism*, Amritsar: SGPC, 1965.

McLeod, W.H., *Evolution of the Sikh Community*, New Delhi: Oxford University Press, 1975.

———, *Guru Nanak and the Sikh Religion*, New Delhi: Oxford University Press, 1968.

———, *The B40, Janam Sakhi*, Amritsar: GNDU, 1980.

Narang, G.D., *Transformation of Sikhism*, Lahore: New Book Society, 1945.

Nayyar, Gurbachan Singh, *Campaigns of Hari Singh Nalwa*, Patiala: Punjabi University, 1995.

———, *Hari Singh Nalwa*, Amritsar: Dharam Parchar Committee, 1993.

———, *Sikh Policy and Political Institutions*, New Delhi: Oriental Publications & Distribution, 1979.

Nijjar, B.S., *Punjab Under Later Mughals*, Jullundur: New Academic Publication Co. 1972.

Prince, Henry T., *Origin of the Sikh Power in Punjab*, Patiala: Language Department, rpt., 1970.

Parmanand, *Veer Bairage*, Delhi: Rajpal & Sons, 1984.

Ray, Nihar Ranjan, *Shiks Gurus and the Sikh Society*, Munshiram Manoharlal, 1975.

Sarkar, Jadunath, *Fall of Mughal Empire* (4 vols.), New Delhi: Orient Longman, 1971.

———, *Aurangzeb* (5 vols), Calcutta: M.C. Sarkar & Sons, 1916.

Sheetal, Sohan Singh, *How Fell the Sikh Kingdom*, Ludhiana: Lyall Book Depot, 1970.

Singh, Daljit, *Sikh Ideology*, New Delhi: Guru Nanak Foundation, 1984.

———, *Sikhism*, Amritsar: Singh Brothers, 1994.

Singh, Fauja, *City of Amritsar*, Patiala: Punjabi University, 1977.

———, *Historians and Historiography of the Sikhs*, New Delhi: Oriental Publishers and Distributors, 1978.

———, *History of Punjab*, Patiala: Punjabi University, 1990.

———, *Maharaja Kharak Singh*, Patiala: Punjabi University, 1977.

———, *Sarhind Through the Ages*, Patiala: Punjabi University, 1984.

———, *Some Aspects of State and Society under Ranjit Singh*, New Delhi: Master Publishers, 1982.

Singh, Ganda, *Ahmad Shah Durrani*, New Delhi: Asia Publishing House, 1959.

———, *Baba Banda Bahadur*, Sirhind: Sarhind Historical Research Society, 1997.

———, *Hukamnamas*, Patiala: Punjabi University, 1985.

———, *Life of Banda Bahadur Singh*, Amritsar: Khalsa College, 1935.

———, *Sardar Jassa Singh Ahluwalia*, Patiala: Punjabi University, 1990.

———, *Select Bibliography of Sikhs and Sikhism*, Amritsar: SGPC, 1965.

Singh, Harbans, *Perspectives on Guru Nanak*, Patiala: Punjabi University, 1990.

Singh, Jagjit, *The Sikh Revolution*, Changdigarh: Bahri Publication Pvt. Ltd., 1981.

———, *The Caravan of Revolution Nanakshai*, SAS Nagar (PB), 2006.

Singh, Kanwaljit, *Political Philosophy of the Sikh Gurus*, New Delhi: Atlantic Publishers & Distributors, 1989.

Singh, Kapur, *Parasaraprasana*, Amritsar: GNDU, 1989.

Singh, Khazan, *History of Sikh Religion*, Punjab: Language Department, rpt., 1988.

Singh, Khushwant, *History of the Sikhs*, New Delhi: Oxford University Press (2 vols.) 1987.

———, *Ranjit Singh*, London: George Allen & Unwin, 1982.

Singh, Patwant, *The Sikhs*, New Delhi: Harper Collins India, 1999.

Singh, Puram, *The Spirit of the Sikhs*, Patiala: Punjabi Universtiy, 1981.

Sing, Ranbir, *The Sikh Way of Life*, New Delhi: Indian Publishers, 1982.

Singh, Seva Ram, *The Divine Master, Guru Nanak*, Lahore: Gulab Singh & Sons, 1904.

Singh, Sher, *Philosophy of Sikhism*, Amritsar: SGPC, rpt., 1986.

Singh, Sohan, *Bandha The Brave*, Published by Bhai Narain Singh, Mazang, Lahore, 1915.

Singh, Surinder, *Sikh Coinage: Symbol of Sikh Sovereignty*, New Delhi: Manohar, 2004.

———, *Banda Singh Bahadur: Battle Strategy Against Mughal Forces*, New Delhi: Har Anand, 2009.

Singh, Teja and Ganda Singh, *A Short History of Sikhs*, Patiala: Punjabi University, 1952.

Sinha, N.K., *Ranjit Singh*, Calcutta: A Mukherjee & Co., 1975.

———, *Rise of Sikh Power*, Calcutta: A Mukherjee & Co., 1973.

Suri, Sohan Lal, *Umdat-ut-Tawairkh*, vol. II, Punjabi tr. Amarnath Singh, Amritsar: GNDU, 1957.

Thornton, T.H., *History of Punjab* (2 vols.), London: Allen & Co., 1846.

Tod, James, *Annals and Antiquities of Rajasthan* (3 vols.), Delhi: Low Price Publications, 2000.

Trump, Ernest, *Adi Granth* (tr.), New Delhi: Munshiram Manoharlal, 1978.

Valentine, W.H., *Copper Coins of India* (2 vols.), New Delhi: Inter-India Publiations, 1983.

Wing, R.L., *Art of Strategy* (*Sun Tzu's Art of War*), London: Thomson, 1988.

B. Journals and Periodicals

Abstract of Sikh Studies, Chandigarh: Institute of Sikh Studies.

Calcutta Review, Calcutta.

Indian Antiquary, Bombay.

Journal of the Asiatic Society of Bengal, Calcutta.

Journal of the History of Sikh Studies, Amritsar: Guru Nanak Dev University.

Journal of The Indian of Advance Studies, Shimla.

Journal of the Numismatic Society of India, Banaras.

Newsletter of Oriental Numismatic Society, Surrey, UK.

Numismatic Digest, Bombay.

Punjab Past & Present, Patiala: Punjabi University.

Punjab University Research Bulletin, Chandigarh: Panjab University.

Proceedings of the Punjab History Conference, Patiala: Punjabi University.

Sikh Review, Calcutta.

Studies in Sikhism and Comparative Religion, New Delhi: Guru Nanak Dev Foundation.

The Spokesman Weekly, Chandigarh.
Bandhai Samarika, Dera Baba Banda Bahadur Riasi (J&K).

C. Select Articles

Ahluwalia, Jasbir Singh, 'Conception of Politiy in Sikh Religion', *P.P.P.*, April 1989, P.U., Patiala.

Alam, Muzzaffar, 'Sikh Uprising under Banda Bahadur', *P.P.P.*, April 1982, P.U., Patiala.

Fauja, Singh, 'Political Ideas of the Sikhs During 18th to 20th Century', *P.P.P.*, October', 1976, P.U., Patiala.

Ganda Singh, 'Development of Sikh Thought during 18th Century', *P.P.P.*, April 1968.

———, 'Banda Singh Bahadur: His Achievements', *P.P.P.*, vol. IX, Pt. II, 1975, P.U., Patiala.

Ganda Singh, 'Character of Sikhs as Seen by Noor Mohammad', *P.P.P.*, P.U., Patiala, 1991.

Gurbux Singh, 'An Analysis of Israr-Smadhi', Panjab History Conference, Punjabi University, Patiala, 1971.

———, 'Bandas Fall', P.H.C., P.U., Patiala, 1972.

———, 'Fuftuhat Nama-i-Smadhi on the Nature of Sikh Revolution under Banda', P.H.C., 1973, P.U., Patiala, 1991.

Harpreet Kaur, 'Liberation Movement under Banda Bahadur', *P.P.P.*, October, 1983, P.U., Patiala.

Irvine, William, 'Guru Gobind Singh & Banda', *Asiatic Society of Bengal*, vol. 63 (1894).

Rehki, Swinder Singh, 'Peasant Movement under Banda Bahadur', *Panjab Past & Present*, P.U., Patiala, 1991.

Index